The Rising Antenna

- a waggler man's journey -

By Jim Baxter

With contributions from: Denis White, Denis Pinkos, Mark Wintle, Jim Macdonald, John Dean, Dave Thomas, Roly Moses, Dave Frost, Terry Moroz, Keith Hobson, John Allerton, Dave Ashmore, Roger Wakenshaw, Terry Payne, Jimmy Randell, Brian Halliwell, Pete Clements, Chris Simmons, Matt Godfrey, Warren Martin, Darren Moyle and Andy Sellars.

First published in October 2016

ISBN number: 978-0-9955630-1-8

Designed and published by mpress (Media) LTD.

Unit 213, Waterhouse Business Centre, 2 Cromar Way,
Chelmsford, Essex, CM1 2QE

Dedications

Thanks go to two friends who helped me probably more than they ever realised. A few wise words from Brian Halliwell convinced me I could become a good angler when results weren't coming easily at club level. Similarly, laid-back Sheffield tackle dealer, Steve Calcott Snr., who took me to Witham matches in his big green van with a random gang of fishing mad youngsters before I had my own transport. Steve also gave me a packet of fine wire size 22 hooks that changed my fortunes. Both encouraged me to study float fishing at a time when ledgering for bream with swing-tips was at its peak and winning the major Fenland prizes. Finally, to my wife Lynne for all her support, enthusiasm and understanding for this constant obsession.

2016 marks the centenary of Benny Ashurst's birth, one of our greatest match anglers and angling brains. His 'Match Fishing' book about stick floats and casters and much more encouraged me to take fishing more seriously. So I also dedicate the book to him and trust he'd have approved.

Contents

Imperial V Metric Measures

The UK angling culture is stuck in a confusion over imperial versus metric measurements. Old habits obviously die hard for we mix up the two systems endlessly and extensively. First we talk of 12′ or 13′ rods yet measure all poles in metres or 'm'. Some anglers still describe a line the old way – eg. '1 1/2lb' strain - while others refer to it by its metric diameter - 0.10mm etc. We order maggots in pints yet if picked for an International squad we have to measure them in litres. Most UK fish are still weighed in pounds but it doesn't end there. We might talk of a stick float as a 'six no. 6 shot' capacity, yet a similar size of pole float (UK-made) will be called 0.5 gram or, confusingly for beginners, a 4 x 16 (in French styl sizes). For this reason I have not changed any measurement in the book where it is common angling parlance. We can all do the conversions. If any angler wants to fish six yards out with a 6m pole, then change to a 12′ rod, and keep both rigs on a 20cm winder, that's fine by me.

Jim Baxter

Contents

Contents

Acknowledgements

First, without the goodwill of others my waggler journey would have fallen well short of where it ended up. For my endless enquiries about floats and the men behind them I am indebted to the following: Tony Bielderman, John Procter, Terry Dorman, Ken Giles, Joe Brennan, Mick Peverley, Edgar Purnell, Ray Smith, Roy Marlow, Geoff Newby, Ian Heaps, Martin Read, Ernie Wilde, Dave Curbishley, Dave Edwards, Dave Parkes, Colin Perry, John Toulson, Roy Toulson, Pete Warren, Bill Watchorn, Brian Richmond, Dick Ward, Gerry Woodcock, Tony Booker, Dave Roberts, Billy Hughes, Johnny McCarthy, Bill Francis, Stan Elkington, Andy Partridge, Tony Scott, and Tony Bryan.

For supplying floats and promotion respectively, thanks to: Gary Barclay and the team at Drennan International, Matt Middleton and Middy Tackle International, Glen Bradley at Drake Floats, Stewart Lister and Karoly Kralik of Cralusso, Angler's Mail magazine and Match Fishing magazine.

Also, to graphic artist Simon Waller, photographer Alain Urruty, proof reader Andrew Griffiths, Dave Roberts for the loan of both his picture and float collections, angling historian John Essex for going way beyond the call of duty, AND to all my upstanding contributors. Finally, a special thanks to my friend Jim Macdonald, who somehow became my editor, for his tireless commitment and enthusiasm for the project.

Foreword

I've known the author for the best part of 40 years. We were teammates in Barnsley Blacks' first Division 1 National Championship win on the Great Ouse and Cam in 1979. We were young and hungry for success back then and beat the mighty Notts Fed team by a mere two points. But, for some reason Jim may tell you about, the following year he took a job in Germany and resigned his place in the squad, returning to fish for us only briefly afterwards.

In 1981 Jim came home and picked up where he'd left off. For much of the rest of the decade he was dominant on the waggler float on the River Witham at Kirkstead. The venue was a 'match mecca', attracting the best anglers in Fenland, and from Yorkshire, Notts. and beyond. Take it from me nobody wanted to draw next to him because he was so hard to beat! I'd call Jim a waggler specialist because this was clearly his number 1 method, but he arrived on the big match scene with a big Trent Open win on a balsa float aged 23, and he also won on the other key methods any good angler needs at his command. Those methods travelled well too, he has won far and wide among the best of company. I should add that back then we fished far bigger contests than most today, where it was necessary to beat 200 or more anglers to win.

Jim confirmed his talent to me when beating me off the next peg in a difficult England trial on the Newry Canal, Northern Ireland, in 1982 by some margin. Fishing pole and bloodworm he was top Yorkshire performer on aggregate over the morning and afternoon trials, but neither of us gained selection that year. Despite the disappointment of missing an England cap however, he has had many highlights and can look back on his fishing career with pride. I hope you enjoy and find inspiration from this well researched book as, believe me, I don't know anyone better qualified to discuss the merits of the waggler method.

Denis White
England International and founding Barnsley Black team member

The first time I saw Jim was when watching him fish the waggler in a Witham match in the late 80s, accompanied by my two match pals, Brian Sullivan and Joe Murray. He was drawn in Kirkstead's Schoolhouse Bend. He seemed to be counting to 20 before striking and hooking a fish every time – small roach of 2-4oz size. He possibly won the match, that detail escapes me, but he certainly came close with a 12lb-plus catch. It was a treat to watch but it left me scratching my head a bit. If Jim knew his float's every movement, I didn't. I never saw the float go under yet the fish kept coming. I had just joined the Doncaster team at the time and was fairly new to Witham Opens, so it was great to witness an angler at the top of his game giving a mesmerising performance. I later got to know Jim better on the River Don circuit when we fished together in the Rotherham Winter League. The fishing could be grim at times but we had many laughs.

Denis Pinkos
Top float angler from Maltby

Introduction

This book is both a memoir and an instructional on my favourite float type: the waggler. It is written from a matchman's perspective because competition fishing using a float is what I do best and have enjoyed doing for over 40 years. I must stress though, that the 'pleasure angler' can get as much from this book as anyone if he or she would like to improve a little, and catch more fish.

The important word that I like to think binds this book together is ENTHUSIASM. I do trust that you'll find plenty of it within all the writing team. Whatever skills you have, whatever method you use and the species you target, if you enjoy it and return home as eager for the next bankside trip as I do, then you have plenty going for you already.

The waggler is an easy float to master in theory, though good bait presentation is not guaranteed. We must get the fundamentals right, before then moving on to the subtleties. When the float is working properly it is a delight to use, and while we have seen a mass shift to pole fishing over the last quarter-century, I'd like to redress the balance, to win back an appreciation for this excellent style of rod and reel fishing.

I'm certain that no two anglers ever fish the same in similar swims with identical equipment, which is a fascination in itself. While I'd never claim to have all the answers on the waggler – there is always something new to learn - I have specialized in it and it has paid me back handsomely.

Unlike many, I do not believe the luck element in fishing is that great. And here the Gary Player maxim about golf – 'the harder I practice, the luckier I get' - always comes to mind, and from a man not blessed with the greatest swing (according to pundits) nor the best physical attributes for his game. But his strength of character, positive thinking and hard work drove him on to greatness.

Yes, of course, we must have some fish in front of us to catch them but that is merely square one. From there in a good swim on a prolific water, and with a reasonable grasp of the basics, almost anyone should bank a few, but that does not mean they are catching anywhere near the potential return for that swim.

Consistent success depends on sound techniques and good tactics. Just how fast, and from whom, and from where we learn those skills however, is an area which I think can be more than chancy, especially if the young aspirant does not come from a fishing family. I was lucky enough to grow up in one, and so my aim is to give you a good start if you haven't.

When I started taking fishing seriously the term 'angling coach' was unheard of. I studied a few fishing books and read weekly magazines, and also met and learnt from many helpful anglers as time went on. Eventually I got the knack of winning matches but it also required much trial and error. Today good instruction is readily available in various forms but there is still nothing like a reference book to keep at hand to check one's progress. I'll be suggesting you write up your fishing days in a diary or similar, to record all those important little details it is so easy to forget.

While I can enjoy catching any fish species, including some fly fishing for trout, the challenge of catching difficult roach is thrilling and still special after 50 years of trying. Described by many as an 'essential therapy', this quiet sport can easily leave us totally drained after a busy match (concentrating on a speck of float tip for hours could be part of it), but in a curious way mentally refreshed and spiritually enriched. Its ups and downs build character, help us think positively, and the memorable days far outweigh the bad.

When it comes to gaining knowledge and skills, I'm certain that table tennis star, Matthew Syed, is right to say in his excellent book: 'Bounce: the myth of talent and the power of practice', that good technique achieved through hard work and practice matters far more in most endeavours than so-called 'natural ability'. He cites 10 years or 10,000 hours-worth of hard work at 'purposeful practice' as the route to the top of every sport he researched.

You may already know and appreciate the visual sensation of seeing the tip of the float begin to move on the water surface then disappear from view. I call this the 'disappearing thrill' because throughout my angling life, and no doubt for most others, that same thrill recurs in that split second when we strike, the line tightens and we feel a live creature pulsating through the rod. And this constant applies whether we are aged 17 or (like me) just 65. The connected enjoyment is the glorious uncertainty of what fish is responsible for the bite – could it be specimen size or even a record? - and the actual playing of the fish. These are the reasons, I think, why the sport always stays fresh and varied and becomes so addictive, the perfect antidote to both the work routine and hustle and bustle of modern life.

While most bites pull the float under however, other bites move the float in different ways. As the shots down the line fall, a fish can hold them up on the way, causing a delay in the float's settling process. Or the shots descend to their limit only for a fish to take the bait and rise in the water, thus lifting the 'tell-tale' shot at least and making the float rise slowly like an emerging periscope, hence the book's title. Also, there's the 'line bite' which is a false bite caused by a fish hitting the line. In theory we should not strike at these unreal bites but we often do so as some of them look identical to the real thing. All these bites and more are part of the diversity of waggler fishing and will be analysed further on.

Part of the joy of writing this book has been to research other anglers' floats in the waggler range, old and new. Some of them are what I'd call 'peacock purists' who use very little else to make their floats, while others include materials like balsa wood, cane, plastic etc. It often comes down to what gives the angler most confidence in this quite personal tackle item. Confidence is a priceless asset and a word you'll be seeing again soon.

Given the many different applications and facets to fishing a waggler, there may be some aspect of the method that the team and I have not covered thoroughly enough for you. If made aware of any startling omission, we will try and address this in a future edition (email address is: jb@therisingantenna.com).

At this point you might say: ‘What about other methods?’ Well, I'm aware that no one float can do everything. There is no float for all occasions, and indeed a ledgered bait is sometimes the best way to catch fish. To be fully versatile we must have other techniques in our armoury, and I discuss some of these alternatives in Chapter 6.

Finally, this crystallizing of all my waggler fishing has been a fun experience. Now I can only sit back and hope that you, the reader, find it inspiring. Good luck and tight lines.

Jim Baxter, 2016

PART 1
The Float for all Seasons

Chapter 1

Why do we Fish?

I have a friend who is well into his eighties. Despite the physical limitations of old age he still thinks young and is passionate about his angling. He has always been sporting, having played golf to a good standard, bowls and pool. A natural gambler too, he also likes a punt on the horses, attends race meetings, and enjoys the odd game of poker. But he always says that nothing comes close to fishing for all round enjoyment and he'd give up all his other hobbies if ever he was restricted to just one.

Another, formerly a keen footballer, describes how angling has a magic and mystery for him that no other sport can replicate. *"The difference between catching fish or not can be most subtle, and the fact we cannot see our target – the quarry, adds to the challenge. Reading the signs on the day and trying to discover how the fish want the bait presented can confound us because every day is different regarding temperature, wind strength and direction, and other governing factors. Fish can also be so contrary. Conditions can look perfect but the fish don't want to know, then on a day it looks hopeless they decide to feed well and we fill our net. So we need tenacity and we can never get even close to knowing all the answers but maybe this is what drives us, makes us want more of it?"*

A third, a fan of tench fishing, summed up his lifelong dedication: *"I love the solitude and oneness with nature, and the glorious uncertainty and elation of the catch, also the wonderful sense of timelessness when at the water's edge."* Timeless indeed, we can certainly lose ourselves in the experience when fish are feeding and all is going well.

A level of escapism drives us perhaps, this yearning to be close to nature? The sport can be a gentle 'contemplative recreation' as Izaac Walton called it, or a hectic numbers game of chasing bigger and better fish. Many love the camaraderie of fishing in a group, others the peace gained from fishing alone.

Does the size of a fish even matter? What serious angler would not drool over fish of the size caught worldwide by Jeremy Wade, of TV and 'River Monsters' fame – stunning creatures like the arapaima, mahseer and tarpon for example? Then there are the sea giants like blue marlin to whet a big game angler's appetite. But most mortals seem content with the comparatively modest-sized fish UK waters have to offer on river or lake. The top Italian match anglers are masters at catching tiny bleak when nothing bigger will feed, so they obviously practice it, while the French have even resorted to fishing for sticklebacks on polluted canals in Normandy.

In 1994 Jeremy Paxman produced a book entitled: 'Fish, Fishing and the meaning of life!' You might think that 'the meaning of life' bit from the feisty TV commentator and fly angler is taking things a shade too far, but for those of us who eat, sleep and breathe the sport it rings true. To any angler on a mission no excuse is ever offered for putting fishing first and everything else off till tomorrow.

In 1960 Robert Traver wrote in his book *'Trout Magic'* that: *'...in a world where many men seem to spend their lives doing things they hate, my fishing is at once an endless source of delight and an act of small rebellion; because trout do not lie or cheat and cannot be bought or bribed or impressed by power, but respond only to quietude and humility... because mercifully there are no telephones on trout waters (or there weren't then!); because bourbon out of an old tin cup always tastes better out there...and finally, not because I regard fishing as being so terribly important but I suspect that so many of the other concerns of men are equally unimportant – and not nearly as much fun.'*

A tale from J.W. Martin, the famous 'Trent Otter' of years past, is another example of dedication to duty. He described how he walked miles from home to the Trent bank, spent all morning in different swims catching chub, then walked as many miles back to see his family. It sounded a perfectly normal routine. The fact that is was Christmas Day seemed totally irrelevant.

I have to include two more eminent writers on this topic. Arthur Ransome, of *'Swallows and Amazons'* children's books fame, was a lifelong angler and I always imagine him writing with a smile on his face. What a strong will his book *'Rod and Line'* shows. His justification for angling is spiky when it comes to observers asking how he can be so patient, but he also touches on some of the humour in angling: *'Nothing is more trying to the patience of fishermen than the remark often made to them by the profane: "I have not patience enough for fishing." It is not so much the remark itself that is annoying (showing a complete and forgivable ignorance of angling as it does) as the manner in which it is said... What are they, these dashing, impatient sparks? Are they d'Artagnans all, rough-riders, playboys of a western world, wild desperate fellows who look for a spice of danger in their pleasures? Not a bit of it. They hit a ball backwards and forwards over a net or submit to the patient trudgery of golf, a laborious form of open-air patience in which you hit a ball, walk earnestly after it and hit it again. These devotees of monotonous artificial pleasures who say that fishing is too slow a game for them seem to imagine that fishing is a sedentary occupation. Let them put on waders and fish up a full river and then walk down it on a hot summer day. Let them combine for an afternoon the arts of the Red Indian and the mountaineer and, in the intervals of crawling through brambles and clambering over boulders, keep cool enough to fill a basket with the upstream worm.*

'... Even in float-fishing so much depends on observation, on watercraft, on the reading of barely perceptible signs, that those who imagine that a good fisherman can watch his float and think of something else beside his fishing are very much mistaken. So completely does fishing occupy a man that if a good angler had murdered one of those people who prate about patience and were allowed to spend his last day at the river instead of in the condemned cell, he would forget the rope.'

That wonderful poetic writer and artist, Bernard Venables – an inspiration to many to take up angling with his 'Mr. Crabtree' stories - said of the roach: *'To its devotees it's almost a reason for living!'* Well, thumbs up, I'm one of that group, preferably when they are caught on a float. I like to think there are other reasons for living, but roach and float fishing have had a hold over me ever since schooldays.

In the following part-introduction to one of his books, Bernard defined the angling attraction most eloquently. Many will relate to his observations:
'Fishing is a subtle compound and only a part of its pleasure is success. Some success sometimes is important, and the desire for it in the early days of fishing can be intense almost beyond bearing…the beginner is lured on by a vision of almost inconceivably big fish that, he feels, lurk within the weedy recesses of every swim he fishes. But there indeed is part of the joy of it, this involvement of the imagination, pricked on by what, if anything is most certainly at the heart of angling – the mystery and fascination of inhabited water. If you had to say what it is in a man that this touches, you could say this it is a sense of wonder. There are many men in whom a sense of wonder never entirely dies, and in any of them there could lie a potential angler.'

So there you have it, he says we might all be driven largely by our mind's eye, the wonder of the unknown, what we cannot see below the water surface, and then actually making contact with a creature from that hidden world. It's hard to dispute anything Bernard suggests, and it could explain why angling has for years been the UK's most popular participant sport. If you have got this far I guess you have more than a spark of interest in it already. I'd like this book to develop this and put beginners especially on the right track. Angling might not only be about catching fish, but it helps.

On only one point would I part company with Mr. Venables. He closed his introduction by saying: *'to become involved in an urge for supremacy, competitive ascendancy, is to lose the essence of fishing.'* Well, if the beginner craves success then why not the more experienced? I am competitive by nature, I cannot help it, but I still have that sense of wonder he describes. To catch the most fish in a given situation is what I'd call success, and is probably why I went down the match angling route.

My aim is to keep on gaining knowledge and improving over the seasons, and trying to hit more bites tomorrow than today. To persist in that relentless search for perfection which we never quite attain as the fish always stay one step ahead. I need good catches of fish and a win now and again to spur me on. Surely this is no bad thing? I don't get carried away and have never succumbed to the 'win at all costs' mentality which is ugly. I can still enjoy the simple 'wetting of a line' on a relaxing day off, or practice day, where there is no need to catch fish quickly within set time limits, and we can take in the delights of nature better - the flash of a kingfisher or the delicate dipping of a tern.

The bonus of seeing wildlife however, should never be used as an excuse for not trying to catch fish, or not varying our approach. Ultimately we ought to try to be, as Dick Walker once described it, 'deadly' in our pursuit of whatever fish we call our quarry. For me it is roach, to others it is carp or pike, but we owe it to ourselves to gain some proficiency with our chosen species.

A reason for living or not, escapism, or an essential therapy for the speed of modern life, there is undeniably something special about this angling game.

Chapter 2

What is a Waggler?

The word 'waggler' relating to a fishing float is not mentioned in any dictionary, yet it has instant recognition by UK coarse anglers and their European counterparts. It is a float with wide application on rivers, lakes and canals. Dick Bowker junior, a Leigh, Lancashire matchman, is credited with the origin of the name, observing over 40 years ago how a peacock quill float 'waggled' from side to side when hanging upside-down from the line. The tag stuck and waggler has become the generic name for almost all bottom only floats.

But the concept is far older. From the very first time someone decided to attach their float from the bottom only, probably in awkward windy conditions, the seed was sown for what was to evolve into the waggler float. Originally of course, it would have been referred to in terms like 'loose float' or 'bottom only', for it began as a minor deviation to style over a hundred years ago. I'll come on to the float's history shortly, but it is fair to say the first floats we officially named wagglers were made from peacock quill in the late 1960s to early 1970s.

These were two key decades which saw the advancement in angling equipment and materials generally, and no doubt this helped the float's progress. Anglers now had casting reels, carbon fibre rods, and could fish floats further out in the stream than with the old drum reel or centre-pin and cane rods and the more cumbersome glass rods. They were looking for floats to match and ready for change, and finally got the message that a waggler could be effective on running water as well as still; in fact bites were often easier to hit this way which is a detail we'll come onto later.

Although the angling grapevine and weekly angling press helped to spread the waggler's popularity, its first written reference came in Billy Lane's book 'Match Fishing to Win', dated 1975. There has been a host of other names given to bottom only floats down the years, but waggler is the one that stuck and has survived, becoming far and away the most common. So for the sake of clarity ALL bottom only attached floats will be called wagglers in this book.

The old saying remains true that 'floats catch more anglers than fish' and is there any true angler who does not somehow get hypnotised by their brightly coloured tips and memories of 'red letter days' while browsing in the tackle shop? We still can't resist a purchase of say a matching pair when we may already have hundreds in our collection. If all the 'unused' floats bought, made or acquired by English anglers over their lifetimes were placed end to end they'd no doubt stretch around the world at least once. But do floats need to be as pretty and immaculate as they appear in the shop? Of course not, and I have always admired the amateur float-makers. Here is match legend and former World Champion, Kevin Ashurst on the subject:

'To hear some people talk you would think that waterproof varnish was essential to prevent floats waterlogging, and thus losing their efficiency...why varnish a piece of peacock quill, when it is quite incapable of taking in water? It won't even absorb most brands of paint to the extent that it will stick all over for very long. And will cane take in water, especially after it has been painted? And will cork? If it did we could never keep wine in a bottle...just because floats in shops are sold neat and straight and beautiful is not an argument that floats have to be neat and straight and beautiful to be used to maximum efficiency...if having a collection which is neat and tidy and beautiful gives you extra confidence then go for it by all means, but my advice is to spend your energy where it matters.' (Taken from: World Class Match Fishing, 1977).

Watching ducks diving for bread thrown by visitors from a bridge at Bakewell, Derbyshire, and competing with the large rainbow trout in the River Wye, I was amazed at how rapidly all the water drained off the birds' feathers when they re-surfaced – almost in the blink of an eye. This strongly supports Kevin's 'leave well alone' theory. But 'confidence' is the key word here. The neat and tidy-minded person will surely prefer a smart-looking float, lovingly painted, and vice versa. As for myself, I take the middle road – not too smart but not too messy seems about right.

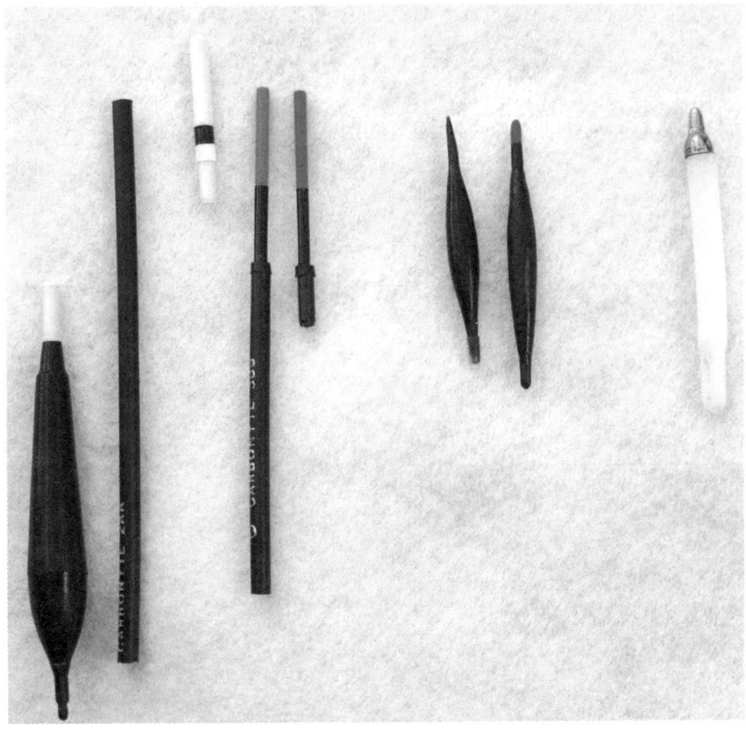

Float 'Oddities' - parts of float group 1 - components of a now obsolete all-plastic Sundridge Carbonyte waggler. All parts were detachable, and offered different tip thicknesses, and for the early Eighties this float was perhaps well ahead of its time. The joints possibly needed strengthening to ensure it had an enduring water seal; pair of floats 2 - Dave Edwards-style 2" balsa on cane micro waggler for fishing with a whip on the Witham. Shot capacity was .2g or four no. 8 shot; float 3 - an all plastic bleak 'splasher' This was an early bleak float used back in the day when bleak were more prolific in our major rivers than they are now.

What is a Waggler?

While writing this book I have pondered on all the times I have spent indoors making different floats including wagglers of every description, especially in my early years on the match circuit, and admit to once being a little obsessed with it. The float in various designs suited how I fished, but what suits my way of fishing may well not suit another's, and this leads to healthy debate. There is no perfect float for every occasion and that alone is good enough reason to keep experimenting and searching for improvement: to reach the unreachable perfection. Suffice to say that all floats described and pictured in this book might change slightly to suit the occasion, but they will all work if you get the other elements to catching fish right.

A trusty servant and reliable fish-catching tool for many years, one waggler or another has served me well on almost every water I've fished. Despite the popularity of the long pole and improved feeder methods in the new millennium, on its day the waggler is still hard to beat, on any water. My mission is to pass on a lifetime of experience using the float, and sincerely wish that through it you might get inspired enough to leave the roach pole to one side now and again and set up a rod and reel to cast a waggler instead.

Because the line immediately above the float is submerged, the way the waggler pulls under when a fish bites offers less resistance from the meniscus than does a float attached top-and-bottom. In effect inertia is reduced. This is why the float appears to get pulled under more smoothly than with a stick float presentation.

I also agree with Dave Thomas (you can find him in chapter 10), that there is a beauty in the float's simplicity. To fish competently with it is within reach of anyone providing a few basic rules are followed, and, together with my guest contributors, I hope to give you the necessary advice and tips to fish the float with renewed confidence. Fishing with confidence is vital, or in the case of a raw beginner we'd want you to try the float without fear. Let's now look at other properties of the float:

1. Built from peacock quill for example, an average waggler is a bit longer than a pencil and slightly slimmer – approximately 8″-12″ in length – 20cm to 30cm and 4mm to 7mm diameter, with or without a thinner insert at the tip. Exceptions exist like the 'Trent Trotter', a mini 3″ float for very shallow water, and specials of up to 24″ long for distance casting or for deep water and/or extreme winds.

A standard waggler appropriate for casting 20 yards with ease, will be something like 10″ or more long, with or without a thin insert of 2mm to 3mm diameter quill, and will have a shot capacity of 3AAA up to 2SSG (Swan shot) - or 2.4g to 3.2g depending on the main quill thickness. At the smaller end of the scale we have dart-type wagglers, lighter and shorter but beautifully streamlined for canal fishing, and these work on the same principle. A third group of short – 4″ to 6″ long - stubby floats of 1cm and more diameter are also now in vogue on carp lakes, called 'pellet wagglers'.

2. By definition all floats are made from a buoyant material, and peacock quill is about the most popular one. Other, slimmer and less buoyant bird quills like crow and pheasant also have their followers. Another excellent material is clear, hollow plastic nicknamed 'crystal' which is similar to a drinking straw but thicker-walled. Balsa wood is another lightweight and robust alternative, as are elder pith and sarkanda reed, while bamboo cane and carbon fibre are used as fine inserts in some of these floats. Essentially, painted or not, varnished or not, the finished float must be waterproof.

An assembled 2AAA Carbonyte waggler.

Wagglers can also be made with the addition of either a balsa, cork or polystyrene body to increase the overall shot capacity, and at the same time this can help to reduce the float's total length for shallower swims. No float needs to be as long as a quarter the depth of water it is being fished in, for example, and a float nearer 6″ would be more suitable to fish a 4′ swim than one of a foot long. I found that a small ¾-inch deep x ½″ wide cork body reduced a Witham waggler from 12″ approx. down to 10 ½″ total length for the same shot carrying capacity. An old but still a good idea is to make detachable float bodies that slide on and off a straight quill. I do like this concept providing the body is made accurately and not too bulbous to hinder smooth casting, eg. a cork body marked 1AAA takes exactly that size of shot, or the operation becomes too fiddly.

3. The float should be aerodynamic, ie. will fly through the air in a nice arc with accuracy when cast, pulled along by the weight at the float's base. This weight can either be the shots used to trap the float in position on the line, and/or loading on the float itself in the form of lead wire or brass or another metal. The lightness of a straight quill body material assists the float's flight through the air, though hollow plastic is equally good and marginally lighter. The addition of a bulbous body to the float can ruin the flight path to some extent and a slim oval shape is preferable.

Options: To load or not load the float with a spiral of lead wire, or a brass base insert, is up to the individual, but I think where locking shot are concerned (the two or more shots that hold the float in position at the required depth) small is good since the outlawing

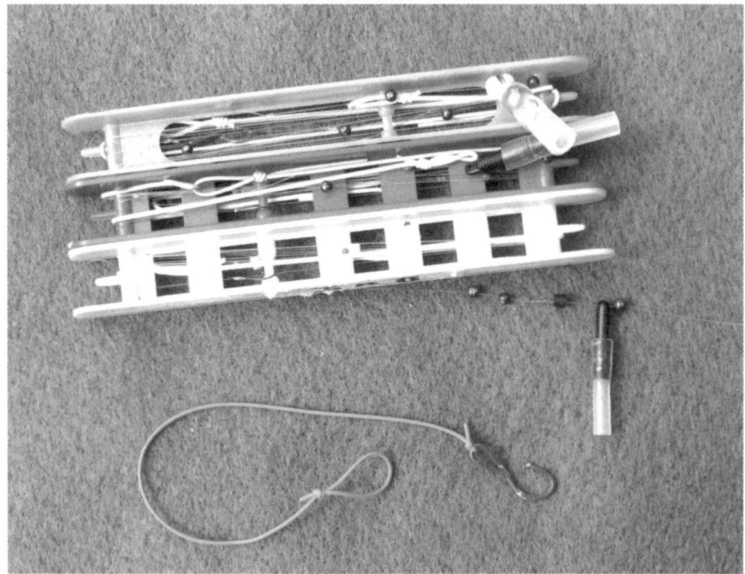

Tidy rigs: Keeping waggler rigs on small tackle winders helps maximise space in the tackle box, and at the same time makes it easy to unwind and finish the rig by simply adding the float. A rig anchor is shown to secure the end of the line neatly on the winder.

of lead shot in the larger sizes. I therefore believe in building around 75% of the float's total shot capacity into the base of the float using lead wire or solder wire (includes 60% lead). This also gives the float stability with a lower centre of gravity, and in strong cross winds this helps it hold station.

4. Most wagglers are given an inch or more of painted colour at the tip (or antenna) end with fluorescent paint (in red, yellow or orange), enabling the angler to see it easily at a range of 20 yards or so, though black is preferred when viewed against a large water with a light-coloured background. In recent years float-makers have begun to introduce tips in hi-viz translucent plastic instead of painted ones as they show up remarkably well in sunlight.

5. As aforementioned, the float is fastened at the base only via an inbuilt small wire eye which slides on the line or, for a quick-change option, can be pressed into a float adaptor - a short length of silicon sleeve on top of a 1" cane or plastic spigot also with the necessary eye attached. The float is then held in place on the line by two or more locking shots, eg. a homemade float marked with the capacity '3AAA+ 5 no. 8' will take 3AAA shot around the float plus five small no. 8 shot down the line.

6. When a fish takes the bait this naturally moves the chain of shots down the line and the float reacts in turn. The visible part of the float - the tip – should signal the bite in whichever direction the fish moves – down, up or sideways. On a personal level, what I call an improved waggler, has a slim cane or carbon insert (or tip or antenna) forming the top 3" of float, and up to a 1" length of this at the very tip is built up in thickness to create what is called a 'sight bob' for improved visibility. This is my idea of a good business end to the float. (Note: a thin tip like this is not suitable when dragging line and/or shots in fast swims.)

7. Another option is to give the waggler a sliding facility, and this can be achieved by adding a wire eye of a precise diameter to hold the float in place when it slides up to a stop knot tied to the line at the required depth. Opinions vary as to whether a sliding float should include loading at the base or not and this will be discussed later. In one camp we have the late, great Billy Lane, sliding float pioneer, who was one of the first to make his float slide up to a stop knot for fishing deep water that made casting difficult with a 12' or 13' rod. Billy did not build weight into his sliding floats but whipped a 15 thou. eye to their base. He also utilised a 'rest shot' above the main weight down the line – the bulk shot – which the float rested against to make the cast. Billy would cast his float with a smooth underhand swing and on the face of it anglers' fears about float fishing deep water were solved.

However, as the sliding method developed other anglers began to question whether some subtle refinements might not make the slider more user-friendly. Many found Billy's rest shot caused them casting difficulties and bad tangles resulted, mainly because the casting weight of the bulk shot and float were separated at the start of the cast. They began discarding the rest shot and letting the float slide down to the bulk shot, and they also started to use bigger base eyes in the float for easier sliding. But even then, with certain casts in varying wind directions, the bulk shot and float might still separate on the cast risking a serious back-tangle. To solve this niggling problem some resorted to partial loading of the slider at the base – up to a third of the float's total weight capacity.

But even these changes do not have a total following. One of my contributors, Brian Halliwell (see chapter 19), while not fully agreeing with Billy about his slider eye diameter – *'too small for the line to slide through smoothly'*, he says - neither does he think that adding weight to pre-load the float is a particularly good idea. He prefers a special sliding adaptor - a wire eye on cane inside a silicone sleeve that the float pushes into - and insists that if the sliding eye is set at a 45-degree angle to help it curve around the bulk shot, the float and shot will remain as one unit when casting, will land together and tangles will be avoided.

New technology and a constant exchange of ideas by European anglers and beyond is forever improving the scope of float fishing and indeed all angling techniques. We have seen some clever refinements to waggler design and application in recent years and no doubt these will continue. In the next chapter however, I want to take us back to the birth of the float and introduce its pioneers.

Chapter 3
History of the Waggler

The origins of the waggler, if simply referring to a float attached bottom only, date back over a century. In 'Angling for Roach', written and first published in 1923, Edward Ensom (pen-name 'Faddist'), introduced it in a sentence: "on quiet waters a useful tip is to use one (float) cap only with which to attach the float to the cast". He obviously meant a cap at the float's base, but this is not the first reference.

Some time ago my angling historian friend, John Essex, sent me an article for his 'Looking Back' section in Angling Star magazine. The article charted the waggler's origin as far back as January 18th 1896 under a title of 'Float Philosophy'. *"It is just slightly more than a single column in length, approximately 1,000 words, and is a real cracker", said John, "because it deals with the 'style' of fishing rather than what sort of float to use, and it goes like this":*

'Every day or hour during which they may fish, may furnish surprising exceptions to some of the best accepted angling rules. "You've lost your top cap!" or "What's the matter with your float?" are among the remarks (not all complimentary) which have been made to me by onlookers and

brother anglers when I have been employing that method of fixing float to the line which dispenses altogether with a top cap, and which is very easily adopted by fastening the float to the line by means of two half hitches at its lower end, the line being prevented from slipping off by the brass ring or loop, which is now furnished on most floats.

Norfolk anglers use this float fastening when fishing running water. To me its advantages are most apparent when it is used on lakes, ponds or very sluggish streams, and especially where the bait is presented to the fish on the bottom of the water.'

This means we can place a bottom only float being used in Norfolk in the Victorian era. As for author 'Clayr Kenwal' (and John does not know if that's his real name or a pseudonym), his message was spot on. He goes on to reveal his method of trotting bottom only: 'With the float fastened at its lower end, little or no angle is formed from the rod top to hooks, and hence the strike is much more direct. Thus an apparently careless method of float fastening is justified, although it is almost solely applicable to the Notts style of angling with the float some distance from the rod.'

Captain L.A. (Leonard) Parker (1886-1959) meanwhile, lifelong angler and writer and landlord of the Bull Inn, Downton, a regular anglers' watering hole next to the Avon on the Wiltshire/Hampshire border, credits the antenna's invention (waggler forerunner) to a Frenchman, Mr. M. Matout, in the early 20th century who made his floats from a thin cork body over a wooden stem, furnished with a 4" piece of thin quill at the tip.

Twice National Champion, the legendary J.H.R. (Jim) Bazley of Leeds however, claims that Dutch anglers were using similar floats a long time before Matout claimed he invented them.

But Leonard Parker wrote on many angling styles, and we have no reason to dispute his findings. The captain once caught 103 roach for 112lb from his local Hampshire Avon, one colossal weight for the old days and the inferior lines in regular use compared to today! In that catch he included 19 fish over 1 1/2lb and two over 2lb up to 2lb 4oz.

He confirms in his 1954 book 'Roach', one of the iconic 'How to Catch Them' series published by Herbert Jenkins, that the antenna-cum-waggler is almost as old as the hills, whether it was a Dutchman or Frenchman who was responsible for its origin. An illustration in that book shows an antenna for general use made from a porcupine stem with a cork or balsa body, and a 'super sensitive' for hemp fishing built from a porcupine stem with a long whalebone antenna at the tip. For floats made over 60 years ago both these are nicely finessed.

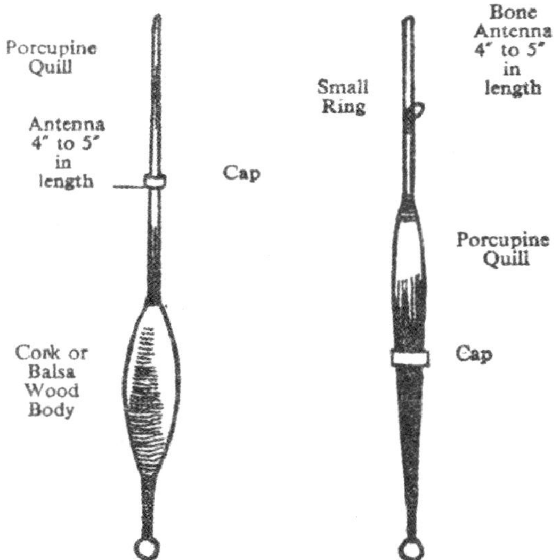

Two antenna floats by Leonard Parker (from his 1954 book).

Sunken Line Method

In the first mention of antenna floats in the book, the two floats are shown with a close fitting cap (or rubber sleeve) or ring an inch from the tip with the latter float, as a means of attaching the float at both ends. But thanks to the base ring the line goes through, it takes little stretch of the imagination to know that the same floats would be converted to a bottom only attachment to beat line drag in rough conditions. And the captain reveals all when describing the 'sunken line' method:

'If the wind is in your face, decide straightway to use a bigger float than you normally do, as it assists you in casting. I strongly recommend a long float in preference to a short stubby one... Antenna floats are my own choice and I advise a normal float without a cap at the top or bottom. [He is saying he's not fishing double rubber or 'cap.] To connect up I double the line and pass it through the small (base) ring and pull

tight. This method sinks the line more readily and makes for more positive striking. I prefer to bind a loop of thick silk to the bottom of the ring in place of the metal ring, as this makes it easier to move the float when altering depth.'

He goes on to say: *'My liking for the sunken line method started many years ago when, on one occasion, I was catching fish at a very fast rate. [By sunken line method he is referring to bottom only presentation.] A wind arose, increasing in force as the minutes went by. Gradually the bites got less and less until they stopped altogether. I promptly pushed my float up at least a foot and almost immediately began to catch fish again, though not as fast as before. I put this down to the fact that the bait was not bobbing up and down to the extent it was before.*

'Every angler at some time or other meets with some such experience: he does something different and starts to catch fish. When this happens the matter should be pondered: every detail connected with it should be studied, for he may have discovered by accident a valuable principle' [Wise words indeed from an experienced angler].

According to his son, Ray, Sheffield's Harold Smith, National Champion in 1934, was already using a bottom only Norwegian crow quill back in the Thirties. Ray passed away recently but was a top matchman in his own right in the 1950s and former Sheffield team skipper. The Norwegian crow quills were larger and took more shot than those from England. Harold's float at 7" to 9" long took up to 3BB plus some lead wire on the float to make it self-cocking.

Ray float-fished in the way his dad taught him on the Witham and popular Fenland drains like the South Forty Foot in the 50s, abandoning the light floats of the old 'Sheffield-style' that offered only a limited fishing range. With the larger Norwegian crow's they could cast further and would fish 'two up, one down' (meaning two BB shot up next to the float and one BB at mid-depth) or one-up, two down (the same shotting in reverse with 2BB down the line), or occasionally three down.

But when Ray stepped up from a crow quill to a heavier float made from a plastic knitting needle material, he gained more distance still. This float, called the 'Windjammer', was introduced by Boston tackle dealer Jack Clayton. It may have been shaped like an Avon, with a cork body situated near the top of the stem, but it was fastened to the line bottom only. Although this might sound a strange float design to us now, it offered a way of defeating a

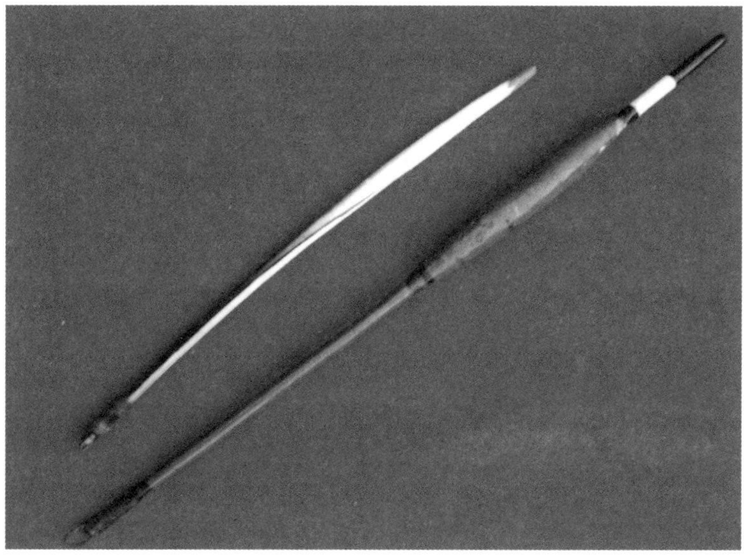

Ray Smith's floats: bottom only fished crow quill and a Clayton Windjammer (knitting needle stem); and (below) two of Len Parker's sunken line fastenings.

skimming wind at a time when good floats were still some way off and was an early form of waggler. Ivan Marks also used a similar float when he was on the road to fame in the early 1950s:

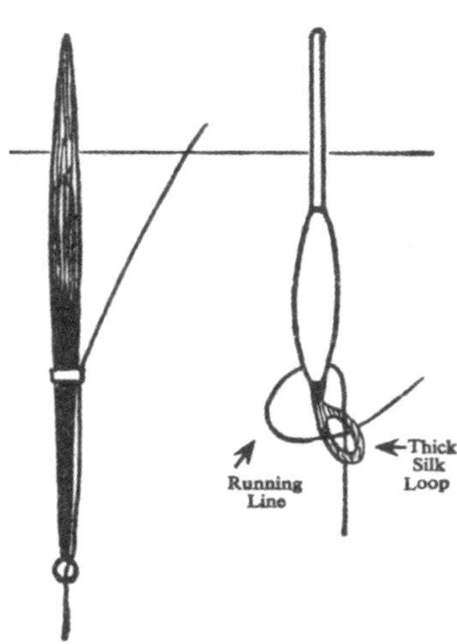

*'I'd met an angler named Roland Hill, he was the best around at the time, and he took me under his wing. Within a short while, we were winning all the matches. Roland was a great innovator and introduced me to the self-cocking float, which was simply a knitting needle with a cork body; that was a milestone.'**

(*Source: 'Ivan Marks and the Likely Lads' by Mark Wintle. He did not say if he used the float bottom only but knowing Ivan's thinking process he would certainly have tried it when combatting a strong wind.)

Did Harold Smith decide for himself to fish his float 'loose', or was he taught the trick by a mentor or another? That is one question I could not find an answer to, so let's just agree he was a pioneer. Other notable 'Yorkies' like Sheffield's Maurice 'lightning' Jackson and York's W.J.C. Noakes, (Bill), were also using bottom attached floats in the years around World War II.

A Flash of Lightning

Former Sheffield Amalgamated AS club secretary Alan Baynes, in his 'Witham Story (1946-1980)' described Maurice Jackson as a *'roach angler supreme'*, for perfecting the *'Sheffield style'* of fishing and becoming its most renowned exponent:

'Nick-named 'lightning' because he was so fast, no one could live with him at catching small fish. He was the fastest angler with the small stuff of his era, one of the impatient breed of anglers who liked to catch fish of any size. Whilst many of the so-called experts were prepared to sit it out and either win or finish with a dry net, Maurice Jackson's intention was to catch plenty of fish. He enjoyed his fishing and if the win came along, as it often did, all the better.' said Alan.

A member of both Sheffield National teams at one time or another, Jackson was the only angler in Yorkshire in his time to win two gold medals in successive years – 1934 and 1935. His top winning catch was 50lb of roach from the River Welland at Market Deeping in five hours. And in one series of seven winter Open sweepstakes on the Witham tributary, Martin's Delph, he won five and came second and third in the other two with an average weight of over 8lb (very good for the venue) against some of the toughest opposition around.

Alan continued: *'Maurice fished a crow quill carrying a maximum of two dust shots placed at least 3ft. from the hook, ensuring that the bait sank naturally through the last part of its descent. Maurice had progressed with his float presentation since the days of the 'old masters' in that he employed it fished LOOSE, i.e. bottom only, so as to avoid wind drift in bad conditions.*

'He was one of the few roach anglers who fished the float loose when most others persisted in fishing it in the conventional manner, and this factor gave him a decided advantage when conditions were far from favourable. His hook size was invariably an 18 round bend baited with a single 'special' liver maggot. In conjunction with this presentation

1934 National winner's team. Maurice Jackson and Harold Smith (centre of front row) behind the team and individual trophies.

Maurice used a fine cloud groundbait and it seemed in match after match that the small fish could not resist swimming through the scintillating mist.

'At the start of a match Maurice Jackson knew exactly where he was going to fish. At the whistle he was off the mark in a flash. A pinch of feeder maggot would be dropped into the pre-mixed groundbait, swiftly worked into a small ball and pitched exactly to the spot. This was done with each cast, and if a bite did not come 'on the drop' the bait was allowed to settle for a short time in the hope of catching a better stamp of fish. But most of them were taken as the bait was falling and his float rarely disappeared, most bites showing only a slight lift of the float and at times onlookers swore they had never seen a bite. Maurice would strike at the slightest movement and, with a gentle lift of the rod top or a leaning over to the left or right, the fish was hooked. The 'secret' of his success, if you can call it a secret, was his superb technique, including the bait presentation aided by the loose float, the groundbaiting method and its accuracy.'

Alan Baynes fondly referred to other 'splendid roach anglers' of that period on the Witham, including: John Arthur Broadhead Snr. and Harold Bennett from Sheffield, and Bob Fuller and Tommy Cotterill (the 1945 National winner) from Worksop but, as good as they sounded, he heaped more praise on another: Joe Emmens. Alan rated Sheffield's Joe Emmens almost as highly as Jackson, saying he also became *'a legend in his own lifetime'*. Joe did not win as often as Maurice but he was more of an all-rounder, winning matches on the Witham and Yorkshire rivers with bream as well as roach. The angling bookie of the day, Joe West, reportedly always gave Emmens the shortest odds irrespective of the match he was taking bets on. Whether Joe fished waggler-style is hard to know however, as Alan Baynes did not say.

These old timers, early post-war, were nothing short of innovative. Another Sheffield National Championship angler of the 'roaring Forties' on the Witham was Bill Hudson, who superseded the crow quills by building a 15" long bottom only job from a cane stem, fattened up for 12" of its length with a slim cork body. It took 4 SSG loading yet despite all that weight, Bill, and his friend Billy Clarke senior (and grandad of the current Sheffield tackle dealer of the same name), won several big open matches. Bill's float was too long to fit easily inside his basket so he carried it in his holdall. Said to be one of the first 'bona fide' bream anglers on the Witham, for a few years Bill was regarded as the best in Sheffield.

The York anglers were highly successful in Witham team events early post-war and most of them fished porcupines and a string of shots well out. Frank Oates, one of their leading anglers, also wrote a book – 'Match Fishing' - in 1957. In it he made what, from a modern perspective, looks like a brave statement: *'Porcupine quill floats are the best for match fishing... sufficiently heavy for accurate casting, yet buoyant enough to carry an adequate amount of lead. They are responsive to most types of bites from taking fish, and their long streamlined bodies allow them to cut through the wind when casting.'*

All the shotting diagrams in Oates' book show 'porkies' with or without cork bodies attached, fastened top and bottom or double rubber. His colleague Bill Noakes however, in a 1949 article in Midland Angler, includes a rig where a 6" porcupine is attached to the line bottom only. It was classed as a 'still water tackle' and he fished it with a 17' Japanese cane rod. Again this shows that different anglers would find their own solutions to weather and water conditions affecting float presentation.

In the angling mad city of Lincoln lies the confluence of the Fossdyke Canal with the end of the upper Witham and start of the lower Witham, and the city's top matchmen were not standing idle. Anglers like Tom Sails, Bill Crane, and brothers Percy and Les Smith Snr. were all gaining competence with the loose float method.

Moving Out

By the start of the 50s anglers generally began to use bigger floats to make longer casts out towards the middle of the Witham. The bream which patrolled there were now within range and the Sheffield, 'rod-end' style for roach was getting left behind. The advent of nylon line and casting reels in these post-war years places the 1950s as the crossroads when the modern angling era began.

These bream anglers possibly got a little carried away with the amount of groundbait taken to a match. A bag of groundbait was one thing, but the keener Sheffield anglers would take a pillowcase full. To quote Frank Oates again, an illustration in his book showing a specimen page from a matchman's diary: *'Used 14lb of biscuit dust together with five pints of feeders (pinkies) all used by 3pm with still one hour to go'*. This was a write-up of a Yorkshire Ouse match where 10lb 10oz won and the author came third with 8lb 2 ¾oz, so had he not run out of bait he might have won.

Some of the more ambitious bream anglers were not content with a bowl or bucket of groundbait, they mixed it in a baby's bath! But to be able to feed half a gallon or more of squatts in groundbait did require a lot of cereal.

In the 50s decade we have much to thank two star Coventry anglers for: Billy Lane, 1963 World Champion elect, and his older compatriot, Harry Wills. This duo were pivotal in their experiments with bottom only floats for Fenland waters. In 1952 Wills, 12 years Billy Lane's senior, won three big Witham open matches with good bream weights. His float was a reversed crow quill, ie. thin end upwards, and shot carrying capacity boosted by a selection of detachable cork bodies, making for a heavier or lighter float to suit the depth and prevailing conditions.

Harry also won the prestigious Trent Championship in that same summer, beating the pride of Nottingham, again on his waggler prototype, with a record 23lb 5oz. This was an incredible catch for just four hours Trent fishing and stood for over 30 years until 1985 when a weight of chub beat it! And it was only ounces short of the five-hour total of Jack Blakey (23lb 12oz) that won the 1961 Trent National. It was probably the first waggler milestone.

Back in 1945 Harry Wills was already using a waggler-style in big matches. In a match report in the April 1951 issue of 'Midland

Angler' a comparison was made of ten different float rigs used in the All-England match. Columnist Frank Oates assessed all ten rigs and said of Wills' rig, as the only bottom only float used: *'Tackle number ten was probably the most efficient of the ten, for H. Wills (Jnr) fishing at I31 put on one of the heaviest bags of roach along the entire section'*. The illustration in the magazine shows what appears to be a porcupine attached by the base ring only.

But by the 1953 Nene National Championship, details of which I discovered from an article on the man in the Nov. '53 Midland Angler, Wills had graduated to a 5" crow quill with the addition of one or two (detachable) cork bodies. In the article the writer refers to Wills' preference for a waggler-type float, and I quote: *'Today he has some very set ideas on match fishing. First and foremost he believes*

Harry Wills in unusual pose (probably) landing a fish. Note the tiny keepnet.

it is the way the bait is presented that really counts, with the wind and drift making all the difference between catching and not catching fish. He maintains that if nature's elements can be overcome and the bait can be offered to the fish in exactly the same way their natural food moves, one is well on the way to success. With this most important point kept to the forefront, Harry devised the LOOSE FLOAT AND SUNKEN LINE METHOD [the caps are mine] *which has produced and is still producing him such excellent results.'*

'He chose the quill with great care. It must be just the right diameter and length; it must be perfectly straight; and when he slips on a specially made cork body it must carry two BB shots, and still show the right amount of tip. When a second of these special bodies is slipped on the float will carry four BB shots'.

A Cool Convertible

Even with a crow quill float as short as 5", with one cork added it took an AAA (or two BB) shot and a dust, and with two corks added it gave it a 2AAA and a dust capacity. In compiling his great Trent catch, Wills set up a 12' rod instead of his usual 13 ½-footer. A great fan of pinkies as feed, he used a cloud groundbait with a few pinkies squeezed into each lump, and with one shot down the line 18" from the hook, he drew the shoal of fish close and got them *'taking the bait only about a foot below the surface'.* So we can conclude his record was set with fish caught close in and on the drop, which adds up to a fast catch rate.

Throughout the match it was said his float rarely dipped under and the majority of bites were 'lift bites'. In previous Trent Championships he had shown his intentions by finishing 11th in successive years and winning three consecutive Trent badges (for a section win).

Harry was a maggot breeder by trade, proprietor of the Five Acre Bait Company, and was noted for his quality pinkies, also called feeders. It was said in the article that they have really earned him his reputation. Harry swears by his feeders and says: *'They are good on the hook too. Put two or three of the plumper ones on a No. 20 hook and they make a very deadly bait for anything.'* [Hard as it was for whoever counted them, there are apparently 14,000 to a pint compared to 5,000 liver maggots (or big maggots)]. *'As fish can only pick them up one by one they certainly do a lot more attracting for a lot less money,'* the writer added.

Alan Baynes summed up the situation: *'During the period leading up to the mid-Fifties the 'pennies started to drop' for Billy Lane and his Coventry friends, who developed and perfected the style and method first pioneered by Harry Wills, and for a number of years they dominated the Witham matches. The loose float and sunken line principle took on a dramatic new phase when fixed spool reels and nylon lines began to seriously emerge and all together gave a new dimension to float fishing in fenland, and Billy Lane must be given the credit for this new style since he was its finest exponent.'*

It is fair to assume that Harry's victories made a big impression on the emerging force and skilful float maker who was Billy Lane. At some point the Wills cork on quill float became the 'Onion' in Billy Lane's hands, and it was only when the float's stem materials changed to balsa on cane that a similar body-down float was christened the 'Ducker'.

Billy Lane swings in a tiny fish on his beloved Nene.

The Rising Antenna

In Billy Lane's 1971 'Encyclopaedia of Float Fishing', he admitted that for a long time he thought peacock quill too buoyant for floats but admired the streamlined quality of a crow quill, reversed or not. Billy softened his view over what he saw as peacock's deficiencies when using it for his giant 16" 'Missile' floats, developed for casts up to 60 yards on the Great Ouse Relief Channel.

The Governor

By the mid-1950s Billy Lane was realising his full potential and his Coventry side had become the top team of the day, winning three team golds in the National Championship – 1956 on the Witham, 1958 on the Welland and 1961 on the Trent.

In the 1956 match on the Witham, Lane caught 19lb of bream for third individual on a large 2SSG-plus size ducker (or heavy waggler), but in the 1961 event he led his team's victory charge with a 4th individual with a float right from other end of the scale - a mini, dumpy waggler he christened the 'Trent Trotter'. This employed a back-shot that dragged on the bottom of his gravelly 2' deep swim that acted like a brake to slow the float's downstream progress.

"Billy Lane was brilliant, and he had the brains to work it all out, exactly which float to put on in any situation," said John Essex, worthy praise by someone who has studied the old records.

Dennis Stringer, a former Coventry team angler, once described to me how the onion float was their main weapon when they won the Welland National. Billy Lane aptly describes its scope in his book: *'It's fine in all still waters, good in canal and in sluggish rivers. I've already mentioned the Middle Nene and another good example would be for reasonably close-in roach fishing in the Lower Welland.'*

In terms of winning ideas, research, and development, I'm not sure anyone (with the exception of Benny Ashurst who we are coming onto) has even got close to the seminal influence on competition angling as Billy Lane. He carried anglers' methods forward in leaps and bounds.

At this point I need to mention two other Fenland pioneers. Peterborough has the deep and windy North Bank of the Nene situated just below the city and it was here that antenna fan Robin Harris learnt his craft. Robin and his team colleague Tug Wilson made some giant balsa-on-cane floats to fish the river here, and Robin later used a bottom only float to win the World Championship in 1969. Both anglers have been credited by Ivan Marks for their forward thinking. Robin was a prolific winner and not just in the Peterborough and Wisbech area, according to John Essex who has pored over the old records. He remains the only man to have won the World Championship and a National Championship – 1969 and 1971 respectively.

This time Billy has fair bagged-up with roach from Scotland's River Tweed.

The other angler, Cambridge star Percy Anderson, lived a bit further South. Although he won the National with swing-tipped bream on the Welland (1974), he also had a mighty reputation with the float on his local River Cam. He influenced Ivan Marks and his 'Likely Lads' team, winning one match at the side of their man Robin Grouse with a quill float all of 24" long. After being given a lesson by Percy, Robin concluded he had a lot more to learn about float-fishing.

World Champions brainstorm; Robin Harris on the Nene watched by Kevin Ashurst.

Percy collaborated float ideas with his friend, Frank Morgan, who he credited as being the 'finest float maker ever'. In the 50s, Frank made a balsa on cane antenna float christened the 'Mardy' which was a squat float with a long cane insert set into the tapered balsa body fat end up, but was intended to be fished top and bottom. He also made a 'Dart' with a longer, slimmer body and shorter cane insert, made for canal fishing bottom only, and a 'Zoomer' which was no different to a ducker in appearance but, heavily loaded with brass, was made famous by Ivan Marks on the Welland for catching bream on a long cast to the far bank.

'Likely Lad' John Essex, would later tackle the often windswept Nene and Welland matches (the 500-plus peggers of the 70s) with an enormous waggler, homemade from a long peacock quill with a slim 3" balsa body and a cane tip, measuring 18 ¾ inches no less. He felt that the length was ideal for burying the reel line well below the surface waves, as a way of making the float travel in the right direction ie. with the flow and against the wind. Although collaborating with Ivan Marks and other team members, he made the floats himself and gained success in events like the Nene Championships. Roy Marlow followed up with an experimental monster of a 20" quill with a shorter 12" quill whipped to it, but eventually the Leicester team abandoned these giants for floats of 8" to 12".* (*Source: Ivan Marks: The People's Champion, article dated 1972).

As tackle and methods improved, big fish were more attainable in matches. Here John Essex with carp caught in the '75 National that helped him to third behind two bream weights.

But Harry Wills aside, were there others trying bottom only in the Trent valley in the 50s and early 60s? As early as 1952, one John R. Cope wrote an article in 'Midland Angler' about two different float presentations on the Trent for fast and slow water: *'Probably you will find it better to fish with a loose float (connected only at the bottom ring) when fishing the slow deeper water, but in the fast shallows a float connected top and bottom is to be preferred.'* Prophetic indeed, this article was published in June, only a few weeks prior to Wills' triumph.

The Enigma

It seems like the waggler style travelled from Fenland to the 'streamier' Trent rather slowly. Jim Sharpe for example, one of Nottingham's best, enjoyed multiple match wins on small top-and-bottom balsa floats in the 50s and 60s. But as stick floats became all the rage in the 60s, there was one man who didn't follow any trend, but relished doing things all his own way: Nottingham's Johnny Moult. Moult turned a bottom only porcupine style on running water into a fine art. I had the pleasure of interviewing 'Moulty' as he was known back in 1984, and it taught me plenty. Come in Sheffield's Terry Payne:

'It was a match at Shelford in the early 1960's. I wasn't feeling too well so decided to pack up and have a walk. I chanced upon John near the bottom of the Cherry Orchard section. He was busy trying to rescue his float, a small porcupine float from the tree behind him. Being taller than he was I offered to help. The peg was what we'd term a 'parrot cage' meaning he had limited room to avoid the tree with his rod. He tackled back up again and when he got the float back in the water it was sheer poetry. With a centre-pin reel and the float attached bottom only, he had too much float showing at the start of the trot. When he reached

the hotspot he leaned back on the float, trimming it nicely, and inching it through to the fish. He caught well; the tree seemed of little consequence and I think he finished second in the match.'

And a word from the late Don Slaymaker, top Trent angler:

'I had the good luck to travel with Johnny for about four months. During that time I learned virtually nothing, only that he was a great angler. He has won more matches than anyone I know with many different styles, most of which confused the opposition. I remember one match in the time when roach were hard to find. So few had been caught all season it seemed like there were none in the river. It was a Notts Fed Clarke Cup match and John was drawn above Stonebridge in the Nelson Field. He landed 9 1/2lb of roach on caster and nobody could believe it. He used his overdepth style with only one micro shot down the line. I often fished the Trent and Mersey Canal at Sandon and one day I took John along to a Stoke DAA Open, an evening match. He drew well, about 40 pegs below Sandon Lock opposite some overhanging trees. I thought he would do well, but he put up an unbelievable 10lb 6oz to break the canal record. He had a 2lb chub, which could be called lucky, but the rest were quality roach and skimmers on caster fished over the far side.'

As a member of the Travellers match group, Johnny Moult did not restrict himself to his home river but took his method to the West Midlands and the Severn. As leading Birmingham angler and former Shakespeare Professionals skipper, Ken Giles recalled in an article on Waggler Fishing in 1981:

'The great Birmingham angler, Billy King, was the first angler in this area to see the potential of the waggler and he did a tremendous amount of work in developing the method. I suppose it was easy to understand anglers' reluctance to use the waggler in those days. It was almost unheard of to run a float down the river at the speed of the current. We used to use bird quills or balsa floats and these were invariably fished overdepth and held back. Shotting was usually a bunch and a dropper on the hooklength. It is also worth remembering that the rivers have changed. We read now about chub weights on the Avon whereas in those days a chub was a bonus fish. It was the same at Evesham and Stourport (Avon and Severn), these were roach venues. As a consequence the waggler wasn't viewed in quite the same way it is today.

'Far bank fishing, especially on the bigger rivers, was unheard of. My generation were brought up on the centre pin reel which is ideal for fishing a slow-moving bait. With the advent of the fixed-spool reel,

A smart operator, Ken Giles at his peak was Birmingham's finest. He pays tribute here to Johnny Moult.

anglers realized that they could now fish further out. What we couldn't get into our heads was the fact that we could catch fish running a bait down at the speed of the current, and this is why it took such a long time for the waggler to really catch on.

'I suppose it was Johnny Moult who finally persuaded the Midlands anglers that the waggler could be a match-winning method. He visited the River Severn and caught fish on the waggler on pegs where you couldn't normally catch anything. It's worth remembering that 10 years ago there weren't the open matches there are today; one a week was as many as you could hope to find, if you were lucky. Consequently we spent much more time pleasure fishing than we do today. Having finally come to terms with the fact that we could catch on the waggler, or 'windcheater' as we called them in those days, we set about developing the method.' (Source: 'Match Fisherman' magazine.)

Ken confirmed that the first occasion when the Birmingham team, of which he was skipper, looked at the waggler as a match-winning method was during practice for the famous 1971 First Division National on the Severn. And history shows this was the year when the peacock waggler became a regular match winner.

And from Johnny Moult himself about waggler-style:
'In the Sixties I started to fish a loose porcupine float; one could call it an early version of the waggler. I found burying the line gave me better presentation and it gave me an edge on the Trent for a long time. Others fished loose float of course, but I shotted very light down the line and caught on the drop. [This conflicts slightly with Slaymaker's

'overdepth' description.]. *Something just happened one day, like things do in fishing, which was like striking gold. I had always dragged back the tackle a yard after casting to keep a tight line. Until the line is released a loose float will stay submerged under a tight line on the Trent because of the flow. On this occasion I delayed releasing the line and kept the float buried. When I finally gave line and the float reappeared it went under again and I had a fish on. I developed this delaying tactic into a countdown system similar to fishing on the drop with a bomb. I couldn't explain why it worked but it did and sometimes the float would never come up at all. Maybe it could be likened to holding back with a stick float.'*

'When the caster boom hit in the Sixties I still liked to use maggot to start with. I found it better to catch from the off on maggot and gradually wean the fish onto caster. Sometimes it would take one hour, sometimes two before I made the changeover. I have also switched to red maggot when caster has been tailing off late in the match. It is really about trial and error I suppose. I remember winning one match at Rolleston with 30lb of roach when I had only pinkies with me. I borrowed a few ordinary maggots as hookbait and caught on the drop. Pinkies sink nice and slow which suits my style of catching high in the water. I have also fed pinkies and switched to casters when the fish got confident. This method once caught me 22lb off the road stretch (Burton Joyce). Of course, when the caster boom was as its peak I sometimes used them on their own to win matches.'

1980 Division One National Championship team winners' pic' (Johnny is furthest left in foreground). They stunned the field with a National record team points total.

What John didn't add was that he also fed tares as a third bait and if he got fish feeding on them his catch rate could go up a level and make him unbeatable.

But even the greats do not always win. The day Kevin Ashurst broke the six-hour Trent match record with 41lb 11oz from Shelford Shallows, finishing just 2lb in front of Ivan Marks at the next peg, John put 33lb 15 1/4oz on the scales from another section on his loose float and caster method. He thought he had won the match, and had every right to with such a big weight, until to his dismay the last section board came in with three better weights on it. Two weeks late at Holme Marsh, John's team colleague, Ted Stokes broke the river's five-hour match record with 37lb 14oz, leaving John second with 32lb 7oz.

The Visionary

At this point I need to mention the Trent 'Raiders from the North-West' Lancastrians led by the great Benny Ashurst and son, the young phenomenon and future World Champion, Kevin, who set both the 4-hr (tidal) and 6-hr (non-tidal) Trent weight records in the 60s. They and friends came and conquered with their deadly stick float and caster combination. But they could also revert to the waggler with deadly effect when conditions demanded.

Ted Stokes with a net of Derwent dace. Widely respected, Ted was an angler others listened to (see Chapter 13).

Benny's book 'Match Fishing' published in 1968 forecast what was to come with inserted peacock quill floats, and in the 1971 Trent Champs he proved it, taking the title with 18lb 3oz of roach on waggler from a shallow swim below Hazelford Weir. He fished a 12" long peacock locked to the depth with two swan shot and a couple of BB 'downstairs'. Baiting with caster on a 16 hook he

Benny Ashurst with a big catch of Trent roach.

realised his long-held ambition but left it late, taking a third of his roach bag in a hectic last 40 minutes!

Benny's book had beforehand extolled the qualities of a short peacock quill float, saying: *'The stick is a good float for a falling bait but it has nothing to counteract the surface drift often evident on canals. The float I have brought out for this purpose is made from peacock quill. It is in two parts, with a thin inset into the top of the lower half. The float measures from four to five inches overall – with the varied lengths allowing for different shot-carrying capacities. The peacock inset extends to an inch and a half. The advantage of this fine tip is that it enables better casting than would a single length of quill. I aim for a shot load of three BB and one No. 4. The float is fastened to the line by running the line through the small base ring. One BB shot is nipped on the line above the float and the remaining two just below it, trapping the float in position. The No. 4 is placed a foot from the hook.'*

Bear in mind that this was a light canal waggler to suit Benny's local waters. But a float twice the size would serve nicely if the wind was bad on the Trent, and they were already using them there by the time his book was published. This is also the first reference I have seen to 'locking shot' used either side of the float's base ring.

Kevin incidentally, fished a peacock and balsa float waggler-style to win an Angling Times Winter League final on Ireland's River Suck as early as 1964. But by general consent the year that the peacock finally spread its wings and became the waggler of choice was 1971.

Rolfe's Rule

Nottingham's Johnny Rolfe was one Trent legend who was at his peak in this breakthrough year, and enjoyed a remarkable run of open match wins that single him out as the first real champion of the float we know today. John had used peacocks on the fenland drains in the summer before he moved to the Trent from September onwards.

Terry Dorman, former Nottingham tackle dealer, bait breeder, team colleague of John's and a more than useful Trent angler in his own right, said: *'We knew a good local angler called Pete Brough and he had watched Billy Lane winning a match on the Nene. He made a peacock float when back home in Nottingham and used it with wheat bait at Burton Joyce and won a match, and when this story got round it made people think.'*

John Rolfe told me himself in the 80s: *'We all had peacocks (the term we gave wagglers at the time) which we used on the Fenland drains in summer but we fished top and bottom on the Trent from September onwards. But were limited with the wind to two or three rod-lengths distance. In the 1971-72 season I fished the peacock further out and the first time I put it on I won with 11lb and 9lb to spare over the second man. The feed was groundbait and casters. The next match was the Worksop at Holme Marsh and I won with 16lb and it carried on from there. I had the middle of the river to myself for a while and won 17 Opens that season and £2,000 in winnings,'* he said.

Johnny's local tackle dealer and float maker, Gerry Woodcock, began making John's floats commercially, which John insisted on calling 'Swingers'. They had a long slim body built onto a ¼" diameter quill and took a lot of shot for their size. This allowed Johnny to fish well out beyond his rivals which gave him an advantage of having all the river downstream to himself to draw fish from.

John Rolfe and his famous 'Swingers'. These floats helped him rule the Trent for a time, often fishing at a range well past his rivals.

By October, following a double win in both the Saturday and Sunday matches (both in the Burton Joyce Nelson Field, the first with 12lb 6 1/2oz which was 1lb more than Johnny Moult at the next peg, and the second with 22lb 2 1/2oz) the angling columnist in the Nottingham Evening News, Clive Brett announced: *'To my knowledge no local matchman has ever had such a run of success as Johnny Rolfe. This is his sixth Fed. success (Nottingham Federation) of the season and in opens he's won eight.'*

Fellow Nottingham team man, Roy Toulson knocked about with Johnny at the time and told me how they both used a BB shot 18" from the hook and a float with a good peacock stem, the typical Swinger being an average 10" long. Roy added: *'At times we'd drag a dust shot (No. 8) and 12" of line on the bottom, other times we'd fish heavier with 2BB shot down but off the deck. My mate, Pete Palmer fished up off the bottom a lot and it worked very well for him.'*

Nottingham AA National Championship angler, Brian Richmond, a miner from Mansfield, topped a 270-strong field to claim the Soar Championship title in 1971 with a respectable 11lb 15oz of roach. Running his peacock float down the middle with an orange caster on a 16 hook, he didn't have a bite for an hour. He was about to go for a walk when on his next trot his peacock float 'juddered and sank'. From then on he caught roach in bursts, usually three in turn between quiet spells and some of them touching a pound apiece. Brian finished up almost 4lb clear to take home £118 and the trophy.* (*Source: Woodbine Angling Yearbook 1972.)

Londoners Spring Suprise

Possibly the biggest shock of this memorable year came again in the Trent Championship from an unexpected quarter. A young five-man London side, 'The Team' (not the most original name) took the five-man team title from under the noses of the pride of Nottingham with a 31lb 11 1/4oz total. This was a stunning achievement, a bit like Millwall going to Old Trafford and scalping them 5-0. Part of the team caught on stick float while others fished waggler.

Billy Hughes remembers this day as the highlight of his fishing career. All five team members were under 26 years old and, according to their man Johnny McCarthy, after they had added up the weights at the presentation and knew they'd won, he (Billy) got up on a table and danced a jig!

Waggler specialist Billy Hughes, member of 'The Team', and a big shield he won for a waggler catch.

"We were a tight-knit group and would meet in a London pub every Monday night to plan matches", said John, who was aged 25 at the time. "We drove up to the match on the morning, and Dick Vetterlein, a little older than us and seen as something of a father figure, was made reserve. When we drew our pegs we chatted with Ian Heaps who said our draw was nothing special. I caught mostly small dace on stick float and maggot at the bottom of the Burton Joyce road stretch, but some of the team caught on waggler. We were 4lb behind with one man to come in, then Billy came back with 6lb meaning we'd clinched it, causing cheering and fist pumps all round."

Views differ as to who was leader of the group. Billy Hughes had done some of his own early research into quill floats, and he lays claim to developing a southern version of the waggler before it got the name, saying how watching Billy Lane encouraged his own experiments. He also gave Andy Partridge the waggler he used in the match. Kenny Collings was also already a fine river angler, and chatty, but Johnny McCarthy was a strong character and just as influential. John later opened Croydon Angling Centre (1978) and, combining with Dells Angling Centre, they formed the renowned DELCAC angling club a year later.

Johnny 'Mac' sold wagglers at his Croydon shop from 1978 onwards, made for him by a chap called Dick Chatland.* They were given a distinctive black and emerald green camouflaged appearance and were all perfectly straight, and at their popularity peak John was selling over 100 a week to his customers! *"Billy Hughes and Micky Thill also made lots of wagglers at the time,"* said John. John once caught 146lb of roach on a 4-Swan waggler on the River Bann at Portadown, in the good years when every fish was 8oz and bigger. He caught them dragging on the bottom with two BBs down the line but was pipped by Denis White with 150lb-plus.

'Team' member Kenny Collings with fish of a size that separate winners from also-rans.

(***Note:** I can vouch for the quality of these floats, having been sent one by John many years ago which often served me well in rough conditions.)

So, by 1972 the cat was finally out of the bag. No longer would anyone be restricted to fishing the margins anywhere. There were now stirrings in the main angling centres in Yorkshire, Lancashire, the

Woodstock? No, it is the victorious 'Team' with lady friends alongside – (l to r): Dick Vetterlein, Eddie Kemp, Micky Thill, Andy Partridge – top scorer with 9lb 15oz for ninth overall, Kenny Collings, Billy Hughes and Johnny McCarthy.

Midland counties and far beyond. From the Trent to the Thames, Witham to the Weaver, and Warwickshire Avon to Bristol Avon, the waggler was a hot topic.

A new breed of river angler was emerging with an understanding that casting and controlling a float at distance was far less of a problem than was once thought. Neither had the peacock gone unnoticed by the likes of Bradford ace John Illingworth and Barnsley's Denis White. They and their followers would not let the legacy of the likes of Ashurst, Wills, Lane, Moult and Rolfe down. Ian Heaps would soon be claiming his 1975 World individual title in Poland on a big slider, Pete Palmer would take the 1977 Gladding Masters on the Trent using a standard waggler, and many others would go on to win big with the method. The peacock waggler was here to stay and would continue to shape angling's future. In 1985 Peter Drennan, long after his quill floats were well established, discovered how tench on his local lakes around Oxford would feed more confidently when he used a semi-transparent, clear plastic float. This led to his famous lightweight Crystal as a handy alternative to peacock. The rest, as they say, is history.

Pete Palmer and his 7lb catch that won the 1977 Gladding Masters title on the Trent.

Footnote: More kudos to the waggler. The 'young lions', in the shape of the England Under-23 squad, underscored the power of the sliding waggler by taking silver medal in the 2013 World Championships. Fishing 18′ deep on the River Villaine, at Rieux, France, they tamed their swims with giant sliders (see more from Matt Godfrey, chapter 20).

Chapter 4
A Personal Journey - Part 1

Life at home

Family life in the Fifties in Walkley, Sheffield was never dull. There were six of us including four children – myself as the eldest, sister Margaret and twin brothers Brian and Matthew, but no pets other than a canary. *'We've got enough two-legged 'uns,'* parents would say. The River Rivelin, a Don tributary, was only about 200 yards away from the house as the crow flies and seeing this rippling stream could have fired my imagination that I'd one day become a fisherman.

My father, Colin, could be cantankerous and sarcastic with the best. But it was not all bad news. He might lose his cool one minute, then in a flash his face could light up and he'd transform into this joker who might burst into song or perform a simple magic trick! He had a rough start in life - his mother died when he was just two, and then apparently a hard step-mother took over. He may even have been relieved to get away when, not long after leaving school he served on Navy landing craft, entering hostile beaches during WW2. He came home physically unscathed but, along with so many others, the war left its mark. Rarely would he share his darker moments, more inclined to blank it out as veterans do. He had mental scars but it was only the family that really knew it, and his strength of character won through in the end.

Colin's lighter moments could be hilarious though. His singular memory of India was 'cheap scent and fried onions', and one particular birthday meal at a local pub he burst out with 'I'm over-faced' when a giant plaice was put down before him over-lapping the plate. The tragi-comic way he announced this was straight out of Fawlty Towers and had everyone in the pub turning round and holding back laughter. He had his own special vocabulary too, all spoken with indignation and possibly navy sourced: *'I'm stood here like CLEM'* (ie delayed), we are *'sitting here like SOUSE'* (fools), or *'he's a SOONER'* (an undesirable person). After a lunch for octogenarians at Sheffield's City Hall he arrived home to cynically describe the meal as: 'a little piece of chicken in some cock-eyed sauce.' He was an ailing man by this time in fairness.

Dad kept fit by walking, either two miles to and from work, or at weekends by the water with his fishing tackle. He'd repair his well-worn boots in the garage with a last and bits of old leather, and

Colin showing off a fly-caught trout from Morehall, North Sheffield, as we enjoy a family picnic (Lynne holding camera).

In a fun mood, Colin would balance his brolly on his foot, swing it up in the air and catch it on his outstretched palm; then challenge any family member with the words: 'not that easy, can you do it?'.

through his lifetime must have made enough furniture to kit out a John Lewis showroom.

His fishing stories harked back to when he was his [own] dad's gopher, fetching the brew of tea from home at Bradfield where they lived in a cottage a stone's throw from Damflask's neck end. My granddad, Willie, would allegedly slowly peel an apple with his penknife before munching most of it then handing the last remnants around the core to Colin. Willie landed some big trout in the Flask's early 20th century days soon after the reservoir's construction, before Sheffield's growing angling community saw its potential. Although Colin learnt with inferior lines and the tackle limitations of the day, the occasional sight of these big ferox trout up to 7lb from this majestic water inspired him.

I look back at his steely resolve and resourcefulness, and know it helped me as an angler. A natural worrier, he found total peace on the bankside even though he played hard. A typical 'dawn till dusk' man, his competitive streak surfaced when fly fishing and he was needing a late fish to avoid a blank. He'd get his head down and try harder. *'And never waste that last yard of retrieve when close to the bank,'* he'd say, either with a fly or spinner.

If Colin was pessimistic, mum Winifred's constantly cheery mood made up for it and kept us all upbeat. Their temperaments balanced out nicely, making for a noisy but generally happy household. Mum would sing as she did the cooking, an extrovert fond of red clothes and outlandish hats, but she could be feisty in her own way and was great with the put-downs, saying dad was *'ruled by the moon'* or he was *'only happy making others miserable'* – ouch!

Winifred's optimism was a joy to know and it must have rubbed off on me because when dipping into any drawbag on the Witham I always imagined a good peg and think I got more than my share. To remember the good days and [to] try forgetting the bad – visualizing good outcomes - certainly helped, as it does in life I'm sure. We achieve nothing by beating ourselves up about bad draws and hard times, and as badly as I could slump after a bad result or two, I always fished well in the match immediately following a good result.

Fortune obviously comes into our peg selection and when I've been on a good run some might conclude I'm lucky, have kissed the Blarney stone or something, but then they might not appreciate the previous bad run. I have observed some strange coincidences at the drawbag though, and sometimes it's like a magnet that draws us to certain places. Only last Spring I won four matches in four weekly tries at Barlow Farm from the same peg. As organizer of these little matches it didn't look good when I won every one from Cabin peg 21, BUT I never drew any of them, always taking the one that was either drawn for me or left in the bag.

Grandad Willie [3rd right] and party dressed up and ready for action in their Sunday best on a Bridlington sea fishing trip.

Lucky or not, the first lucky person in our family who definitely had it was my kid sister Margaret, 18 months my junior. Going to Saturday dance classes aged 10, she arrived home with a box of Milk Tray for winning the raffle almost every week. Her winning streak was uncanny and always gained from only one ticket. She learnt how to jive, she said, and had to dance plenty to burn off those calories. Did this mean my mother had some gypsy DNA somewhere beneath that radiant smile and raven black hair, I wonder?

The Baxters

The Baxter side of the family has a musical leaning, which is sadly lost on myself. Dad would sing in local pubs and/or play the mouth organ on request. His elder brother, Les, was an accomplished pianist, as is his son and my cousin, Steve. Dad was also fascinated by astronomy and space travel, and Patrick Moore, eccentric host of 'The sky at night' TV show, was a bit of a hero. He loved any kind of challenge, physical or mental. Apart from creating things from old scraps of wood, or growing flowers and tomatoes in his greenhouse, he loved to receive a good puzzle for a present. The best (or possibly worst?) challenge he ever got was the Rubik's cube which he was enthralled with but couldn't solve. He cussedly twisted it for months until we all grew tired of it. He'd never as the saying goes tolerate fools gladly and had no time for anyone he thought lazy. For years when he fly fished at Morehall Reservoir he'd catch a bus, or set off walking then shamelessly hitch a lift on a passing vehicle. Few anglers would do that today I'm sure, and far fewer over 70! Uncle Les built a houseboat in his cellar and garden that made its way from the Sheffield Canal via Fossdyke Canal to the River Witham at Kirkstead (on the famed Chicken Run stretch) where it is still berthed. As for the Hurrells, mum's side of the family, they were all good people, always up for a laugh, and some of them also fished, keenest of them being my other Uncle Les (Oxley) which was at times a shade confusing, cousin Paul, now living in Ireland, and nephew Dave, a carp and barbel angler.

The hardest of waters

My early fishing life was limited to one large water, invariably wild and windy and gin clear, where the good fish were notoriously crafty. Damflask Reservoir, Bradfield, had its moments, but at first they amounted to tiny bullheads and gudgeon, or a small perch that took pity on me, fishing amongst the rocks in the deep bay area. This was fascinating in itself as a kid of eight, for anything was better than a dry net, but even the adults who knew their stuff would struggle at the difficult 'Flask'.

Hooking one of those elusive, silver-sided roach was the ambition, but achieving it was beyond me and would be for some time. The fish immediately knew the difference between the loose maggots and the one with the metal hook inside it, and so I came up dry. Because of this (and the bullheads never quite meeting the criteria of a fish to brag about) my early angling interest wavered.

This windy expanse of water, 3 ½ miles in circumference, had the added handicap of being very deep. An experienced friend later explained how to find swims where I could 'bottom it', ie. find the depth near the end of a 12-foot rod, but in some areas even this was difficult. The great Billy Lane fished the dam once and, two roach later, the world champion described it as the hardest lake he'd ever fished, which from a legend who had fished almost everywhere was really saying something.

Billy Lane contemplates a change of float in trying to catch roach at Damflask Reservoir (neck end of dam).

When still at school my whole tackle outfit was handed down from Colin, but unfortunately I could not take pride in any of it; a short cane rod and part-rusted barbed hooks were a handicap even if some were named 'Allcock's model perfect'. But probably what I needed most was some good instruction. Dad was mustard keen but a bit of a lone wolf as a fisherman, and didn't know or socialise with many good anglers.

Neither did we have any easy local fishing to learn from, or none that we knew. The now cleaned up River Don was a soup of industrial effluent, and few would have thought of wasting a day there. They might have caught something but it wouldn't have been fish. The adjacent Sheffield Canal was no better as far as I know and the whole local angling scene was more parochial then; yes, a long trip to the Witham gave the chance to net a few bream, but as a schoolboy reliant upon public transport such adventures were not that regular.

Sometimes I was invited on Dad's firm's 'factory match': a coach trip to far off venues. Places with evocative names in the Fens like Guyerne, Anton's Gowt and Swineshead, and I marvelled at the expanse of the river when one year the coach arrived at a windswept North Bank of the Nene. I could only have been about thirteen and remember missing stacks of bites from bleak while catching a few suicidal ones.

Some anglers at the time though, were working out how to defeat the difficult Flask roach. Derek Hinchliffe, now a veteran Sheffield angler, told me how he tackled it: "We used a boss peacock waggler of 16" long with a double insert. This helped us bury the reel line a bit easier and trip the bottom at 12'-13' deep. The float had to pick up the flow and run against the wind to get bites, and we'd put a no. 6 and no. 8 shot in the last yard of line above the hook. In company with anglers like Bill Bartles, Jack Andrews, Ian Wiggins and Mick Higginbottom, we found that the 'dumping' style of feeding caster – a small handful and then leaving it alone for a few fish – kept the fish down on the bottom. We could only hit bites on the bottom, and sometimes feeding clay off the bankside helped the fish feed more confidently, especially in the bay near Hughill Point."

While we eventually found that a few roach could be caught on the bottom and close in with cheese, a bait the trout also seemed partial to, Derek's way was probably the best for hooking the tricky roach on maggot. When the fish were flashing around up in the water they were a nightmare to hook. I knew of certain anglers outsmarting them shallow, notably with wasp grub fished three-foot deep in the warmer months. Of course an 18 hook in a queen wasp grub cannot be seen anything like as easily as in a maggot only a third of its size. Another angler called Jeff Capper had some success by almost burying a 24 hook in the maggot.

To stress the difficulty of this lake, in 26 years of the Damflask Championship from 1965 to 1990 (fished by 150 or more) a catch of 4lb or less was good enough to win half of the matches (with a 1lb 7 3/4oz low); in the others it often took a bream or two to make the top weight look respectable.

Colin the specimen hunter

In time bigger bream started to figure in catches and anglers switched to long range feeder to reach them. Some huge chub up to 6lb were also caught by a small group of big fish anglers. Back in the fifties and sixties though, carp never got a mention and neither did bigger fish of other species, with the exception of pike of which the Flask held some proper leviathans. The specimen fish likely grew fat on the trout that were stocked each new season when it was a mixed trout and coarse fishery. The

Sheffield's Keith Mottram with a stunning 19lb 9oz pike from Damflask.

best I heard about was a 34lb-er caught by a local called Paul Chivers, but he told me he'd seen a much bigger fish in the deep Hughill bay area.

We only saw the local fishing scene from a basic level, I should add. Dad was more of a trout angler and occasional coarse angler who fished his firm's two annual matches, an allotments society match and not many others each summer, turning to spinning for pike in Lincolnshire in winter.

He caught a 'pb' 5lb 2oz trout at Damflask just hours before I entered the world in June 1950, and on another special day he caught two of 3lb. And one red-letter day when I was with him, aged 10, he said he'd just have one more 'chuck' on the low side of the bay with his usual fat and juicy lobworm (he called them 'dew worms'). We had only twenty minutes left before catching the last bus back to Sheffield so it was really a long shot on getting a bite. But looking across the bay at the beautiful pink sunset I remember so well, his rod bounced into action, the tin lid bite indicator flew off the spinning centre-pin, and he hooked into a heavy fish. Three minutes later this huge trout came up and cleared the water by a good yard when it jumped, then jumped again. A magnificent sight, the airborne fish looked 10lb to my young eyes but scaled 4lb exactly. A full-spotted brownie, the fish's flanks were every bit as rosy as the sunset. This was an event, a capture worth talking about for weeks.

Although Dad's methods were a bit crude he made them work and turned up several big fish, often when I least expected him to.

Dad never owned a car and our holidays were spent in a caravan at Filey or Flamborough on the East Coast. We knew a local fisherman who'd take us out on the North Sea for the day and we caught codling, whiting and mackerel. At last, I hooked fish that pulled back and pulling up three mackerel at once on a set of jiggers gave a terrific fight that nearly had me over the boat gunnel! Dad, as an ex-navy man, knew all the dodges about fishing from boats. On any pub trip it was essential to be 'cute' (a word he liked) and get an early position on the boat 'up forard or down aft', he'd say. They were in effect end pegs on a small boat. Fishing shoulder to shoulder amidships was not advisable, being a tangle of lines and lures waiting to happen. And exploiting this theory he'd often win pub trip boat competitions.

On one less happy seaside day, we were out digging for sandworms or those prized, darting, silver sand eels, and I saw a flash in the wet sand, plunged my hand in to investigate and got stung by a small weaver fish. It spiked me on the finger and felt like three wasp stings in one hit, and the worming session was cut short.

It was other trips that rekindled my early coarse fishing interest. First with school pals to small ponds along the Rivelin valley near to home, then at last when we took the train to the Fossdyke Canal at Saxilby. The smell of the lush grassy bankside instead of the usual Flask's rocks was invigorating, and the sense of freedom a joy. Catching even hand-sized fish was still not easy but at least we were now seeing our floats go under more often.

A progress check

A ticket for the Sheffield and District AA juvenile match on the Witham at Kirkstead, along with over a hundred other under-16s as I recall, was seen as a good opportunity to return to the river I'd fished before and hopefully catch on an 'easier water'. I was to learn that competing in a match was trickier than the newspaper angling columns always implied; ending up totally demoralized though was not part of the plan.

A talented 1980s Richardson's-sponsored [cutlers] Sheffield Amalgamated Junior side.

I could only muster four tiny roach for 2oz, while the bigger youth drawn beside me, called Pearce, caught 1lb. The result left me feeling lonely and depressed as I walked back to Kirkstead station to catch the train home. From my (age 12) standpoint, my old cane rod was too short and whippy for a good strike, the rest of the kit a bit makeshift, and casting my small float past the marginal weed growth wasn't easy. Counter intuition told me Pearce had coped well enough though and his tackle wasn't that much better than mine? His 1lb would have easily got him in the top 20 prizes – so my excuses would sound lame back home. It was a day that took some recovering from.

It was three summers later at Kirkstead when I made my next attempt at a junior match. This time lady luck helped me out. Fishing the opposite (railway) bank, upstream towards the landmark called Ivy Cottage, I hooked a decent fish. Trouble was I'd actually dozed in mid-match when the fish took the bait. After what could have been one minute or an eternity of five, I awoke to find the float underwater, the line tight and a roach on the end which not surprisingly had swallowed the bait and was duly landed. Result: one fish for 9oz.

Amazingly this low weight got me ninth overall, with 5lb of small bream winning the match from some child genius using swing-tipped ledger and gozzer maggots. Any lad topping 5lb when most mortals could manage 2lb at best was permitted serious bragging rights but his name is long forgotten. I was obviously still lacking in a few departments, but that large slice of good fortune gave my shaky confidence a real boost.

Hardly a day passed in my youth without dad talking about fishing – planning a trip, making some item of tackle, or attending to our bait ahead of the morning we actually set off on the big excursion. And a cliché it may be, but I could never sleep easily for the excitement and would wake before the alarm clock. Dad's boundless enthusiasm far surpassed mine however, as I had so much to learn and had not yet made a good catch anywhere.

If he didn't have the knowledge to teach me the finer points of match fishing, Dad made up for it with his passion and snippets of wisdom. He drilled it into me to tread quietly and keep a low profile, never making quick arm movements or jumping about or the fish would scare at our presence. And to this day I always set my landing net up as the first job like he always told me, after placing my box gently on the peg. Lots of little things add up. But it was not until I reached senior school age and was starting to catch a few silver fish that I realized fishing might become an important part of my life.

Summer coach trips to the South Forty Foot Drain at '88 gate', a railway access point to the drain near Wyberton, Boston, were always good and got the adrenalin flowing. This involved crossing the live railway line to reach the bankside. I only have happy memories of the often weed strewn drain that offered better roach and skimmer catches than other places I knew - Dad's on bread paste or flake over hemp, mine on maggot, though one day I tricked a jack pike onto a plug after seeing it first sunbathing in the weed. Even better were the 'Angler's Special' train journeys down to the lower Witham, usually Bardney for us. There was always a frantic rush for the train and the bustle of the anglers on the platform had its own special atmosphere; grimy Sheffield (as it was then) lost its significance with each station passed towards the river and its lush, grassy banks. I'd play pencil cricket, a form of solitaire with two hexagonal pencils, to while the journey away. Once the river came into view though, we'd soon be looking out of the window onto the water for promising signs of rising fish.

My mate, Dave Curbishley, reminded me recently, just how frantic it could be when the packed train pulled in at Bardney station or any other along the Witham's course. Tackle was sparser then and carryalls full of accessories and gadgets had not been thought of. All most anglers had was a basket or wooden box over their left shoulder carrying all the reels and smaller items and bait, plus, of course, a keepnet and landing net in a bag. The rod bag, net pole and bank-stick formed a slim holdall under the arm or over the other shoulder.

The train would grind to a halt and well before the whistle sounded for it to set off again, the race was on to reach the best pegs. I remember the sickly sweet smell of the sugar beet factory as we walked that long, sweeping inside bend below Bardney Bridge (I still associate the smell with roach as it also comes from Newark's sugar factory and we could smell it on the Trent from a couple of miles away at Winthorpe when carried on the wind). On sunny days, or if a club match had booked the first field, the train would be crammed full and it almost became a sprint off that platform to find a peg that wasn't a mile away.

But to me, the mad dash to get to pegs, clambering over stiles and the like, didn't matter; the river was beautiful, meandering and inviting, and seemed greener then than ever it did in later years. This is quite natural as things always seem much better when looking back. I tried with bigger baits here but never caught any bream. The power of good groundbaiting was still unknown to me. The general pattern was: I'd catch 20 or so small roach over the first three hours then dad would hit back with the better quality roach on hemp in the afternoon, always topping my weight.

Other trips were made with schoolmates, including Roger Cotton who had earlier won respect for taking a 10oz roach from Rivelin's Round Dam – an almost impossible feat in our young eyes from a pond where roach in the hand were as rare as a lunar eclipse. On the Fossdyke Canal at Saxilby, some five miles shy of Lincoln and the nearest station on the line where we could access fishing, wily Rog would fish down the margin while I thought it best to cast into the boat track near the middle. The usual outcome was I'd get most fish but he'd beat me on weight thanks to three or four hand-sized skimmers. One up for his watercraft against my fancy casting. We fished maggots but every season tales would circulate about the old canal men catching big roach on 'seed' – 1lb fish, mostly on hemp and tares, occasionally wheat, and at other times bread.

On one return journey from Bardney (an adventure for us aged 14), a sunny afternoon after we'd caught very little, I saw another youngster still fishing as the train passed, and he swung a roach in. At the same time a story was doing the rounds of a young angler who had won a junior match with 5lb of small fish on pinkie bait. Why couldn't I do that? I wanted to step up to that kind of weight yet the chance looked remote; I'd no idea how with my limited knowledge.

A while later I saw a more experienced lad on our 'youth club' match announce his intentions by opening up a sizeable tinful of pinkies, and this was only half his bait supply. Could this be the way to those catches? My heart sank when I looked at my own smaller tin. As it turned out he didn't do that well with them; it was a bad day - cold and misty - but another mate of mine, Phil Goss, won it with four good roach for 1 1/2lb. The details escape me as I never kept a diary until 1972, but feel sure my old faithful porcupine float hardly moved that day. Phil, bless him, a lad who was always smiling and liked by everyone, sadly died in a car accident before he was out of his teens.

Underbank Reservoir, Stocksbridge, brought a ray of hope. Armed with my new glass rod bought as a 15th birthday present by Mum, I rigged up with an Arlesey bomb and a butt bite indicator. It must have been a good day because after an hour I landed a 'pb' roach weighing 1lb 4oz on my Samson spring balance. The next time the aluminium indicator hit the rod I landed another 'big' roach, and then a third, and they were both a mirror image of the first, and uncannily weighing close to 1lb 4oz.

The ledgered bait had changed my fortunes, and I began to try it with some success on perch at Damflask. I have often thought in later life how badly I needed some coaching at this point in my angling. Someone like the legendary Eddie Outram would have knocked me into shape. Eddie, I found out too late, caught more Flask fish than anyone in the Sixties with his canal methods brought over from Leigh, Lancashire. He could turn his hand to float and bread punch, or a small feeder with squatts when the method was still in its infancy. Unfortunately I was still not keen enough to go out and search for good anglers like him to learn from.

The Breakthrough

My younger by eight years twin brothers, Brian and Matthew, were only aged 7 by this time, but were already showing some fishing interest. They could not escape it, of course, as the main topic of dad's conversation. Of different temperaments, Brian was a competitor who later progressed to do well in some club competitions while Matthew was content with pleasure fishing. Brian's time was taken up playing other sports - table tennis for Yorkshire boys and then going on to become a good snooker player in his teens. I was perhaps too self-centred to give the lads any help at this point, busy looking for answers to my own angling questions.

Angling title for 17-year-old

Sheffield Newspapers Ltd. Welfare Club angling section prizewinners were presented with their awards by the president, Mr. J. F. Goulden, Director and General Manager, in the firm's canteen.

Winner of the Championship Cup and Chairman's Prize was 17-year-old Jim Baxter, an apprentice in the Composing Department, with a weight of 21lb. 10½oz. He is the youngest competitor ever to win the cup.

Runner-up was Bill Fieldsend of the Maintenance Department with 10lb. 10½oz. He received a hors d'oeuvres dish.

Prizewinners were introduced by the chairman, Jack Richardson.

But my own fishing world was about to change in dramatic fashion. Armed with one good GCE o-level in art, which I was proud of as my other academic achievements were poor (I was rebellious and did not work for the exams, later having to take them at college), I somehow clinched a job with Sheffield Newspapers as an apprentice compositor. This involved keyboard work, making the linotype that formed the words in the finished paper, and page make-up – building up pages of the same type, headlines and pictures in a frame. The finished page became a semi-circular 'stereo' that fitted onto the printing press.

At the first opportunity the following spring I signed on for the company's Welfare AC annual summer match, together with fellow apprentice, Brian Redfearn. From the reaction of some of the men in the machine room where the deafening printing presses rolled out the morning and evening papers, we were just making up the numbers. It was a case of: *'are you going to win it then?'* to smiles at their certainty that we weren't.

For some reason that escapes me Brian never turned up on the day. The venue was Bull's Bridge on Popham's Eau, a tributary of the Middle Level drain in Cambridgeshire. I drew somewhere in the middle of the match length and can see the little porcupine float I put on as if it were yesterday, slightly curved on the centimetre of red tip which was the point I shotted it down to. Soon after the start, following two pinches of maggots, the float sailed away nice and slowly. I struck and swung to hand a small white bream (or skimmer as we'd now call it) of around 3oz. A great start for me.

Before long these skimmers got slightly bigger, and there were a few bubbles and bow-waves showing, signs of bigger fish in the swim. Then it came - a slower, more deliberate bite with the float running an inch or two on the surface before disappearing, followed by a solid strike and healthy bend in the rod. As my eyes grew wider this bigger (bronze-coloured) bream reluctantly rose to the surface and slid into the ready net. And this better fish came less than an hour into the match. I could hardly believe what was happening - my best hour's fishing by miles!

I had obviously drawn smack on what we now call a flier, or a 'Mr. Crabtree' peg, and the more maggots I fed the more lively the swim became and the skimmers just kept coming. But it was not all plain sailing. My reel was a cheap and inferior 'Norman' lacking a back-wind facility, and was no match for my half-decent rod. In mid-match I hooked a proper 'slab' of 3lb or more and coaxed it to the surface and onto its side a mite too eagerly. I was horrified to see it right itself, get its fins moving again and dive deep, at which point I could not release line from the reel and ended up pointing the rod lower and lower until hearing that pitiful 'zip' when the line parted. This brought me back to earth for a few minutes.

Inexperience could have cost me at this point as I felt more nervous than at any stage, but luckily I wasn't too fazed. Feeding the swim as before, the smaller skimmers did not appear troubled by the lost 'grandad' and I picked up the catch rate again. Bushes on either side prevented me seeing how other people were doing which helped me concentrate on that red tip.

The hours flew by and then suddenly it was all over. 'Time' was shouted and I reluctantly had to bring the tackle in. The scales arrived and burly Bill Fieldsend, my next peg neighbour, weighed 10lb. He was to end up third behind a 15lb catch. I secretly thought I had more and, dare I say it, hit the bulls-eye with a 21lb 10 1/2oz winner. This was my best catch so far by a few divisions. The sun had beamed down on us all day long and I was now soaking up the thrill of a win.

I have never felt more of a buzz after a match, even shading the thrill when in 1979 we won the National as Barnsley Blacks. I was holding back a smile as wide as t'Wicker Arches (as we say in steel city) all the coach ride home, before bursting back inside the house

Barnsley Blacks 1979 National winning squad.

to tell the family. Wherever cloud nine is I think I was still on it six months later. Finally, I'd enjoyed a day that every beginner needs for the confidence to flow and generate the belief that there could be more good days to come.

Of course, having this new-found success was one thing, but back at the Damflask roach academy they seemingly hadn't got the news yet, and the senior redfins were avoiding me as always. I soon came back to earth with the return of all those missed bites. I'd still much learning to do, but Popham's was a turning point.

Branching out

Around this time I was spending some summer holidays at Kirkstead on the Witham, staying at Daubney's Farm (Fred and Iris) who owned the chickens that lived on the bankside in what was the 'Chicken Run' section. We'd wake up to the cry of the cockerel, and one day before breakfast I tackled up the swing-tip rod and made a nice bream catch of over 30lb on bread. I also met Benny Ashurst one Sunday during a big match, and both these events played a part in me wanting to learn more about this river.

Aged 19, I'd just saved up enough to buy my first car - a green Mini van - and was enjoying the new-found independence it gave. Getting to the Witham and Trent was now much easier and I was starting to catch more fish, but it was still a case of one step forward then two back. One particularly bad match dampened any feelings of progress in more ways than one. After a dull and wet day at Kirkstead, where I assessed the river all wrong and caught next to nothing, the car distributor flooded on the way home and spluttered to a standstill in Lincoln where I had to call out and join the AA.

The image is still fresh in mind, of rain dripping off my nose as I stepped out of the car into the deluge to check under the bonnet that dark evening. This was not helped by agonising over how all the men downstream of me, but round a bend out of sight, had fished for bream and caught far more fish – plundering a shoal stretching for 10 pegs. A tactical blunder saw me blithely targeting roach on a stick float to weigh in 2lb-ish when the bream were feeding further out – argh. I have no positive memory of that day, or if there was one it has long gone. This is why I value the diaries that I kept for years after. We can all forget the small but important details over time, but angling patterns do repeat and we can make good use of them if we have a point of reference.

This disaster was one of many tentative early ventures into the world of the big open matches. For most of my teens fishing took a backseat to enjoying life and any bankside progress was a case of hope over expectation. But gradually things started to take shape.

The big match (competition) scene was flourishing even though winning a match on the waggler was not easy because swing-tipping for bream was ruling Fenland throughout the Sixties. The level of anticipation when 300-400 keen anglers were gathered in a crowd, even more for a river championship or an Eastern Region Winter League round, and 1,000-plus on a National Championship, was nothing short of electric. These anglers arrived from all points on the compass, paid their pools (had a bet) and amidst all the banter prepared to battle for supremacy. I wanted to get established and make my mark but for now I still couldn't get off first base.

Early waggler success

Armed with the one match win I now entered some club matches and pleasure (or practice) fishing became more enjoyable. Together with my pal, Ian Bray, we notched up a few half-decent results. I met Ian one day on one of the Darnall Horticultural AC winter bus trips, in the company of some of Sheffield's finest anglers. We were introduced to the likes of 'gentleman' George Sands, the larger than life Keith 'Bozzy' Boswell, Brian Halliwell, Jack Eaton, Denis Hodgetts and the club secretary, a very friendly guy called Gordon Bradley.

George Sands, a former Sheffield National skipper and veteran by then, was a father figure to the group and greatly respected. He'd tour the bus with a tin of his home-grown gozzers and encourage anyone to take a pinch of his 'specials'. He had a genuine wish for others to catch fish and enjoy their day, and it never bothered him that sharing his bait was levelling the field up, reducing his own chances of winning.

I looked like winning one match on the River Nene's Fitzwilliam Bridge section. I caught 8lb of roach on waggler and caster, only to see Mick Higginbottom – the Damflask regular mentioned earlier, drawn a few pegs away - land four bream in the last two hours to deny me victory. He had a bigger 8lb than mine, and when he hooked his fourth bream with 20 minutes or so left I knew it was one bream too many. But I was getting closer. As for

George's gozzers, I tried them but only briefly. They were perfect for the bream but caster was the more popular bait for roach and I had a growing confidence in them.

The craziest aspect to fishing caster back then was the large hook size. Popular wisdom at the time described a round bend size 18 or 16 as being the ideal hook size for burying deep inside the caster bait with no metal showing. What many seemed to overlook was the fact that roach would take a maggot with all the hook exposed, and that the fish could detect the weight of this 'heavier' caster with the bigger hook inside when sucking it in, then rapidly blow it back out. Gradually we scaled down to size 20 hooks and pinned the caster on so all the hook point was showing, and this remains the situation on most UK waters today.

On the Witham at Kirkstead I met Pete Glossop – who now owns Woodland Farm fishery at, Barlborough, North Derbyshire - Derek Powell and John Rimmington. They were all a similar age to myself and trying just as hard to find early success in the matches, and Rimmo was showing most promise on the bream, and was the most confident of us youngsters. One day I played a 'blinder' of the wrong sort. Together with my pal, Ian Bray, we made up a four-man team with John and Sheffield tackle dealer Eric Thackeray. I had ended up with the team card in my pocket which had to be handed in after the match with the weights totalled for any potential winnings to be claimed. Neither Ian nor myself had caught much so we concluded the team card was worthless and 'decided' to drive home. Trouble was John won the match with 15lb of bream and almost won the team event single-handed. Whoops. On discovering this news I hardly dare call Eric – the most senior of the four, to apologize for costing him a few quid. When I built up the courage to pick the phone up, his response was predictably grumpy: *'never mind, there's one born every minute'*, he fumed. That comment stung and took me some time to get over, but it taught me not to make assumptions again about others' catches in any match, certainly not one stretching over four miles of bankside.

A Trent challenge

Getting keener now, I took on the role of secretary for my local pub's club, Florist Inn AC. We met every Thursday evening in the snooker room, and I got to know more capable anglers like George Thompson and Albert Taylor. I also met John Yeardley who joined me on a few Trent visits soon after. Ex-merchant navy, John was a force of nature - a born comedian, cheeky and irreverent - and everyone in the pub took to him. I think I'd only seen him twice before when he threw down the gauntlet for a Trent challenge on the coming weekend. He offered me and Ian a couple of pounds start each, but had not seen either of us fish. In short, we ended up scratching for bleak on a hard scorcher of a day at Torksey, the handicap system went out of the window and John ended up third. He got some verbal 'stick' for that encounter but nothing was taken too seriously.

Author with a roach catch from Farndon.

George Thompson, related to the former Sheffield National angler Ernest, introduced us to the upper Trent at Bass Island, Burton, a stretch belonging to the local brewery. He got us permission to fish through a friend at the brewery, and it would lead to the odd Sheffield v Burton club challenge matches. This was my first taste of some good 'streamier' water and it was full of fish. Here the Trent splits into two to circumvent a massive island and is full of character with fast glides, pools and eddies, and we enjoyed some wonderful sport on nearly every visit. Ian once drew the bottom peg where the river re-joins into one and won the match with his float travelling straight out beyond his rod tip – a strange way to trot as if from an anchored boat, but he'd 20lb of fish from this natural holding spot.

Ian and John were with me when I reached another milestone - my first Trent Open match win, age 23. From 350 anglers lined up at Winthorpe, I came good with a lowly 8lb 10oz including three sizeable chub on a balsa float and caster. I was proud knowing that John Allerton was not too far away – he had 6lb-plus, and even that early he was an angler John Yeardley had seen before and respected highly. Mr Allerton would prove a good luck charm on a few more occasions when I saw him in my section.

Another friendly challenge around this time had some significance for winter fishing locally. Pete Dixon, who ran the Walkley Working Men's Club AC, might have heard me banging on about one of the Florist's matches one day and announced his gang would challenge us and kick our bums, or similar words of bravado. This led to a match at Dog Dyke on the Witham. I cannot remember which team won, but the river was flooded and Walt Glaves was top scorer for Florist with three bream for 7lb. Walkley angler Terry 'Ivan' Ambler then ran another match soon after with the same crowd, and this in turn became the hilarious, or should I say manic Walkley Winter Bus. Thanks to Terry's personality and dedication as organizer, this proud club is still running today even though they now travel by cars instead of hiring an expensive coach.

Trying my luck in the Opens prevented me going on that many of these bus trips, but whenever I went they were always a laugh a minute, despite the grimmest conditions winter could throw at us. When the Witham was flooded almost up to the road one winter, we fished Billinghay Skirth, a tributary, and I did enough to win with 6lb of fry roach on whip and pinkie, and another time I won a proper grueller on a chocolate coloured Coronation Channel with 1lb 5oz. That was a day of perseverance – lots of black weed fouling the hook, and about eight roach tempted on a laid-on stick rig from not many more bites.

Swing-tip stylists

Before the 60s were over I had some mixed results on the swing-tip and had considerable soul-searching to do. I drew Kirkstead's Reedy Bay (220s pegs) on one match and we were all ready for the off when this big old car with the extended arched wheel covers pulled up a couple of pegs away. A burly guy emerged and with the minutes counting down to the starting gun, he was in no hurry. He tackled up and the match had already started when he made his first cast (I think), but first he launched two good balls of groundbait right across the river. The river at this point sweeps round an inside bend and is wider than all the straights. He then cast his bomb into the middle of the rings the balls had created on the surface. I was both impressed and surprised. My first thought was I might just make the same long cast with my 9'6" tip rod, my second was more daunting: no way could I throw my groundbait that far. I had to settle for targeting an area just past the middle.

No catapults were in use at this time (they came in around 1973) and if you couldn't physically throw well you were in effect a no-hoper on a bream shoal. The angler finished with four bream and his 8lb or so got him in the top four in the match to win big money at the time. His name was Len Chapman and he later became a maggot farmer at Woodhall Spa. It was all done in an easy, matter-of-fact way that told me he could do it anytime.

Talking about laid-back anglers reminds me of the great Freddie Foster, of Swinton (S. Yorks.) and there was no one finer on the swing-tip ledger method. Although Freddie also had float skills, he was the acknowledged king of the 'swinger' for bream. He had great patience, and I love the quote from the late Sheffield journalist Colin Graham: *'he could take bream from a shoal like guests disappearing from a vicar's tea party'*, meaning so quietly that no other bream noticed. He had great patience to leave his bait in – usually double gozzer in summer or redworm in winter - until he got a response. As for his groundbait throwing ability, it was said that if an imaginary pint glass was sitting just over the middle of the Witham he could land every one of four balls inside it, and I'm not sure this skill can be taught.

I was starting to catch a few bream, and had ended up on the right side of a draw next to Brian Lakey of Cambridge, who not long before had won a National Championship. I messed up a few pegs along the way but also got my best result in a brewery match in 1972 with four bream for 11lb in the Bass Charrington Gala (previously called the Wm. Stones match) that gave me a section win and 8th out of 1,100. Progress.

One day I was in the Pound Length section, the first 50 pegs below Kirkstead Bridge. My peg jutted out slightly allowing me a clear view of all that was happening a fair way downstream. Ten pegs or so below me sat Freddie, swing-tipping as usual. I was catching small roach steadily and after two hours knew I was well placed to win the section. And it was then like a double take: I glanced at Freddie the same instant as he glanced at me and just as I was swinging in a fish. He weighed up the situation in a flash and, you can guess the rest. He set up his float rod and caught me up then overtook me with 5lb to my 3 1/2lb, winning the 50-peg section and putting me second.

There were some fine Sheffield tippers, of course – Terry Payne, Joe Waldron, Ernest Stamford and Trevor Leigh to name just four. Also the Rotherham anglers, the best after Freddie being Mick 'Pev' Peverley, Stuart Foster (Fred's son), and Russ Foster (Fred's nephew) who had a mighty record on the Welland to rival that of Ivan Marks. Peverley is arguably the man with the best Witham match record after the great Sammy Buxton of a former era. Dave Smith fished for Mick's successful Conisbrough Ivanhoe team, and when I drew near him once I got a lesson I wouldn't forget in a hurry. Again it was a case of being near an excellent caster and accurate feeder. He caught bream and framed in this particular match while I returned ounces.

Crocodile Smith

As good as his bream record was however, Dave is possibly best remembered for a pike. The Conisborough lads had a knack of catching pike in winter when no other fish would feed, and this paid off handsomely in the 1973 Angling Telegraph match fished by 600. Drawn on peg 111 at Timberland Lane End, with less than half an hour of the match gone he hooked a big pike on swing-tipped caster. The idea was to slowly coax a pike towards the net under minimal pressure. After an estimated 12-minute battle he half-netted the fish only for his landing net to collapse under it. Seeing the pike and appreciating its full size, and knowing to lose it he'd likely lose the match too, Dave decided on his only course of action. He jumped into the river, grabbed the pike by the gills and wrestled it onto the bank. It weighed 20lb 12oz and won him £500 and a holiday in Sweden. George Sands, drawn next to him said it was the finest angling feat he'd ever seen.

My progress was still erratic but, without realizing it at first, my '73 Trent win probably set me up for future successes in the mid-70s and long after. When I started to gain some consistency and win a few matches I became quite nervous when tackling up. The first hour would set the tone of the other four hours and I'd feel the pressure to get it right in that first period – pulling in some fish, keeping them there with the right feeding level and not missing bites. Whatever the draw was like my constant thought was that if I avoided any serious mistakes I would be right up there in the prizes at the finish.

Again it came back to Damflask, if I could catch there I could catch anywhere, or that was at least the theory. Looking back I think I was better technically than tactically as I could sometimes read the swim badly. I was always a bit pro-float, anti-feeder, but on big fish this policy could be costly. My diaries also show many occasions where I fished the wrong method for too long, made changes at the wrong times, or fed too much or too little of one bait or another.

There was a period when eels, won many Witham matches. I sometimes won with the help of eels but they generally liked a few more maggots than I was inclined to feed which is possibly why I never won with eels alone. From June to early September bream could also put the kibosh on a roach catch even framing, and so a hot roach draw was necessary to figure highly. Many top Witham float men I know can relate to the dreaded day when they'd done all the hard work, beaten every angler with only the last section board still to come in to match HQ with a weight of say 10lb, only

Ivan Marks with a typical large audience, landing a nice fish at Evesham, [Warks. Avon] with his protege Phil Coles taking it all in [left].

Left: Bob Nudd signs a petition at the NEC, Birmingham against cormorant predation [led by Martin Read in Angling Star magazine]; Right: Dave Thomas with a big bag of quality Trent roach when the river was showing great form.

for the straggler section to throw up the winner with four or five bream for 11lb. Once the river settled down to roach fishing in autumn however, when the fish were feeding up ahead of winter, bream took a backseat and I'd feel the confidence surge. Apart from the odd day when the river was gin clear, I always fancied the job and those early frustrations were long gone.

I never liked anglers who strutted around with a brash attitude, and there were some.

One angler on the crest of a wave from a good win in a sponsored match was overheard boasting: *'I'm the best in the world on pole and even better on a feeder'*. That would take some living down the next time he got slaughtered by the anglers either side of him. I always thought the quieter ones could be more dangerous. If you were good you didn't need to shout it from the rooftops to wind people up. I tried keeping my confidence on the inside, but I was cocky within – which snooker legend Steve Davis calls *'a superiority complex that you need'* – even if it was not always justified. We can all make mistakes, but my confidence returned just as fast with any small success.

Chapter 5
A Personal Journey - Part 2

The Witham years

At what point do we make the jump from being only average to becoming a consistent winner? I'd made a decent stab at the club match circuit after years in the wilderness at Damflask, but to score in open matches I still needed more confidence. My diaries tell of fewer successes than disappointments up to 1975, but by the drought summer of 1976 the balance was starting to shift the other way. The Witham had also changed from the Sixties when bream dominated prize lists to them taking more of a backseat to roach.

Thanks to tackle dealer Steve Calcott taking me on Witham trips I got to know Ian Wiggins, a 'thinking' angler of some repute who was hardly older than me but more experienced. He won the Damflask Championship when still in his early twenties, and his homemade floats were top drawer. I also befriended Dave Edwards, and this pair were both excellent small fish catchers. All three of us in fact began to take prizes on the Witham with roach and skimmers on a short whip and squatt method sometimes fed with regular 'slop', a black cloud groundbait. We gained confidence by winning sections (50 in size at first, later reducing to 25) and catches on a good day ranged from 5lb up to 9lb. Such a weight could get us into the frame or top six positions whether some bream fed or not. And more and more, the bream were starting to play second fiddle to roach on the river.

Ian Bray and I joined Bill Bartles and Mick Higginbottom to win the team prize in the first Lincoln Cathedral Open, where Ian won the individual with 12lb from the Pound length, Bill chipped in with 8lb, and the other half of the team, let's say, didn't contribute that much more. Ian's results matched mine at Damflask but he'd tend to miss out on the Witham. He put plenty of casters in his groundbait this day and it obviously worked. I was well chuffed for him winning his first big open.

In this early Witham period of the early to mid-70s, Dave and I had not graduated to big wagglers but fished small floats just beyond the marginal weed – 4m or 5m to hand. Dave opted for a micro sized waggler – a slim oval-shaped 2" piece of balsa on cane attached bottom only, while I fished a peacock on wire dibber flat to the surface. I thought Dave's float worked better than mine in a skimming wind but I tried to get away with fishing the dibber top and bottom and continually mending the line (straightening out the bow) when it was windy.

Thanks to the flat-top peacock on wire float I was able to do dad a favour at this time, a case of mature student showing the teacher a new trick. His firm's annual match was destined for Five Mile House, a tough stretch of the shallower and narrower part of the Lower Witham, five miles from Lincoln. I set him up with a short 4m whip, including an old-style crook on the end to which 15" of elastic was added, and four lightly shotted rigs on winders. Bait would be squatt on a 22 hook over some black groundbait consisting of peat and a little binder and fed in marble-sized balls. The target weight was never high at this venue. He arrived home with a smirk on his face. *'I did it'*, he announced. Going into the final (fifth) hour he'd managed to tangle up all four rigs, but by that time had caught 3lb 4oz of small roach. In the last hour he reverted to his old porcupine method and caught no more, but he won the match easily with the bonus of seeing the long-time club champ, Harry Cooper well adrift.

Downstream at Kirkstead, the Witham was undergoing a change and the bream catches of old were less reliable in the big matches. Some of Leeds finest float men in the shape of Dave Thomas, Stu Thompson and Tim Harrison, along with colleagues Howard Robson, Trevor Bentley, John Gray and others, all started taking advantage as the Witham experienced a roach boom. Horncastle's Colin Freeman and Keith Lidgett, and Ripley's John Dean also joined the party. For a time yet though, my attentions were divided between trying to win the match with bream on swing-tip and targeting roach when drawn in harder sections.

Destruction by Dean

Despite my first big match win in 1973 my confidence was still rather shaky. The following summer, I fished with a float too small for the conditions and John Dean clearly demonstrated from the next peg that the middle of the river was a place I hardly knew but that was where the better roach lived. The thrashing he gave me took some time to recover from but this turned out to be a pivotal moment - a life-changing day.

I paid great attention to getting the float just right for the Witham from that day on. I'd learnt about catching roach on small maggots like gozzer and pinkie, but with a small dart-type float with limited casting power of up to three rod-lengths. For some time at the club match stage this was good enough, but no longer. I was determined to get my tackle fully up to scratch and experiments at Damflask were ongoing.

Once I scaled up to peacock wagglers of 2SSG size that could reach the middle of the Witham easily I knew I was getting closer, but were they right? I'll say more about the waggler shortly, but a 'sight bob' on top of a slim cane insert, and a small cork body at the base, took the float a stage further and it seemed to perform better. At the same time I was improving my other tackle, including new lines from France and a packet of Mustad hooks given to me one day by Steve Calcott Snr. in his tackle shop. It took me a month or two to try this hook but once I'd caught a fish with it I never really looked back.

Better catches followed and a little more belief in my ability. By the late 70s I was using a quality glass rod – the Shakespeare Professional – which I guess I must thank Ken Giles and Clive Smith for, and my tackle generally had a good feel about it, which naturally spurred me on. But there was never room for complacency. As soon as I had a good match and thought I was about to crack the Witham, on the next visit nothing would work and I'd blow out. That was the nature of this tricky river, up one day and down the next.

But I sensed that this homemade float of 10.5" long and 2-swan size (3.2g) including lead wire at the base was going to work. My feeding method had developed over four seasons to the point where I was putting fewer maggots in an average swim, but feeding more often, up to three times per cast and spreading them around early in a session. As the match wore on and the hotspot for bites became obvious, the trick was to place the feed in a tighter area, always with a reserve swim in mind which was fed only lightly and occasionally.

In 1979, my second year with the Barnsley Blacks team, we were young and hungry. We returned from Cambridgeshire to the Witham jubilant on the Saturday evening having won the Div. 1 National Championship team event on the Ouse and Cam. We'd beat Notts Fed by just 2 points to take the title, and it remains one of my proudest moments. The celebrations continued for some of us with an overnight stay at the Fortesque Arms, Tattershall. Tom Pickering, captain on the day, was ironically the only team member to blank on the dreaded Ouse, while the rest of us (11 anglers) did enough to just nick the title.

Author proudly shows trophies after a good year in 1978 [includes some for snooker].

With the match split in half between the Rivers Ouse and Cam, I drew the Cam to my great relief, as the Ouse was tipped to be a death draw. The Cam wasn't exactly good fishing either. I fished a small stick float and a 26 hook to catch a little over 1 1/2lb of tiny roach for an average team points score of 57, but it was mainly eels that beat me in the section. Over on the Ouse however, they sat like garden gnomes praying for one decent fish; three of our men netting only an eel or two to save their bacon for massive section points.

By now, as my diary notes show, I was becoming more positive and confident with every match. In 1979 my average catch of roach on most venues had improved from four years earlier by about a third, e.g. the 4lb nets had gone up to 5lb-plus, the 6s become 8s etc. I'd also enjoyed a breakthrough on the Witham, winning my first Open at Southery in the Tom Sails Memorial. Curiously, this win was in the event where I'd been trounced by John Dean at the next peg three years earlier when the match was held at Kirkstead. Moving the match upstream to Southery proved a one-off as the returns were abysmal. But Southery's loss was my gain as I did enough to win with 1-10-8 of bits on pole and squatt.

By 1980 the Witham was fishing quite hard for roach compared to five or more years earlier when the Leeds aces, along with the Trent legend in waiting, John Dean, scored so well with the species. I'd missed out on this mid 70s roach boom but was ready for the scratching matches of the 80s. So I'll now try and assess why my Witham waggler approach was consistent: what were the magic ingredients needed to do well on a slow-paced river around 8ft deep where roach and skimmers were the chosen species?

1. Two Floats

From about 1977 onwards I used two quite different wagglers - one for summer though it could take me up to and into October, another for winter, though they were never confined to set months and there was some cross-over. The summer float was designed for a still or gently flowing Witham or lakes, and small fish. It sported a small cork body and double insert of quill then 2mm diameter cane. The fine cane insert was intended for catching roach and skimmers either shallow (on the drop) or at full depth, and was usually set no deeper than to fish just tripping the bottom. The winter float was simply an inserted peacock quill (minus body) with a fatter tip for fishing over-depth, scouring the river bed on a stronger flowing river for easier to catch, sometimes better quality fish.

2. Feeding - Little and Often

For an average summer match the bait list included: 2 pints bronze (ie. chrysoidine-dyed) maggots, 1 pint pinkies (also bronze dyed), and ½ pint of hemp. Groundbait would occasionally also be used if the skimmers or bigger bream were showing, and a change bait colour - a few red maggots mostly - was added, though bronze was the favourite. In later years fluorescent or fluoro' pink was available as a good alternative colour to bronze or red.

The key to the feeding system, part of which was fully realized years later, lay in trying to attract roach or skimmers at all levels in the water column with a view to catching them at different depths. This could be 'on the drop' if the fish were active, mostly in mild water temperatures, or just as the bait settled on the bottom, or running through in the flow slightly overdepth which we called 'tripping' the bottom, or presenting the bait hard on the bottom when the fish were lethargic (usually in cold water) which we termed 'dragging on'.

The first job therefore, was to attract the fish into the swim, for we have no reason to expect them to be in front of us to start with – it is possible but cannot be relied on. The game only ever really starts when there are a few fish in the swim willing to play. To attract and hold the fish in the swim I'd feed the three baits as follows:

Bronze maggot (or 'big' maggot, bluebottle larva) was fed lightly but constantly – firing 3-10 maggots two or three times per cast - to attract fish at all levels. The maggots were usually fresh although older, fridge-toughened maggots could work well in near zero winter water temperatures. The theory behind this was that a fresh maggot would be stunned easier by the icy water than one that was accustomed to the cold, so the older, 'fridge-prepared' maggot would stay lively for longer in the river.

Hemp (ie. hempseed) to hold fish on the bottom. Other than bloodworm (midge larva) and 'joker' (gnat larva), I believe hemp is the finest holding bait of all. I never fished it on the hook on the Witham (which might sound illogical) but always fed it in small quantities. I'd put in at least two or three catapult pouches of hemp, possibly six, at the start then top up at intervals according to how well the fish were feeding. Diary details describe light hemp feed to heavy - varying from one pouch every 15 minutes, 30 minutes or one hour, up to an all-out attack with 15 pouchfuls at the start then five more after an hour. The latter was probably for a Trent match as a 1/3-pint would always be enough for the Witham.

Pinkies (smaller maggot, greenbottle larva) were also to attract and hold small fish in the peg, which in turn might attract the bigger fish. Pinkies sink at a slower rate than big maggots, meaning on difficult days it might pay to continually fire ten pinkies instead of five big maggots to get a slightly wider spread of bait over the target area. At times I'd mix both maggots and pinkies together in the maggot pouch (or tub) but only feed them lightly until some response was achieved and an approximate hotspot found where bites came regularly.

Getting those first two or three bites was the sign we always looked for in a session's early stages, and it offered a green light to feed more boldly, but care was always the byword as the green feeding light could rapidly turn to amber then flick over to red in an instant. Witham roach were notoriously fickle and it was essential to have a sensitive 'radar' in case they suddenly decided enough bait was enough. And exactly where in the swim those bites came was vital knowledge for where to continue feeding the next pinch of bait.

Sometimes I'd attack with a 2:1 ratio of big maggots, on a less promising day it would be vice versa with pinkies dominating. This was decided by how well I thought the fish would respond or were showing early on. And if at all in doubt, I'd not mix the two maggots together but fire them separately until a pattern emerged. The hemp would always go in the top pouch of the bait apron, taking care not to put too much in the pouch at once as it had to remain moist. When hemp is exposed to the air too long it dries out and floats.

I was convinced about the value of good pinkies and would say my all-time favourite summer hookbait for the Witham was a fresh and fat bronze pinkie, or two of the same. (Note: this was before 'fluoro's' - fluorescent pink - became a popular colour. Today I would be as happy with a fluoro pinkie as a bronze.) In winter the pinkie would be replaced by a single big maggot or sometimes double maggot. Winter fish eat only a third of the bait they eat in summer, but when they burn the energy to swim up to and take a bait, they can prefer a mouthful – or at least two maggots instead of one. I've had many a good winter result where only two maggots on the hook would get a bite and single was a waste of time.

I fish more often with casters today than I ever did on the Witham and I cannot deny being a little unfairly biased against the caster back then. That said, the size of the target roach, bonus fish excepted, were mostly what we'd call 'maggot fish', in the 2-3oz range. I don't think a roach really becomes a 'caster roach' until it's bigger than that. Also, if the stamp of fish were around 1oz size they were definitely 'pinkie fish'.

Regarding the hemp, this was in place to hold bigger roach on the bottom until a lively and succulent maggot or two caught their attention. Even if these bonus roach might have taken a caster before a maggot, in order to play the percentages and take enough of the smaller fish I had to offer them maggot instead.

3. The Target Zone

Where to feed the baits? This is a big question. Unlike today when pole anglers feed bait tightly with a cup on the end of the pole to concentrate feed into no more than a bin lid size area with great accuracy, I was looking to feed a much larger area – at least three square yards in the first hour or two of a match, possibly tightening up the area later. The first job was to attract some fish into the swim that might well not be there. Subject to the flow on the river, usually sluggish to slow, I'd start by aiming the feed slightly downstream – about one yard from my standing position – and to a distance of 14m-16m, towards or just beyond mid-river. To feed even slightly upstream would risk the fish being dragged further upstream by a rival feeding his bait well downstream and joining up the two trails of bait. This would have been what we might call a schoolboy error.

By force of habit therefore, I'd turn my stance a few degrees to face slightly downstream and catapult the maggots up to mid-river and beyond, but rarely would I feed as far as two-thirds across. Let's say it would be an area beyond 11m but short of 16m pole range (subject to the width of the river which varies by several yards section to section, on a bend or straight). At times I might have to chase the fish further out to three-quarters across, but would only do this if nothing came of my first swim, if it failed altogether. And any swim must be given a chance to work. If I caught ten fish in the first hour then the signs were good that sport might continue and even improve. If that running total was as low as only three or four fish then I could be in trouble but not necessarily. If no anglers near me had got 10 and most far less, then it would make sense to keep on persevering at the same time as trying the odd longer cast to the far edge of the feed area.

Something which is obvious to me now but took some time to grasp, relates to what I call the epicentre of the feed, or centre of the feeding hotspot. If you imagine the feed area as a square (on river or lake) and you continually pull fish across that square from the far side, or low side on a river, then the fish in the middle of the shoal – the epicentre – will sooner or later wise up to what is happening and scare. I tried to avoid catching a fish that would cross the the rest of the shoal during play. True, I did not know exactly where all the fish in the shoal were, and could only get clues from where the most bites occurred, but I would try to take fish off the nearside, upstream edge of the feed area wherever possible. And on a lake it pays off to pick a line that is just to the left or right of where you are placing your feed. In this way you can minimize any hooked fish swimming and flashing amongst the main shoal. It is not always possible to stick to this rule, but it is always worth being mindful of it.

Note that pinkies will fall short of big maggots by a yard or more when fed in the catapult together, which creates both a far line and an inside line to exploit. The majority of fish would be expected on the far line where the fish felt safest, but not always. Sometimes, surprisingly, the bigger fish, will come from the near line at around 11m-12m. But this mark would often coincide with where the river bed shelves away into the deepest channel.

4. Running the Float Fast at the Fish or Slowing it Down?
Although the River Witham is generally a slow-moving river, there are times when it doesn't flow at all and times when the rain never seems to stop and it carries extra water and the flow is akin to the Trent. How fast the fish want the bait presenting on a given day in relation to the flow speed is a key question. Every angler must come up with an answer, a 'plan A', as he studies his swim on arrival at the bankside.

The usual pattern was that the river flowed only gently in summer, allowing use of my 'summer' float with its fine cane insert to catch on the drop, or just as it reached the bottom. When the river took on a stronger flow in winter, a thicker peacock insert allowed me to drag line and even shots on the river bed. But beyond these obvious seasonal difference came some subtle questions. Was the water cold enough to make the fish lethargic and reluctant to chase a bait? Maybe we had had two frosty mornings in October; or flowing slightly faster than usual after some cold August rain had topped it up the previous day making them equally slow to respond? On the other hand if the water was flowing and warm, it could generate a feeding spree.

Did the water conditions mean the float wanted to be run at the fish fast (and when fish are willing the bites are easier to hit this way) OR slower, with the float held back to some degree to put the bait right up to the nose of the fish slowly or dead stop, teasing it to take? In the latter case I might not even fish the waggler and revert to a stick float presentation or even a ledger. The only downside with ledger is that you rely on the fish coming to the bait instead of the float carrying it to them, covering more area of the swim. But sometimes that's the only way to catch.

It was vital to find out as soon as possible how the fish wanted the bait presented on the day. It is the fish which govern our method choices, they dictate the rules and we have to adapt to suit. To illustrate how my system was working in practice look at the three situations below (noting this was before the pole became widely popular):

a. Good river/warm water, normal level, lots of bites potential = waggler set roughly to depth and trotted at flow speed with float slightly checked, or river not flowing at all when fish could often be caught on drop.

b. Cold air and/or water, or river slightly up with possibly a lower target weight in mind = waggler set overdepth to slow float down, either dragging 12″ of line or more and occasionally also dragging at least one shot, or a stick float held back to slow presentation even further.

c. Icy cold, still river in winter = sometimes scouring a wide area with waggler could tempt a few bites; or failing that a small bomb (ledger) and still bait could do the trick. A cold river with extra flow would see the waggler replaced by a heavy (average 7 no. 4) stick float, and held back very hard, as bomb's best alternative.

5. Defensive Feeding

When and how much to feed? This is THE question which often decides our fate. The amount of feed used in any match and the regularity of feeding was a constant source of debate and speculation amongst me and my contemporaries. You had attacking anglers (often Trent lovers) who fed boldly and made it pay when the fish were hungry, and others who fed more defensively but came good whenever the fish were in a finicky mood. I could attack with the best of them on the Trent but for the slower Witham I erred on the defensive side. This may well have cost me a few matches but, equally, it likely won me my share too. Some anglers fed less than I did and made it work; others fed heavier of course (note: see my lowest winning weights at the back of the book before saying I fed negatively).

On a good day, when fishing for say a 10lb target catch and regular bites, I'd feed possibly 1 ½ pints of big maggot and a ½-pint of pinkies, plus a good handful of hemp. On a hard day where bites were scarce and as little as 2lb was the target, I'd cut back seriously on the big maggot and feed mainly pinkies in a 60/40 ratio, perhaps feeding only a pint of combined maggots total, plus a smaller handful of hemp. The hemp would always go in because I never felt it did any harm and almost every time I made a decent catch I'd get a quality roach or two at some stage – fish of 8oz and more - and even if it was just one fish in the catch I'd credit the hemp for it.

Obviously the target species can determine a change in the feeding pattern. Eels for example, demanded more bait if they came into the swim. An occasional warm winter's day too would warrant an increase in the feed rate. Conversely, when it got frosty, firing as little as half a dozen pinkies and a couple of big maggots per cast could keep a decent shoal of fish feeding for long periods. If the water was freezing cold – below say 40 degrees F (4.5 degrees C), then I'd find double maggot would regularly score over a single – not much different you might think but, double the size and more of a 'mouthful' to a 6oz roach, a fish that might hesitate to burn the energy to move otherwise. I have won winter matches where double has caught every fish and single maggot got nothing.

To summarize then; my feeding strategy was about trying to play the percentages, to get a few fish of any size to start with and then taking it from there, adjusting the feed rate to how quickly the bites came and how confidently the fish fed when they arrived. It is no good tackling any shoal of fish like a bull at a gate. It is only natural to speed up when bites start coming quickly, but the danger then is that we might feed too often and/or too much. Pace yourself. If you start pushing the feed at them too hard it can backfire, if you manage to scare them a blank spell could follow and they might stop feeding altogether. But equally, and possibly a worse fault, is to leave a hungry shoal too long without feeding them at all.

6. A Sideways Cast
For added distance we can all propel a float with an overhead cast in the manner Benny Ashurst once described in his book as a 'howitzer cast'. BUT if the bankside foliage is sparse, is low cut and there are no tall reeds, bushes or trees in the way, I always prefer a side-cast where the rod is pulled forward from the wrist a bit like a hoopla throw at the fair. In tennis terminology this cast is made with a pronation of the wrist, starting with the palm facing down, then punching the rod forward by turning the hand 180 degrees over so the palm faces upwards.

This cast gives the tackle a lower trajectory and with a gentle check or feathering of the line just before the float hits the water it sends the shotted rig out beyond the float in a straight line which minimises tangles. It makes sense if you think about it that a high cast leaves the tackle in the air longer than a low one, and in flat and windy places like Fenland, where I have seen mini whirlwinds, I don't want my tackle airborn any longer than necessary.

Some anglers cast light floats further with the help of an open face reel and a more skyward pointed cast than I can ever reach with the same weight float. My way is for a low flight, under the radar if you like, with a closed face reel and a bit heavier float, or at least that's what happens when the bankside is not overgrown with reeds or a bush or tree on my left-hand side.

7. The 'Link'
I met a Rotherham angler in strange circumstances while on holiday in Ireland. Whilst we fished he drew up alongside in a cruiser he was skippering, stopping to go through the adjacent lock on the River Woodford to our left. Noticing his Yorkshire accent (sorry but the name escapes me) we exchanged hellos and he remembered me from the 1980s Witham scene.

Then he recalled an anecdote from the time, something I always did that he never forgot: my insistence at using a length of fine line all the way up to the float - eg. if for example my 8″ hooklength (or trace) was 0.08mm diameter line, I'd join this to a two-yard or more length of 0.10mm line – which we might call a 'link' - that extended right up to just below the float and was rarely less than 7′ long for an average swim depth of 8′. I always wanted as much fine line under the float as possible, rather than have the reel line terminate say a yard from the hook or less. Apart from the reduced scare factor of using finer line from inches below the float down, the main benefit was it gave more stretch on the strike. More elasticity equalled more fish in the net in my book. The extra joining loops were no handicap as I never encountered a problem with loop-to-loop attachments.

The only downside of this link was if I ever got snagged and the trace line refused to break before the link line. Then I could lose the whole rig, but if you step up from 0.08mm to 0.10mm link in turn to a 0.12mm reel line it should not happen. The major gain was whenever I made a mistake and struck too hard on a fish, the extra elasticity meant I rarely 'cracked off'. And I didn't lose many fish either.

8. An Extra-fine, Lightweight Hook
Another reason for my using the longer piece of light line below the float and the extra stretch it gave, was because I used the lightest fine wire hook available. This hook was so fine that if I struck at a bite carelessly I could very easily bump a fish and find the hook had opened up (we sometimes say 'straightened' but let's settle on 'sprained', where the gape opens wider and the fish comes off). I was obsessed with an extra-fine wire being convinced this got me the maximum number of bites but it meant I had to be extra careful on the strike, especially with those bites where the float was pulled under at an angle to show the fish was running away as some speed.

The two hooks of choice were Mustad 5715 in bronze and Au Lion D'Or 1217B in blue, both size 22 barbless, with the blue being slightly stronger and thicker wire. The 5715 wire thickness compares with the Kamasan B511 or the modern Green Gamakatsu hook, said to be as light as any on the market. Only on the Trent would I scale up to a thicker wire – a Daiwa MLB or a Kamasan B510. I said to myself at the time, and stand by it today, I never wanted anyone to 'outfine' me, ie. to offer the fish a finer line or finer wire hook and, right or wrong, felt this gave me an edge.

9. A Light Shotting Pattern
Unlike the 'streamy' Trent, the Witham flows at a gentler pace, often it only creeps through. Years of trial and error led me towards a light shotting pattern. I had total faith in a bulk of 3 no. 8s placed just over a yard from the hook and two more 8s spread out below that. These droppers would often be adjusted a few inches during the match but rarely would I move the bulk.

In summer, the rig was usually fished at full depth so the bait was just touching the bottom. In winter, I'd go deeper to fish over-depth with up to a foot of line on the bottom (possibly including a shot dragging). Now it's no coincidence to me that 5 x 8s equates to approximately 0.25g total weight, little more than the popular 4x12 (styl weight) float capacity today's anglers use on a pole rig in good conditions in 6′ to 7′ of water. I have won matches with heavier shotting but light was usually right for me on the Witham.

Another point about shotting must be mentioned. Whatever amount of shot used down the line, it is always wise to start a session by putting the tell-tale shot well away from the hook to give a nice slow fall to the bait. Or to put it the other way round, only place the tell-tale as close to the hook as you need to to hit bites. This comes from experience of a 24″ gap invariably getting a bite when a 12″ gap did not. Ergo, there can be no excuse for putting that first shot too close so it deters bites as you'll never be any wiser; by placing it further away and getting a bite (even if it results in a miss and a burst maggot) it tells you there are fish in the swim. You can then start moving the shot closer to make the rig more sensitive until you connect.

Finally, whatever size of shot used down the line – mostly 8s, sometimes 7s or 6s, never bigger, I only ever saw the need for three shot positions below the float, locking shot excluded. This would be three single shot spaced out, or a bulk of up three shot together and two droppers. Occasionally I might go up to a four shot bulk, and at times would use a styl weight and a shot together to form the bulk. Other anglers preferred to spread the shot wider, shirt button style, but three placements were enough for me.

10. An 0.08mm Trace

My old mate Dave Edwards and I used to swap notes about tackle in the early days. At that time we only fished for small fish and good French lines were starting to find their way into our tackle shops - clear lines that were harder for the fish to see than brown-coloured Bayer or Maxima. Before long I had graduated to Racine Tortue green on the reel – 2 1/4lb, and a 0.08mm Kroic GT (neutral grey) hooklength, and for several years saw no reason to change. Geoff Newby once remarked that the green Racine seemed to get better the longer it was on the reel, because after it had lost its shine it would sink better. The Kroic and other clear 0.08mm lines gave me little trouble when I had at least 5′ of it below the float, but I'm no great believer in the pre-stretched types. Give me stretchy lines any day for this all-important connection. This allows you to hang on to those occasional fish that you strike at that are running in the opposite direction. The wily Damflask roach taught me that.

11. A Dotted Float

A dotted, or super-dotted float came up trumps for me so many times at Damflask that it became essential to use it everywhere - a certainty that I'd set my float tip low to the surface in matches, with just enough left out to see it. I confess I took this to extremes sometimes, to the point where I was peering to see a ridiculously trimmed float in a bad light, but when young with good eyesight this is the last thing you worry about. Generally speaking, if the float tip sat 5mm above the surface after all the shots had settled that was about right. 'Super-dotting', which I might do on a calm day in a good light, would leave a mere 1mm of float show, or as little as possible for the fish to pull under. Whether you believe in dotting the float right down or not, the truth is clear: the surface film of water is sticky (or viscous), but once that float tip is underwater the resistance to the fish is negligible. So get that float dotted pronto!

Flask roach - always hard-earnt.

12. The Twitch

No, this is not an affliction but a way of imparting movement to the bait. On the Witham I'd cast out the float, sink the line with a couple of reel turns, and let the shots do their work and the hookbait drop to full depth. If it made it there, ie. without a bite on the way down, I'd leave the float still and give the fish a chance to find the hookbait. But I would ALWAYS, after a time lapse of say 20, 30 or 40 seconds, wind in a few inches of line with a short turn of the reel handle. This is the twitch which can be a deadly way of attracting a bite from a fish that might not bother without it. It can be likened to a cat chasing a piece of wool, it will only pounce when the wool is moved.

13. Delaying the Change

My final point is a funny one that on the face of it has no rhyme or reason behind it. If I ever thought I needed a method change, I always decided to have one more cast with the old method before picking up the change rod. This refusal, cussedness even, to change over immediately served me well and I still do this today. That final cast with the old has caught me more fish than I would have believed possible, often after a 10-minute blank spell. I can't explain it, it is illogical, but it does work.

Chapter 4
A Personal Journey - Part 3

A new fishing partner

I met Lynne, soon to become my wife and fishing buddy, at what was then called a disco (night club) in Sheffield in 1984. She only watched me fish Damflask once before asking for some of her own tackle to fish with. She had been on one previous fishing trip, taking a class to the Fossdyke Canal with her job as a biology teacher. It appealed to her imagination. Also, as a young girl she had been shown how to tickle trout on Derbyshire's River Noe by her dad, so there was already a link to the piscatorial world.

And so began her rapid development as a float angler, mostly with the waggler as this was winning me lots of prizes by then and was the method I practiced most. Before long this competitive apprentice was able to beat me by the odd fish, and when I beat her she'd grill me over why I'd won. I couldn't always give an honest answer other than reminding her that 15 years hard experience had to count for something. The first time I let her loose on the Open match scene was in a Damflask autumn sweepstake in 1985. I was missing on another match and Lynne finished fourth from over 100 anglers. I knew she was already capable enough to beat men but the result was still a happy surprise.

In '87 she stunned me more by winning the Ladies National Championship on the Suffolk Stour. Husband and wife angling team, Brian and Pat Needham, took her to the match while I fished one at Rudyard Lake. Lynne's friend, Pat, had won the Ladies the previous year and this gave Lynne a little extra incentive to do well. Having won my match at Rudyard Lake, it was a happy homecoming when I opened the door of our old flat to find a beaming Lynne surrounded by her prizes and trophies. We just hugged each other and fell apart. Her 5lb score on waggler and maggot was only 1 3/4oz better than York's Rita Bell's on stick float and caster, from the next peg. Lynne gained from it being the first year Calor (the Gas people) had sponsored the event. She caught small roach, dace, perch and gudgeon right up to the final whistle – 'four or five fish in last 15 minutes', giving a great example of how razor blade differences have great significance on outcomes.

And she carried on doing well from there, putting up good results in opens against all-comers, male or female. She second-placed at Long Higgin with 11lb 15oz on stick float, won at Damflask and came second at Rudyard Lake, both times on waggler, and added a

The 1988 Leeds Anglers World Div. 5 National-winning squad that won on the Witham with a huge 942 points. Lynne, the only lady member, was named a reserve. Elated skipper, Stan Haigh holds the trophy.

few more good male scalps with a place in the Cutlers Arms (Sheffield) Winter League, also helping me to cope with the occasional beatings I got! I only taught her the basics, the speed she grasped it was I'm sure down to natural ability.

My match fishing priorities did not change that much by helping Lynne, but when our daughters, Frances and Sophie were born (in 1989 and '91), that's when both our lives changed. Lynne went on to fish trials and qualified for the first Ladies World Championships in Bulgaria in '94 where she ended up as reserve but they came home with the bronze team medal, while I was losing my match focus a little.

The demands of life as a parent is something that crept up on me. At first we'd bundle up the babies and take them to the Witham in the back of my white van, and they'd be no trouble while we both fished a match. But once they outgrew that and were making 'demands' of Mum, a compromise on our fishing time was just around the corner. The consequence for me was I burnt out as a team angler, no longer having the time to work hard for others when I'd not enough time for my own preparation. The team element of match fishing has brought me lasting friendships and some glory so it was a shame to lose it.

Team Fishing

The camaraderie and fun of involvement with a successful team can never be underestimated, and the obvious advantage gained is the pooling of ideas and information to learn faster than you would going it alone. Even two anglers who travel together can gain similarly, flattening the learning curve and sharing information; the 'two minds are better than one' theory. I have learnt plenty from many different anglers, including many team-mates.

Sheaf AC – Steve Calcott's team – was named after his first tackle shop on Sheaf Street. Steve (that is Steve senior) would take me and a group of youngsters to the Witham in his big van and we'd sometimes enter two four-man teams in the match. I only really had a close-in dart waggler style for roach but caught enough to get picked for the B team. Aspiration was the driving force behind every fish caught or lost. If I'd weighed 2lb of fish I'd go home racking my brain as to why angler X had caught 3lb or 4lb. This is how we improve. My small float scratching method got exposed for what it was on the fateful day John Dean drew beside me (a story told earlier).

Barnsley Blacks, Yorkshire's finest match team, is the most talented team I was part of and I fished for them in two separate spells. When we won the '79 National we enjoyed that little bit of good fortune to beat the mighty Notts. Fed. outfit by just two points. Two or three eels caught on the dreaded Ouse (half the match was pegged there, the other six sections were on the slightly better Cam) earnt big section point scores for us. The Fed. team showed how good they were by winning the Trent National a year later with record points.

Together with my Sheffield mate Steve Koc [his unusual surname is Polish], I also signed up for the Rotherham Raiders team for a time, and I skippered Sheffield Amalgamated in Nationals and other team events. Both these teams included some very good anglers without having the strength and depth of Barnsley. Sheffield Amalgamated finished tenth in the National on the Huntspill, but our situation became difficult when Barnsley nicked three of our best men in one swoop – Tim Hannon, Andy Sellars and Andy Kinder. This was fair game but I could hardly complain having earlier fished for the Blacks myself.

1983 Sheffield Amalgamated team (l to r): Kevin Rice, George Bracegirdle, Alan Bateman, Ian Wiggins, Denis Bateman, Brian Shaw (half-hidden), Dave Hall, Tim Hannon, Dave Pearson, JB, Andy Sellars, Dave Goodwin, Dave Speight and Dave Edwards. A Whitbread team challenge on a windy Holme Pierrepont became a local derby, with Sheffield beating Rotherham and Barnsley at surrounding pegs.

Coaching a junior on the Trent's Burton Joyce road stretch. Aside from the one good roach the lad holds, we crashed.

There is nothing quite like seeing the excitement on a young angler's face when he gets some instruction and he immediately catches a fish or two to appreciate its value. It is always so rewarding for the coach. I spent many happy hours coaching youngsters during the 80s, from 1982, when Sheffield Amalgamated entered its first team in the Junior National. We came fifth on the Thames and second to Leicester the following year on the Suffolk Stour, and were placed a couple more times but never managed to win it. On the Stour match we were beaten by a strong Leicester side which had bloodworm as a back-up bait. Having no 'worm' with us was a chink in our armour, as it can always attract a few tiny fish that won't take a maggot, and it could have helped certain anglers like our skipper, Tony Bell, who had drawn in a featureless section.

With particular help from Dave Hodkinson and Tony Stones, two dedicated dads, we handled some fine young talent in those years. Dave's lad, Kevin was the standout performer, who made the Young England squad at age 15. The likes of Steve Fretwell, Tony Bell, Andy Kinder, Wayne Bartholomew and Jamie Hall also had star quality and it shone through when they joined the senior ranks.

When I left the juniors the coaching mantle was taken up by Andy Kinder and the late Tony Hall and they won two consecutive Nationals which made me feel proud even if I'd made mistakes. Andy did tell me that the team they assembled was so good they always fancied winning it at their first attempt.

Leaving the Witham behind

Although the Witham was my home river throughout the 80s, for some time all roads had not taken me there. In 1983 I first fished the beautiful Crown Meadow at Evesham on the Warwickshire Avon, and later travelled two winters there with Jan Porter, a top Trentman. Before that I discovered how good Holme Pierrepont was, and the waggler potential of the North Bank of the Nene. The Trent of course was another happy hunting ground – Long Higgin mainly and at times Burton Joyce on the non-tidal, and Dunham on the tidal.

Captaining Sheffield and fishing for Barnsley at times, and putting myself around new venues generally, gained me invites to a few quality little challenges. Two of my most memorable were England v Select matches in November 1983, the first being a close battle at Long Higgin where I came third on waggler, 2oz adrift of Tony Scott in second. My rueful diary comment said: 'changed to the right hook too late – a 20 fine wire.'

In the second match on Mallory Park's Foundation lake I made up for the first slip. The format was a 'rod' versus 'pole' match and, thanks to winning the match for the rod team, Ivan Marks nicknamed me the 'robot' which I took as a nice compliment on my work rate.

I put 27lb 11 1/2oz on the scales, ahead of Joe Brennan on 25lb 5oz and Pete Lee on 20lb 11 1/2oz. Five full internationals fished for the pole team but the pole was no match for the waggler men on the day. Tony Scott (somehow borrowed from England for our team) was sixth from our seven showing the up and down nature of match fishing. I was drawn well but in good company, between Bob Nudd and Richie Borley. Bob finished top in the pole team with 15lb 5oz on long pole but I had the advantage of fishing waggler at 25-30 yards range. I caught two roach of 1lb-plus, a 1lb perch and lots of good skimmers. Ivan was drawn badly and could only muster 2lb 10 1/2oz on pole, but he could still laugh and joke about it. My diary comment this time said: 'Wonderful – float kept going under for three hours.'

Occasional trips to the Soar, Stainforth Canal and Coronation Channel were also enjoyable and all responded to the waggler. From 1984 Rudyard Lake was on my radar where the matches were six hours long and it was a big day out including the three-hour round trip in the car. Then a bit further west I discovered the Weaver in 1985 (thanks to a suggestion from Dave Thomas) which incidentally was not such a good year for me on the Witham – that year's diary shows a modest six prizes won from nineteen visits for a 32% success rate. But on all these venues a variation of the Witham waggler method worked nicely.

The Witham was still a worthy venue I thought, and I nearly won the Super League again in 1989/90 season, chucking it away on the last round by foolishly fishing an 8oz Bayer trace and breaking on two good fish that cost me the section.* No disrespect to Grimsby's Tony Woods who was fishing very well and deserved a win, but after that something in me changed.

(*First, 8oz Bayer, like every Bayer line grade, was not quite as fragile as it sounds and had a slightly higher breaking strain. But the river was coloured and so risking an extra fine line was ridiculous. I rarely ever dropped below 12oz line and it was like common sense deserted me that day!)

It came about quite suddenly. I now had a family and was not fishing so often in midweek. It was the first time in my life I had

The biggest trophy I ever won - Sheffield Amalgamated's 'Angler of the Year' c.1983.

ever heard of – or had to think about - 'time management'. My job was not going that well and I was also trying to come to terms with a leaner than normal time on the Witham with the roach.

It was one of those grey and cold winter days at Kirkstead. The river was supposedly having extra water flushed away fast through the night. We'd lately been arriving for the Saturday matches to find the river at low level but coloured and fishing hard. The exposed mud was wet suggesting the water level had been higher not long before. Where a gentle pull on the river usually made the fish feed, now it fished better with no flow because when it ran it usually ran too fast.

We'd also had seals run up the river, one popping his head up in a match right in front of Joe Murray, which nearly gave him a heart attack. I think cormorant predation was also adding to the river's poor form. With hardly a fish to show after three hours on a river that was gaining speed, I packed up early and think my patience snapped there and then. As I drove back along the roadside adjacent to the flood bank, most anglers had a feeder rod stuck up in the air to hold line off the water, Trent-style. Their thinking was they had more chance of catching a bream than a roach, and maybe I said to myself this was not the Witham I'd always known and was not worth the long round trip to fish it.

I did not return for at least six years and so, most unexpectedly, my Witham years were over. Did I sack it five years too early? Possibly, but it has continued to deteriorate to the point where few from South Yorkshire fish the river any more, and those who do generally either have a caravan down there or have moved to live in Lincolnshire permanently.

What replaced the Witham? That's a question I would ask myself many times as I'm not sure any fishery has done so in terms of pleasure. I ran matches on the Fossdyke Canal for nine winters, and enjoyed it – bloodworm and joker fishing mainly with the pole, but the matches got smaller and so did the catches as each season passed.

Bob Nudd was a regular big name guest in these matches on the Fossdyke, and sometimes he brought his Dutch international friend, Jan van Schendel. I'd say Bob was by some measure the best bloodworm angler in the country at the time (I likened his smoothness to a Rolls Royce), but it was Jan who took the top all-roach winning weight – 106 fish for 14lb. Sadly however, with every winter that passed it got harder and attendances suffered. When we started, 4lb of fish would not even get in the frame; by the finish a good 2lb score would come close to winning.

I started looking for new venues. I was still a fan of Rudyard Lake, and the Weaver at Northwich and Winsford. Driving in the same direction but closer to home, I also became a regular at Combs Reservoir, Chapel-en-le-Frith. By getting to know the Stockport anglers this led me to their Compstall Reservoir. The waggler worked well for me at Combs, where I could compete with the bream men adopting the same style as at Rudyard catching small roach on the drop.

In the 80s I was taking note of other anglers' floats, like the one used by a chap called Alec Tissington. Alec was a 'Flask regular who I first met when running a series of midweek evening matches. On the very first match Dave Thomas came down from Leeds and arrived late, but drew the end peg and won the match with 5lb of fish. I came second with 4lb and Alec third with a few ounces less. Later matches revealed how Alec (a man in his sixties with poor eyesight) fished a 24 hook to 12oz line. He tied many hooks on at home because he had no chance of tying one on the bankside, and even struggled to attach the trace loop-to-loop. Alec also stood up

A spell with the Rotherham UAF National team, alias Rotherham Raiders, was fun [1980s].

to fish when sitting down would have made him less conspicuous beside the clear lake. He'd cast only as far out as he could throw his bait (never using a catapult) then slowly wind his float back through the feed area. Whenever he put his catch on the scales it included some big roach over 1lb and it became clear that these specimens liked the trolled bait. His unusual waggler had a long, flexible wire stem that bent when he struck, with a balsa body above. By hitting into the bendy wire he avoided that bump effect on the strike when the weight of the float's locking shots is felt just before the fish.

I also turned the clock back with an ancient looking float made from a pheasant quill spliced into a crow quill with a polystyrene body. In 1990 this helped me to finally win the Damflask Championship. Two things about this float were impressive: one, with the tip being as thin as a pole float bristle, and with a centimetre of black tip against a white water background, the bites were very positive; two, the 'pick out', or the way the float pulled out of the swim on the strike, was very smooth. Any quill other than peacock is regarded as old-fashioned but fashion should not enter into when judging a float's efficiency.

I'd always missed out on the good chub fishing on the Derbyshire Derwent at Borrowash, but now ventured to the Derwent at Belper, winning my first match fished there – the Bert Russell Memorial - with a near 30lb chub haul, but was only able to make the frame in matches afterwards. The river was a bit 'peggy' with some good roach and perch swims, but a draw on chub was essential to win. Even some of the Belper locals had a love-hate relationship with the river as they regarded it as being so patchy.

This was also my roach pole period when the waggler would, at times, be left in the holdall. Two enjoyable and lucrative matches on pole deserve a mention. Thanks to the National Federation of Anglers' sponsorship link with Embassy, I was invited (as editor of Angling Star) to a day out at Bobby George's Lake not far from Colchester, Essex, and met the extrovert TV darts pundit. As a nice bonus I won the match with carp on the pole and dapped bread. (Thanks to Mark Wragg for such a winning bait tip, and for the loan of his second string 16m pole.) The best bit by far was when we all trooped off the bankside and out of the hot sun, 30-odd anglers parched to a man, and found a row of ice cold pints of lager waiting there for us on the bar of his snooker room. Heaven in a glass! I swept the board with prizes including a watch and a large barometer. Bobby called me a greedy bastard (with his trademark beaming smile) for going up so often for them!

After the 9/11 tragedy I got invited by the York tackle company, 'Tek-Neek', to join a charity team match at Roy Marlow's Glebe fishery, in aid of the New York Fire and Police. We had one man too many so, Ivan Marks, no less, generously agreed to run the bank for our team. This was outrageous: someone of Ivan's calibre acting as our runner, and on his local commercial at that! But thanks to Ivan I won a holiday. Ivan came up to see me with half an hour of the match gone. At this point I had only caught three small perch and admitting this to my hero was bad form. He watched me for a few seconds then gave me a jokey clip at the back of the head, saying: 'get more maggots in, you're feeding like you are on roach'. I did as was told and less than a minute later I was suddenly attached to my first carp. Ivan cheered then almost fell over, convulsed with laughter. I was drawn well at the windy end of the lake, and won the lake with 50lb-plus. Later at the presentation all the lake winners went into a draw and guess whose name came out to win a holiday in Brittany? I could have kissed the famous Likely Lad skipper. Happy days.

A local fishery called Fusion Ponds at Chesterfield then caught my interest. The fishing was hard but fair, a poor substitute for the rivers really, but for years I could not resist the place and its convenience, only a10-minute drive from home. I made some good friends at Fusion and enjoyed many happy hours there, also managing three wins in the winter league run originally by Chris Mann then Martin Lievers, two members who had the enthusiasm and dedication to run matches even in the foulest of weathers.

After a decade I had got in a bit of a rut at Fusion and finally realised it. Looking for fresh fields early in 2008, I booked in a 10-leg Spring League on KJS Aston's big pond, Sheffield. This proved to be a great move as I renewed old friendships and caught ide and roach in the early rounds in March, before taking carp in three later rounds when the weather warmed up. Although I was told I'd need carp to win the league, I won it mainly my own way on various methods including waggler but with silvers the mainstay of my weights. The following year the clientele and format changed slightly and I finished second, one point adrift of young Mosborough hotshot Leon Hardwick. All told it was a great two-year campaign.

WITHAM 'CRACKERS'

BREAM have been winning most of the big River Witham Opens at Kirkstead, but Sheffield Amalgamated National Championship skipper Jim Baxter reversed the trend in the Witham Joint Championships.

Drawn 74 on the Aggies length, Jim produced 12-4-8 of top quality roach on the waggler float and maggot, to end a lean spell which has lasted since a few early wins in June.

"I'd just about given up on the Witham," said Jim. "It was great to win it with roach, and I had some cracking fish. But the biggest of the lot was swiped off by a pike."

Paul Andrews (Lincoln) took second with 11-10-0 at 147 in the Chicken Run, and he had third-placed George Newby (Rotherham) at the next peg. They both netted bream.

Result: 1. J Baxter (Sheffield) 12-4-8; 2. P Andrews (Lincoln) 11-10-0; 3. G Newby (Rotherham) 11-1-0; 4. T McCarthy (Lincoln) 10-5-0; 5. F Parker (Sheffield) 9-8-0; 6. F Woods (Rotherham) 9-3-0; 7. E Tattersall (Lincoln) 8-13-0; 8. M Peverley (Rotherham) 7-7-0.

BIG WITHAM WEIGH-IN

ON CHRISTMAS Sunday, in almost perfect conditions, Grimsby ASA staged one of the best open events of the season on the River Witham at Kirkstead. The first 27 anglers – the only ones who bothered to weigh in – had 238 lb 2 oz of fish, mostly top quality roach.

Winner was Rotherham National Championship angler Barry Stoakes, whose nearest challenge came from his Rotherham team-mates Mick Peverley and Roger Downing. Drawn 39 in the pound length, Stoakes fished stick float and maggot for 15-10-0 of roach.

Peverley, fished the same way and had 14-14-0 or roach, edging out Downing by just 7 oz. They were drawn 34 and 27 respectively.

Results: Peg 39 B. Stoakes (Rotherham) 15-10-0, 34 M. Peverley (Rotherham) 14-14-0, 27 R. Downing (Rotherham) 14-7-0, 36 D. Ashmore (Grimsby) 13-0-0, 1 T. Asher (Grimsby) 12-8-0, T. Hepburn (Grimsby) 11-15-0, 3 G. Carratt (Lincoln) 11-5-0, 5 J. Pugh (Rotherham) 11-0-0, 33 E. Purnell (Ruskington) 9-15-0, 35 J. Baxter (Sheffield) 9-7-0.

After their Christmas Sunday Bonanza, Grimsby ASA expected a sell-out for their Boxing Day Open, but half the pegs were unsold.

Only 16 anglers bothered to weigh-in but they totalled 173 lb, led by Grimsby's Dave Ashmore with 19-15-0 of roach on float and maggot at Timberland peg 138.

Sheffield Amalgamated National skipper Jim Baxter won a close race for second, taking 16-11-0 from peg 128, and beating Grimsby's Tony Hepburn by just 7 oz.

Results: D. Ashmore (Grimsby) 19-15-0, 128 J. Baxter (Sheffield) 16-11-0, T. Hepburn (Grimsby) 16-4-0, 120 M. Talbot (RAF) 13-7-0, E. Purnell (Ruskington) 11-4-0, 121 C. Roberts (Grimsby) 10-15-0, 104 A. Cockerell (Grimsby) 10-12-0, 140 N. Verschoor (Grimsby) 10-9-0.

Local men disappoint

IF SOUTH Yorkshire representation in the World Championship team rests on the results of the trials matches on the Newry Canal, there may not be a Tyke in the squad.

Leader after the two trials had been fished was Ivan Marks, who might be considered an honorary Yorkshireman after joining the Barnsley National Championship team. The Leicester lad totalled over 8lb., and raised his hopes of regaining the place he lost last year.

Runner-up was Alan McAtee, from Bolton, with Harry Settle (Leigh) third. Izaak Walton (Preston) anglers Dave Brogden and Dave Roper also did well, but former Barnsley internationals Tom Pickering and Denis White returned unhappy.

Tom came eighth overall, but had been soundly beaten in one match by McAtee at the next peg, a fate shared by ever-present England international Kevin Ashurst. White barely topped the pound in both matches, and Eckington's Dave Edwards got no chance to shine.

Top South Yorkshire performer was Sheffield Amalgamated skipper Jim Baxter, who finished just in front of Pickering, but the exercise may have confused England manager Stan Smith rather more than it helped him.

The match length was very "peggy," and the events were staged at a time when bloodworm — the key bait on the Newry Canal — was difficult to obtain in sufficient quantities.

★ The Pennine Championship at Dam Flask is a traditionally poor match, and the latest was no exception. There are, in fact, suggestions that it should in future be switched to Underbank, which is fishing much better.

Wisewood angler Jeff Capper won the title with 3lb. 8oz. — three bream and two roach from a peg between the boathouse and the first pipe. Runner-up was Sheffield Amalgamated's National Championship skipper Jim Baxter, who has made a good start to the season.

Jim drew peg 77, topped 7lb. and won £77 in the Leeds-Liverpool Canal Championship over the first weekend. "Talk about lucky seven," said Jim, who had 12 perch for 3lb. in the Flask match, all on waggler float and bloodworm from a peg between the plantation and Hugill Point.

Other weights: John Rimington 2-5-0; G. Fox 2-1-8. Veteran winner, George Crookes 0-6-0; junior, S. Brown 0-9-0.

★ Barnsley team

Big win boosts a Tyke's earnings

● Long Higgin Open

SEVENTY-six anglers found the River Trent in perfect condition in Saturday's Long Higgin Open, and Sheffield's Jim Baxter took his season's winnings to over £1,500 with his first placed 21 lb 8 oz.

Pegged towards the bottom end of the wood, Jim took a carp of 5 lb 4 oz, five chub to 2 lb and roach and skimmer bream on stick float and bronze maggot with a size 22 hook.

Bronze

Nottingham's Ken Parr took second with 17 lb from a peg in the Earl Manvers AC length. He also fished bronze maggot and stick float to take two chub and a lot of roach.

Phil Raw, from Doncaster, was third with 15 lb 14½ oz.

Result: 1 J. Baxter, Sheffield, 21 lb 8 oz; 2 K. Parr, Nottingham, 17 lb; 3 P. Raw, Doncaster, 15 lb 14½ oz; 4 J. Allerton, Selby, 14 lb 10½ oz; 5 L. Smedley, Long Eaton, 12 lb 4 oz; 6 T. Moroz, Nottingham, 11 lb 15½ oz.

Super league title won by a single point

● Witham Super League

SHEFFIELD'S Jim Baxter snatched victory by a single point in the Witham Super League final table, thanks to a second place in the last match, on the River Witham.

Drawn 33 in the Pound length, Baxter fished both the stick float and the waggler, with single bronze maggot on a 22 hook, taking roach to 14 oz in his 14 lb 15½ oz haul.

It wasn't quite good enough to win on the day, for Eckington's Dave Edwards had 15 lb 8 oz of roach to 1 lb 6 oz. He was drawn 74 on Aggies, taking his fish two thirds of the way across on a 2AAA waggler float and single and double bronze maggot.

But Baxter's haul was just enough to beat Rotherham's Geoff Newby to the overall prize. Newby finished fourth on the day with 10 lb 11 oz, one point behind Baxter and one ahead of Oundle's John Castledine.

Result: 1 D. J. Edwards, Eckington 15 lb 8 oz; 2 J. Baxter, Sheffield, 14 lb 15 oz 8 dr; 3 N. Baxter, Oundle, 13 lb 8 oz; 4 G. Newby, Rotherham 10 lb 11 oz; 5 A. Rowan, Chesterfield, 10 lb 9 oz; 6 J. Murray, Ruskington 10 lb 5½; 8 D. Thomas, Leeds 9 lb 5 oz.

Overall: J. Baxter 16 pts (£450), G. Newby 159 (£320), J. Castledine 158 (£210), E. Purnell, a. Rowan and M. Peverley all 154. Decided on weight, Purnell winning £100, Rowan £60 and Peverley £30.

Grimsby ASA Open

IN a disappointing Witham match, last Sunday, the Grimsby Open produced low weights — but a tight finish with only an ounce separating the top two men, and two ounces covering the first four.

Rotherham publican Eric Booth was drawn just below Schoolhouse bend and had three bream on swingtipped worm to weigh in 5 lb 2 oz, while Sheffield ASA skipper Jim Baxter was just an ounce behind.

In contrast to winner Eric, who had to wait until the end of the match for two of his three bream, Jim had roach and smaller skimmer bream on float tackle for his 5 lb 1 oz from a swim at Timberland.

Result: 1 (Permanent peg [illegible]) E. Booth, Rotherham, 5 lb 2 oz; 2 ([illegible]) J. Baxter, Sheffield, 5 lb 1 oz; 3 ([illegible]) H. Sapey, Rotherham, 5 lb [illegible] oz; 4 ([illegible]) T. Moroz, Chesterfield, 5 lb; 6 ([illegible]) P. Bacon, Rotherham, 3 lb 9 oz.

Angling Star magazine

Anyone who has the luxury of doing a job they enjoy is to my mind a rich person. It didn't happen for me until my forties but I finally managed to combine my sport with a career in angling journalism. I had edited and published two small independent angling magazines, with only the second being a partial success, and I had also edited Coarse Angler in the last months of its life when it was at a crisis point, before finally folding.

A 1995 meeting with Sheffield Newspapers when they wanted a new magazine to replace their former and much-respected Angling Telegraph was the start of an 18-year spell as editor of Angling Star. For most of that time I could write in the morning and take off fishing in the afternoon, which also gave me more free time with the girls. Once we got over the first few months, when I had to call up many friends and ask for writing favours, the editing task became quite easy and such a privilege to be a part of this popular regional magazine. I must thank all those largely amateur writers

MATCH

PUZZLED BY HIS OWN SUCCESS!

SHEFFIELD Amalgamated angler Jim Baxter claimed his second River Witham title in three weeks – but he had to go home and work out how he had done it.

Jim won the Witham championship, then missed the river for a week before taking on the Lincolnshire Championship, run by the Lincs and South Humberside Federation.

He drew 106 below Timberland, and after taking just over 2 lb in the first hour he began to struggle. A bad fourth hour persuaded him to try another waggler float rig on a second rod, and he hit three big roach in four casts.

He went on to take more, finishing with 9-7-8 and picked up over £200 in winnings.

"It was uncanny," said Jim. "I suppose the second waggler was a bit heavier and set just a few inches deeper, but it worked. I wound both tackle onto winders so I could study them at home and figure out the difference a bit more."

Result: J. Baxter (Sheffield) 9-7-8; S. Thompson (Leeds) 8-1-0; K. Lidgett (Bardney) 7-8-0; C. Freeman (Horncastle) 7-7-0; E. Purnell (Ruskington) 6-6-8; J. Pugh (Rotherham) 5-12-0; P. Smith (Lincoln) 5-2-0; H. Sayles (Rotherham) and F. Austin (Rotherham) both 5-0-0.

Worksop Open

SHEFFIELD angler Dave Speight was one of only two to break double-figures in the Worksop DAA Open — fished on the River Witham at Kirkstead — when he took a mixed net for 12 lb 7 oz.

Drawn 64 on the bend below Schoolhouse, David was biteless for the first 90 minutes. In the next hour his swingtipped worm accounted for four bream, but then the peg went dead again. Eventually he decided to switch to waggler float and maggot, and that's what won it for him.

The switch brought him around 2½ lb of roach and eels, and they edged him ahead of local angler Keith Lidgett, from Bardney. Keith, drawn 174 at Tilney Lane End, fished waggler float and maggot one third of the way across, taking about 6 lb of roach. The rest of his 11 lb 2 oz catch was all eels, and he had 80 fish altogether.

Sheffield Amalgamated National championship skipper Jim Baxter took third with 7 lb 1 oz — all roach from Pound Length peg 42.

Result: 1 D. Speight, Sheffield, 12 lb 7 oz; 2 K. Lidgett, Bardney, 11 lb 2 oz; 3 J. Baxter, Sheffield, 7 lb 1 oz; 4 T. Hazleton, Bircotes, 6 lb 15 oz; 5 B Thacker, Sheffield, 6 lb 6 oz; 6 F. Butler, Lincoln, 5 lb 5 oz; 7 T. F. Tunaley, Nottingham, 5 lb 0½ oz; 8 M. Thacker, Lincoln, 4 lb 8½ oz.

Jim's £600-an-hour finish

BIGGEST prize of the week fell to Sheffield Amalgamated National Championship skipper Jim Baxter in the Woodhouse (Sheffield) Syndicate match on the north bank of the River Nene at Peterborough.

Jim picked up over £600 for a 7lb. 10½oz. roach catch — 25 fish on waggler float and maggot. He edged ahead of Barnsley National angler Dick Clegg (7lb. 1oz.), drawn three pegs away, inside the final hour when he caught five roach. Clegg won nearly £400.

Top quality roach showed in the first Cheshire Winter League fixture on the River Weaver. Liverpool's Ken Dooley, drawn on Hulse's Island above Vale Royal Lock, landed a 2lb. 1oz. roach and another only two ounces smaller turned up in the winning catch.

Bobby Watson, fishing for the Cheshire team Deva, fished pole and caster for 3lb. 15oz. of roach. But that top weight didn't help his team to victory which went to Liverpool (70 points) with Chorley on 69.

Chesterfield angler Joe Shaw took home-bred gozzers to Holbeach AC's 220-peg open on the South Holland Drain and landed top honours with 24lb. 2½oz. of roach, bream, perch and rudd.

DAILY MIRROR OCT '81

Witham eels were welcome

THE bream failed to show in the Newark PF Witham Open at Kirkstead and Sheffield ASA skipper Jim Baxter sealed things with a roach and eels net totalling 7-11-8.

He drew below Timberland Lane End and waggler fished single bronze maggot on a 22. He began by picking up 30 roach but eels eventually made up half his catch.

Result: (permanent peg 124) J. Baxter (Sheffield) 7-11-8; (46) W. Eyre (Hull) 7-3-8; (70) D. Edwards (Eckington) 6-12-8; (69) D. Nicholson (Chesterfield) 6-11-8.

It's lucky Jim

Clayton-Pearson Memorial

THERE seems to be no stopping Sheffield's National team skipper Jim Baxter . . .

He kept up his winning ways with victory in Boston AA's tough Clayton-Pearson Memorial match on the River Witham at Kirkstead.

Jim, whose results this season are outstanding on the Witham, picked up over £600 in the big Woodhouse Syndicate match on the River Nene two weeks ago. He added another £100 after taking 4 lb 1½ oz at peg 74, below Schoolhouse Bend.

He took mainly small roach on waggler float and chrysodine maggot, and only just scraped home. His margin over Boston's Jack Richardson was one ounce. Richardson was drawn 22 in the Pound length, and had two nice bream and a smaller one on quivertipped worm and a small swimfeeder.

Result: 1 (permanent peg 74) J. Baxter, Sheffield, 4 lb 1½ oz; 2 (22) J. Richardson, Boston, 4 lb 0½ oz; 3 (150) D. Edwards, Eckington, 3 lb 2 oz; 4 (52) G. Atkinson, Conisbrough, 2 lb 6 oz; 5 (26) D. Speight, Sheffield, 1 lb 14½ oz; 6 (1) S. Borrill, Lincoln, 1 lb 11 oz; 7 (55) F. Butler, Lincoln and (73) G. Bracegirdle, Sheffield, both 1 lb 10½ oz; 9 (54) B. Shaw, Sheffield, 1 lb 8 oz; 10 (143), D. Maguire, Boston, 1 lb 5 oz.

Sibsey Trader Championships

MANY of the 200 competitors in Sunday's Sibsey Trader Championships held in Lincolnshire stuck it out for bream — but not a single one found their quarry.

Best man of the day was Boston National squad skipper Don Green with 8 lb 2 oz from a peg on ... on of the drain. ... the method so ... lers have made ... — pole-fished ... took a net of ... h — but no big ...

... just an ounce in ... xt three anglers ... Clive Checkley ... second with 5 lb ...

... first peg above ... waggler-fished ... rumoured after the match to have lost a big fish, believed to have been a tench or a carp, which might well have made him the winner.

Result: 1 (Permanent peg 23) D. Green, Boston, 8 lb 2 oz; 2 (76) C. Checkley, Newark, 5 lb 7 oz; 3 (43) J. Baxter, Sheffield, 5 lb 6½ oz; 4 (224) B. Weatherley, Northampton, 5 lb 6 oz; 5 (7) J. Porter, Nottingham, 4 lb 8½ oz; 6 (173) P. Allen, Ruskington, 4 lb 1½ oz; 7 (26) P. Tomlinson, Nottingham, 3 lb 15 oz; 8 (50) N. Stephens, Boston, 3 lb 5 oz; 9 (67) P. Taylor, Boston, 3 lb 2½ oz; 10 (52) M. Lewis, Boston, 2 lb 14 oz.

Baxter leads Super League

SHEFFIELD ASA's National Championship squad skipper Jim Baxter won the latest leg of the Witham Super League on Saturday and moved into top place in the league table.

Jim, who has been challenging all the way in this series, won the latest round on the Kirkstead match length of the Witham at a peg which doesn't normally produce, permanent peg 57 in Schoolhouse Bend.

He fished single bronze maggot three rods out on a 20 with a waggler to pick up roach to 12 oz.

He won with 11-9-8 and is now one point ahead of the previous league leader, Geoff Newby of Rotherham, with two matches still to go.

Runner-up at peg in "Bomb Alley" was Doncaster's Reg Fearn, who stick-floated single bronze maggot to take a small-fish net weighing 9-11-0.

Results: Permanent peg 57, J. Baxter (Sheffield) 11-9-8, 129 R. Fearn (Doncaster) 9-11-0, 77 P.R. A W Doncaster, 9-9-0, 67 M. Peverley (Rotherham) 9-0-0, 62 J. Pugh (Rotherham) 8-10-0, 54 R. Downing (Rotherham) 7-7-0, 35 K. Smith (Leeds) 7-6-8, 69 M. Thacker (Lincoln) 7-4-0.

League leaders: J. Baxter (Sheffield) 156 pts, G. Newby (Rotherham) 155, C. Roberts (Grimsby) 151, J. Castledine (Oundle) 150, K. Lidgett (Bardney) and A. Rowan (Chesterfield) both 148.

for their boundless enthusiasm in putting pen to paper, some of them for years, for only modest pay. I always said it was a good team and I salute the likes of John Essex, Jim Macdonald, Dave Pilgrim and Martin Read for their consistent quality output, along with many others too numerous to mention.

The waggler today

So where is my waggler method today? Back in the Witham years I could set up the same rig week after week almost blindfolded. These days I have had to change a few things, largely because I now fish on lakes more than rivers. Some aspects have never changed, like the side-cast and the dotted float, but let me outline the odd change in the last 10 years that has helped me catch more fish, in matches at Aston Park and Poolsbrook Country Park, Staveley - on a lovely lake called Markham, for example. Alos, in recent waggler matches at Barlow Farm, another favourite venue, I have been able to fish lighter shotting than ever before and score well with it:

An Elastic insurance policy

How many times do you bump fish off in an average season and can you cut your losses? I'd say yes if you put more stretch in the system from reel to hook. My way is to use a short elastic shock absorber below the float and it has made a big difference to my waggler bite conversion rate. It pays off mainly on those fish that are charging away from us on the strike, those that Bernard Bryan termed 'roadrunners', with the problem of opposing forces as we take the rod back. These are usually good fish which take on the drop, the way I like to catch them. The elastic is tied loop to loop and it also gets me out of trouble if ever I strike a bit carelessly. Just 4"-6" of no. 3 or 4 elastic is sufficient to land more of those lightly-hooked fish, and make no mistake, we all encounter them. If you prefer to fish commercials for carp then a no. 6 minimum elastic grade is more suitable. Try this system and I promise you will never look back.

The 91215 or 121518 express

There was a time when I would load the tell-tale shot to try generating a more positive bite. A no. 6 with an added no. 12 butted up next to it, would sometimes give a better bite and more fish in the net. It did not always work, of course, and care must be taken not to shot too boldly when the fish are backing off, going shy. I have now reached a better shotting compromise with what I call the 91215 express. This employs two micros placed 9″ and 12″ from the hook – what I term the 'canary shot', then the real tell-tale, a no. 8, at 15″ from the hook, hence the number 9-12-15. The second six- figure number indicates when these same three shots are all moved back 3″ – to 12″, 15″ and 18″ - for a slightly slower drop. Both these shot permutations have worked well for me in the last five years.

Even lighter shotting

It's fair to say that shotting for most UK coarse anglers has lightened up over the years, with most Pellet wagglers for carp not even carrying a shot down the line at all! Rarely now do I ever see any BB shot used down a line on a waggler rig, or at least it's rare on the waters I fish. At the same time we might sometimes use a bunch of four no. 6s on a tackle or an equivalent small olivette. On one of my favourite local waters, Barlow Farm, I have never shotted lighter. Here the fish will come up to mid-depth or so shallow that they cause swirls on the surface when the bait goes in, proving they are only inches down, so we can seriously lighten the shotting. I will only use three no. 11 shot max. spread out down the line, or even just three no. 7 styls which equates to one no. 10 shot! With heavier shotting my bait drops through the water column too quickly and bites are fewer.

More use of the reel

In keeping with the light shotting mentioned, I will turn my reel more than ever these days to keep the bait moving and tantalizing the fish to follow. It does not always work, but a moving bait can prove irresistible to lively fish, whereas a still bait means a longer wait for a bite.

Brighter float tips

As far as float tips go – the tiny part we observe that indicates the bite – modern materials are helping our eyes enormously. Translucent plastic lights up in the sunshine and is far superior to painted cane. We should take advantage of this. By all means use a cane insert (or antenna), or solid carbon is also possible now (like a carbon pole float stem), but by capping it with a bright plastic tip you'll get the best of both worlds.

The Float - the benefits of a slim tip

Some of my first peacock wagglers, influenced by books, magazines and my own experiments, were slim 12"to 15" long and took 3AAA+, with a 3BB bulk down the line and a couple of dust shot droppers. When getting more ambitious and fishing the Witham and other Fenland venues, 3BB down was not regarded as overly heavy with a couple of no. 8s below. I got one float working well enough to land 5lb of roach at Bardney one cold October day – a very modest catch in today's big weight terms, but consisting of mainly net-sized fish it was good for me at the time.

Experiments at Damflask however, convinced me that a thinner tip than the standard straight, 4mm peacock was required to hit shy bites. This led me to a long cane insert let into a ¼" peacock main stem with a small cork body and a 3mm cane peg at the base to plug into the quick-change float adaptor. Spiralled lead wire was also wound onto the cane as partial loading. By the mid-Seventies this float was catching me roach and perch at Damflask and it would soon be doing the same on the Witham where it became my 'summer float'. It caught fish both 'on the drop' (up in the water) or on the bottom, more of which later.

The float was painted matt dark green with a red tip and a slim collar of base white. The 3" cane antenna with a 'sight bob' built onto the top inch of cane for improved visibility was the important feature. I made the first sight bob from a whipping of cotton smeared with Araldite epoxy resin then painted blaze red over white. I also made versions of the float with a black tip, but for any shadows on the water, such as those created by the surrounding trees on the dam, the red tip was best to see.

The extra confidence this float gave me cannot be overstated and by the early 1980s I'd convinced myself that with all other factors being equal, NOBODY could beat me from the next peg on waggler. Obviously conditions varied greatly and so those other factors were not always equal, but we have to accept the bad draws with the good.

The most important feature of any float has to be the part that shows the bite – the tip. To consistently achieve a good 'fish to bites' ratio (when catching roach in particular) and hit the optimum number of bites, the tip needs to be slim and sensitive enough to register the bite easily, but also be easily visible in all manner of different light conditions. Our eyes need to respond quickly and tell our brain to strike a millisecond before the fish rejects the bait as it feels that piece of metal (the hook) attached to it. We should then feel the solid resistance of a hooked fish.

To achieve this rapid connection I wanted a tip as thin as practically possible, maybe only 2-3mm diameter, which moves further than a thicker, say 6mm tip for the same downward pull. I am sure too that the material the tip is made from matters hugely in this regard. Peacock quill is very buoyant and though I rate it highly for the fat body of any waggler, I'm less keen on it for thin inserts which form the tips of most of my floats. (* See footnote.)

For me cane (not that buoyant but slim and strong) is the best antenna material by a long way, these days capped by a hi-viz plastic tip, solid rather than hollow and made from either a sinking or floating plastic. A sinking plastic might sound like a contradiction but it isn't. A sinking float tip will still stand proud of the water providing the whole float is not overloaded. As for the fine cane insert it is stronger and more durable than one of a similar diameter peacock, and will move further on the bite than peacock. Roly Moses, one of the guest writers, has even made float tips from beech wood which is heavier than cane.

Roly Moses describes cane as 'inert', in the way it neither wants to float or sink – it floats but only just due to its minimal buoyancy. To prove this, take a 3" piece of 2mm cane and suspend a no. 10 shot at one end. The cane will upend easily, will almost sink. But by taking a similar piece of slim peacock quill, and adding the same shot to one end, it might not even be enough weight to cock it as the quill is so buoyant in comparison. This is where a cane insert pays dividends when we are wanting the float to show the gentlest of bites.

One consideration about the colourful sight bob. If the slimmest of tips make sense for converting shy bites into hooked fish on a pole float, then why not use them for waggler work too? Well, if the light conditions are good, and remembering the waggler is mostly fished beyond pole range, we obviously can. Given calm water, a good light and a consistent background colour, there is no need for a sight bob at all, and the thinner tip diameter the better. So some of my more recent floats are made without a sight bob. Try something like a 3" tip of 1mm carbon, painted red if necessary, or a fined down length of 2mm cane, and you'll soon notice how good the bites are compared to fatter tips.

Generally however, the sight bob helps me see bites easier in less than perfect conditions. Take a waggler I have just been working on. The body is a lightweight Drennan 4gm loaded giant crystal, a semi-self-cocking float. The original (detachable) tip was also made of hollow plastic and was an inch too short in length for me. I like a 3″ insert at least. So first I removed this old tip. I then took a cut-down piece of white plastic toothpick (I collect and squirrel away such things for the purpose) and spliced and superglued an inch piece of hollow (white) plastic curtain rod into it, with a layer of fly-tying silk over the junction made by the two. The toothpick piece then fitted as the male 'ferrule' into the top of the float body, while the thinner curtain rod section fitted neatly into that before a red plastic tip was added.

The final piece of the jigsaw was novel; a float tip from an original Hungarian Cralusso waggler which was slightly trimmed down. It is a high-viz orangey/red colour and fluted like a dart flight. Importantly this new tip gave me the profile I was after – a slim 3″ tip that will show lift bites as well as sinkers, and a sight bob in the form of the red fluted tip that gives great visibility at long range. Voila!

*Footnote: An exception to my slim tip rule is when dragging line, and sometimes a shot or shots as well, on the bottom of a river. Here a buoyant tip is vital and it is where a peacock tip, sometimes a very thick one to counter the drag effect, is unbeatable.

Tips to Improve your catch rate:

-Inspect that bait closely
Denis White has often asked the question to juniors on his coaching classes: 'Would you like to eat a sandwich that someone else had taken a bite out of?' No, is the obvious answer. And it was his good metaphor for the hook maggot that we bring back after a missed bite. It might still be moving but has it been stunned or injured with a couple of teeth marks. Look closely and if in doubt replace it at once. The only way to maximize bite chances is to make every cast with a maggot that is lightly hooked and in pristine condition.

-Think smaller not bigger if struggling
Kevin Ashurst made a telling comment in his book: 'World Class Match Fishing', ghosted by Colin Dyson and dated 1977. Any angler would be wise to heed it. After discussing match hooks in

sizes 18 and 20 he said: 'On occasions I find I cannot get bites on anything bigger than a 24. Now I know I am probably in trouble if I hook a big fish on a 24, but I am in a lot more trouble with an 18 which won't produce bites.'

-Shot inside the float adaptor

When using a silicone float adaptor, there is often a short gap left between the float's cane base peg and the peg or swivel in the other end of the silicon when the float is pushed in place. This gap can be useful for adding a no. 8 shot or two of same. Suppose the float is dotted down and two shots have been added to the adaptor, the light level drops and the float tip becomes hard to see. We now need a bit more float showing and could do with removing at least one shot? It's quicker to remove the shots from the adaptor by tapping them out than it is to take them off the line.

-Lentils

If you like to fish with tares in summer but do not like the preparation of the cooking process, and it can be tricky, then there is a good solution. Buy a pack of 'Sainsbury's green lentils'. Sold in a plastic sachet like various brands of easy-cook rice, it's a simple case of two minutes in the microwave then opening up. I was amazed. The lentils are more brown than green when they emerge, and though the smell is not exactly that of a tare it's a fair imitation and the texture is perfect. I have a mate who is slaughtering bream on this bait. His feed hemp he cooks in a flask.

-Floating maggot

As a hook-bait, a floating maggot will counter the weight of the hook and mimic a free maggot, making it easier for the fish to suck it in. In all forms of fishing this can be an advantage. To make fresh maggots float, place a handful in a plastic maggot box with just enough fizzy (carbonated) water to cover them. They will float almost immediately. The lid of the maggot box needs a square hole cutting in the centre of the lid, big enough to get the hand in, but not so big that the wet maggots can easily crawl out.

-Plastic corn

Imitation baits have grown to a new level of popularity in recent years, thanks to companies like 'Enterprise' making very close copies of the real thing – maggots, casters, corn etc. I used some false corn on a recent trip to Holland - buying some of the 'Balzer Feeder Master Soft Corn' (40 grains/pack, made in Germany) and, being a floating material, tried tipping a bunch of three maggots or a worm on a 14 hook with a piece. In 16′ deep, gin clear water, I caught some good bream, helped I'm convinced by the slow fall to the hook-bait this blob of plastic gave. Apart from counterbalancing the hook's weight, the corn is such a vivid yellow that it's logical to me that the fish will find the worm quicker. From the four colours in the pack it figures that the white might be taken as a piece of bread though I did not find the fish more partial to one colour over another; I caught on the white, vivid red/pink and the yellow. Plastic maggots in the 'Berkeley Power Bait' range are also said to be deadly and they have a powerful scent. I will be using this corn again which can also be trimmed down with scissors to suit small hooks.

-Banded caster

Where every second counts in competition fishing, every time we do not have to re-bait the hook is time saved. In today's world of hair-rigged* baits it is possible to tie a rubber pellet band onto the hair but to use a caster inside the band instead. Mounting caster this way several fish can be caught on the same bait. It has been found that the fish do not damage the caster because they do not take the bait as far back as the throat teeth. Maggot can also be presented the same way by ensuring the band is a tightish fit on the maggot.

* **Note:** To the uninitiated a hair-rig is where a tag end of line extends from the hook knot and the bait is mounted on that line (called a 'hair' because in early experiments a human hair was used for the job, before changing to fine nylon). An extension of this attachment is to tie a tiny rubber band (or pellet band) to the hair, inside which a pellet hookbait is placed, leaving all the hook showing. The fish, usually carp, sometimes bream, happily accept this form or bait presentation.

-Sour bran specials

When fishing squatt on canals, or difficult lakes, a maggot that is now out of fashion could give your catches a real boost – the sour bran special. This maggot can be bred without too much smell in a shed or outhouse. Scalded bran is put into a plastic breeding tray with a few small bits of fish mixed in, and sour milk poured over the top. Two or three trays are placed on shelves in the darkest part of the shed and soon the fly will 'blow' ie. lay its eggs on the milk. In around 10 days, pure white maggots should appear. These small maggots for some reason crawl backwards and are plumper than a fresh squatt.* (*Source: 'Baits', by Frank Oates.)

-For a roach treat, try wheat

Sweetcorn is a popular bait for carp and is known to sort out the bigger roach on some waters. A great cereal bait to team up with it is wheat as it can both be fed and used on the hook. It is also a filling bait so a little goes a long way. Wheat is a surprisingly neglected bait yet is so easy to prepare. Just soak it for 24 hours then bring to the boil and the white kernel should appear.

-Try two hooks in practice

It goes without saying that if we were to fish with two hooks say 18″ apart, we'd get twice as many chances of a bite. When fishing a feeder on harder waters in particular this can be a good way of learning which bait the fish prefer sooner rather than later. But two hooks under a float with a different bait on each can also teach us which is the favourite - if local rules allow it (always check to be sure). In each case tie the top hook on a short 3″ paternoster.

-Removing a shot

You have added a shot too many and need to remove it? With the reel line taut, grab the offending shot between left finger and thumb. Place the closed split in the face of the shot on your fingertip so the back of the shot is facing upwards, then squeeze the shot endways on across the split with scissors or small pliers and the shot will loosen enough to pull free.

-Resting the swim

When fishing is difficult and the fish are likely to get shy after a few have been taken from the shoal we need to think about having a secondary swim, or back-up line.

A friend of mine, Barry Moat, has a unique way of resting the swim when pole fishing on lakes in winter, to keep the fish interested without overfeeding them. On whatever length of pole he decides to fish, he'll feed two swims - at 10 to the hour and 10 past on the clock face. Here's the clever bit: he feeds very lightly in one and a bit heavier in the other, but he always alternates swims every time he lays his float in. Assuming swim A is on the left and B is right, he feeds swim A and fishes B, and for the next cast, he does the opposite. In this way he's feeding both swims lightly but less often than if he fished just the one swim. I've known him win matches with over 20lb on difficult days this way, and the same system can be adapted to fishing with rod and reel and a waggler.

Big Fish

I have never really craved big fish, though do enjoy watching Jeremy Wade's 'River Monsters'. Back in 2000 Lynne and I were lucky enough to fish a five-day safari on Lake Nasser, Egypt, among a party of 18 anglers. The trip was organised by well-known pike angler Barrie Rickards, and sponsored by Shakespeare and Harris Angling. To say the fishing was sensational is an understatement. My dream was to land a 50lb perch (they grow to over 200lb), and I managed to top it with a 76lb-er – the fourth biggest of the trip behind one of 118lb taken by Russ Manning on the last morning. The lake was low and was said to have 'fished difficult', with 40 perch landed in total. Although I was fortunate enough to enjoy a great result, my week could have been much better. I lost four other big fish, one of which was played for 2 ½ hours before I made a fatal mistake. I had finally got the fish close under the boat, but in trying to keep it clear of the boat I brushed my line (65lb braid) against a nick in the metal stern rail which cut the line and cost me the fish. The fish was thought to be a big vundu catfish but I never saw it. The perch I caught came in like a baby in comparison taking 20 minutes to land.

Attached to a monster on Lake Nasser, 2000.

A 76lb Nile perch, fish of a lifetime, but a bigger fish was lost on the five-day safari.

Homemade hooks

On a trip to France I was introduced to the fine wire (blue) hooks made by some of the leading French matchmen like Jackie Morzieres. Nicholas Beroud, our host, gave me information as to how they were made and I followed it up when back in England. I made some hooks that were not quite as good as the originals, but was determined to use them in a Witham match. The points were nice and long but I think the temper let them down. I caught a respectable weight of 13lb 11 1/2oz for sixth spot (as shown on the same page of the diary as hook details) BUT little over 1lb more, 14lb 15oz, won the match. How I'd have loved to fish that match again with my regular hook!. Truth is I should have gone the extra step of perfecting the hooks first and only then tried them in a match. 'Too risky' was the cry for this vital piece of equipment.
An entry in my 1986 diary suggested how to make the hooks as follows:

1. Start with a piano wire as follows: 15 ("thou" (size 26), 20 "thou") (size 24 and 22);
2. Spade: place the wire in between two matching pieces of flat steel - and hand press the spade, or hammer it against a corner of steel;

3. Point: using a three-jaw chuck from RS Components, put the wire in the chuck and apply 80 grit stone to form a spear point on wire;
4. Cut a wire length of 12+mm for a size 22 hook;
5. Bend the hook into desired shape;
6. Hardening: Heat furnace to 790-810 degrees and leave inside for 45 minutes. Quench in quenching oil. Consult a machine tool hardener re temper. Tempering is done from 200 degrees C in 5-degree stages until hook hardness is perfect.
Also noted was a phone number for Terry Emms, my advisor on the experiment.

Diary extracts

Throughout this chapter I've made references to the diary I keep to record my fishing trips. My first diary is dated 1978 but I have match records included in there dating back to 1972, showing I kept them earlier. Keeping diaries isn't just to jog the memory about the best fishing days (though it is great for that), it helped me to learn from experience, from both successes and failures. The need to write things down helps the facts stick, but what do we need to put in these diaries - how much detail? I certainly write more about the good fishing days than the bad, but am never scared to be self-critical, and that has to be a good thing.

What follows is a selection of actual diary entries from 1981, the first year I began adding more comments about results, and trying to add those key details that might come in handy later. The first entry describes an easy holiday session, the kind of day that is all about relaxation and enjoyment. Next come three near miss seconds in matches. These show how a little luck either way plays a big part in shaping a result and that we don't always get what we deserve. In the first of this trio I lost the match by a few ounces but had no complaints at all. In the second I fished badly and hardly deserved to get close to winning, while the third was a special day, one of the best matches I have ever fished, on the Nene's North Bank, yet I got beat by a feeder weight. The final entry tells of a lovely match win, also on the Nene. What's striking about these matches is they could all have turned out so differently with a couple more fish netted or lost. But that's how it was in the silver fish era of low weight matches where every ounce mattered.

1. Holiday Pleasure session, final day, Sat. 18/7/81 (Four-day holiday with Bob Fox, Bob Walker and Mick Nicholson.)
'Caught 29lb of roach at 141 peg on Forty Foot fishing simply. Fed only

big maggot. Shotting: 8 8 86 (bulk) – (drew mini diagram here to show this pattern). Used a 14"-18" tail to an 18 hook. Cast 1/3 across drain with a straight peacock and cane insert. Roach fed well – 20 hook at first then an 18. Bit late in day they got cagey and needed longer tail and more time (to take bait properly). It was useful to strike before float was well submerged. Earlier though 90% were spewing up maggots and hook was ½" inside mouth when struck perfect. Also, some cracking fish gave ½" slow lift on float after settling. Oh yes, enjoyed this day very much! In one hour I caught 20 fish including two for 2lb+ (probably 9lb).'
(The South Forty Foot drain, near Boston, was easier roach fishing with better bites than on the Witham, even with a gift of a good draw as can be seen below.)

2. 29/7/81 Chesterfield AA. Royal Wedding day Open (Another day off, courtesy of Charles and Diana's marriage.)
'What a marvellous day! Instead of watching TV we were on the Witham in blazing sunshine and have finally broke my duck. A poor turnout (70 fished) gave me four empty pegs upstream from pound peg 47. Of course it helped and I was happy enough with my catch including 6lb of roach and a 14oz bream and 4lb of eels. Caught roach from start about 8 ½' with river backing up strong. Fed about four pouches of hemp and when roach arrived I thought I'd not put enough in to keep 'em. Well, they stayed long enough to get a 14oz fish, but I suppose 6 or 7 pouches in Pound length is better. Eels kept invading to interrupt catching rhythm but caught roach in between, some mid-depth but mostly at depth. My float hardly lifted all day except on a bleak. After 3 hrs a skim developed pushing float off line a little and simultaneously river pulled off and continued for last 2 hrs. It was mostly eels from then on in. I caught 4 roach on 20 hook on 3 hr mark then it became harder. Lost 2 good eels in last 20 mins and just one would have given me 4 1/2oz needed to win. That is fishing and I'm not complaining. Feed: bowl of g'bait, ½ squatts and hemp in g'bait, 2-2 ½ of bronze.'

(I wrote 'broke my duck' but Boston's Dick 'Cherry' Brocklesby beat me into second - 12-2 to my 11-14 - from six pegs away at peg 41. A close one but my 'no complaints' verdict for such a near-miss looks out of place. On the previous weekend Nottingham's Paul Cope had beat me for the section 4-6 to 3-10, so I think I was happy to improve amidst a few early season match struggles.)

3. 16/9/81 Grimsby Open, R.Witham at Kirkstead
'As I write I feel embarrassed. I know I didn't fish well and a tight scrap saw me 2nd – 5lb 2oz, 5lb 1oz, 5lb 0 ½oz and 5lb 0oz. I can only thank the gods as I had 2 spare left and 2 spare right at peg 94. It was like

pleasure fishing but I couldn't interest fish after a brilliant opening hour burst. Wind killed it and I fished a bigger waggler with - 8 8 6 (dropper shots) 88666 (bulk). This caught me roach, but again I missed many eels. In opening hour took 17 roach, but it couldn't last and I should have leaded up 10 mins. Sooner. Normal 2AAA skimmed through too fast for too long and when I did change I fished a 20 to 1lb (ie. 1425 Trent hook). This cost me match. Instead I should have swapped to fine hook before mid-match. Badly needed a third rod with a stick float to catch two eels when I couldn't get a bite for 5-10 minute periods. Next week I will have three rods with me. My saving grace was a three-cast burst for 9oz of fish in last five minutes. A fish last throw would have been enough to win. I CAN'T ASK FOR THE STARS! To be fair I fed the swim well if not a shade too heavy – 2 ½ (pints) was right, fed nearer 3. Hemp worked – 8 pouches. My inclination to feed heavy is still better than the reverse due to eels, eels, eels. In the eel department I did very badly today. I don't know why I missed so many – 9 in 10. I nearly lost a fish in edge. This means use a plastic sheet to ensure no fish get back that have been swung to supposed safety. (Drawing added showing edge of a plastic sheet hanging over front of keepnet.) Catapult pocket must be given some thought, it is not safe. Note: Don't mix and waste so much groundbait.'

(This report tells me it was still early days for my method as I rarely fished with as light a float as 2AAA as the 80s wore on. And to get so close to a win when missing so many eel bites was a minor miracle.)
1/8/81 British Sugar Open – R. Nene, North Bank:
'This was my best ever day in a match. I beat the field on roach then lost out to a net of bream. Started with 6-7 hemp pouches just over and in the middle. Struggled for four roach in 1st hour but fed lightly and built up swim – 3 to 4 feeds per cast instead of one. This put more feed on target as gusting wind blew some off line – overhead and upstream. This feeding was secret of later success – made fish compete. In hours 2 and 4 swim erupted with roach taking as near as 2' to 3' down (in 11' of water). If I missed a fish on drop I often took one trotting through just clear of bottom. My timing was excellent and if I left float to travel beyond expected bite range I often had a bonus fish! Had 70 fish in all and 65 roach. Sat on box and used only one hook catching an eel in process. Interesting factors were: 1/ When swim died a little I fed pinkies before maggot and it immediately produced again (used 2 or 3 tiny balls of hemped groundbait also in quiet spells, although I was scared to use bread); 2/ Twice in match I had bleak moving into action and pushing roach underneath. At these times I was catching high up, to find bleak everywhere, and if I could avoid a bleak bait got down and I had a roach bite. In first instance when fish came high in water to feed I shallowed up to catch easier but fish went down. Next time I compromised as I was also catching down and fished

6" off bottom. It had no detrimental effect and I hit most bites. Used 4 - 4 1/2 pints of maggots with fennel and turmeric and loads of maize. Fished Witham pattern 10 ½-11' deep with about a 15" tail. Had the pleasure of beating my namesake and former winner of this match, Nigel, at 75 peg. Good pegs are supposedly 120s to 140s. Section prizes were so good this is by far the best match I've ever entered. One sad point was we didn't put a team in and Nottingham won it. We could have won it with three weights (including travelling partners Kev Rice and Dave Hall!). Winner caught 12 small bream for 16lb 10oz.'

4. 4/10/81 Woodhouse Syndicate, R. Nene, North Bank:
'Well a big win at last! Made up for yesterday's slip with a prestige win in this expensive little match. Drew round point at 234 as I'd hoped. 180-200 is a bit rubbish so I was relieved to get below. Cleggy (Dick Clegg) drew 237 so I knew I had a good 'un to beat. Had a good start with 8 good roach to Dick's 4 after about 30 mins. River was backing up and water was cold. We were ruined with 2 factors: 1/ On ¾-hr mark four rowing boats came through swims; 2/ River started pulling. This killed it for almost an hour before we started catching odd fish again. I'd caught early on light shotting, 13" tail, after an 8-9 pouch hemp carpet was laid beyond middle. In struggle period I went onto heavy float and shotting, but today it didn't work so well. After about 4 fish on heavier rig I eventually went back to light one, but switched floats as I needed a longer throw. Line sinking was awkward as it was a bit flat (too calm) and to fish 2/3 (across river) I had to cast 3/4+. Dick used open face (reel) and fished 3/4 over, and when he had his good spell I'd settled for 2nd. He must have had 10 fish to my 1 with about 3 hours gone and I'd no answer. Anyway I persevered and adjusted ending with light shotting but 2 x 8s set at 17 ½" (ie. to tell-tale), about 11' deep. I had caught 1'-2' overdepth but in last 40 mins shallowed to 11' and tripped bottom, taking 5 roach when Dick didn't get one. This swung match in my favour. Omitted mention of a hemp top-up in a very quiet spell mid-match – a calculated risk. In fact I had about 25 bites for 20 roach + 1 eel. I was lucky I never lost a fish today as they weren't all hooked well, whereas Dick lost half a dozen at net. We need some luck at this game and I'm grateful. Denis White lost a big chub I'm pleased to note as he came close with 6-14 of chub for 3rd at 175 peg. Upstream of road are good pegs and I would have fished a bit closer if drawn there (being away from traffic). My feeding was right today – 2 – 2 ¼ pints, about 10+10 per throw. My last fish were caught as river ran but rest of day we did better when it stood and wind put a ripple on. Make some heavier floats for open face reel use, Nene and Holme Pierrepont in mind. 200 fished won £600.'

(Result: JB 7lb 10 1/2oz, Dick Clegg 7lb 1oz, Denis White 6-14)

Chapter 5
Float-making Made Easy - In 10 Steps

Materials:

- Full peacock quills,
- Stanley knife or modelling knife with new blade,
- Cane barbecue skewers (or 2mm and 3mm float canes if available),
- Araldite Rapid (or a similar epoxy resin),
- Lead wire or solder wire (1mm grade) for loading,
- 18 thou guitar string or other hard wire such as piano wire,
- Wire cutters,
- Small swivels,
- Hollow fluorescent plastic float tips (red, yellow and black),
- Superglue or Unibond sealer,
- A 1.5″ sewing needle and a 2.5″ bodkin (like a big blunt needle 2mm thick),
- Scissors,
- Medium sandpaper or emery paper,
- Invisible nylon sewing thread, or Fly-tying silk,
- Modelling paint, Humbrol or similar - matt black or green for the body quill, and base white, blaze red or orange for the tips (these tip colours only required IF you cannot buy the plastic float tips).

To catch a fish on a float I have made myself is considerably more satisfying than catching one on a shop-bought model. Float-making is also a challenge because while most wagglers I have ever made have worked to some extent, there has also been the odd reject and even hideous failure. This drives me on to further experiment and to continue refining and perfecting them. It is a hobby in itself, and is far more rewarding than watching filler TV shows.

This does not mean that I don't buy floats in tackle shops; indeed I do whenever one takes my fancy. But I have spent countless hours making my own or customising those bought from shops to suit my purposes. Adding a finer or longer insert to a float then capping it with a translucent sight bob is where I'm prone to interfere, as a 3" or longer insert suits me better for lake fishing in particular.

First, by trial and error you must decide which wagglers suit your style and the waters you fish, and then take it from there. Whether you want to make wagglers from scratch or just modify shop-bought ones is up to you, but the materials listed below will fulfil your requirements.

Some anglers are untidy or cavalier by nature, and I wouldn't say I'm overly tidy myself, but I do try to take a pride in my

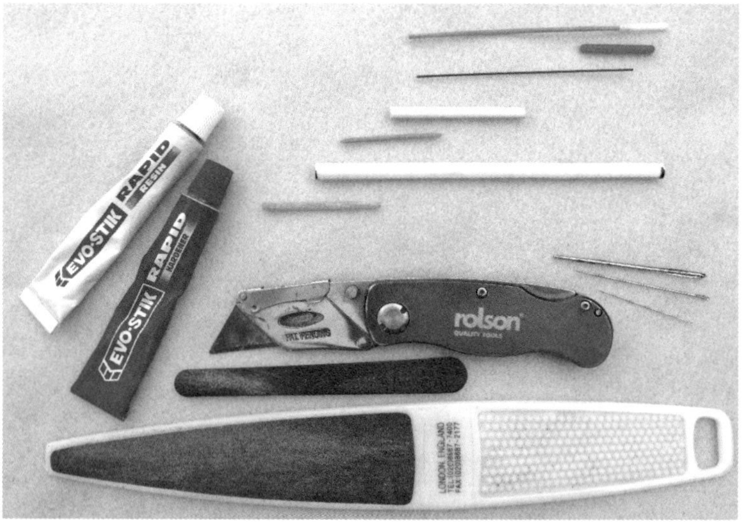

The float's components and the tools for assembly.

floats more than with other tackle items. I would not be happy if the float paint at the tip was messy or chipped for example, as it's only a minute's job to repair it. Nor would I ever like to arrive at the bankside with little idea of how much shot a particular float takes. It is never a bad idea either to make floats in pairs. This is an insurance against the occasion when you break one, or lose one when it seems to be working to perfection and catching fish to order. If you wish to have a go I have outlined the stages of construction below. I hope you find the process as rewarding as I do.

Stage 1: Buy some peacock quills either from a tackle shop or on-line, or even from a bird sanctuary or zoo if you know of one not too far from home. Using a very sharp blade, carefully cut a 7″ length from the thick end (1/4″ diameter) of the peacock quill by running the knife blade around the tough shell of the feather. Don't press on too hard or the knife may suddenly go through into the soft pith inside and the quill will tear, but slowly keep on revolving and scoring until the blade goes right through.

2. Trim off all the herls with scissors then sand down the remaining stumps to give a smooth finish. (Note: ensure these fall into a bin or container and not over the best carpet.) Now you are left with the main stem of the float.

3. Insert the point of the sewing needle into the dead centre of each end of the quill to a depth of approx. ¾″, slowly pushing the needle down in a straight line. Checking for straightness over the first half inch of the hole will ensure a straight drill. Enlarge the hole by inserting the bodkin and slowly rotating it, going down to the same depth, and then repeat with the wider eye end of the bodkin. You should end up with a hole at either end of ¾″ deep by 1/16″ diameter which will allow for the insertion of the canes.

4. Cut a 1 1/2″ length of cane for the base (the fatter end of the quill) and a 3″ length for the top, again by scoring the cane around its circumference repeatedly and without using any force. If using a cane skewer that seems a shade too fat for the insert, whittle it down with the Stanley knife to nearer 2mm diameter.

5. Smooth down the canes with sandpaper then glue both sections in place at opposite ends of the quill, taking care to squeeze out the epoxy resin in two equal halves before mixing. Check that the plastic tip will fit neatly over the longer cane piece (the insert). You

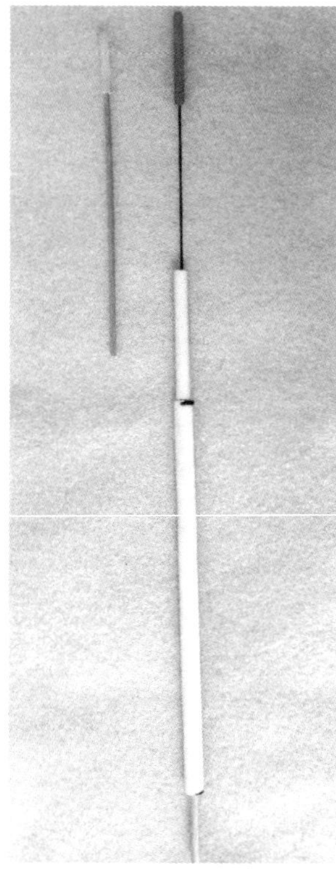

Pinned together with the cane spigots and ready for gluing, with an alternative cane insert (left).

may need to whittle the cane down a shade with the knife or even build up its diameter with a whipping of the thread or silk if it needs more bulk. Now glue the plastic tip onto the upper cane piece. Thanks to modern technology we also now have slim but strong, solid carbon fibre inserts and hollow plastic tips that fit them. Cralusso coloured float tips (an imported float from Hungary) are sold in packs separate to the floats and will fit the bill for all light conditions on different waters.

6. At this point there's a choice to make. If you prefer a quick-change float facility where you simply insert the float's base cane into a silicone adaptor (widely available) then the swivels and guitar string are surplus to requirements. But if you like the idea of a swivel at the float base then you take an inch of the wire, bend it into a narrow u-shape, and whip onto the cane after first sliding the swivel onto it. This facility helps the float collapse on the strike which some believe gives a much smoother strike (see Roly Moses chapter).

7. All we now have to do is finish the float. You can cover all the quill with sanding sealer or Superglue as this forms a good base for the paint to bond to, though some float-makers see it as unnecessary, leaving the quill as it is apart from the top half-inch to inch of coloured tip. It comes down to personal taste but paint does not adhere that well to the shiny quill.

8. This stage is optional and you will need to buy some cylindrical corks (5/8" wide or similar) or cut down the same from wine/champagne corks. These will then need a central hole drilling in them. This can be done by hand with a drill chuck or similarly with a hollow metal tube. The advantage of a small cork body is that it reduces the overall length of float for the same shot capacity.

For very shallow waters, especially with clear water, it makes no sense to use a float that's too long and this is where a small body at the base comes in handy. You can also make these cork bodies detachable. You can widen the scope of any waggler by making two transferable bodies of 1 BB shot and 1 AAA respectively. This is an old idea but still a very good one. In effect it gives you three floats in one, but the bodies must be accurately made so that when added they take exactly the one extra shot and no more or the system becomes too fiddly.

9. The float may now be turning out just as you wanted it to. However, the key feature of any float for me is the business end, the bit we see on the surface – that 1/4" to 1" of float tip. At this point we are looking at the finishing touches and it helps if we know something about the venue we will be fishing, and how good or bad the background is for seeing the float tip easily. This is where the addition of a 'sight bob' can help. If you are fishing an open expanse of water offering a whitish surface you may not need a coloured tip at all; black will suffice. If not, and you have mounted a plastic hi-viz tip on the cane, then do not interfere with that; you cannot really thicken it up or it will destroy its light reflective quality.

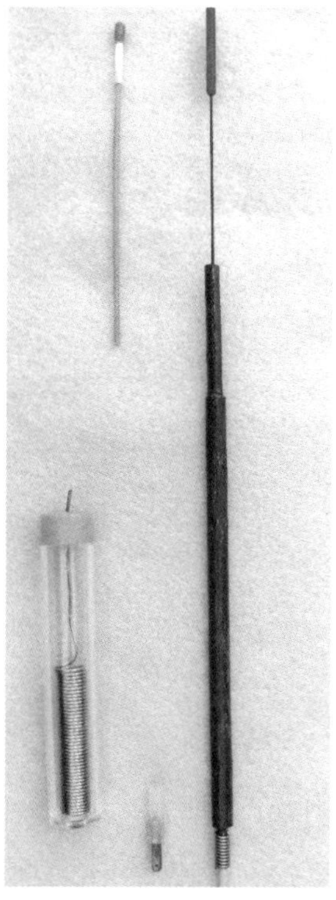

The almost-finished float, plus lead (solder) wire for possible extra loading, and an adaptor for attaching float to line (left).

10. Now we can paint the float tip, if we haven't bothered with the ready-made plastic float tip idea. We can add a coat of base white straight onto the cane followed by one of blaze red, but first we should stop and think for a minute. Ask yourself whether you will be able to see this 3mm tip at say four rod-lengths out, which is the distance this 3AAA float is designed to cast? You may need to see 4mm or 5mm diameter of red tip for comfort, a tip at least 25% thicker. All we need do is to halt the painting job. Get hold of the invisible thread and start building up the tip of the float in tight wraps over the cane. Superglue to tighten the finish. For a fatter sight bob simply cut off a mini ½" or ¾" length of peacock of the desired diameter, insert the bodkin to make a ¼" or ½" depth hole in it, and glue onto the cane. This peacock sight bob can be strengthened with a coat of superglue but this is optional. Now finally, we add a couple of coats of base white and then red, orange or black on top as described, and voila, your float is finished.

Note: lead wire can be wound round the float's base to reduce the amount of locking shot either side of the float. Technically there is no need for lead wire at all, but I do not like using lead substitute shot, so by adding the wire to make the float self-cocking it allows me to lock the float with two or three small shots only.

Other float designs, thick and thin:
To make a float for fast rivers and dragging line on the bottom, it requires buoyancy in the tip. Take a leaf out of John Dean's book and cut a 12" length of peacock quill, thicker the better, using the fatter end for the tip and gluing the cane base peg in the thin end. A coat of Superglue will add strength but is optional, as only the float tip really needs painting to finish.

To make a slim lake float, white plastic curtain rail can be used as a thin but strong stem, plugging the tip with a piece of pole float bristle, and gluing the bottom end into a cork body or thick piece of quill. Thin sections of hollow carbon fibre, 12" off-cuts from the ends of carbon poles (when they are cut back for threading an internal elastic for example), will also fit the bill for a good float stem and are stronger than the plastic. For an even finer tip we have solid carbon fibre, and this can be married to the hollow carbon described. Various modern commercial wagglers incorporate these solid carbon inserts – see point 5, but the DIY float-maker can replicate them with a stem off an old or damaged carbon-stemmed pole float.

Plastic baby buds also make light float stems for small canal wagglers, with 2mm cane or carbon inserts.

Chapter 6
Floats for Special Jobs

Darts, rockets, swingers, crystals, and trick-ems? Fancy names are bestowed on commercially made floats in the knowledge that if they sound catchy and also look pretty they will sell, and we should be mindful of this. I have sometimes done very well with a homemade float that has looked like it was fit for the scrapheap, so floats need not be aesthetically pleasing to catch fish. What is essential though is to ensure the chosen float does the job required of it, and picking the right size of waggler for a given swim is one area that I feel is important. Around 90 per cent of my waggler work has been done with a 3AAA to 2 Swan shot capacity float of 8″ to 12″ long by ¼″ thick with a 3″ fine insert in the tip. But there are many other wagglers for a host of different applications. This section covers the others, floats that I might use only rarely but which may suit different anglers for other situations perfectly. Depth of water and how fast it flows are two governing factors, but there are other considerations which dictate our choice…

Where finesse matters

At one time many youngsters began their fishing lives on local canals, now it is more likely to be carp lakes, but there is still some good canal fishing around the UK for anyone prepared to look for it. Fishing scaled down tackle on a canal for roach and perch can be a magical experience for a beginner before he ventures onto bigger things.

Let us then first look at the smaller wagglers for canals and slightly bigger floats for small ponds. All these floats require light shotting and a delicate approach, usually with small baits like squatt, pinkie and bread punch, but this does not rule out the use of bigger baits for big fish. Sometimes specimen fish can be caught in the margins where a small float will do nicely...

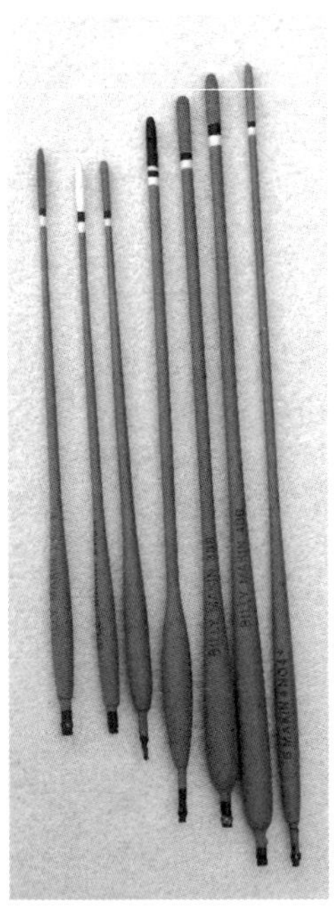

A. Makin Canal Grey

These all-balsa floats originated on Midlands canals in conjunction with either the squatt method – which consisted of feeding loose squatts with squatt on the hook for small roach and skimmers, or sometimes the float would be fished with bloodworm and joker or bread punch. The squatt style was taken to its full potential by top canal anglers with rod and reel such as Jimmy Byrne, Billy Makin and Ray Mills, before lighter and longer carbon poles robbed them of their advantage of being able to cast tightly into small gaps on the far bank. Billy Makin, the most successful of this group, launched the 'Canal Grey' when he set up a float-making company. There is a beauty in the streamlined profile of this slimmest of floats and its maker enjoyed scores of victories with it on small roach and gudgeon, often caught with the aid of a 17' rod and centre-pin reel.

B. The Image Squatt

The Image Squatt float in tapered balsa is size for size a little shorter and more compact than the Canal Grey, but equally successful for its followers. It was developed as an alternative to the Grey by Mark Pollard and his team at the Image Float Company, Luton. Mark was one of the next generation of top canal anglers on the Grand Union Canal. Like the Makin float, this would often be fished in 2BB or 3BB size with just a few dust shot or micro shot (sizes 10 to

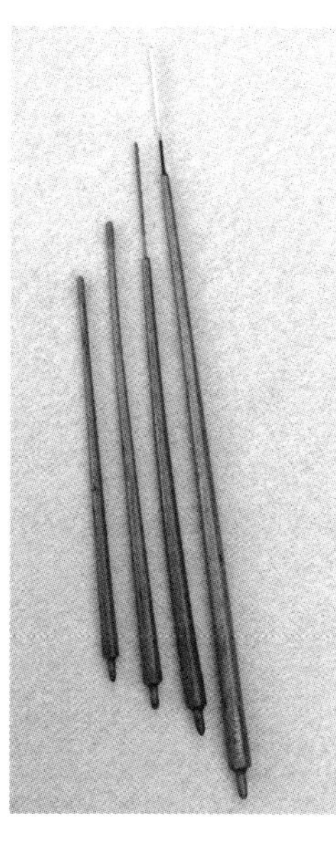

13) or styl* leads down the line. The only real difference with this float was the fine plastic bristle forming the tip that was sometimes used for even greater sensitivity, but both floats were highly successful in their respective eras.
(* The styl is a small cylindrical lead weight that originates from France. Sizes go from the tiniest at .010g up to .320g. Some anglers find these easier to attach to line than micro shot. Special styl pliers are available for the purpose).

C. Reversed Crow quill

This float must date back centuries, certainly over 100 years to the pioneers of the old Sheffield style of angling, where short 9-10′ rods were used and all the action happened close to the rod tip. The thinner end of the quill, no thicker than a 1mm pole bristle, was moved from its old downward position at the bottom of this float to the tip, which made for super sensitivity. An eye is either whipped to the base or it can be attached to the line with around ½″ of tight rubber sleeve.

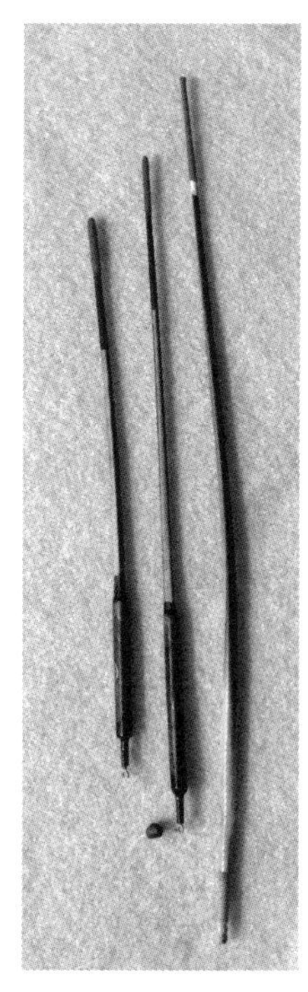

I have used these floats both with a 4m whip and a longer pole and short line. I have also made a 3AAA scaled up version of 9″ long with the crow quill spliced into a slightly thicker pheasant quill and a small polystyrene body added. To make the simplest of these floats all that's required is a discarded, fairly straight crow quill from a field. The quill can be straightened over the steam of a kettle but a slightly bent quill will still catch fish.

In the smaller sizes the neatest quills I have seen are made by Drake Floats involving a crow quill spliced into a short piece of peacock quill (pictured). Old-fashioned this float may be, but it's a superb canal float and more durable than a similar float made from light balsa.

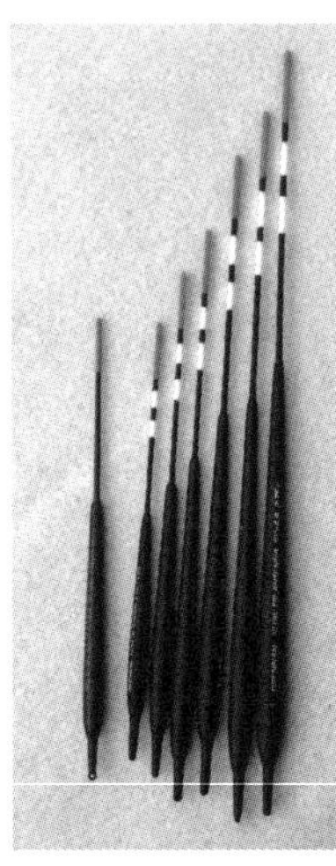

D. Drennan Glow-tip (formerly the Stillwater Blue)

Gary Barclay of Drennan International kindly sent me a set of their Glow-tip wagglers and they really are lovely floats, as neatly finished as any I have seen. This is the second generation of the old Stillwater Blue (pic, left), a very popular float for close-in work on small waters. The float now has a matt black finish but its shape has hardly altered. The only real difference is what the name suggests: the Glow-tip, a hi-viz plastic antenna replacing the old painted cane one. By holding the float up with the sun behind the effect of the plastic is remarkable. The glow-tip lights up where the old cane tip remains dull. It's a massive advantage for all, but especially for those with poor eyesight. I like the long antenna too, 3 ½″ on the longest float in the range, my kind of tip.

Of the six floats in this set the heaviest is marked up as '3 1/2 AAA (2.75g)'* which is 8 5/8″ long and would suit lake and pond swims, or medium width drains and canals up to a depth of 10 feet. The smallest are 2 no. 1 and 2BB and between 5″ and 6″ long and these are more suited to smaller canals.

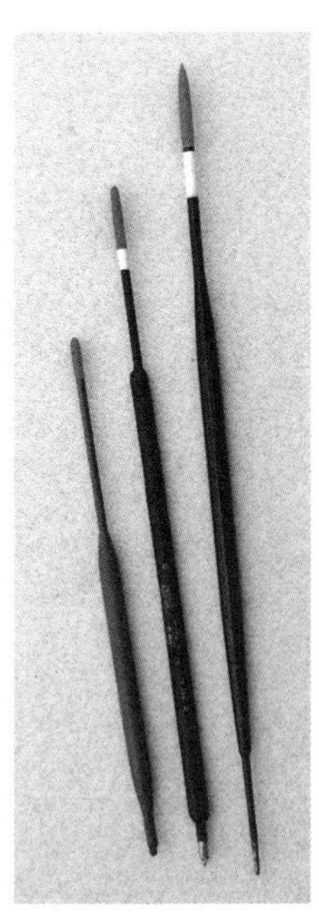

Note: Stillwater Blues are still available online from other makers.

*One AAA shot weighs 0.8g meaning 3 1/2AAA equals 2.8g. This grammage is slightly heavier than marked on the float, but my example of this float takes 3 1/2 AAA – 3AAA and one BB - with some float to spare to shot it down fully (Anchor brand).

E. The Dart

The Dart is a small canal float, loaded to make it semi-self-cocking, made from a balsa body and cane insert. The loading helps the float fly straight through the air like an arrow on the cast. Sizes range from 5″ up to 7″ total length with 3/5ths of the float being balsa of ¼″ diameter, and the float generally takes around three dust shot (no.8) down the line. Billy Lane said of the Dart that it will do everything the reversed crow quill will do and more. It's more sensitive and easier to shot up, and because it is straight it eliminates the 'lean' that can affect a crow quill.

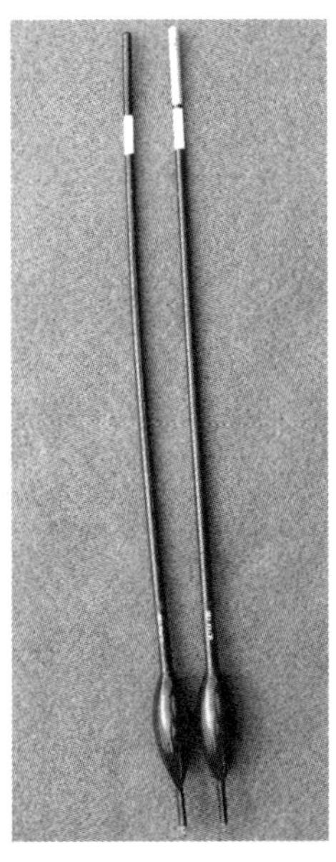

F. The Onion

This is an old float but one that would still catch fish today. It was Billy Lane's scaled up version of 'The Dart', made from a crow quill with a cork body added at the base plus a few turns of lead wire to give the float partial loading. Made to fish in around 8' of depth, Billy described how well the float rises on a lift bite: *"One of the first things you'll find about 'The Onion' is that a lift bite with it becomes a real cracker. No other float I know gives a more positive lift reaction. The tip fairly looms up out of the water in a way which makes the bite absolutely unmistakable – and of course, that much easier to hit."* Billy and his Coventry teammates won two National Championships in 1956 and 1958 (River Witham and River Welland respectively) with the aid of this float.

G. The Dumpy

As the name implies, 'The Dumpy' was a compact, slim, cane-stemmed float, with a bulbous balsa body, of only 5-8" long. It was created by London's Pat Richardson for fishing Kent's slow and deep River Medway at places like Tovil and Allington. Pat is said to have got the idea from a bleak float used by Colin 'Nozzer' Naylor, of Leicester, when fishing the Cam at Dimmock's Cote. Although originally it was a top and bottom attached float, anglers like John McCarthy later used a bottom only version with a peacock stem to win Thames matches at Reading Prom and elsewhere. The float also served well for different anglers on Southern lakes with one shot down the line.

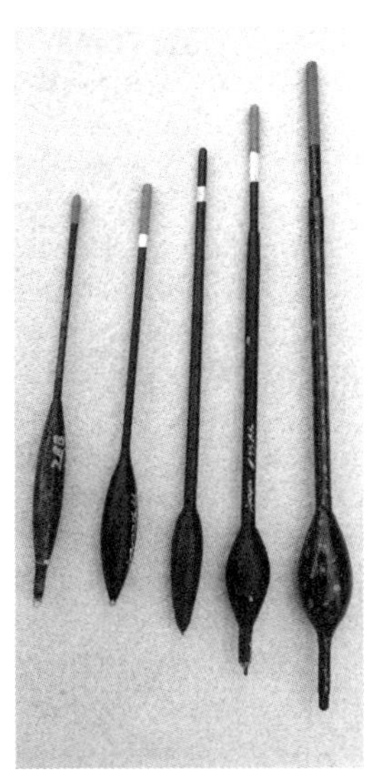

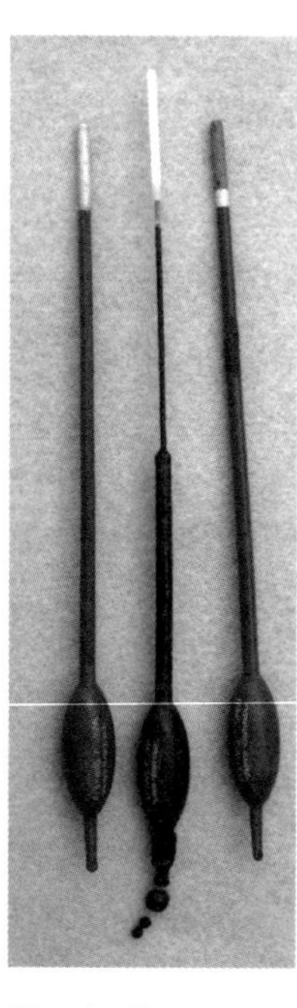

H. The Polywag

This stocky Drennan waggler is now obsolete but was a brilliant float in its time for casting across wider canals like Yorkshire's Stainforth and Keadby. Not unlike the second generation 'Dumpy', it was heavy for its size thanks to the rugby ball-shaped polystyrene body mounted on a stem of slim peacock.

I. The Double Decker

Former England international and Shakespeare Professionals skipper, Ken Giles, is widely regarded as one of angling's true gentleman and is famous as a 'thinking' angler. Apart from all his individual and team successes, the angling world owes him a great debt for pioneering the use of barbless hooks in the UK. Back in the Seventies Ken wanted a short but buoyant float for his local River Severn. He explains how a double peacock quill float emerged, which I have named 'The Double Decker' as it seemed so fitting:

"In shallow, pacey swims of 4'-7' deep on my local Severn we required a float of 2 Swan shot (SSG) size but one that was not too long. After a few experiments that went wrong, the penny dropped of how to make a float of 5"-7" long by strapping two pieces of thick peacock quill together, creating an oval shape if seen end on from an aerial viewpoint – approx. ½" by ¼" cross section. Peacock was all the rage as THE float material back in 1972 and, although we had tried balsa wood, peacock was lighter and cast better, and was therefore the ideal material.

"These floats were a little tricky to make as first the quills were glued together then whipped all the way up, before fitting a cane peg in the base. But the end result was a short, stubby float, very buoyant at the tip, that worked brilliantly. The float could be fished at least two feet overdepth in fast, shallow swims at popular venues like

Stourport. It proved a regular winner but the clever bit was in the way we learnt to shot the line below the float. A Swan and an AAA locked the float in place leaving around a BB to split up into smaller shot down the line.

"The use of micro shot was key to slowing the bait down without the float pulling under on any small obstruction. Two or three no. 6 shot would be placed as bulk around halfway down the line, then in the last 30" of line towards the hook anything up to a dozen micros were placed 2" apart. This allowed the float to ride the current, dragging the shotted part of line over a rough bottom with an inch of float showing, and tangles were minimised compared to using bigger shot. It worked like a dream. Today the peacock waggler is universally popular so after 45 years and still going strong it says it all about this great material!"

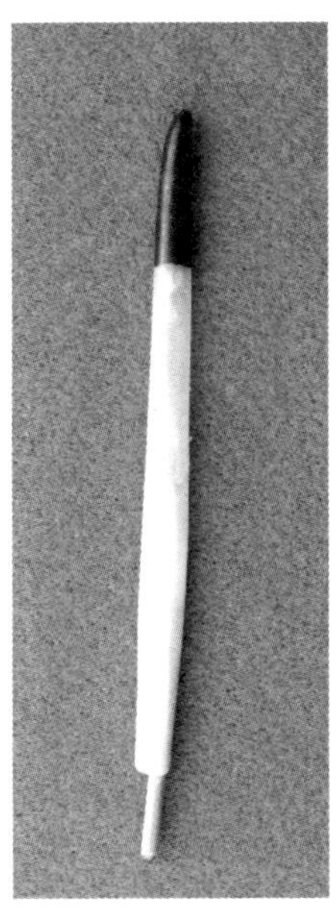

J. The Sawn-off Goose Quill - by Tony Scott

This is another excellent float for dragging shots on the bottom in fairly swift, shallow water. Former England International Tony Scott, from Burton-on-Trent, made a name for himself by winning some good matches on his local Trent and Mersey Canal before graduating to rivers. He represented England in the World Championships on seven occasions between 1974 and 1981. He was a superb waggler angler on the Rivers Trent and Warwickshire Avon and he specialised in groundbait and caster. He won the Trent Championship in 1972:

"In the peak years of the Trent in the 70s-80s, a draw on Shelford Shallows was always favourable and the opportunity of a frame place or match win was on the cards. But you needed a special float to cope with the fast, shallow water as here the river careers round a long outside bend. In swims no deeper than three feet a short float was essential, and I made one from a cut down goose quill which placed the fattest, hollow end of the quill, the most buoyant part, at the tip. It held up perfectly when running over small underwater obstructions like stones and it caught me stacks of fish. Obviously the quill need not be from a goose, there are other big bird feathers that would also fit the bill, but it's as good as any. If you can't find a discarded one then a trip to a bird sanctuary should give you the basic material – a giant feather."

A good alternative to Tony's float would be Ken Giles' double quill (above) while John Moult tackled it in a different way. John bought some square 3/8" balsa dowel and sanded down and rounded off only the top inch of it, adding a cane peg to the base. This float might sound a bit clumsy but a 4-6" float would take plenty of shot to cast well out. Ken insists that the peacock suited him better than balsa as it was lighter and therefore easier to cast.

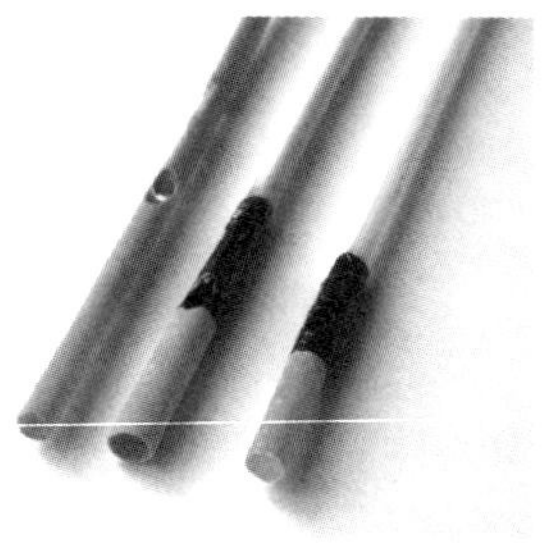

K. The Hollow Tip Waggler - by Mark Wintle

[Angling author Mark Wintle spent more than three decades match fishing, mainly at club level; he also fished many team events including winter leagues and National Championships plus opens, and enjoyed more than his share of success. He co-wrote three books with Graham Marsden: 'Pole Fishing – A Complete Guide', 'Practical Carp Fishing', 'Practical Barbel Fishing' (all Crowood Press) and has written three as sole author: 'Big Roach', 'Big Roach 2', and 'Ivan Marks and the Likely Lads' (all Mpress). He now introduces the hollow tip concept:]

The waggler angler sometimes has the challenge of needing a float that is sensitive yet visible at medium to long range in difficult light (or slowly failing eyesight in my case). The problem is that the thicker a tip becomes its sensitivity to shy bites diminishes. In simple terms if you double the thickness of the tip it is twice as visible but four times less sensitive.

This problem is an old one. The solution lies in increasing the visible surface area of the float tip without increasing its volume. Back in the 1960s balsa trotting floats were available with inset plastic fluted tips. These floats never really caught on but they did give a highly sensitive yet visible float for long trotting. In the 1970s, Lancashire angler Harold Pattison (later based in Ireland) came up with another solution, described in 'Coarse Angler', which was to use a short length of plastic drinking straw for the waggler tip. The innovation came from having the tube open at both ends. This reduces the volume of the tip yet it is highly visible. The hole at the bottom of the float tip is best described as a shallow scoop. He publicised this idea in the now defunct 'Coarse Angler' magazine. Commercially made wagglers with hollow tips were available in the 1980s but the idea didn't really catch on.

I can't remember when I decided to try this idea out but guess it was sometime in the late 1980s. I soon discovered that it worked best when the tip diameter was either 4mm or 5mm. It still works with 3mm but diameters less than this don't fill up with water through the hole so well. I use either 4mm drinking straws or cut down sections of Drennan Canal Crystals. To get the fluorescent paint to key onto the plastic I sanded it very lightly. The hollow tip has an additional benefit in that when the sun was shining the light shining through it made it extremely easy to see. I also made some tips with matt black plastic that did not require painting. Some float makers have tried having several pinholes instead of a much larger scoop hole but it is vital that the water can flow in and out of the tip freely and I'm not convinced the pinholes work properly.

In terms of sensitivity a 4mm hollow tip is as sensitive as a 2mm solid tip but twice as visible. There is no exact science to this because the thickness of the tube wall in the hollow tip has a bearing on its volume but the general principle holds.

Because I was using these floats at ranges of 20 to 25 yards I incorporated the hollow tips into straight peacock floats that typically had a shot load of 4AAA to 5AAA. I also made some bodied peacock stem slider floats. I found these floats worked very well on still waters. On a river, you generally need a more buoyant tip to stop the flow dragging the float under and a solid tip is generally the way to fish.

L. The Driftbeater – by Jim Macdonald

In his groundbreaking 1953 book 'Stillwater Angling', Richard Walker explained the effects of the various elements on lakes, ponds, reservoirs and pits and showed how they create all kinds of currents, undertows, rises and falls so that water which appears to be still actually is not. These movements may be insufficient to require fish to lie head on to them or to move food particles along the bottom, but can be strong enough to drag a float through a swim and cause a static bait to move unnaturally on the bottom.

The driftbeater is a waggler designed solely for the purpose of doing just that - beating the drift - and is used exclusively on stillwaters. It has no place on running water. The float has a unique appearance:

an oval body from which extends a thin antenna which is topped with a bulbous, buoyant sight tip, and it must be fished in a very specific way to be effective. The float must be attached to the line bottom end only, using either a couple of float stops or a quick change float adaptor. Split shot will do, but needs to be small to permit as much weight as possible to be concentrated below mid water. The hook should be tied and split shot bulked somewhere between mid-depth and 18 inches from the hook. The amount of shot should just sink the body but leave the antenna proud of the surface.

The depth must then be accurately plumbed and a single shot placed between 2" and 12" from the hook. This shot must lie on the bottom and be heavy enough to sink the antenna down to the sight tip. When the tackle is cast, the bulk shot will cock the float and the single shot sink it further so that only the tip is showing. The set-up is completed by sinking the line between the rod and float and resting the rod so that its tip is submerged. The shot on the bottom will anchor the bait and the buoyant bob-tip will prevent the float from being pulled under by any drag. If the drift is exceptional and the rig still moving through the swim, an increase in float setting will decrease the angle from float to anchor shot and the problem should be remedied. If it is not, simply increase the size of the tell-tale shot.

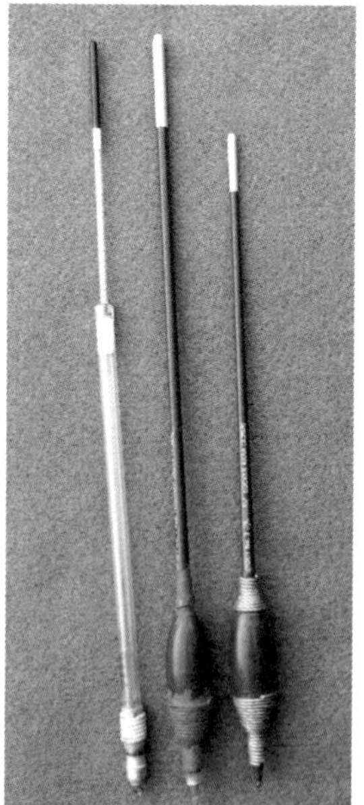

Bite indications using this method may vary with the distance from anchor shot to hook. If the bait is fished close to the anchor shot the chances are that as the fish takes the bait and dislodges the bottom shot, the float will rise up to the body - a lift bite - but if the tail is long, the float will tend to just disappear. Whatever, takes are generally very positive indeed.

M. The Puller Waggler

This float can be any waggler that is adapted by extra loading, usually with lead wire, to make it fully self-cocking apart from approximately one no. 8 shot (which is split up into micro shot or styl weights down the line) and is used for trolling baits on lakes. This can be a deadly tactic in the warmer months whenever fish are feeding subsurface and swirling at loose-fed bait when it hits the water. The float mimics the sliding stick float method (aka the 'puller' method) as pioneered by Sheffield's Bernard Bryan, and is a handy alternative when a cross wind makes presenting the stick float difficult. Bernard was a real innovator, always trying out new methods on his local waters like Ecclesfield Dam and the Sheffield Canal. The sliding stick made him something of a local legend for catching big roach on the drop. It is never used on rivers I will quickly add, but it can be superb for tricky roach on lakes.

The only trouble with the trolled stick float style is when a cross wind puts a bow in the line. Back-shotting the sliding stick can sometimes beat such a bow, but in strong winds even this won't be good enough. This is when the waggler version comes into its own. The float fishes bottom only like all wagglers, but the big difference is it slides on the line via its base eye down to a bottom stop, with no locking shot or stop of any kind used above the float. The fully loaded float takes on average five or six no. 7 styl weights to be shotted down fully. It slides down to a small shot at the end of the reel line or a cushioning piece of ethafoam above a double overhand loop. The float is cast straight out then drawn back slowly through the loose feed directly to the rod tip. The line can be retrieved by winding the reel slowly, which literally winds the fish onto the hook (no strike is necessary) or line can be pulled with the left hand, similar to retrieving a fly line when fly fishing still waters.

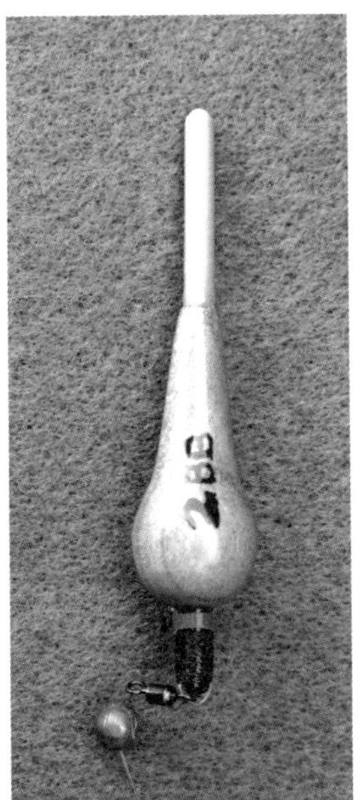

N. The Trent Trotter – by Billy Lane

This is a remarkable little float that paid dividends for the great Billy Lane, 1963 World Champion from Coventry, for fishing a River Trent swim a mere 12″ deep at 30 yards range. The same man who fished giant sliding floats on such as the River Nene went from the sublime to the ridiculous with this 2″ long Trent float incorporating a 1 ½″ x ½″ pear-shaped piece of cork or balsa with a ring glued in the base and a ½″ cane tip. In such a seemingly hopeless shallow swim above Stoke Weir in the 1961 National

Championship, he caught 17lb 4oz of roach to finish fourth individual. Billy hit upon the idea by accident when using an Avon float in an earlier Trent Championship. Late in the contest his float broke in two, but with the short stump remaining he proceeded to total 7lb 12oz to win his section. The float will perform well in water from 6″ up to 2′ deep, said Billy.

The information source for this float, and the Dart, Onion and Missile, is Colin Graham's 1971 book which he ghost wrote for Billy Lane entitled 'Billy Lane's Encyclopaedia of Float Fishing'.

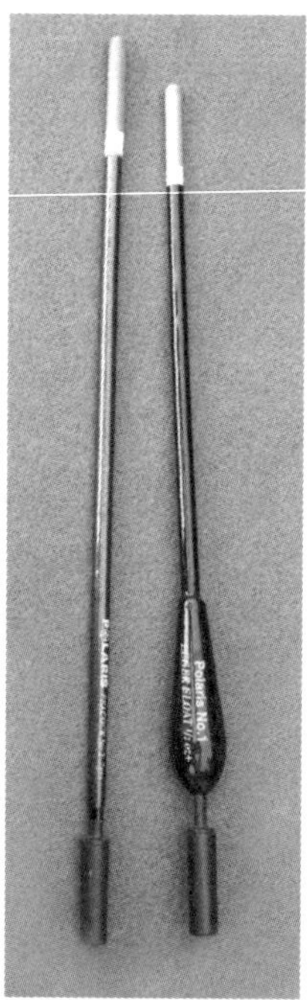

O. The Polaris Self-locking Slider
This cleverly conceived sliding float works on the principle that the float will run freely on a slack line but will lock in position once some tension is applied. In deep swims, the shots (or a small leger or feeder) will pull the line through the float until they hit the bottom, then as soon as the line is wound back enough to tighten to the float it will stay put at that depth. The cylinder built into the float's base has two separate channels for the line to run through and these spiral around the interior of the cylinder. One channel opening is a tiny hole that accepts a fine line; the other takes a thicker one. The key to the float's success is matching the right thickness of reel line to whichever hole the float is threaded on by.

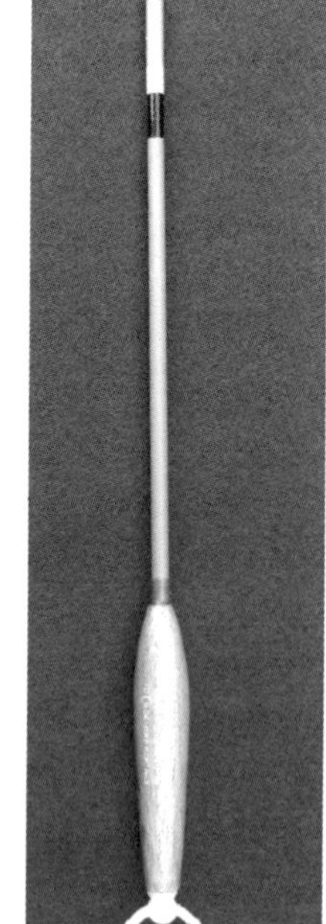

P. The Dave Thomas Locslide Leger Float
This slider works on the same principle as the 'Polaris' (above) but the line slides in a semi-circular channel at the base of the float. This version is ideal for fishing float-leger on big waters in rough conditions that might make life difficult for a normal waggler presentation, and is certainly worth a try if you prefer to fish a float to a feeder.

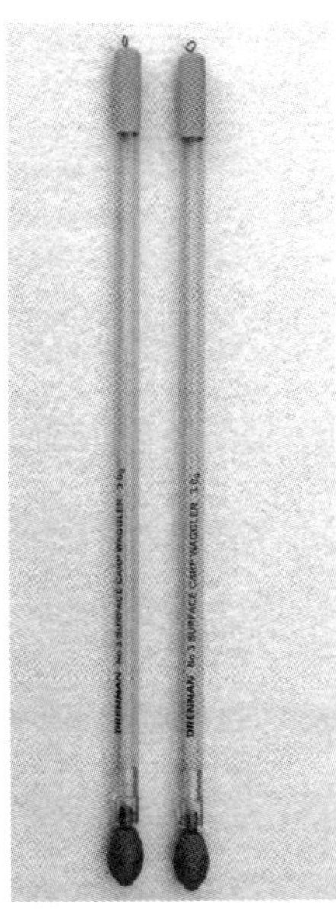

Q. Drennan Surface Carp Waggler

In Sheffield this waggler, in this case a hollow plastic crystal, is called an 'upside-downer'. The line runs through an eye at the tip of the float and is fully self-cocking with all the weight built into the base. It is used for fishing the surface layers of water, with or without floating baits, with minimal shot or no shot down the line. Any time that carp are showing on or near the surface this float is worth considering as with a floating line it offers a direct line of contact between the rod tip and the bait. While some fish it with a greased line float to bait, I prefer to sink all the line below the float, though not too deeply, with just a small size 10 or 11 shot when fishing a bait like dog biscuit. The float scores best in calm conditions when the fish are up in the water basking in the summer sunshine.

AND NOW FOR THE HEAVY MOB!

R. The Feeder Float

What do we do when fishing in a strong facing wind that makes it almost impossible to fire out maggots beyond 10 metres when we know that the fish are well beyond that, but where ground-baiting is not ideal? The answer could be to use any one of these three interesting floats below. The first is a UK-made Dave Thomas 4AAA (or 3.2g) feeder float with a balsa stem, and the second is an Italian option almost twice the size at 6g.

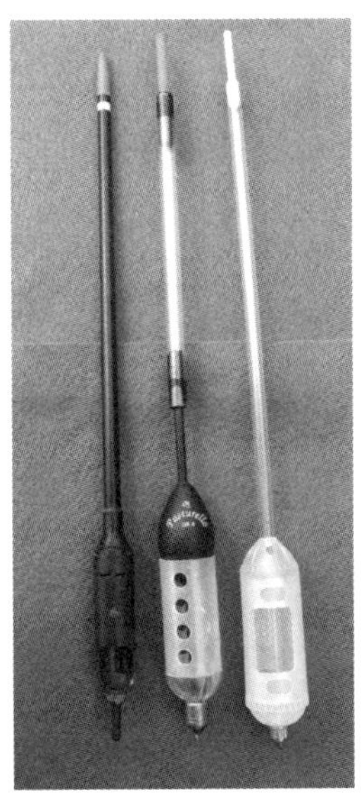

As the name suggests this float combines a waggler and a maggot feeder. The first float requires locking shots adding to the base, whereas the other two need fewer shot to hold it in place as it is part-loaded with a brass weight mounted below a central column running through the feeder section.

The bait chamber on the simpler Thomas design is open and must therefore be loaded with the float in the upside-down position. However, the bulbous body of the Italian Colmic float slides upwards to allow maggots to be poured into the gap created, then is replaced to trap them in the feeder ready for casting.

The Thomas holds at least 20 maggots while the Colmic takes over 60. But to fill either chamber is not always necessary. Indeed jamming them too tightly into the Colmic will prevent their escape. Its also worth noting that in warm water the bait will release easily, but for cold temperatures the holes in the feeder on this bigger float might need enlarging for the bait to drip out quickly. The float would serve no purpose if on most strikes the majority of maggots were still in the feeder.

Dave Thomas admits that while he has never won a match on his own branded float, he has come close several times and it has caught him fish when all else has failed:
"The first time was in a shallow peg on the tidal Trent at North Clifton, where the prevailing wind is mostly downstream and with an outgoing tide, the fish were out of reach of the catapult. I came second with 10lb. I always carried one after that but changed the top half of the balsa stem to lighter peacock quill. In coloured water it generally pays to concentrate the feed more tightly like this float does, and in such conditions in one of the TV 'Hooked' series rounds at Longleat, again I made second."

Suffolk company NISA also make a smaller but fatter modern adaptation called the 'Chomper' that has earnt a fine reputation for catching carp on the surface. Difficult gusting winds will always limit feeding range and accuracy with a catapult, and this type of float offers a neat solution.

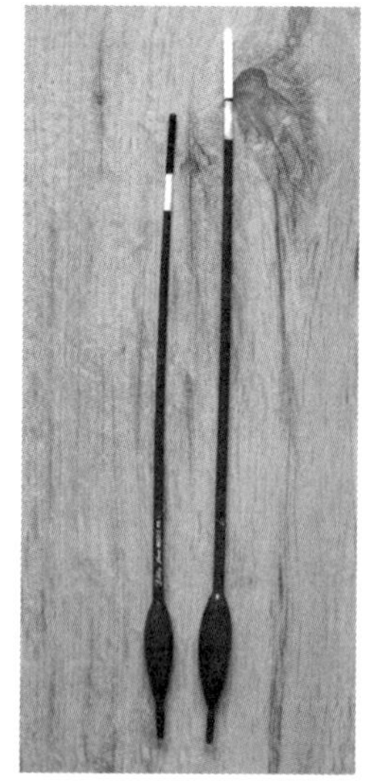

S. The Missile

Billy Lane coined the name 'Missile' for a giant waggler capable of casting up to 60 yards distance on Cambridgeshire's Relief Channel, but the name could be applied to any of the longer peacock quills or other big wagglers for fishing at such a range. How far out can we fish, is the question? If the float is heavy enough then the actual casting

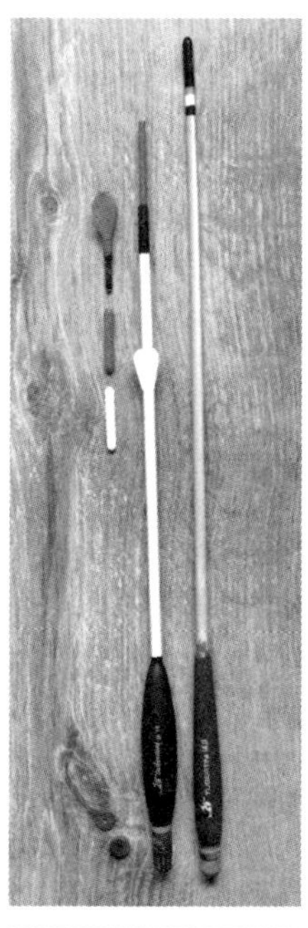

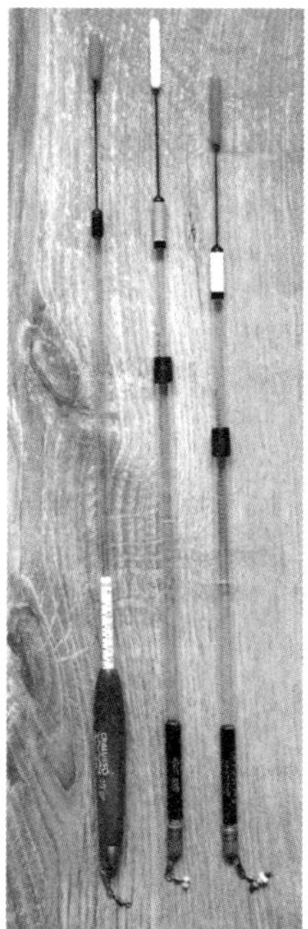

distance is not the issue. Feeding the swim is by far the more tricky part with casts of 50 yards or more. It all depends on one's skill with a catapult, and regular practice is called for. I say groundbait for preference, but there is also a time for 'sticky mag' - a ball of maggots bound up in Horlicks or similar sticky powder then fired to the float, when it is well beyond the range of loose feed. (See how contributor Dave Frost explains this in chapter 12).

T. Tubertini Giant Wagglers 14g and 16g

These are more examples of some of the huge floats available for long casting to distant swims. Adjustable loading in the shape of metal discs are incorporated in the base of the body, which allow different shot sizes to be used down the line. These are not new floats and the coloured tips could be improved. A fluorescent plastic tip from the 'Cralusso' range (below) would greatly help visibility at the sort of distance this float is likely to be cast, knowing how far the right rod and reel could project such a 16g or 10 Swan shot float! It's claimed the flutes in the stem are to help casting accuracy.

U. Cralusso Wagglers

These are the large wagglers preferred by Dave Frost and feature excellent fluoro plastic sight tips on top of solid carbon inserts. They also have a unique telescopic feature to change the length. (See also Dave Frost chapter).

V. The Bagging Waggler

It takes considerable physical effort to fish this macho float for a whole day on a prolific carp water. It is the heaviest float I know purely because a ball of groundbait is moulded around a wire frame at its base before casting. It works in the same way as the feeder float but is like its big brother! Instead of feeding a pinch of maggots inside the float every cast, a groundbait ball the size

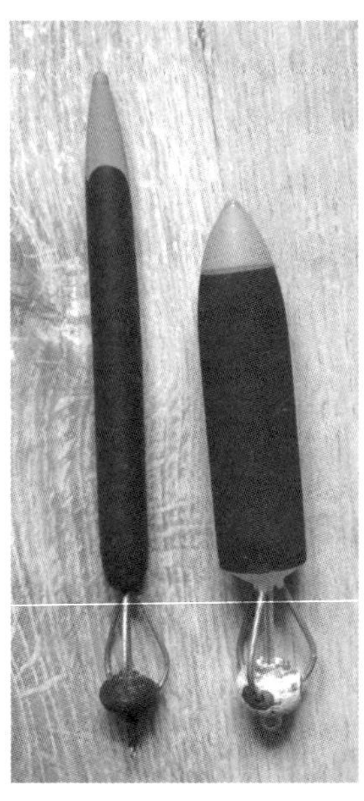

of a golf ball or bigger, weighing 2oz or more, is moulded around the already weighty base frame, requiring a powerful rod to cast any serious distance with accuracy. On a prolific carp fishery it's possible to get through a full large (Sensas-type) groundbait bucket and more of bait in five hours. The float was pioneered in Sheffield by Tony Hutchinson who went on to take huge catches of carp at Midlands Lakes like Drayton and Boddingtons. Tony used a Tri-cast 2x2 rod for the job but there are many sturdy feeder rods that will take the casting strain. It is said to work best with a groundbait that creates a good cloud as the float impacts the surface and, when the angler leaves the float where it lands, in typical bolt-rig style, the carp will self-hook against the float's weight.

W. The Hinged Waggler

This unusual float, featured on former World Champion Clive Branson's website 'Gold Medal Floats', is hinged in the middle as the name suggests. I first saw a version of this float made from two pieces of porcupine quill in Sheffield back in the early sixties, but this particular model was developed by the late Albert Friswell, of Newport, Gwent. It is constructed from a 10" peacock quill cut in half, then the two halves glued back together at either end of a connecting swivel.

The float can be fished in two ways. For the first, enough shot is added to sink the lower half of the float with the top half laying flat on the surface at a 90-degree angle to the other. This makes bites easy to see by people with poor vision, because when a bite occurs the top half of the float will stand up. Alternatively, the float can be shotted normally so both halves sit underwater apart from a ¼" of tip left showing on the surface, with 2AAA or 2SSG shot locking it in place depending on quill thickness, and small shot down the line. The advantage of this latter configuration is a slightly smoother strike because the float collapses halfway up at the hinge. Clive highlights a match he won on the River Usk with an impressive 20lb-plus of big dace when fishing this way after struggling to hit bites on a standard waggler.

Reducing the bump effect of hitting the float on the strike with this second use of the hinged waggler can only be a good thing. But as for the first option, the half-cocked, half-flat float setting, I'm wary about the float's inertia at the point where the fish has to pull down one end of the upper half of the float to cock it. Were the upper section reduced to only 2" long it would need less force to up-end it, but then wouldn't a normal thick-tipped waggler, with a bit more float showing, be just as easy to see and be more sensitive?

X. Floats of a former era.

See 'History of the Waggler' (chapter 3) for more on the bottom only porcupine quill, 'The Ducker', and the 'The Swinger'. 'The Sarkandas Reed Waggler' is covered by Dave Thomas, and 'The Drinking Straw' by Terry Payne and Jim Randell.

The Fluted Tip

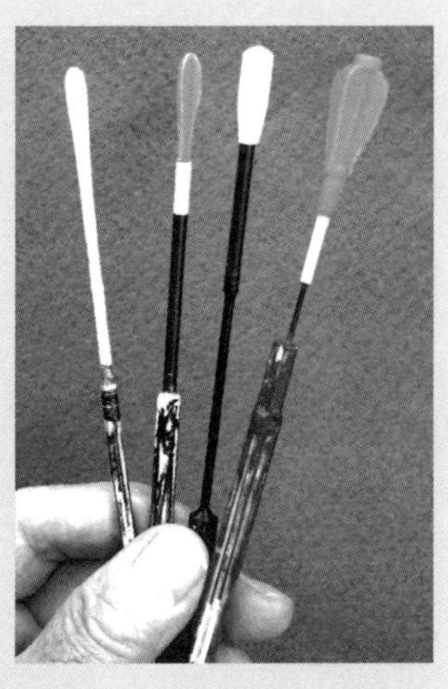

This really is the future for waggler tip design in my opinion. As someone who has spent years experimenting with different versions of sight bobs to make float tips easier to see, I now think that the fluted tip in a hi-viz plastic is the ultimate for building onto the top of any waggler for lakes or slow rivers, only becoming too sensitive on faster rivers where buoyancy is required for dragging a bait over depth. The great advantage of this design is that it gives the necessary diameter for good visibility but is twice as sensitive as a solid tip. An aerial view shows the volume - and therefore the resistance to the fish - and is around half that of a solid tip. The hollow tip also offers the dual advantage of good visibility with less resistance, but I think the fluted tip will pick out of the water a shade smoother on the strike.

Note: It was decided that two floats deserved more coverage than this section provided: The 'Sliding Waggler' for deep water, and the widely popular 'Pellet Waggler' for catching carp in shallow water. These two floats are featured in chapters 19 and 20, and 21 and 22 respectively.

Chapter 7
Alternative Methods to the Waggler

Give me a warm and windy day, or one with at least a ripple on the water which ideally also carries a tinge of colour, and we can expect bites on the waggler. As much as I love fishing the method however, it is not always the smartest choice as it cannot do everything. The match angler must have other strings to his bow - both float and ledger methods – to cope with different water and weather conditions.

In my best years on the rivers I relied on three methods – waggler, stick, and bomb in the main – that covered most situations. Back in 2008 however, I won a league at Aston Ponds where I fished seven different methods over 10 rounds, including: sliding stick float (also known as the 'puller', see method no. 5 below), pole, small bomb and maggot, larger bomb and meat, pellet waggler, my standard slim waggler for roach, and one other. The target fish varied from 2oz-6oz roach, ide from 6oz-1lb, small skimmers and sizeable big bream, and carp in the later rounds. These days, on all sorts of venues, the best anglers have almost as many methods at their fingertips as the golfer has clubs in his bag. So let's briefly consider a few alternatives to the waggler for lake or river:

1. Whip: If ever small fish will feed confidently for long periods very close in, the area we call 'under the rod tip' or no further than 3m-4m range from the margin, then the whip is superior to all other methods. Originally a whip was a short, soft-actioned, telescopic pole and made for tiny fish like bleak or gudgeon, but today's whips are often 'take apart', where spare sections can be added during play, and they can also be elasticated (with internal elastic) for coping with bigger fish. The best feature about fishing a whip is the 'line to hand' facility, meaning that fish can be swung in quickly to meet the waiting free hand. The only proviso is that the line strength and elastic must be strong enough to cope with most of the fish hooked. If fish are all of a similar size and will feed close in, then the whip can be unbeatable. Floats for the whip can be either top and bottom or a small waggler-type, and a pole waggler of 6"-7" long is a good choice for a shallowish swim (1.5m) when faced with a cross wind. This is because any whip longer than 4m has a long line between pole tip and float, therefore burying that line below the surface is the way to avoid wind drag, and bottom only makes this task easy.

2. Pole – up to 14 metres long, sometimes longer: What must be the most popular method in use by younger anglers today, the long pole is really an extended version of my no. 1 above, the whip (elasticated). The pole's efficiency can beat all other methods hands down when fish are feeding fairly close in and are tricky to catch, on all kinds of venue. It also performs very well at the other end of the scale on bigger fish, especially since the introduction of side puller kits and the like where the elastic can be shortened/tightened as the fish tires. In many situations in between however, I think the waggler has a chance of out-fishing the pole. It's not hard to appreciate why the pole is good when fish are shy. A 4m rod casting a waggler to 14m distance equates to 14m of line, mostly with a slight bow in it, plus a 90-degree angle formed between the float base and the baited hook when it's reached the bottom. All this line must be tightened on the strike to hook the fish. Knowing how a fish can both suck in and eject the bait in the blink of an eye, it means that some bites will be missed. Now compare the ease with which a long pole and just an 18" lash of line hanging vertically from its tip to the float, tightening the line to the fish is now rapid and requires only a couple of inches of lift to set the hook. Far fewer bites are missed on difficult days.

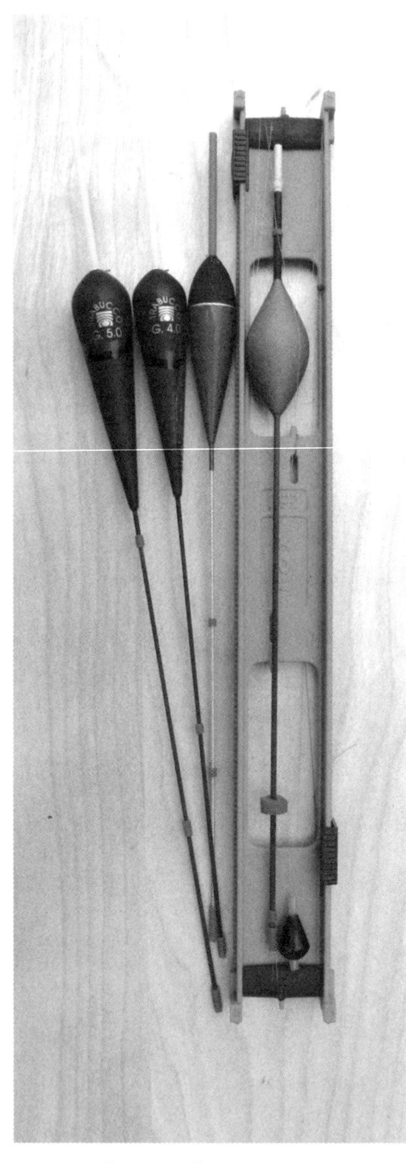

3g-5g Bolognese floats.

I mention 14m pole, but many fish are caught on the so-called 'long pole/short line' method at 8m to 10m and shorter lengths. If you can catch fish all day at 8m then this is a lovely, comfy range to fish, and the same goes for 10m or 11m, and obviously it's faster to bring the fish in to shore when you have fewer sections to remove to land it. The waggler chips back the pole's advantage when it comes to distance and strong winds. Even a top quality 16m pole will take some handling in a gale but the waggler man can cast 17m or more to take fish that are out of the pole man's reach.

3. Stick float: Simply put, the stick float is the waggler's close cousin for trotting on rivers and making full use of every yard of the swim. These two float types have long ruled our premier rivers like the Trent, Severn, Warks. Avon, Thames etc. The one obvious advantage the stick has over the waggler when the fish want the bait slowing down considerably, is that the line is fixed to the top of the float, making it easier to hold back the float without it sinking. Most top anglers say it's harder to master the stick float method than waggler. I think it's hard to generalise but if a stick is dotted down fully so only a pimple is

A Stick float selection, light to heavy.

showing it is not difficult to fish it well, providing the line above the float is kept reasonably straight. To do this it is vital to back-shot a stick if ever the wind is downstream or adverse. The stick is a wonderful method to use when working well.

4. 'Bolognese': Where once UK anglers fished an all-balsa float on a river when heavier shotting was required for boily or deep swims, sometimes a sliding one, the modern answer to 'leading up' (using extra weight down the line) is the 'Bolognese' method. Imported from the top Italian anglers, this style incorporates a rod of up to 20′ long (5m-6m) originally of the telescopic kind, and floats of 3g and bigger. Picture the scene: 18′ of water on the Upper Erne at Belleek in the 1991 World Championships. Helped by an upstream wind so he could hold the line up like a sail to slow the float down, Italian master Roberto Trabucco fished his swim with a 6m rod and something like a 10g float carrying a big chunk of lead at 2/3 depth. I watched him inch his float through slower than the flow and catch enough bream to win his section and lead his team to the gold medal. No other method with a float could have got close to fishing that vast depth as efficiently on that day, easing the bait through the swim at the perfect slow speed the fish liked.

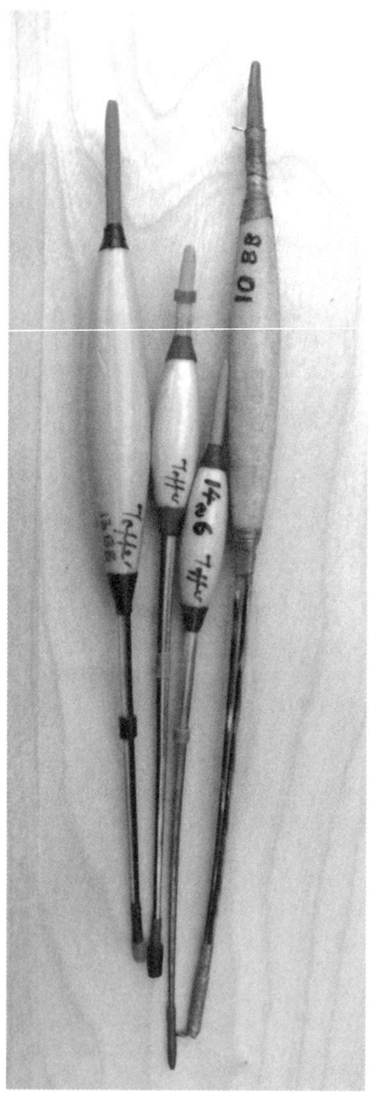

Bolo' alternatives, 'Topper' Haskins floats (and a homemade version).

5. Sliding stick float (aka 'Puller' method): This is a specialised method that peaks in those warm summer conditions when fish swirl as the loose feed is thrown in, rising up in the water to take it. Whenever we see a mini vortex it is a tell-tale sign that fish are feeding close to the surface, and this is my cue to consider this float. Trolled baits are as old as the hills but I'm fairly sure it was Sheffield's Bernard Bryan who first used a sliding stick float for catching roach on lakes. It has been tagged the puller because the float is cast straight out then pulled back to the rod tip by taking a bite of line in the left hand just beyond the butt ring and slowly pulling the float back by extending the arm away from the rod and behind. A fish sucks in the bait, turns its head, and hooks itself in the corner of the mouth. The only downside of the method is when fish of an ounce or less get in the way, as they hardly have enough body weight to set the hook when they grab the bait. On the plus side it can single out the bigger fish in a roach/rudd/ide or skimmer shoal, and it is a method where you hardly ever need a disgorger – few fish having chance to swallow the bait before they're hooked.

6. Bomb or Maggot Feeder and Spring-tip: These two alternatives are for the other end of the scale when the weather is inclement. When winter bites in particular, when we sometimes have to break the ice on lakes to make a gap to fish in, or merely when a cold easterly or northerly is blowing and the fish almost shut up shop, this is when the springer (spring-tip) reigns supreme for me. These are days when I have to sit and wait for a bite knowing that if one occurs it is unlikely to be that positive, often a slow pull round of an inch or less. If a fish sucks in a bait and does not swim anywhere then we have to detect a gentle pull on the line or we come back with a sucked maggot. The springer gives me the best chance of hitting these shyest of bites.

On rivers that are out of sorts when scratching for bites with a bomb this way, then keep the loose feed to a minimum and try a tail length of around 30" to a fine wire 22 hook. If on a lake then I'd say a small maggot feeder is better, one taking only around 50 maggots maximum, but this does not mean you should fill it. Put only 6-10 maggots in the feeder and a sprinkling of cloud groundbait to leave an enticing scent trail for the fish to investigate.

7. Bubble Feeder: This method was developed in the Sheffield area way back in the mid-Sixties. The innovator we have to credit for it was Eddie Outram, a Lancastrian who came to live in Sheffield at that time. Eddie had a canal background and made his feeders from those oval capsules containing sweets and novelties from slot machines located outside newsagents or 'sweets shops'. Four ¼" holes were burnt into each half of the capsule to enable maggots, groundbait etc. to release, and a swivel glued into one half to attach it to the line, or a short piece of line attached and a swivel tied to that.

The finished 'bubble' was loaded with squatts and sand by Eddie to catch roach and perch from the difficult Damflask Reservoir in 30' of depth, and he won consecutive Damflask Championships in 1970 and '71 doing so. Eddie passed away soon after but years later his former work colleague, Tony Wills, reprieved the method and began to catch big roach with it from the lake when all other methods failed. He broke both the 3-hour and 5-hour Flask match records and was so hot for a few years he earnt the nickname 'bubble man'. Take it from me that on its day this method will out-perform all others, tempting fish that manage to evade capture on more popular techniques and traditional forms of bait presentation.

8. Method Feeder: Although this is a method I do not use, as I do not fish the ledger very often and rarely fish for carp, I do fish for bream and therefore feel obliged to mention it. Many anglers in my area have great success with this feeder, or variations of it – one being the pellet scoop, another the shallow banjo feeder. It's a fact that carp and bream everywhere simply adore fishmeal, and with a fishmeal pellet on the hook (various sizes) and micro pellets in the feeder it can be the ultimate way of catching fish on the bottom. With a method feeder the micros are moulded onto it and the hookbait fished close to the feed, and it has blown apart the old theory that a long 2′-6′ tail was necessary to catch bream. Not any more! I'd advise any youngster out there to learn this method well, even though feeder is not my strong suit and I am not best qualified to give more details.

Chapter 8
Masterclass - What These Anglers Taught Me

1. Benny Ashurst – I still occasionally read Benny Ashurst's Match Fishing book of 1968 which inspired me in my youth, and believe that most of the wide-ranging advice given was years ahead of its time. Benny possibly taught me most that anglers who work harder than others at practice and preparation, and reduce the chance element in fishing, will be rewarded for their efforts. Examples include: reducing the weight of hooks for canal fishing by filing down oversize spade ends, adding an extra 'v' to shots for easy opening with a fingernail, and cutting up small redworms into inch long pieces to make a bloodworm substitute. This is not to mention how he developed the stick float, circa 1956, and even before that pioneered the sinking casters as a superior bait to the darker floating maggot chrysalis or 'husks'. The influence of the stick and caster was monumental and far reaching, combining into a method that improved the fortunes of future generations of river anglers.

The book highlights Benny's confidence from all his achievements, but also has a thread of humility running through it. Here was a champion angler aged 52, suggesting, for example, how he'd only made limited progress with some methods like ledgered caster for roach on a flooded river when he suffered lightning fast bites. Some anglers get carried away with early success and think they know it all; Benny was too wise to think like that.

Benny Ashurst with his 18lb 3oz Trent Championship winning catch 1971.

A quick word on 'Kevin', the son of the maestro who became a 'great' in his own right when still young, going on to become an England regular and 1982 World Champion. Whenever I've seen Kevin in action his unwavering self-belief forged on beating most anglers he ever came up against could be spotted a mile away. He now lives in Northern Ireland where he fishes the Erne system; what a wonderful place to retire to.

2. Johnny Moult – This enigmatic Trent genius taught me many things, an important one being the need to experiment with baits. He learnt how feeding different baits into one swim could win matches. Before knowing this I wrongly assumed that to change baits mid-match, like he did from maggot to caster and then occasionally on to tares, could kill a swim. Not so. Johnny said: "It was all maggot on the Trent at one time but experimentation led me to try wheat. I started to lay down a carpet of wheat and fished maggot over the top of it. It worked and was the basis of my mixed baiting idea which stuck with me throughout my career."

Johnny also made me realise that light shotting could work in deep water, once trouncing the opposition on waggler and tare with 27lb. This was a Trent match at Burton Joyce which I fished myself where 10lb was regarded as a good return. The swim was 13' deep but he used only one no. 8 shot down the line. The tare is a not the lightest of baits I should add, and to some extent behaved like a second small shot.

Johnny Moult pioneered waggler on the Trent in the 1960s.

But the best tip I got from this modest and unassuming man was about holding back a waggler, as described to me when I interviewed him back in 1984: *"Something just happened one day, like things do in fishing, which was like striking gold. Everybody fishes a bit different but I have always dragged back the tackle a yard after casting to keep a tight line. Until the line is released a loose float (waggler) will stay submerged under a tight line on the Trent due to the flow. On this occasion I delayed releasing the line and kept the float buried. When I finally gave line and the float reappeared it went under again and I had a fish on. I developed this delaying tactic into a countdown system similar to fishing on the drop with a bomb. I couldn't explain why it worked but sometimes the float would never come back up at all. Maybe it could be likened to holding back with a stick float. I have no doubt that some of the modern waggler artists have done something similar to catch fish."* This tactic lifts the bait to tantalise the fish and it has caught me stacks of fish, particularly on the Witham and tidal Trent at Dunham.

3. Johnny Rolfe – Another of the famous Trentmen called 'John' from Nottingham. Johnny was the first angler to score multiple Trent wins on a genuine peacock waggler in one spectacular season 1971-2. By all accounts, and from the size of floats he used, part of his success was that he could present a bait well beyond other anglers around him, certainly well out of range of anglers on a stick float, so at times he had that part of the river to himself.

John Rolfe in action with a big Trent waggler (alias Swinger) on his line.

I once drew next to Johnny on a lake - the rowing course at Holme Pierrepont - in an evening match. He won it with 18-1 but it was a close battle and afterwards he was most generous with his advice. It gave him five wins from six matches in that particular series but he was quite laid-back about it. I came third with 17-2, also behind Stef Josko on 17-14 but a whisker ahead of Wayne Swinscoe on 17-1. John said I'd fed too often and fished too far out, possibly 15m to his 12m. We were on a lot of roach and by feeding twice per cast I'd got the fish darting about too excitedly. I made more strikes than John but he had more hits by feeding a good pouchful of bait then taking at least four fish off it before re-feeding. Lesson learnt from a top bloke.

4. Ivan Marks – First and foremost Ivan put on the best show I have ever seen from an angler anywhere in the 1973 Witham National at Langrick, when I stood with 200 others behind him on the flood bank, straining my neck to watch his every movement. He was both angler and entertainer, playing to the crowd throughout, but every ball of groundbait he threw landed within a foot of his float and he plundered 14lb of skimmers from a swim where most mortals would have struggled for double figures. That put him second in his 80-peg section, only beaten by a 40lb bream catch from the National Champion as I recall. A Nottingham angler of some repute was drawn not too far away from Ivan and he returned a modest 5lb-odd.

Here's three more key lessons that Ivan taught me about lines and floats, partly drawn from his Angling times columns (source, all bar the last reference: 'Ivan Marks – the People's Champion'):
I. Line stretch: *'Flying in the face of modern pre-stretched lines, Ivan always wanted elasticity, saying: 'Stretch is one of monofil's most important features. It is your defence against shock impact; the line stretches instead of breaks. Manufacturers don't apparently look at it quite like that. Some are trying to sell us pre-stretched line with the elasticity removed. I can't see they are doing us any sort of service.'*

II. Using fine line only below the float: *'We favour a heavy 3lb reel line (.14mm) that sinks quickly but usually a 5' hook-length of 1lb 8oz (.10mm) to get the bait fall we favour.' Dated 1972, this was my cue to try finer line from the float down, terminating the reel line just below the float. This use of what I called the 'link' – fine line running down from just below the float to join to an 8" hook length, puts less pressure on the hook-hold with every fish hooked. When fishing 6' deep for example, the stretch is twice that of a yard-long hook-length, and this pays dividends when hooking a fish by only a sliver of skin which often happens with roach and skimmers. Problems mount on any strike when a fish is running outwards creating an opposing force to the rod's pull to the rear, so more cushion in the line the better.'*

The ultimate 'thinking angler'.

III. The float: *'A peacock quill float between 10" and 12" long with a small cork body is our major weapon.' (Referring to the Leicester anglers' dominance in Fenland. I probably read this in 1972 when it was first published and the thought stuck.) Regarding sight bobs and thin inserts: 'Ivan figured that a waggler with a cocktail stick insert and just ½" of peacock quill at the tip would show lift bites really well when the chub held up the small shot down the line, yet resist pulling under once it had settled.'* (Written by Ivan's successful apprentice, Phil Coles, about the float he used in 1977 in the Ladbrokes Super League at Evesham, Warks Avon. The float worked pretty well; Ivan won the match with 22-15-8 leaving Phil second in the quality field on 22-5-0, but Phil came top individual in the league overall. Source: 'Ivan Marks and the Likely Lads' book by Mark Wintle, 2015.)

5. Tony Scott – I watched and admired Tony Scott's style when I was still a relative newcomer to matches in the early 70s. His big method was groundbait and caster and he always looked neat and smart, smoothly efficient. His rod and basket (yes, it was that far back!) were painted matt black and for a few seasons this was the fashion. Twice on the Trent I saw him casting a waggler well out

Tony Scott (2nd from the left) with the successful Cofton Hackett squad from Birmingham.

and feeding groundbait accurately to it. When he won the Trent Championship in 1972 with roach he got through four pints of caster in 10lb of brown groundbait and molehill soil to add weight. If ever any team manager was after star quality he hardly needed to look further when Tony was at his peak. He won seven full England caps. Over the few hours I watched 'Scotty' he taught me most to be single-minded. When he threw that ball of groundbait out and deftly put his float among it, he didn't appear to waste a second looking around at what others were doing. He was fully committed to his own swim.

6. Bill Francis – I learnt plenty from London angler Bill in one phone call as part of my book research. Few anglers surely can have slaughtered Ivan Marks off the next peg on a float with over 35lb to spare, but Bill achieved this (44lb – 7lb) with waggler-caught crucian carp at Whitley Park, Surrey! But when Bill, now 67, told me how he shotted his float the result made sense. Come in Bill: *"I'd caught these crucians before after finding out that any amount of float showing above the water meant I missed nearly every bite. But once I shotted the waggler down so the tip was in the surface film, obviously casting fairly short to be able to see it, I hit almost all of them. I'd won a match with just under 80lb and drew next to Ivan the next time out. A bush separated us and I managed to land 30 fish, quietly picking them out of the water and avoiding use of the landing net. Ivan could not have heard much by his reaction at the scales: his chin almost hit the floor!"* Bill's low float position tallies with my long-held belief that the less waggler the fish have to pull under the better, while ensuring that the float is still visible.

Bill Francis and some quality bream.

Billy Hughes and a fine 'slab'.

7. Billy Hughes – Billy, also now in his sixties, was respected as one of the London area's top waggler men for many years. He confirmed to me that an unshakeable confidence in one's method – in his case the waggler - can always make good things happen. From long wagglers used to catch the undertow on a lake, to pheasant and crow quills spliced together for a canal waggler, to making his own centre-pin reels, this man was a force to be reckoned with. Billy travelled with Bob Nudd for over a decade and they shared winnings which tells its own story (Billy's proudest team fishing moment was described in chapter 3).

8. John Toulson – I chatted to the affable John, a Nottingham butcher, on a Trent match at Winthorpe. He demonstrated how a medium size balsa float simply shotted with three AAAs down the line was a great method wherever a river flow was strong to powerful. Up to that day I'd never seen a float with a shot heavier than a BB down. He fished positively this way to win Trent matches, later high framing for Birmingham (3rd and 4th) in consecutive Nationals on the Severn and Bristol Avon, the latter on a sliding waggler after a lesson given by team-mate, Kevin Ashurst.

Johnny Toulson won an England v France friendly on the waggler with groundbait and caster feed. Here he is using the basket top as a bait waiter on an uncomfy-looking Trent peg.

9. Dick Ward – Apart from having a fine Trent match record, Dick, from Stockport, was the man of the 'long drop' in one particular Boston match he won on the Witham. The match report told how on waggler and caster from the second hour onwards (he used a stick float to start) he kept pushing his tell-tale dust shot further and further away from the hook to keep the bites coming, until it was a full five feet away! He won the 400 peg match with 7lb 2oz leaving a trail of big names behind - Edgar Purnell, Jim Todd and John Dean among them, and with only 2lb of fish separating the top 10. This long drop was exceptional, rarely do anglers leave more than a yard of line between the bottom shot and the hook,

Dick Ward flanked by Alan Mayer (left) and Ken Booth, of the successful four-man Stockport team 'The Method'. Fourth man was Bobby Watson.

but to me it's a better option than shotting too close. Up next though, is an angler who totally contradicts the theory, proving there are no set rules with shotting.

10. Bill Watchorn - My way of placing shot well away from the hook was not always right. I won one Dunham, Trent match by putting the shots very close to the hook – a string of 'dusts' only inches away, similar to how Kirkstead's Bill Watchorn did it on the Witham. He shotted his waggler in a reverse taper starting 8" from the hook. From there a typical pattern had narrower gaps than even a stick float 'shirt button' shotting pattern, but it obviously worked well for Bill when the fish wanted a bait stiller than the one I was offering them. Placing a no. 10 as tell-tale, he'd have another no. 10 and four no. 8s in the bottom 18" of line, plus four more no. 8s spaced out above that for a total of ten shots down the line. The gaps between the bottom six shots were tight but gradually got wider moving up the line, as follows: 1" 1.5" 2" 2.5" 3.5", with the top four shots set wider apart at 6" to 10". I'd not like to get in a tangle with such a pattern, but one man's meat and all that.

Lincoln's 'Lead down' Les Smith also made a habit of fishing a stabilising chunk of lead on winter Witham matches. He had a good run of success with a 1g olivette placed two-thirds down the line below his waggler and nothing else. This was heavy shotting for Witham roach to my mind but it proved there is always another way of doing things.

11. Geoff Newby – My old pairs partner and Rotherham Raider was one of Yorkshire's finest match anglers before he emigrated to Australia. I'd have put him in any team of mine and together we won the 1983 Sheffield Amalgamated Pairs on the Witham. Geoff once walked at least 10 pegs to watch me on a mean Witham match, stayed for a few minutes, then returned to his peg only to start catching better and beat me for the section. What cheek! The lesson here is, if you are not catching then do something about it. I'd never advise sky-lining others but, providing you keep a low profile, studying good anglers' methods is the best way to learn. At one time a young Ivan Marks was renowned for 'getting on his bike' (walking the bank when he could not catch) and look where it got him. Geoff also used only three no. 6 shot to lock his wagglers in position and made the rest of the weight up with lead wire wound around the float's base, which for the 70s was quite an advanced idea.

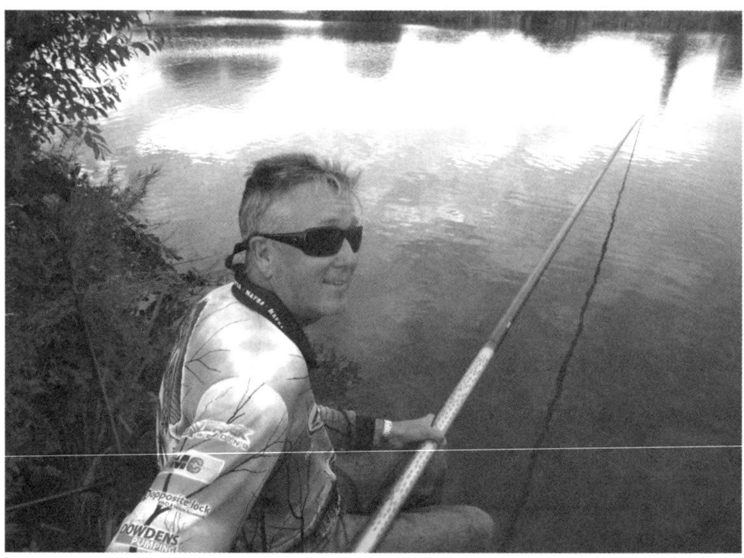

Geoff Newby on the pole (top); and Bernard Bryan (below right) together with his protege Roger Pryor and a massive net of roach (pic courtesy of Jim Tyree).

12. Ian McNeil – This Oundle team angler took some terrific waggler roach catches from the Welland in a brief period in the 80s/90s. He was piling lots of maggots in – up to four pints, and his winning catches often topped the 20lb mark which was exceptional. I knew Ian fished light down the line and asked him (at Ivan Marks' funeral of all places, but to talk fishing is what Ivan would have wanted) just how light. He surprised me when he said: 'a 10 and a 12'. Now that's extremely light but, knowing what I know now, I think there are times in warm weather when most of us fish far too heavy shotting down

the line. Just think of a pellet waggler; carp aren't the only fish that will feed shallow and Ian obviously caught his Welland roach on the drop.

13. Bernard Bryan – the Sheffield 'roach professor' taught me new things about tackle presentation which totally changed my outlook. Having experimented for years on local lakes, he perfected several methods for catching roach, and like a good wine, he improved with age until he could win local matches consistently in his fifties. Bernard's most famous legacy was the 'puller' method, which is in essence a trolled stick float. The stick is made to slide by adding eyes at either end, and it lays semi-cocked in the water while being slowly pulled back to the rod tip by winding the reel or pulling line off the rod from just above the butt ring in trout fishing style. Once a fish mouths the bait, which is already in motion as the angler is retrieving line, it feels the hook, turns its head in classic bolt-rig style and hooks itself. For the method to work properly the line between rod tip and float must form a straight line. When a cross wind puts a curve in the line and spoils things, a small sliding waggler can be used as an alternative (see chapter 6 - floats for special jobs)

14. Ken Giles – Birmingham and Shakespeare Professionals skipper, Ken taught me and thousands of others that barbless hooks could not only hold fish well but they were more efficient than barbed ones. He brought some Mustad 90340 hooks back from France in the 1960s, caught fish with them and then told his friends about their advantages. But anglers were not swayed that easily and it took a few years for the barbless hook to gain wide acceptance. It was not until 1979 that Ivan Marks advised anglers in his weekly Angling Times column to: 'Go barbless, you won't regret it', citing the example of Ken winning the Embassy final on Denmark's

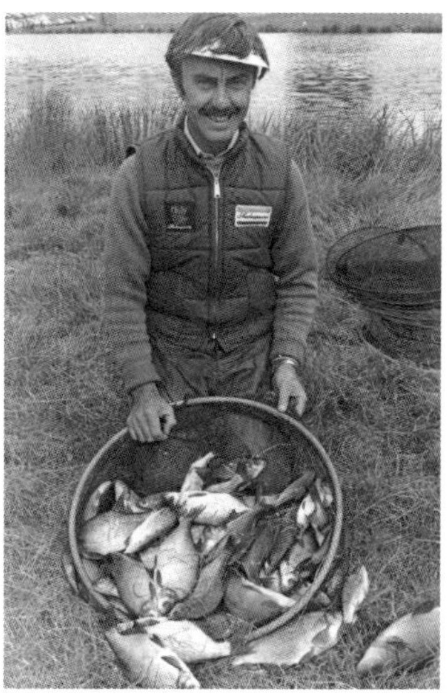

Ken Giles and a winning catch from Coombe Abbey lake, Coventry.

fast River Guden with 110lb, half made up of bream, half of roach, and all caught on a barbless size 18. But even Ivan was slow to change, on his own admission. How was it possible for anglers to be so reluctant to switch to the hook so universally used today?

15. Terry Fidler, Trev Cutts, John Yeardley and Terry Dorman. Let's call these four the jokers in the pack. The first three are from Sheffield and the other from Nottingham. They each taught me, often with a one-liner, that we must never forget that fishing is supposed to be FUN. These characters could entertain a crowd to the point where they'd be splitting their sides with laughter. Any fishing meeting would need a strong chairman to keep order with one of these lads in full flow.

Note: Over nearly half a century many anglers have been good enough to share their secrets with me, but the ones included here, along with my contributors in Part 2, have obviously stood out and made me ask searching questions. Hopefully some of their ideas can help you, the reader, similarly.

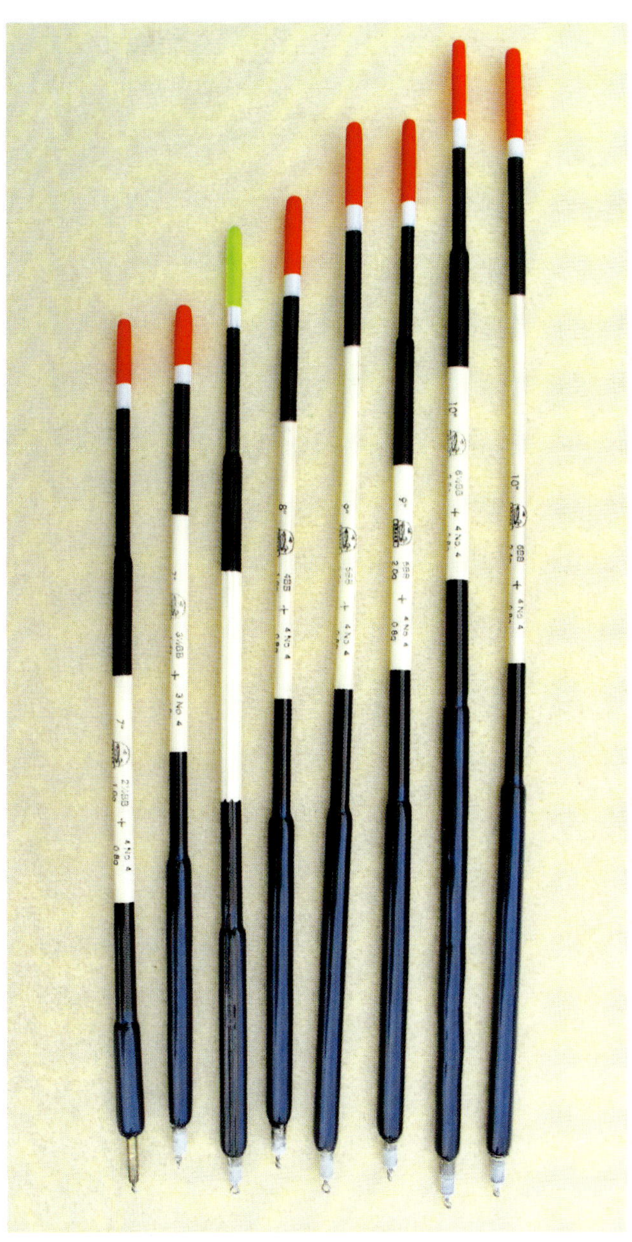

Drake 'blue and whites' – beautifully streamlined inserted wagglers, part-loaded and accurately marked with the shot capacity in the white section.

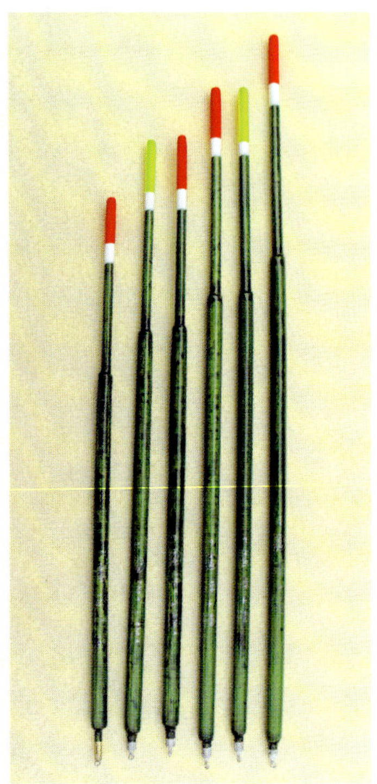

Drake inserted wagglers and painted tips – for river or lake when the light is favourable.

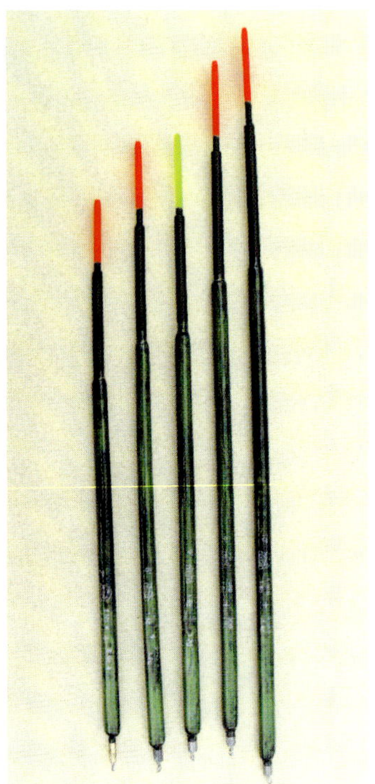

Drake two-stepped wagglers with hi-viz plastic tips. They light up with the sun on them and also show up well in dim light.

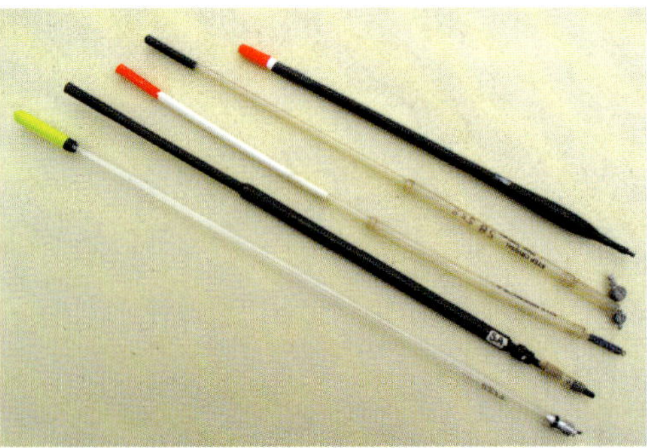

Draggers. Fatter-tipped floats the author would use for dragging line and shots on the bottom in faster river swims. They include peacock with the thicker end of the insert at the tip, Drennan crystal, and a combination of the two.

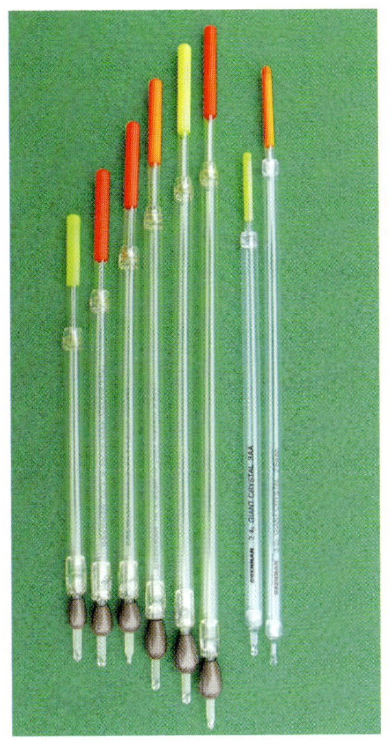

Drennan Crystals inserted and loaded (modern shorter version) plus two unloaded. Some makes of crystal have walls that are a shade heavy, but these are just right – superb all-round quality.

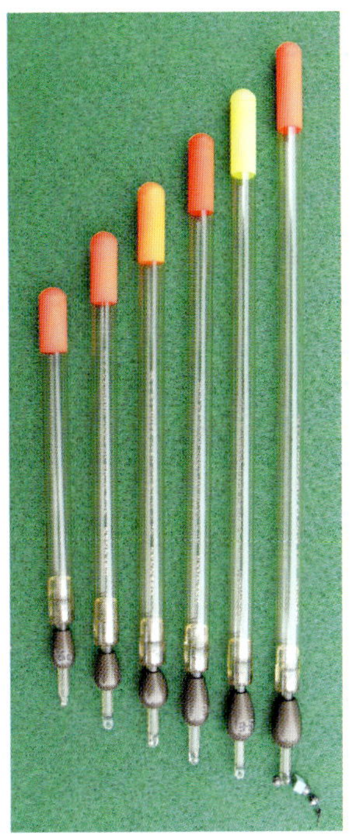

Drennan Crystals straight and loaded.

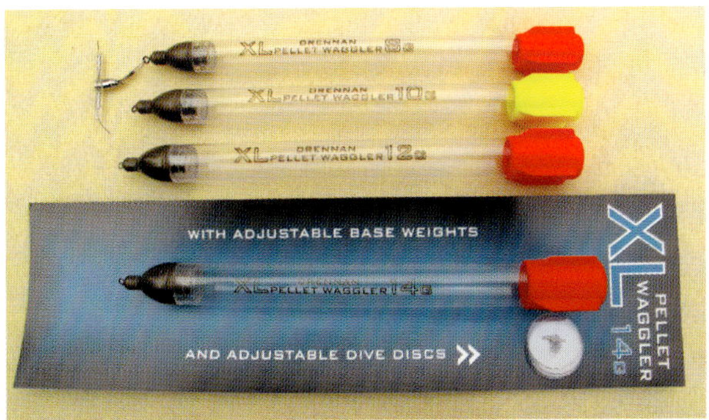

Drennan Pellet Wagglers 8g to 14g for long casts to shallow carp typically on commercials.

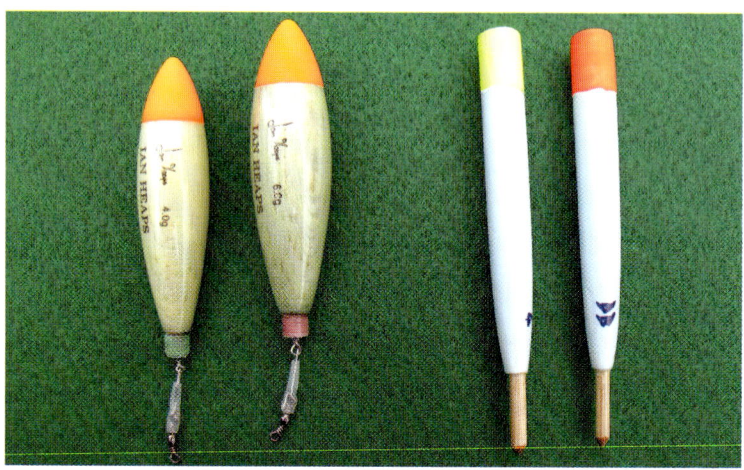

Ian Heaps PWs 4g and 6g. Made by Drake, this is the former World Champion's design for a float that does not dive when cast. A diving Pellet Waggler defeats the object as it can scare fish in the surface layers. This balsa float contains a metal ball within a channel in the float's interior and, as the ball sits in the tip end of the float when casting, it flies out tip end first. After hitting the water the ball runs to the bottom of the float and cocks it upright. Clever! Also pictured are two 4-gram polystyrene floats made by Dave Brittain. Also short for their capacity, they are strengthened by the central 3mm cane that runs the entire length of the float.

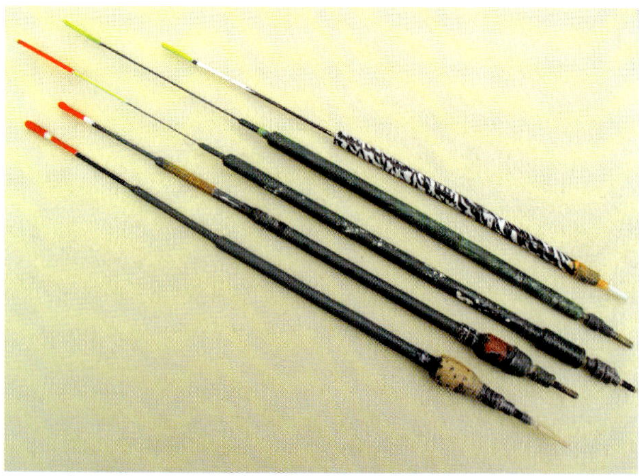

The author's treasured Witham summer float (left) and a spare, alongside three lake wagglers.

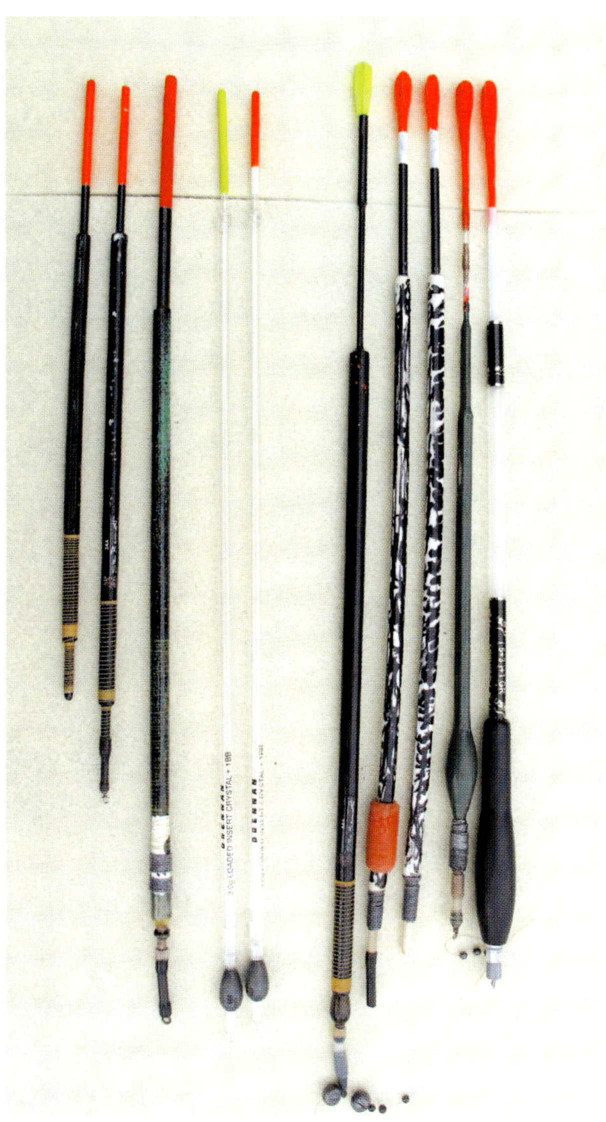

(L to R) Stan Bennett insert wagglers (with trademark yellow whipping at the base), A Johnny McCarthy camo-finished waggler the author occasionally used on the Witham in adverse conditions, original long Drennan Crystals (loaded) of the type used by Roger Wakenshaw, and a selection of wagglers with fluted tips cut down from Cralusso fluted tips.

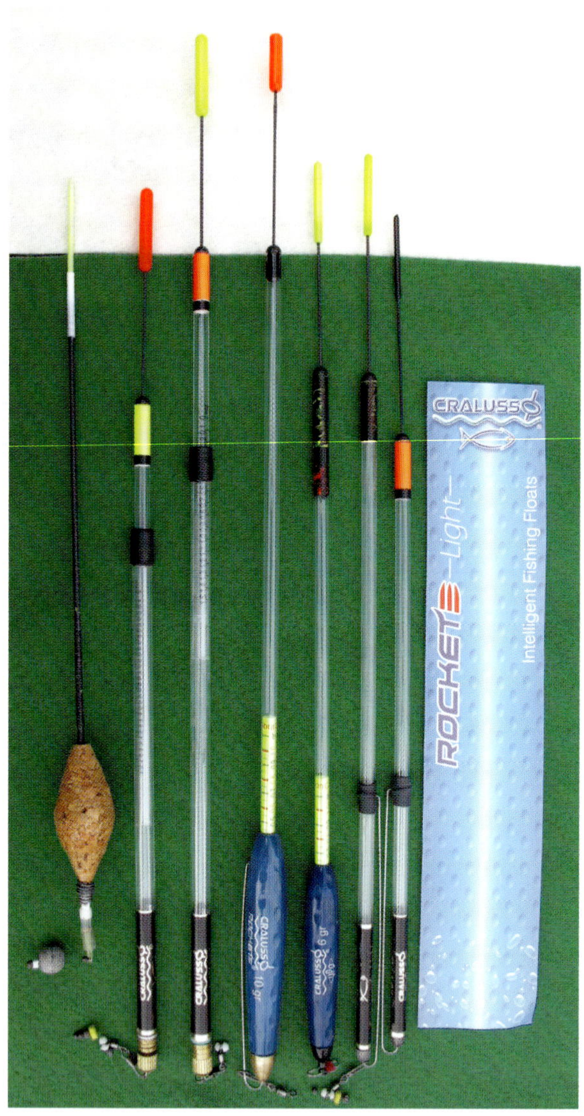

A homemade 6g slider made from a hollow carbon stem and a wine cork body, left, together with a selection of Cralusso wagglers. Note the three 'Rockets' (right) which have a unique wire boom that the float adaptor clips onto, claimed to make the float more aerodynamic with 20% extra casting distance over a normal base connection.

Rods old and new (from bottom up): 1/ Middy Carbon Live 3g (four-piece) pellet waggler rod. It can be fished at 11′ 7″ or with the short butt extension added at 12′7″. In the longer length it puts the butt ring well away from the reel and this aids casting distance. A soft-actioned rod but with inbuilt power. 2/ My trusty old Mitchell Excellence multi-quiver 10′ bomb rod, with quiver-tip replaced by a spring-tip. 3/ My newest rod, the Fox Waggler Lite 12′ – has to be the softest rod I've ever owned and a delight to fish with. 4/ My well-used Shakespeare Excelsior Match 13′. Possibly the red trim first caught my attention in the tackle shop and, bought second-hand from the dealer for £70 after it was returned by a previous owner, it has paid me back many times over with good catches. Note the thicker diameter of the tip close to the tip ring compared to the Fox tip (1mm approx.), but the rod still has a forgiving action in the important middle and tip sections.

Reels old and new: three original Abu 507s for general float-fishing and bomb work. The tape around the spool housing is optional, an old idea for stopping dirt or bait getting into the reel. The smarter looking reel is a modern Daiwa 2508 Tournament Airity used for pellet waggler or feeder.

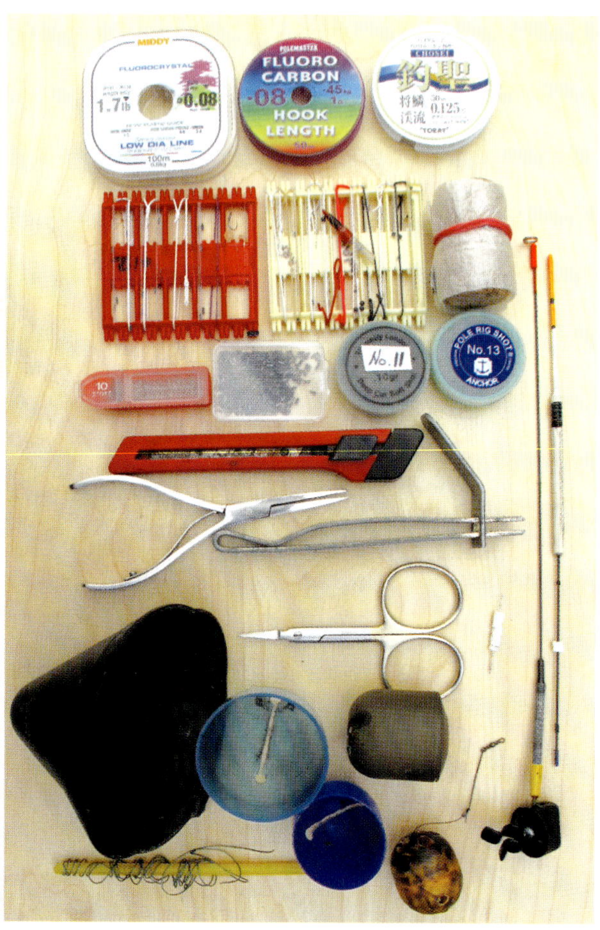

A selection of accessories (top to bottom and l. to r.): 1. Fine lines including a Toray 0.059mm brought back from Japan by the missus. This is a canal grade line reserved for the hardest of days. 2. Plastic winders for storing tackles neatly, and an emergency cork winder. 3. Various lead weights: Preston Stotz which are ideal for use with thicker lines, styls for finer presentation, and micro shot. 4. Metalware - Sharp fly-tying scissors, fine-nosed pliers, styl pincers and modelling knife. 5. Feeding cups large and small, bought and home-made. 6. Disgorger on a string (35lb braid). 7. A slow-sinking bubble feeder for lake fishing. (Right of pic): 8. tiny plastazote foam pieces on a needle. 9. Side-winder bite indicator with a twist - an added spring to improve shy bites. 10. Pole float with two foam pieces added to stem to adjust shotting.

PART 2
Guest Stars

Chapter 9
John Dean - In a Class of his own

In Part 2 we can study the different approaches used on the waggler by guest anglers. Some are lifelong friends, others I got to know only recently, like Jimmy Randell who I first met three years ago in Norfolk, but who sadly passed away not long ago. Most of the team hail from Yorkshire, or the North of England down to the Midlands, and I make no apology for this. It is where most of my fishing has been done and is a hotbed of angling, though our birthplace is irrelevant in regard to our achievements. I'm proud that such brilliant anglers agreed to participate in the project and tell their stories with typical enthusiasm for the benefit of future float anglers. We start with the man widely considered to be the greatest Trentman of all time – John Dean.

In a class of his own

For over a decade on the River Trent – c. 1974-84, it is fair to say that John Dean, 69, from Selston, near Nottingham, was in a class of his own. There was an intensity of purpose about him that I have rarely known in another angler. On top form he seemed able to make the frame (money list) from average pegs and win from anything like a flier.

In his short and distinguished match career he developed an aura, where some rivals when drawn nearby must have trembled and lost confidence before the match even started. At his best he was simply a winning machine.

Acting as professionally as it is possible to become in a largely amateur sport, John always prepared fully for a match and religiously practiced the venue ahead of a weekend contest. With hard work added to natural ability – he claimed to be largely self-taught - he also remained cool and modest about his achievements.

Away from the Trent he could be just as formidable, managing to win titles on many other venues. Of all his rivals Dave Thomas probably got the closest to matching his Trent record, and they both fished for England in 1981 on the Warwickshire Avon at Luddington when Dave took individual gold. But I think even Dave looked up to the master.

Inspired by angling friend Malcolm Levy, of Blidworth, with whom he fished regularly for five years from 1966 to the early 70s, John was also a member of Ripley AC's four-man team that enjoyed early successes on the Witham (alongside Jeff Stokes, Al Birks and Terry Harrod). Framing in Witham matches was one thing, however, winning them was surprisingly elusive for John at this time. It proved a jinx water but it probably developed his tenacity. He did everything bar win on the Kirkstead match length, despite being one of the river's most consistent anglers in 1974, but with hindsight he was still only tuning up for the concert that was to follow.

John then started winning opens on the Trent and never looked back. He progressed to join the mighty Trentmen side in 1978. A shy and private man, he soon established himself and won the respect of the group.

In 1975 John served notice of what was to follow. In August he qualified for the Woodbine Final in Denmark – the biggest sponsored match on the calendar later to become the Embassy Challenge. Come October he would finish fourth with 80lb 7 1/4oz in that 80-peg final on the River Guden behind Ken Giles' winning 110lb 5oz, so came closer to nailing a major prize. But in between he took fourth in the Division 2 National on the Trent with 10lb 1 1/2oz also winning his section in the Holme Marsh Weir Field. Winner Alan Webber had 16lb 2 1/2oz but it was a tight race for second with Goole team men Barry Rudge and John Allerton (on 11-10-8 and 11-5-0) edging him out of the medals.

From any good Trent peg John then started threatening to win, taking lots of runner-up places for a time, from Burton Joyce or anywhere else on the middle or tidal Trent. He was tagged the 'Selston wizard', and at the start of the 1980 season such was his success that others would have been forgiven for throwing in the towel before the season was a month old.

John started by winning the first match of the season (a Wednesday match) at Burton Joyce with 41lb 6oz on stick float and maggot, a personal best weight of Trent roach that few others have surpassed. He won again with 31lb 13oz on Saturday's Open, then produced his third big weight in five days - 22lb 1oz to take second. Keeping the momentum he added another second spot with 15lb 8oz and a third win with 15lb 7oz all within the first six weeks.

All bar one of these wins came on the stick float (which this book is not really about) yet John thought he was better on the waggler! A year or two earlier he'd joined the float-making business, putting his name to both stick floats and wagglers made commercially by Nottingham tackle dealer and float-maker Gerry Woodcock, and the venture was lucrative with sales booming. He obviously promoted his own floats nicely by winning so often with them.

As stunning as the above weights were, John managed to top them when he drew peg 342B near Stoke Weir in 1984. He fed nine pints of maggots plus three more of hemp (he rarely fed hemp but on this day the fish were ravenous) to put 44lb 2oz of chub on the scales. He fished a 6BB balsa float in the turbulent swim, setting a new weight record weight for the Saturday Opens at the time.

On lakes too, he seemed to revel in the challenge no matter how classy the opposition. The 1980 Sundridge 'Champion of Europe' match on the rowing course at Holme Pierrepont, Nottingham, was contested by the best teams from England and France, including many full England internationals. Fishing for the North of England team, John put 35lb 12 1/2oz on the scales to both put his team on course for victory and earn himself a great individual win on the waggler. The team actually tied with France on 18 section points but won it on weight countback 92lb 12 ½oz to 71lb 9 1/2oz.

The pinnacle of John's career was his England cap for the home World Championships in September 1981 at Luddington on the Warks Avon where he showed he could also scratch for a low team weight. Dave Thomas won both days of the event on the flooded river, becoming World Champion in the individual event on day two. Even though France won the team event on day one, John's 2lb 1 1/4oz section third was the joint second best performance for England, equal to Kevin Ashurst's placing.

The shape of things to come. John's 80lb 7 1/4oz fourth place net in the 1975 Woodbine final on Denmark's R. Guden. A month earlier he just missed a medal with fourth in the Div. 2 Trent National with 10lb 1 1/2oz.

But only a month before this on 15th August in a friendly international against Germany at Edgbaston Reservoir, Birmingham, John led England to victory with a stunning 26lb 4oz of waggler-caught roach. This was a four-hour afternoon match and his weight beat the old five-hour record of 25lb of bream. He may have surprised a few locals at the time but no member of the Trentman team would have batted an eyelid – he'd been doing similar for years back home.

"My peg was so deep I never actually managed to plumb it with the 13' rod. But setting up a small waggler 5' deep with an AAA and a BB locking and a no. 6 and an 8 bunched a yard from the hook, I got sailaway bites and caught roach to 12oz on the drop. We fished from 2pm to 6pm and I attacked it with 3 1/2pints of bronze maggots and the fish responded. Surprisingly we had no team discussion or plan and everyone else fished for bream," said John.

John had learnt the value of an almost identical rig to this on the Trent. He found that placing three no. 8s together as a bulk 30" from the hook, with no droppers below, was a great way of catching the better quality roach on the drop. It won him several matches in 1980 and beyond (see page 340).

He won one match with 20lb 3oz from the Mangold Field, Shelford, and another with 26lb 4oz from peg 155, on Burton Joyce Rack. He also caught 19lb fishing 5' deep in a 14' deep peg at Stone Bridge, Nelson Field (not a great draw). All these were roach catches on the shotting pattern mentioned. At the other end of the scale, using the same rig, again at Shelford, with a 10" reversed taper waggler (thick end at the tip), he dragged on 10' deep in 6' of water and won a match with 20lb 15oz of chub.

Never shy of experimenting, he would alter his depth and shuffle shots around until he got the exact presentation he thought the fish wanted, but was always ready to make further quick changes to suit the fishes' mood. In an early interview with John he had struggled at first to name me a standard shotting pattern for the waggler because those shots never stayed put on the line long enough.

John was outstanding in the Angler's Mail Kamasan Matchman of the Year competition. He announced his intentions with a fourth in the competition's inaugural year in 1977/78 when Dave Thomas won the title. He claimed runner-up spot in 78/79 (behind Billy

Makin), then won it in seasons 1979/80 and 1980/81 with 125 and 87 points respectively.* When he won it the second time he'd started as the 2-1 bookies' favourite – ridiculously short odds for a competition where every angler in the country is eligible. (*In this competition points were awarded 3-2-1 for the top three in all matches with entries of 60 or over.)

John's midweek practice sessions helped him formulate a feeding pattern for the roach or chub, giving him a head start for the weekend's matches if the river conditions did not change too much. John was single and his job allowed him a day off to fish midweek.

Surprising as it may seem now with the modern multi-rod and pole set-ups, he was one of the first anglers in the 70s to set up three rods to fish any peg he drew, and on a good river they'd all be float rods – carrying two wagglers and a stick or the other way round. If two stick rods were assembled one might incorporate a centre-pin reel, bringing a new slant on an old reel on days when the fish wanted the bait slowed down almost to a standstill. But whatever float method was called for he usually had an edge with it.

He was also fussy about selecting the right colour shade of maggot to suit the fish on the day, and noted how this changed from match to match. He'd take some week-old maggots of a darker colour than the fresh ones, and would experiment between the two. He was also one of the first to carry a thermometer and religiously took the water temperature before he started a match as a guide to his feed rate later.

He was always ready to customise tackle to improve it too. He used the Abu 507 reel but did not like the spool (its main fault) so he made some of his own! Other anglers I know have doctored Abu spools, but John also changed the black central bale button to one of his own design. And at a time when hooks were not quite up to today's top quality, having bigger barbs and spades, he'd cut the spades off to leave a tiny bump (visions of Benny Ashurst) which he smoothed off with a file. Then he would tie and varnish the knot to that, as a way of reducing the line spin which could result in a tangle, especially when the river was flowing fast and a double maggot was required. His one-time travelling partner Colin Perry was most impressed with the time and commitment John put into the hook department alone.

Not long after Dave Thomas started his bronze maggot revolution on the Trent, John's promising form on the Witham made people start to sit up and take notice, including Dave himself who admitted: *"He was so good, I hoped he didn't start fishing Trent matches or we'd all have a job on to beat him!"* And so it proved, while Dave kept up his winning ways, his prophecy came true.

Then, while still at his peak, John's focus suddenly changed when he decided to enter the fishing tackle business, partnered by Mansfield friend and match colleague, Colin Perry. It meant he could no longer fish the Burton Joyce Saturday matches and this was half his weekend's agenda. But while some would not have missed his dynamic presence, the change had to be angling's loss. What records John could have gone on to set had he continued match fishing for another 10 years or more is anyone's guess, but they'd have been worthy.

The following interview comes from two discussions and fishing sessions we spent together, where I asked him to hark back to those great Trent matches and describe his waggler method. John also kindly gave me access to his diaries, press cuttings and notes:

JB: You once said you were self-taught, but who did you study, and did you have a mentor or hero in the Trentmen side?

JD: No one taught me really, but I always read a lot about the sport, and studied the greats like Ivan Marks, Kevin Ashurst, and Johnny Moult, and even older press cuttings from Jim Sharpe. The latter two were Nottingham legends, and they all impressed and inspired me. I also learnt from Johnny Rolfe and Ted Stokes, senior members of the Trentmen team when I joined them.

JB: Trentmen had some great anglers of course, and fishing as Nottingham Federation you won the 1980 Trent National with a superb record points score of 883*, averaging a top 10 place in each 80-peg section. You led the way with a section win, and John Moult in the twilight of his career was second. Some team! Were you close friends with any of the lads? (*In a National section of 80 anglers for example, points were awarded 80 for the winner down to 1 for the last, or zero for a dry net, with 12 anglers in a team. This meant Notts Fed had averaged over 70 points per man.).

JD: I travelled with Paul Cope so knew him best. He was a very tidy and precise angler, good at everything and certainly much underrated.

JB: So catching roach on the Trent was your speciality, can you remember an all-time best match, and/or a favourite swim?

JD: Possibly a Rotherham Open win at Dunham Bridge with 22lb. The wind was very strong and a facer making it hard to keep the float running through straight. I fished a big waggler – a thick quill of a foot long with reverse taper so the fatter end was at the tip - and cast it as far as I could catapult maggots which wasn't that far. Whenever it is windy longer floats seem to produce more bites. Denis White came second in the match. One swim that I always loved to draw, always 'ran to it' as we might say, was 151 peg on the Burton Joyce Rack. It had a nice depth and flow and was a bit shallower than those around it, and I won a few bob off it.

JB: You once fished me off the bank on the Witham John, yet though you often came so close, you never actually won a big Witham match. You also came out of retirement to guest for our Sheffield team in the Eastern Region Winter League in 1986 and I remember you finished third not that far from me when I got 6th overall. I'm astounded that you never won there. A jinx river, is that why you switched to the Trent?

JD: For the number of times I fished the Witham maybe I was a shade unlucky. I attacked the river with maggots and did well, including a few frame scores with punched bread. I can't explain why I came close so often but never got over the line.*

(*John's 'shade unlucky' is an understatement here. He finished in the top 10 nine times in the 1974/75 season, and six of those events was in the top four. In July 1975 he came second to a bream weight 2lb heavier, and in August added a third when he lost by 10oz!)

JB: But from there things really started to happen. You came fourth in the Trent National, fourth in the Woodbine Final and it worked like a booster rocket. In five years on the Trent 1976-80 you took control. Checking your results you won 37 Trent matches, plus 18 seconds. You won the Nene Championship in 1979 which together with 1980 looked like your stand-out years.

JD: I'll take your word for it without checking. They were great times.

JB: Like myself, you have always kept a diary, but you would also test the water temperature. Would you advise the young anglers of today to be so thorough?

JD: Absolutely, patterns repeat so the diary can come in handy, and you can never have enough current information about fish behaviour; naturally, when it's cold their metabolism slows down so they eat less.

JB: So let me take you back there John, to your three rod outfit on the river, what would your rigs look like?

JD: Three Bruce and Walker 'John Dean' rods, the stick float rods would have a spliced solid carbon tip while the waggler rod had a hollow (fly rod) tip, and the reel was a customized Abu 507 closed face. My pin reel might be on the second stick float rod, a Harlow with the check mechanism and handles removed. I bought this from Tom Watson's shop in Nottingham in the Sixties. I practiced the pin on trips with Malcolm Levy especially when there was extra water on the river, with the float over-shotted and held back. The idea was to inch it through and as we sometimes say 'put the bait in the fish's mouth'. The Harlow made this easy and offered perfect presentation.

JB: And what were your waggler floats and set-ups like?

JD: For an average 8'-9' deep swim I'd rig up two home-made 3AAA peacock wagglers - one with a 3" insert incorporated, and the other a bit longer and heavier of 10" long approx. and taking upwards of eight no. 4 shot down the line, spaced out shirt button-style to start with, for dragging a bait on the bottom. This was a straight peacock made in reverse so the thicker end was at the tip to make it more buoyant.

The second waggler with the insert of thinner quill was a bit shorter at around 8" long and for catching fish off the bottom. This would take only around three no. 8 shot down, bunched as described earlier. I'd likely start by fishing this second float 6' deep trying to catch on the drop and take it from there.

JB: How shallow might you set the float to catch fish on drop?

JD: Five feet minimum to retain that slow fall of the bait.

JB: What hook patterns and lines did you prefer?

JD: Mustad 90340 in sizes 18, 20 and 22, tied to 1.1lb or 1.7lb Bayer Perlon trace and a reel line of 2 1/4lb Racine Tortue (green) for the waggler and 1 2/3lb for the stick. These days I'm using Sensas Classic on the reel in 0.14mm or 0.16mm which is a bit like the old Racine in that it's not too heavy. You don't want a waggler line to sink too deep. Another hook I liked for when the fish got really shy was a bit of a secret weapon in the shape of an Au Lion D'or (gilt) in size 22, a barbed hook but with the barb flattened. This would often bring me a few extra bonus fish in the closing stages of matches.

JB: Did you ever back-shot the waggler?

JD: No, I never felt one necessary on a waggler but did use at least a couple with the stick float method to facilitate burying the reel line in a downstream wind.

JB: Did you ever use micro shot?

JD: No, the smallest shot would be an 8 on the Trent though I might use a no. 10 tell-tale on the Witham.

John and some of his old favourite river wagglers.

JB: How low to the surface did you shot down your wagglers as a rule?

JD: I didn't dot them down far, usually preferring an inch of float up top.

JB: Did you follow Ian Heaps' example, or Ivan Marks when it came to sliding floats - a sliding waggler?

JD: No, I never really needed a slider on the Trent, the one exception was a peg I drew in Dunham Dubs that was 20-foot deep which I tackled with a top and bottom sliding balsa float.

JB: Moving on to hookbaits – which maggot colour did you favour and were you a single or double maggot fan?

JD: It was always bronze (chrysiodine) maggots for most of us back then with a few reds mixed in. But occasionally I fished a yellow maggot as a change bait, and even yellows dyed bronze, and this did win me the odd match. This taught me that a subtle change of colour in the orange/yellow range could make a big difference and more than I thought previously. And I'd vary from a single maggot to a double, depending on how the bites were coming. If not getting bites then the way is to keep ringing the changes.

JB: There are big differences with all anglers' feed rates from sparingly to very heavy, and surely how we feed any swim decides our success, providing our method or technique is sound. How did you approach feeding an average Trent swim for an estimated frame catch of say 10lb?

JD: Well absolutely right, feeding is the key, the secret to catching fish consistently in any situation. But it was totally different between winter and summer. On the Trent in summer I'd normally take four to five pints of maggots and would expect to feed most of them. But on a cold winter river I might feed just half a pint with far fewer bites expected. You have to play it by ear and experience counts for a lot. Taking extra bait is not a bad idea. On one Welland match I was lucky in that I ran out of bait an hour from the end but was able to borrow some more on route to winning with 20lb.

JB: We know there were a few fish in every swim on the Trent at this time, some more than others of course. If you weren't catching

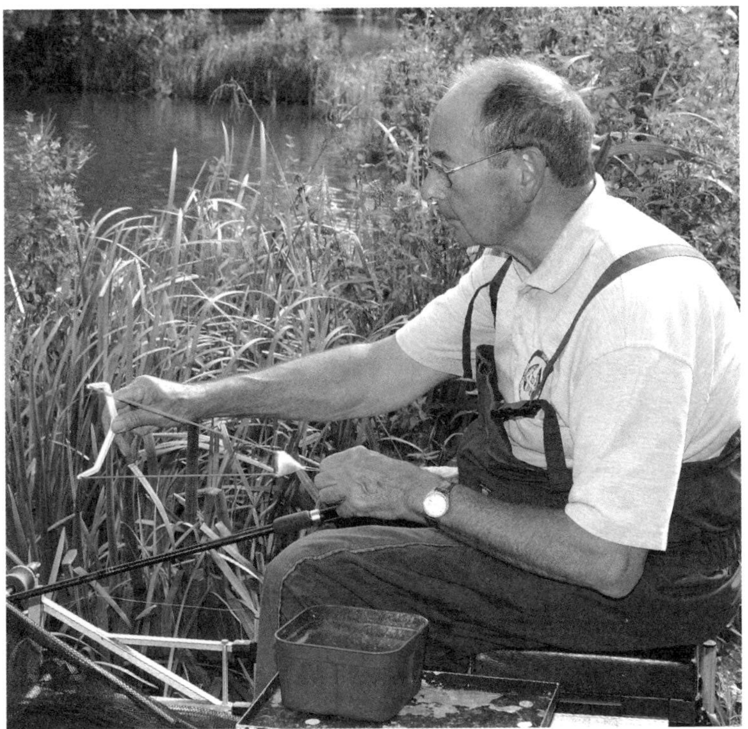

John fishes Barlow Farm, Derbyshire, in 2015.

well, was it down to a bad swim, or incorrect feeding or shotting, and how would you know?

JD: I think in the 80s the Trent (at Burton Joyce especially) held vast amounts of roach and they could be drawn to your peg with correct feeding. This might be a pint of maggots or it might be eight pints or even more depending on the day. This meant regular fishing at least three times a week to give an idea of what the fish wanted.

If you had another good angler nearby who knew what he was doing, you had to share the fish. The one that got the feeding right won.

I like to believe that if I wasn't catching there were few fish in the swim, but maybe there were fish there, I just couldn't catch them. Shotting could make a difference but feeding mattered more.

JB: Some anglers gained a reputation for 'giving em a gallon' of bait when the Trent was in its heyday, so 'blasting it' obviously worked on some days on a lot of fish. What is the most bait you have fed on the Trent?

JD: I once had a pile of bait left over after a Bristol Avon National and decided to feed heavily the next day at Burton Joyce (peg 204 on Stone Bridge). I fed 12 pints for 18lb of roach and it put me second or third in the match. I might have overdone it. Half a gallon of bait would serve me very well as a rule.

JB: Did you use other baits like hemp, caster and groundbait?

JD: I switched to caster occasionally in summer, but seemed to do better with maggot, and rarely bothered with hemp.

JB: You told me you always experimented in matches, in what ways?

JD: I was always moving the shot up and down and changing depth to see if it made a difference. I was never content even when catching well, so kept on trying things out, pushing the boundaries.

JB: How long would you give one shotting pattern a chance before trying another?

JD: Hard to say how long, it was more of a gut feeling when a change seemed appropriate.

JB: What was your greatest asset that helped you to all those match victories?

JD: I used to think about my fishing a lot. You could safely say it was an obsession. I'd also make and customize tackle to suit changing circumstances on the river. It might be a cliché but I lived, ate, and breathed it.

JB: How confident were you to frame off a good peg?

JD: Very confident.

JB: 100 per cent?

JD: Well it was very rare that I got next-pegged, though it did happen of course.

JB: What's your best fish?

JD: A salmon estimated at 25lb from the River Spey, number 3 beat at Castle Grant, Grantown-on-Spey.

JB: What kind of fishing do you do these days?

JD: I spend a lot of time after Trent barbel, and catch a few chub and bream in the process. I still enjoy pleasure fishing as much as ever.

JB: Finally John, why did you pack the game in so early while still at the top?

JD: One big reason was when taking on the tackle shop I suddenly had to work Saturdays and therefore could only fish a Sunday match at weekends. In those matches I'd nothing to draw on from the previous day and so it meant I was playing catch-up for half the match. My edge was gone as I was no more in tune with the river.

Top Tip

When trotting a waggler down to the next angler, just before the float reaches the bottom of the peg, say with a yard still to trot, put a big mend in the reel line to ease the float back slightly and briefly sink the float. This changes the bait presentation. Now release the line so the float pops back up again, and a bite often follows in the last second of the trot. I told my mate, Col Perry this, and it gave him enough extra fish in a match at Shelford to beat me.

The last word from travelling partner Col Perry:

In my opinion, a lot of John's success was down to his keen attention to detail. Many anglers will comment that their preparations are very thorough, but I will give you an example of how far John would go to be better than the rest. Please remember, this period of angling was at a time when tackle was not at the standard of today.

To give younger anglers an idea of how tackle has improved, when John started his climb to fame, most of the floats we used, ie, stick floats and wagglers, had to be made by hand, and the hooks we could buy were of average quality. Mustad was the famous brand but many of their hooks featured big barbs and big spade ends. The popular patterns were 90340 barbless and 90210 for caster fishing etc., and these hooks allow me to describe John's rigorous attention to detail. He spent an unbelievable amount of time on his hooks. Today there are several quality hook-tying machines available, like the Periott from France, but John made his own.

When I got to know John reasonably well, I called at his home once to find him tying hooks. He had made his own hook-tying machine with an arm so that all his hook lengths were the same length, but that was only the start. I was astonished to find that on every hook, he would cut the spade in half with a pair of wire cutters (approx. depending on the batch), he'd then stone off the sharp edges, turn the hook round and stone the hook point, and then either squash the barb or break it off to his choice. He'd then tie the hook on his machine and then dope the tying and hang it to dry while he repeated the process. He explained that he felt it important for presentation that the hook was the very best it could be, and make no mistake his hooks were the very best I had ever seen. The hooks we have today are superb, they have mini spades and barbs, so many of today's anglers would not appreciate these details, but this explains the lengths John would go to to be the best. (By the way, I tried to copy John's method of tying but found it far too messy for me. I would probably have arrived at the bank with just two hooks tied up.)

I have thought hard about the next reason why John was so good, and again it comes down to presentation and also to getting on to the best method early in the match. Again things were so different in the old days compared to today. Almost every angler was maggot or caster fishing with either float or feeder. When you arrived at your peg, it was either stick or waggler or a feeder for the bigger fish, either a block-end and maggot or groundbait feeder and caster. What I am saying is that in today's match scene the choice of method/bait can vary greatly - from pellet, corn, paste, and meat, 4mm pellet, 8mm pellet, fished either on pole, method feeder, waggler shallow, wag deep etc, etc. – whereas in the old days to some extent the decisions were so much simpler. We were all virtually doing the same thing, but the class angler did it so much better than the rest, and John was to my mind the VERY BEST.

We were almost all river anglers, and when it came to float fishing John was simply a genius. When you watched him fish it was simply effortless, he had a fantastic knack of fiddling about with his shotting pattern like we all do at times, but often this would increase his catch rate and then he'd leave me standing - scratching my head as to why he was getting three or four fish to my one. There are many matches where John stood head and shoulders above the competition around him. He had an uncanny instinct for presenting the bait just how the fish wanted it on the day. I'd like to highlight one particular match that I remember well.

We were on the famous road stretch at Burton Joyce fishing one of the superb winter matches run by Roy Toulson and Peter Palmer. As we all know, at this time the match was full of all the top Trent anglers from across England, and although I cannot remember the anglers drawn around John, one can be assured they would have been competent. John had drawn towards the bottom end of the road and there were a few inches on the river, not a flood or anything but enough to make it difficult. There was also a difficult downstream wind making fishing a stick float at any distance virtually impossible.

The river at this time was full of fish, and in particular those big-eyed hybrids as well as roach and a few chublets (to the uninitiated, baby chub up to 8" or so long). John fished a waggler at about three rod-lengths out, any further and the river was too fast. He spun his usual magic, weighing in 14lb-plus, consisting mostly of postage stamp hybrids with a sprinkling of roach. He had obviously caught a fish a throw as the fish were only small, and yet all the anglers in the area were only weighing in 3lb to 5lb. This was not just casting out a waggler and letting it go through - the river was pushing hard, it was more about holding back the waggler slightly to slow it down a fraction more than the river's speed. But by getting it right there were bites and fish available - perfect conditions for a master float angler to shine. In such conditions very few anglers could compete with John. I know this was so as I was about six pegs above John, and although I thought I had done well with my 6lb, when I saw John's catch I was just amazed, so much so that 30 years on it still sticks in my mind. A brilliant catch, only one of many that John made look so easy.

John, when pleasure fishing on the Ferry Field at Burton Joyce, once caught 120lb of roach. Yes I did say 120lb, weighed and witnessed by Ted Stokes and Pete Warren. Many times John and I fished on Shelford shallows when there were no matches on we fancied. I remember fishing for about three hours on one particular day and catching well. I probably had caught 25lb in this time and thought I would have a sandwich and walk up to John who was just round the bend upstream. As I walked up I was thinking how well I had done and feeling quite self-satisfied. I sat behind John chatting however, and after watching for about 15 minutes, he was obviously 'emptying' the river. Fishing three to four rods out, changing between stick and wag, he was catching chub and roach one after the other. I ended with about 40lb plus to John's 80lb plus. That is why despite his short match career everyone remembers him. He was totally outstanding. I have nothing but complete admiration for a fabulous angler - a genius and for me the BEST.

Chapter 10
Dave Thomas - The Revolutionary

Born in Leeds and introduced to angling by his elder brother, Jack, Dave Thomas spent his teen years fishing venues he could reach by bus, such as the Wharfe at Boston Spa and Tadcaster, where the dace - abundant, but never easy to catch - provided him with a good grounding to develop his skills with the float on running water.

From age 15, together with a few pals, he would enter local club matches, mostly on Yorkshire rivers, such as the Swale, Nidd, Derwent and Ouse, and later the Trent for which he developed a particular liking. He managed to get a lift to fish his first open aged 19, a 300-plus pegger at Dunham Bridge on the Trent. It was at the start of the caster revolution and the Lancashire anglers were cleaning up on the river. Everyone expected it to be another rout but the venue fished badly and Dave was amazed to win with 6lb 6 1/2oz on bronze maggot.

Lack of transport confined Dave to club matches for the next nine years, until in 1972 at age 28 he married Avis and bought a car. Brother Jack said he had left it too late to make his mark in match fishing. This only made Dave more determined to have a crack at the Trent Opens. His pals Stan Haigh and Stu Thompson joined him.

Around 12 months later, after some encouraging placings and section wins, he won another big Rotherham Open at Dunham Bridge with roach on caster, then three weeks later won the match he wanted to win above all others, the Burton Joyce Saturday Open. He considered it the hardest match in the country to win and it meant a lot to him. He did it on caster with a catch of 15lb but came away convinced that, contrary to all the advice he'd received, he would have had more on maggot. Three weeks later in the same match he was going nowhere on the caster and decided to switch to maggot; it paid off and he won again with 10lb of roach on a windy day. It was the start of several years of outstanding success during which he won numerous Trent Opens, 16 in his two best seasons including eight of the prestigious Burton Joyce Opens.

Apart from individual success, Dave's team honours included two Angling Times Finals with Barnsley and the Division 5 and Division 2 National Winners' Medals with Leeds Anglers World.

In the 1977/78 season he won the first ever Matchman of the Year, picking up points on the Trent, Wharfe, Tees, Soar and Welbeck Lakes, and recognition came in the same year when he was named as reserve for England at the World Championships in Austria. He also fished several friendly and home Internationals.

In 1981 he was selected for the World Championships on the Warwickshire Avon at Luddington. Dave shone in practice and three weeks prior to the event, the spotlight was on the England Team at the Evesham Bank Holiday Festival. Dave recorded a win and two seconds over the three days, beaten twice by the Bridge Peg which threw up some bigger chub. It was a feat which Ivan *Marks said would never be equalled: "Take that peg out and you've won all three"* he said, and history proved Ivan right.

Three weeks later in spite of the river carrying extra water, Dave made no mistake at Luddington, winning both team and individual matches outright to become World Champion. Sadly, some would say almost criminally, Dave never got the chance to defend his title as he was never capped again...

Waggler Fishing – by Dave Thomas

If I had to choose one style of angling or one type of float to fish with rod and line for the rest of my life, it would have to be the waggler. There are several reasons for this. First, its versatility: it catches fish on most waters, be it river, lake or canal, and it's the best float there is for beating the wind, of which we get plenty on this island of ours. Then there's the sheer pleasure of it. For me the ultimate experience in angling is catching roach, dace or chub, at say three to five rod lengths out on a river with a moderate flow. I am thinking specifically of the Trent when I say this, but would also include the Yorkshire rivers, the Warwickshire Avon, the Severn and the Witham when it flows.

That said, I am happy to catch fish with a waggler whether there is movement on the water or not.

I have often wondered why I enjoy it so much and I think it must be something to do with that silent strike, no disturbance to the surface of the water and the moment of instant and direct contact through the bottom of the float to the fish; it's just a great feeling. It may seem strange to hear a match angler talking like this but, although I was as clinical as anyone in a match situation, I never forgot to enjoy it and that is important.

Having experimented with and caught fish using various float materials over the years, including balsa and sarkandas reed - sarkandas was particular good when catching fish up in the water on the Witham - I arrived at the conclusion that there is nothing to touch peacock quill. It is buoyant, natural and its density is perfect. For maybe 80 per cent of the waggler fishing I have ever done I have used a straight rather than a bodied float and strung out shot rather than bulked shotting patterns.

I still make most of my own wagglers because it's enjoyable and easy, and you can make various sizes to suit the particular venues you are fishing. I nearly always make them with an insert which will vary in thickness depending on the venue - thinner inserts for still and slow moving waters and thicker ones to cope with faster flowing rivers.

Once you have decided on and cut the stem and insert to size, make a suitable hole with a bodkin then just push the insert into the stem, something like a centimetre depth is ample. Then all it needs is gluing, preferably with some fast drying epoxy resin so that you just have enough time to make sure the overall float is as straight as you can get it. All that remains is to glue a peg of some sort, be it cane or plastic for example, into the bottom for the waggler adaptor to push onto, and finally to paint the tip whatever colour you prefer.

I don't even bother to paint the rest of the float now, just the tip, and I have never had one leak, to take on water and ruin the shotting capacity. Some anglers like to make their floats look pretty but I am more interested in the job they do, how they perform, and to my mind the less you interfere with the natural qualities of your chosen material the better.

Many shop-bought floats have too many layers of paint on them for my liking which I think can make a difference to how they fish. That said though, if you don't have the time to do your own there is a better selection in the shops these days than ever before, and if you can't find the right ones in peacock, some of those crystal varieties are well worth a try. Balsa comes into its own with canal floats, and anglers of more senior years might fondly remember the Makin greys with the ultra slim stem which were perfect for light shotting and short casting into shallow waters.

I have often heard anglers say that it doesn't matter too much, within reason, what size of waggler you use so long as it is shotted right. Well, to some extent there might be a wider margin for error with the waggler whereby you will catch fish regardless, but the right float will catch more, and quite often when the fish are, let's say fussy, it can be a lot more.

To illustrate the point, when I first started fishing the Warwickshire Avon at Evesham, the accepted standard set up was a 2AAA peacock waggler with a few small shot down the line. Initially I followed suit but eventually just got the feeling it was slightly too heavy, particularly during summer when the fish were up in the water. So I changed to one that took 3BB locking instead, and this move made a big difference to my catches.

As a general guide, however, I would say you are always better off fishing a bit too heavy with a waggler than too light; err on that side and you will be a lot safer. Too light can result in no bites if the float is affected by the wind for example, whereas too heavy will still get you some. And anyway, you don't want to be struggling to cast to where you want to get, you need sufficient weight on to do it comfortably.

Shotting the waggler is simple enough with most of the weight going either side of the float, normally AAAs or BBs or a combination of both. You can use a bit of silicone under your locking shot to protect the line if you wish and, dependant on depth, leave enough scope on average to place maybe three or four number 8s and three or four 10s down the line. Just allow yourself enough to play with. The shot can be evenly spaced to start with and then adjusted as required throughout the day.

If you find the fish are coming up in the water, or prefer a slower fall of the bait, you can slide some of those 8s up under the float and experiment with the spacing of the other shots. It is so easy to sit back and think that making small changes won't make a difference, but it can and it does, so make the effort is my advice.

One thing that can make a massive difference is the distance of the bottom shot, the so-called tell-tale, from the hook. The closer you can get away with it, the earlier you will see the bite. However, if the fish are what I call 'shot shy', it may be necessary to place it 18 inches or more from the hook. A prime example was the Trent in the Seventies, when more often than not you had to fish with it at least 24" from the hook to get bites, something I doubt many anglers realised at the time.

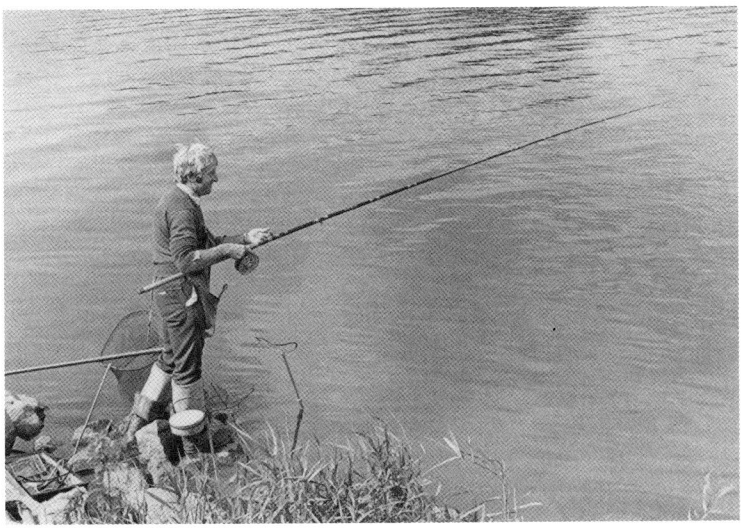

Dave relished tackling the Trent with a pin reel and stick float when there was extra water on.

The Trent in those days was under a lot of angling pressure and unless you got your presentation and feeding spot-on they wouldn't play ball, and the placement of that small shot had to be adjusted an inch at a time to get it right. In fact the placement of any shot in the last few feet of the rig is very important, as this is where fish are watching the bait fall through the water and taking a decision, in effect, as to whether it looks safe to eat or not.

Once again, adjustments may be required during the course of the session to stay in contact with the fish. If you stick with fairly evenly spaced shotting patterns you should not have a problem with tangles. As for weighted floats, they have their uses, for instance they might cast further and fly truer, but I am not a great lover of them. Though it may be a personal thing, I don't think they fish as well as a shotted one [Dave is referring here to loaded or self-cocking floats with weight built into the base].

I recall as a young angler that information and advice were pretty hard to come by. Most of the top anglers tended to be quite secretive which meant I, along with my fishing pals, without the benefit of any expert guidance, had to work things out between us. That said, I was more fortunate than a lot of other anglers thanks to my brother Jack who got me interested in angling and was able to give me a good grounding. Jack himself improved sufficiently in later years to win a Veterans National and is still going strong at 82.

Nowadays, things have changed dramatically and there is any amount of information available both on the Internet and in magazines, books and DVDs and I think that's how it should be. When it comes to rigs and shotting patterns and floats and so on, it's all there. The problem is that even armed with all the right info, good tackle and everything, if you are making one simple mistake in your application on the day you might struggle to catch fish or, if you do, it might only be a fraction of what it could have been. That's why I think it would be beneficial if I talk about some of the things I see anglers doing wrong, some of the mistakes that make the difference between an odd fish and bagging up. Success or lack of it might not depend on all the things that you are doing right, but just one basic mistake which could ruin the whole show.

The important thing with any style of float fishing on a river is that it has to be what I describe as 'going through right'. Therefore, the question you have to keep asking yourself, throughout the session is simply: 'does it look right and is it going through right?' and if not, 'why not and what can I do about it?'

The first thing to look at is the pace of the river and the relative pace the float is going through at; if it's going through faster than the river is moving then something is causing it to be pulled or dragged through too quickly and no self-respecting fish is likely to look at it. One of the main reasons for this as often as not is the wind. The line gets ahead of the float if it's a downstreamer, and this drags the float with it as well as pulling it off line, which is obviously unnatural and no good. The obvious remedy to try is sinking the reel line but the big mistake you can so easily make with this is in not making sure you have sunk all of it. If you leave the tiniest bit on the surface, the wind will very quickly push it into a bow, pull the float with it and ruin your presentation. The same applies on a still water I might add.

Another massive pitfall, that so many anglers I have watched don't realise is happening, is one that's apparently easy to be oblivious to. Quite simply, it relates to how close you place the rod tip to the water surface when trotting. The length of line left above the surface may only be a few inches long but even this small length can still be enough to ruin everything. In other words you may have done the right thing in ensuring that you have sunk all your line but, unless you keep your rod tip just under the surface, the effect of the wind on that little bit of exposed line will drag your float to some extent and possibly put an end to any chance of catching, and it will take effect very quickly. It surprises me how many anglers are not aware of it and never guess why their float is skating along all of a sudden.

I witnessed a prime example quite recently, watching an experienced angler fishing a lake. There was nothing wrong with his float, his shotting, or the way he was feeding. There was a slight breeze just skimming the surface (often the worst kind), but not enough to make a ripple, and he was sinking all his line; so far so good. After casting and sinking his line, he would put the rod on the rest and pick up his catapult and feed a few maggots. All fine, except for the fact that his rod tip was a good 12 to 18 inches above the water and the breeze latched onto that exposed line on the surface which in turn started to pull his float along in a very unnatural manner even before he had put his catty down. He had fish in front of him for potentially a bite a chuck but, although he did catch an odd one, it was nothing like what he should have caught. If only he had he positioned his rod rest so that his rod tip was two or three inches under the surface, thereby eliminating the problem, he could have had a field day.

Aerial views showing a bowed line and how to correct it: by Dave Thomas

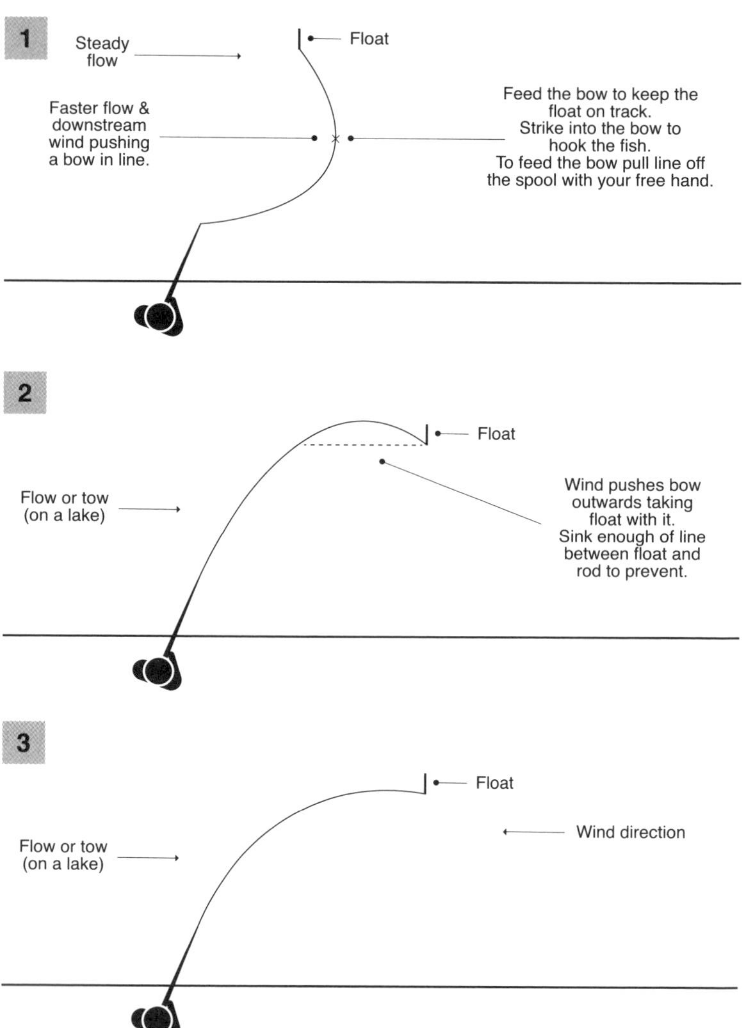
1
Steady flow
Float
Faster flow & downstream wind pushing a bow in line.
Feed the bow to keep the float on track.
Strike into the bow to hook the fish.
To feed the bow pull line off the spool with your free hand.
2
Float
Flow or tow (on a lake)
Wind pushes bow outwards taking float with it.
Sink enough of line between float and rod to prevent.
3
Float
Wind direction
Flow or tow (on a lake)

In this situation, instead of sinking the line, lay it on the surface and allow the wind to create an upstream bow, using this to slow the float's progress down or even stop it. This can be a deadly tactic on the right day.

There are situations where even sinking the line does not provide the answer. The obvious one is where you have faster water in front of you than the steadier water further across that you are trying to fish. Unless the wind is favourable and you can hold the line up off the faster water, the only way round it is to feed the bow in the line. What this means is that you simply feed enough line out to ensure that the float stays on track and is not interfered with for as long as possible, before the ever increasing bow eventually starts to pull it off line. I had this very problem on the first day of the World Championships on the Warwickshire Avon. The river was carrying extra water, it was pacey down the middle and I had a very inviting looking small area of steadier water at the far side, in front of some reeds. I attacked this by casting as close as possible to the reeds and feeding the bow until it got the better of me and dragged my float off line and I had to retrieve and cast again. I managed to keep it going through right for only a few seconds but it proved long enough for me to snare four or five precious chub to add to those I caught on the stick float.

Another example that springs to mind was on a Burton Joyce Open on the Trent. I was pegged in the Ferry Field, the wind was one of those you can get at times where sinking the reel line and plunging the rod tip underwater doesn't work. The wind was coming across, blowing diagonally towards me and downstream. I tried everything but I knew the float was still dragging slightly.

The only answer once again was to feed the bow, but I had to pay out so much line to make this happen that when a bite came I knew I would never connect with it by striking in the normal way. The only option was to strike into the bow. It's like a chain reaction and instead of trying to pick the line up with an overhead strike and going direct to the float, an impossibility with that amount of line out, I just struck to the side and into the bend or bow in the line, which in turn pulled the float and hooked the fish. It's a case of doing what you have to do to get the bites and then working out how to hit them. It worked like a dream on this particular day and I went on to win with 17lb of roach. Although they were decent fish - 8 to 10oz samples, when I hit one I could barely feel anything until I wound some of that slack in. And surprisingly, I hardly lost a fish. It was as if the bow cushioned the strike. It was clear that a lot of other anglers on the day had found the wind impossible to deal with judging by the gallery behind me. One angler asked me afterwards why I had struck at bites the way I did. I had to think for a second or two before explaining, as I had done it instinctively at the time.

One more I recall was in an open match at Welbeck Lake when a strong wind blew up and created a big tow on the lake. Feeding the bow got me one precious bite on the waggler and a good roach of 1lb, which helped win the match and gave me vital points towards winning the Matchman of the Year title. On this occasion I had so much line out I had to walk back about four yards and strike three times before I eventually made contact with the fish, honestly! It's an extreme example but as I said earlier, sometimes you must do what you have to to get bites before worrying about hitting them.

Another scenario where the bow can be used to great advantage is when there is an upstream wind blowing on a river, or on a still water where you often find the tow going in the opposite direction to the wind. In both cases instead of sinking all the line you can actually use the bow to slow the float down which can be deadly if that's how the fish want it on the day. This is always likely on a still water if there is a strong tow and the fish will not accept the bait running at that speed. At times it is possible to stop the float dead for several seconds, which can be very effective.

It's often a case of finding a balance between how much line to sink and how much to leave on the surface to give you the right degree of bow. Quite often it may not be necessary to sink any line. One thing to be aware of is that if the wind is coming slightly from behind, it can push a bow in the line, which will consequently pull the float further out with it. In this case you would have to bury enough line behind the float to defeat the wind.

Another way of slowing the float down in these conditions is to hold the rod higher and hang the line on the breeze. In this instance the bow is in the air acting like a sail on a yacht rather than on the surface of the water. It works brilliantly when conditions allow. At times on a river if it's a strong upstream wind and not much flow and the fish want it running at the speed of the river, then it's time to revert to sinking the line to get the float to go through. When feeding the bow I always pay out line with my left hand to ensure I am in total control.

Still on the subject of bites, I have noticed that on still waters in particular, most anglers strike at everything with no concept of 'reading' the bite. Ideally we should only strike at bites we have a good chance of hitting but it is not easy. It's even difficult to describe a hittable bite in writing, it's something you learn through experience and even then you will still miss some. The best way I can explain it is that when my float does something unexpected, I ask myself: "Has the fish got hold of the bait, has it got the bait in it's mouth?" You might only have a split second to decide whether to strike or leave it and wait for the float to move more positively. It's not a case of whether the float goes under or not, it doesn't have to move more than a millimetre to be a hittable bite. For example, if the float only lowers a fraction but holds there I would strike. It indicates that the fish has the bait in its mouth, and a slight movement like this is often a better bite than one that flies under at 90 mph.

Whenever I get anyone watching me on a lake they are always surprised at the number of indications I don't strike at. They often tell me I have just had a bite, and they might think I have been too slow to respond or gone to sleep or something, but the fact that they mention it suggests that they would have struck at what I considered to be an unhittable bite.

One day at my local Roundhay Park Lake, Leeds, a group of anglers from a local club came and sat behind me. I was fishing caster with the waggler for roach. I had learned in previous sessions that the bites were very finicky with all manner of indications, some of which might have looked hittable. But recent experience told me not to strike until eventually the float slid away. I could soon hear the comments coming from behind me: *"He just had a bite then, why didn't he strike?"* or: *"I'd have struck at that."* The bites took several seconds to develop, and it seemed like minutes, but the fish were of good quality and I was connecting with about four out of five, ending up in a few hours with 16lb in the net.

I was talking to one of the group many months later and he referred to the time he and his mates had watched me, and said: *"We learned more about roach fishing that day than we ever knew."* I think they had learned the value of reading the bite. Undoubtedly on that particular day, had I struck at all those slight indications I'd have been lucky to have caught 3 or 4lb. It would never be possible to hit every bite when roach fishing and I still miss plenty, that's the nature and fascination of it, but to win a match we just have to connect with more than our rivals and thus put more fish in the net.

So if you are missing all those bobs, touches and sharp bites, try leaving a few to see what happens. It takes discipline, but it's worth it in the long run as you will eventually learn when to strike and when not and your catches will improve accordingly. Sometimes it can vary from one venue to another. I remember a period when I was fishing two stretches of the same canal only a few miles apart. On one stretch, when the float lifted slightly, the fish was always on, yet on the other stretch, striking at these indications was rarely successful and I had to wait for the float to go under, which again proves that we could miss bites all day without learning the difference.

Again, if missing lots of bites you should make every attempt to manufacture a better bite by playing around with depth and shotting, combined with checking the hook size or pattern and rate of feeding the swim. You don't normally want too much float showing either, on average depending on conditions and bites on the day. I will fish mine between dotted and a quarter inch showing and occasionally up to half an inch, for example, if it's particularly choppy. I think any float fishes better when it is properly balanced and that means shotted well down.

Talking of reading bites brings me to the next simple mistake; that of not fishing a black top against a sky background. It's an absolute must in my book, simply because you will see so much more with a black top than you ever will with any other colour, and it makes a massive difference to reading the bite. That's why I always carry some black-topped floats and a black marker pen in case I find myself in this situation.

Finally, learn to feather the float, touching the reel line with your forefinger to stop the float just before it lands. This way the rig lays out in a straight line on the surface, rather than landing in a heap. It's tidier, avoids tangles and sets you up for a bite on the drop.

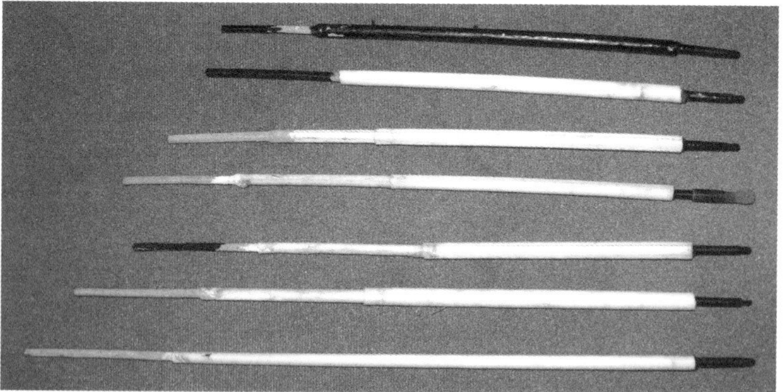

Dave's homemade floats - left in their natural white state apart from the tip.

A lot of swims on rivers scream waggler or stick float, but don't fall into the trap of assuming it is an out-and-out one float choice or the other. I invariably tackle both up and have often caught on a waggler in a peg that looked a dead cert for the stick, and vice versa. I remember winning a match on the tidal Trent on a very hard day. My peg was very fast and shallow and after a spell on the stick the bites dried up. The tide was running off and the pace got faster and faster. I could see nothing amiss about my presentation with the stick, and at least I could hold back slightly to slow it down.

In the end, after a lengthy spell with no bites, I decided to run the waggler through on the same line. It effectively flew about three quarters of the way down the peg but then suddenly buried. I struck and was into a decent roach. Even though I had experienced such surprises before, on this particular day I couldn't see any reason why the fish would have it that way in preference to the stick. I winkled a few more out and luckily it was just enough to win.

There are times, situations and venues where a straight quill waggler with relatively light shotting has to give way to a heavier approach with bodied wagglers and bulk shotting, fixed or sliding, depending on the depth. It's not complicated really, you just need a selection with varying shotting capacities and, depending on the waters you fish, you will probably find you are using the same two or three floats all the time.

For a bodied waggler the shotting is still straightforward. Most of it goes round the float – eg. 4AAA locking - and the bulk shot down the line is the equivalent of two to four BB, or even an olivette placed around 3 to 4 foot from the hook, with maybe two or three no. 8 droppers. Sliders in deeper water may warrant bigger samples but of course there would be no shot around the float; it would be mostly bulked a few feet from the hook, again with a few droppers below. A degree of weight in the float itself, and lead wire is one option, helps to ensure it flies with the shot and doesn't climb back up the line when casting.

I have had a few eye openers with bulk shotting and one I always recall happened on a Post Office National on the River Nene. I was pegged on a lovely part of the river at Water Newton, above Peterborough. My peg was about 9 to 10 feet deep down the middle with a very steady flow.

I chose a straight peacock insert waggler carrying 3AAA around the float and some 8s and 10s spaced out down the line. My float appeared to be performing well enough but all I could catch was an odd small roach. I began to think something was not quite right but couldn't put my finger on it. Then I noticed an angler about three pegs above me swing in a roach of around 3oz which was a much better stamp than mine. I kept an eye on him and saw him catch another. It was plain to see he was using a bodied waggler with some bulk down. I quickly sorted one out and made the necessary changes to my rig.

First cast, as soon as the float settled, I could tell it was going through a fraction slower than my original set-up. The float travelled a yard or so and buried and I was into a 4oz roach. I continued to catch steadily and ended up with over 8lb, a decent weight on the day. I never forgot that lesson, that's what bulk can do at times and as on that particular day it made all the difference. I noticed how well-known Lincoln angler, Les Smith enjoyed a lot of success fishing a waggler on the Witham with a 1gram olivette down his line placed a yard from the hook approx. and with no droppers below it (equivalent to 2.5BB shot). Slowing the bait down more on a cold winter river probably made a vital difference to how the bait behaved, judging by his results.

I have always maintained when fishing abroad, be it Ireland, Holland or Denmark that I would rather catch 50lb on the waggler than 100lb on the tip, matches aside of course, simply because it is so much more enjoyable. I do enjoy feeder fishing, but don't think anything compares to seeing that float go under and if I am pleasure fishing there is no contest, I'd take the lower weight on the waggler every time. The other thing is that you also get to enjoy some of the stunning scenery those big lakes have to offer, something that can't be said for looking down at a tip all day. That's not to say that on many occasions you wouldn't catch more on the waggler, especially if the bream come close enough or if roach and skimmers are the quarry.

The thing to remember in any country I have ever travelled to is to forget your light floats and delicate shotting. What you want are bodied wagglers that carry plenty of lead and a bulk rather than strung out shotting; all my experience says you have to be positive. Of course, there might be the odd exception to this rule, but mostly not and I think it is due to the use of groundbait.

Unlike many UK waters where loose-fed bait to a float is standard practice, groundbaiting is more the tradition on the Continent in countries like France, Holland, and Denmark. The fish seem to respond better to groundbait on the bottom and so bigger floats with heavy bulk shotting are suitable for getting the bait down quickly to them. This also applies to some of our deeper waters in Yorkshire of at least 12-foot deep, like the Aire and Calder Canal, Yorkshire Ouse and deeper sections of the River Don. But experience shows that a bigger float and bulk shotting pays off when abroad even in swims that aren't too deep.

I once fished next to a fellow English angler on a trip to Sweden. We sat on landing stages fishing only three or four yards apart and three rod lengths out in seven feet of water in calm conditions. I fished a bodied waggler with some bulk down while he fished his usual English style with a straight waggler and a few small shot spaced out. In effect we were both fishing the same baited area of the lake, and I couldn't believe it when my float kept going under and his didn't. In those conditions there was no apparent reason why he shouldn't get bites with the tackle he was using, it was incredible. I realised it must be his rig and I tried to explain to him that it was just not positive enough. Initially he couldn't believe that altering his set-up would make any difference and it took me a while to persuade him to change. But once he did what an eye opener it turned out to be. He was into bream straight away and we both went on to amass a good weight of fish. It just emphasises the point that positive shotting works well when fishing abroad.

If you have neglected to fish the waggler for some time, as I suspect a lot of anglers have in this age of poles, I hope I have rekindled your appetite for a bit of proper fishing. As for the younger anglers who have only ever fished commercials and don't even own a rod, all I would say is, life does exist beyond the pole and if you're not exploring it with the waggler you don't know what you are missing. Treat yourself and give it a try.

Top Tip

Something that sticks out like a sore thumb to me when I watch certain anglers is that they seem to forget to feed. To stand any chance of building a swim it is essential to keep some feed going in on a regular basis. The old maxim of 'little and often' feeding is reliable and is almost always better than feeding only rarely. Then if you feel you might improve the situation or catch a better stamp of fish by upping the quantity, try it, as that's how we learn. If it kills the swim then too bad, but you will have gained from the experience. We must all make mistakes to learn. Always go with your gut feeling but keep that feed going in.

The Bronze Maggot Revolution

Dave Thomas almost single-handedly changed the Trent culture by winning matches on bronze maggot. In the early Seventies the maggot's chances of beating the more popular caster bait on the Trent were regarded by most of the river's regulars as remote. Dave was to change their minds. The Lancashire anglers had raided from across the Pennines and enjoyed a period of domination over the locals, mainly with light stick floats and caster, that had lasted over a decade. But suddenly the waggler was coming more into anglers' thinking, and Dave and his Leeds pals were about to put a spanner in the caster works. A new class of star anglers from Nottingham and beyond would emerge from this change. But even for Dave it didn't happen immediately such was the great faith in the dark red 'shell'. He takes us back to the events at the start of winter 1973...

Coming off the back of a 220-peg Open win three weeks earlier at Dunham Bridge on caster.

On 3 November 1973 I achieved my burning ambition to win a Burton Joyce Open to prove to myself I could compete at the very highest level. It was the first match of the Saturday Open Series that year and I did it off a peg in the Nelson Field with 15lb 13 1/2oz on caster, following the advice I had been given when I first took the step from club matches to the Opens, 18 months previously, that I would be wasting my time on the maggot at this level, it had to be caster.

Although I won this match by a clear margin, I came away convinced that I would have caught a lot more on the maggot. Its difficult to explain, but I think it was the quality of the bites I got that day. The fish seemed very wary of the caster and a lot of the bites were not that confident - very touchy, tentative. I felt pretty sure in my own mind, that it might have been 20lb or more on the maggot? Was I right, that was the burning question.

So here I was three weeks later, halfway through a Burton Joyce Open, going nowhere on the caster. Once again, finicky bites, odd small fish, but dare I do the unthinkable, the one thing no other angler in this match would dream of doing? Everyone knew that the caster ruled, it was written in tablets of stone that 'caster was king', with maggot confined long ago to mere serfdom. The urge became overpowering. If I didn't do it now I would spend another week wondering, agonising over it and deep down I was so sure, so certain, those fickle bites and the enormous confidence I had built through years of winning club matches on the maggot, were urging me on.

I had realised some time ago that the only way to find my true potential as a match angler was to always go with my gut feeling – that way whether I got it right or wrong I had learnt something. We learn as much if not more from our mistakes as our successes, but more importantly we develop what can only be described as a knowing, setting ourselves free to follow and develop our own instinct, without fear of failure – it's a win-win attitude (mindset).

And so, it had to be. I could stand it no longer. I had to go with it. My hand reached into the bag of maggots now around my neck, in went about 30 bronzies. A huge sense of relief came over me. I'd done it. No turning back. Soon I would find out if my theory was right. The peg had only given me a few small roach and shown no sign of anything better, so I hardly knew what to expect, but I didn't have to wait long. Five to ten minutes elapsed before my stick float buried and I struck into a quality roach of 8-10oz – BINGO! They came steadily for the remaining two hours, good roach that happily accepted two maggots on an 18. At the scales, I was delighted to weigh in 10lb 5 1/2oz to win on what had been a very windy day. Two Burton Joyce Opens in the space of three weeks, beyond my wildest dreams and for sure it would be maggot for me from now on.

The secret was soon out. It's difficult to conceal chrysoidine-dyed hands of course, not that I tried to. Frank Barlow (*see footnote) would look at them after a match and query: *"All on caster again, Dave?"*. I'd hold up my hands with a smile and say *"Aye Frank, caster again"*. However, the caster religion had too strong a hold. Pete Warren* in particular kept the faith alive by continuing to score well. Also, many had little confidence in maggot, having fished caster almost exclusively for the past 10 to 15 years.

Then came the match that for many was the turning point, when Pete and I drew next to each other in the Ferry Field in a

Burton Joyce Open on 21 December 1974. All eyes were on this one, aptly labelled by Denis White*: 'The Battle of Burton Joyce'. I remember conditions were good, the scene was set for an epic encounter, maggot v caster between two anglers at the top of their game.

We battled fish for fish for the full five hours, a brilliant match and at the end, I wasn't sure, but felt I might just have the edge. The scales confirmed it, with my 17lb 14oz to Pete's 14lb 11oz, putting us first and second in the match. The result decided many of the caster faithful that it was time for a change, although they were to find it was not quite as simple as changing baits, there was a bit more to it than that. One thing was for sure, the bronze maggot revolution had begun.

Other areas were slow to catch on, they probably looked at what was happening on the Trent and thought it could never happen on their own river, but it did. One prime example was the Warwickshire Avon, which I thought had been crying out for it for a long time. I also loved the story about Wayne Swinscoe* turning up to fish an open on the Thames at Medley with a bucketful of bronze. The regulars told him he wouldn't catch with those - *'not here'*, but Wayne had other ideas and obliterated the match with 30lb.

Footnote: The late Frank Barlow, was the larger than life Trent ace and Angler's Mail regular match columnist, whose articles about the Midlands match circuit were famous for their humour and sarcasm. He had a huge following. Barnsley Black, Denis White was another character who became an England International not long after. Pete Warren was famous for his winning nets of roach on stick float and caster. Wayne Swinscoe was an up and coming star from Nottingham who was to become an outstanding river performer, also winning honours at team level with Notts Fed, Shakespeare Professionals and Essex County.

Chapter 11
Roly Moses - The Tidal Trent King

Roly Moses is a gentle giant with a mighty reputation. Despite standing 6' 4" and with the shoulders of a rugby prop forward, he talks in a quiet, measured way. He also has the measure of the tidal Trent, with scores of victories over the last 20 years, mainly with roach. His success at South Clifton in particular is second to none, winning the regular Thursday Open series (formerly run by Sheffield Amalgamated, now by Scunthorpe DAA) no less than 13 occasions in the last 15 years at the time of writing in 2014. Incredible form.

But despite this domination he claims: *"the success in competitions when targeting roach is secondary for me to the catching of them. I have splashed down into most of our country's rivers at one time or other, and many lakes too, mostly wild venues, all in pursuit of roach, and it has been a wonderful experience. I have also forged many friendships along the way, with like-minded anglers."*

Roly's father, George, introduced him to the joy of river fishing at an early age. This soon developed into what he describes as 'roach fever', and throughout his angling life he has pursued this species which he describes as 'the most beautiful' of all fish.

Above all else Roly still loves his redfins but sadly for him the roach fishing on UK rivers is not what it used to be. He says he's witnessed the decline of our rivers, due entirely [in his humble opinion] to mismanagement by the powers that be.

After reaching his 65th birthday, the ex-police officer describes what was once a raging fire in angling terms has now become a warm glow. Yet, while he enjoys other angling disciplines like fly fishing for trout, he is still driven to float-fish in at least one match a week for what he calls those 'pristine' river roach. And river decline or not, he's probably caught more 20lb roach match bags from the river than anyone else, dead or alive, and most of these have fallen to a waggler float.

I'd not want to swap shoes with any EA official trying to convince Roly that there is little wrong with the River Trent compared to yesteryear, but that's by the by. Let's get on with his story...

Part 1 – River roach on the waggler

There was a time when the River Trent was a roach-filled, nutrient-laden waterway, with a smell and colour all of its own, which drew anglers like me to its banks like a magnet.

I make no secret of the fact that I have enjoyed a privileged journey in search of roach, one that has taken me many, many thousands of miles, the length and breadth of that river, over many years, meeting many like-minded anglers along the way.

The spell I fell under all those years ago was borne out of the aspiration and obsession to become 'a roach angler', for of all the species in the River Trent, none were more sought after than this one. When I look back and recall all the names of the day that lined the Trent banks, not just in matches, but just in pleasure fishing, at every opportunity in search of those roach, it really is awe-inspiring.

Even today there still remain windows of opportunity where the same passions that drove us then can be applied, but we are at the mercy of regulations that demand 'clearer water'. Most significant in roach angling terms is the fact that we are now totally dependant on an influx of rain water and colour to sample the Trent roach fishing of old.

A man in his element – Roly Moses with a Trent redfin.

These opportunities are rare now, for the roach in large numbers have gone. We rely instead on huge, nomadic shoals that are seeking colour and safety, and tend to stay feeding only for brief periods in safe havens before moving on. It is at these times that the roach angler has an opportunity to sample the halcyon days of old, when you could literally put down your tackle anywhere on the river, top to bottom, and catch roach.

I have pursued these fish to the exclusion of all others, and in matches have fished for roach just in order to catch a weight of them, forsaking the need to catch a framing weight, which may well have entailed fishing the feeder, which I was loathe to do. It may well sound suicidal to fish matches, and knowingly fish feeder pegs with the float just to catch roach, but for good or ill I was doing that. I'd happily take a lesser weight of roach from a peg that to the feeder man may well have been a winner. I just wanted to catch them.

The benefit of this seemingly foolish strategy was, from clumsy beginnings, that I became a competent roach angler. The desire to catch roach fuelled a need to have the best tackle to catch them with, and this did not involve a great expense. I believed the single most important aspect then, and now, was the actual float used to catch them. Floats are personal, that which suits one angler might well not suit another. They must suit the 'style' of the angler and what he is trying to achieve.

For me the best way to catch roach was to get them to come up in the water, and that is not always easy. But when it happens you can guarantee that some of the biggest roach in any shoal will fall to a method that stands alone: waggler. I think I have exhausted all avenues of waggler fishing in pursuit of 'rutilus'. I have been down the plastic road [here Roly means the hollow plastic commercially sold as a 'crystal'], I have fished with many float materials, but I always come back to the peacock waggler.

I have copied other anglers who seemed to have good floats, but as soon as I realized they had good floats for themselves but not necessarily for me, I moved on at a fast rate of knots.

In fact it all fell into place for me when I mastered the art of making my own floats, designed to do what I wanted them to, and not the things that other anglers wanted me to. What I'm trying to say is that because a certain float is raved about in a magazine article it does not follow that you will be successful with it.

Just because a float carries the name of an angler known to the angling press does not mean, for instance, that it will catch you roach. It may suit him, and he may sell a lot of floats but, more often than not, the float being endorsed is not quite the same as the one being used by that same angler. So my advice to any would-be roach angler-cum-float maker would be to get away from other people's input, develop your own, and you are halfway there to becoming a 'thinking' angler.

Peacock quill was to me the perfect float-making material, a natural product which offered all the attributes I was looking for, and it was not long before I was making peacock inserted wagglers that caught plenty of fish. And I still use them today, with a longer fine insert than most shop-bought models, designed for fishing 'on the drop'. The construction marries two different quill thicknesses, with the insert as fine as necessary to register bites clearly.

This float, the insert peacock, is available in a myriad of forms, and thanks to today's tackle advances some really good ones are available commercially, BUT I can guarantee none are as good as the best home-made ones if you make them properly.

For me the wagglers always have to be loaded. I want them working the minute they enter the water. The perfect loading is in the eye of the beholder, but this is a 'must have' attribute to my floats.

There are many other features that contribute to a float's performance, too many really to cover in a single chapter, but suffice to say that all floats coming off my small production line had to do exactly what I wanted them to do.

Finesse was the key – fine lines, fine floats, neat shotting, fine hooks – for example, the balancing of 12oz bottoms to 1.5lb main line as opposed to 1lb bottoms and 2lb main line. I know that modern pre-stretched lines offer different parameters, but I'm referring here to more traditional lines, for old habits die hard, and I sometimes think that old is best.

As for the Trent in the old roach-filled days, even given the finest tackle available, you also had to perfect the art of feeding the swim. I'd say this is arguably the second most important factor of all, second only to the float, though each in fact complements the other.

What bait(s) you may ask? For me it had to be maggots and hemp. Never did I go to the river without both of these and, being totally honest, the single most important ingredient to any Trent session was the hemp.

I always used to have a second waggler rod set up - a 'hemp waggler'. Simply put, a hemp waggler is the same float but with a grain of hemp on the hook at the ready.

This was a back-up method for me, possibly never noticed, just another waggler rod, but armed with that magic seed, and the float nearly always set at about four-foot deep. The times are legion when maggot bites were 'iffy' and I would pick up that second rod and find the peg solid with 'hemp roach'.

It was amazing how quickly a good weight could be assembled with this method, even if they were there and feeding for only an hour. Combined with the regular maggot waggler, the hemp method gave me a real boost in performance.

The above is, or was probably the best kept secret of mine, until the late Alan Baynes started sitting with me at South Clifton on a regular basis (that is the tidal Trent Clifton). Alan used to tell me I would be found out, but it was a lot of years before I was, though the method has been used to good effect in recent times by one or two of the top South Clifton anglers.

I remember once taking 24lb of roach against the 22lb off the next peg angler at South Clifton, a scalp I still carry with pride, and make no apology for doing so. This man was a real gent in my eyes and we shared a truly memorable day; treasured memories for me, although I recall the man in question challenged my parentage! I'm referring to the Trent maestro from Leeds, Mr. Dave Thomas.

Little did the recently crowned World Champion realize what a massive boost that gave to my roach fishing. Yes Dave, you were one of the waggler anglers of the day who inspired me. The roach 'disease' is so infectious that if it catches you you are at risk of succumbing at whatever age.

I remember the penny dropping for my friend Bob Pearson who is, like myself, now of senior years. Bob became so enthusiastic to learn and it all fell into place for him one day several years back. I will never forget the excitement generated by his discoveries about fishing the waggler for roach and it reminded me of my own journey years earlier.

I must digress at this point because with the passage of time, and the changes in water management on the Trent which resulted in a 'clearer' river, everything moved away from the angler, literally, and a new approach was required. The 'mini bolo' (alias small version of the top and bottom float, the Bolognese) was born, designed for the days when the roach would feed.

Again I resorted to making the floats to my own specification, allowing me the facility to cast the rig down the peg to the fish (out of range of most stick floats) or even down the middle of the river in perfect conditions, now incorporating olivette leads and carbon-stemmed floats, to target the far off roach of today. Sadly, the opportunities to catch roach this way on the tidal river are more limited to those rare occasions when the wind permits it.

There are other challenges as a roach angler, notably cormorant predation on almost all the venues I know. The fish have become more shoaled in areas where there are people, houses, or marinas for example. No more are the far off, remote locations the best.

For me the River Trent is totally feeder dominated, and as a match angler/roach angler/float angler, I am, to say the least, really saddened, for I am anxious I will never see it return to the way it was, when you could tackle up at any peg on the Trent and catch roach.

But, if ever you want good company and optimistic anglers, then come and visit us at South Clifton. I can promise you the best breakfasts bar none, and the best run matches bar none. As a bonus you might just catch the river with a bit of fresh water in, with the roach in a feeding mood, allowing you to sample roach fever. For there are still those who fish nowhere else in the hope that things will be as they once were.

One such day last year, a memorable day with fresh water and a bit of colour prevailing, I caught 18lb of roach. There is no greater feeling in the world than being regarded by your peers as a roach angler, to see those wagglers and 'mini bolos' seeking out rutilus is a sight to behold, and it still gives an old man a great deal of pleasure.

Part 2 – The Float itself

As this book is all about the waggler I will now describe my way of making wagglers. I would love you to experience the satisfaction of fishing waggler for roach, and would get great personal pleasure if it was with a float I'd told you how to make.

First, you will need some FRESH peacock quills, not those that have been sitting on a tackle shop shelf for months or years. There is a stark difference in the way they perform in my opinion. I think that a piece of fresh quill, treated so to seal in the internal 'pith', will last a very long time without losing any of its buoyancy. That's my own view, but if you are happy to make floats from shop-bought quills then so be it, many anglers do.

Here's a little tale I cannot resist. At one of our regular Monday night meetings of Brigg A.C., I made it known that I was in need of some fresh quills. Well, a good friend of mine, a like-minded countryman, took me at my word, and the following Monday night he appeared with this great big smile, clutching a bundle of peacock quills.

He thrust them into my arms and just said: "Let me have a couple of the finished article," (that to me was a great exchange rate). I nearly fell off my chair having got hold of these quills, for I swear they were still warm and carrying fresh blood on their base. I looked at him and he just said: "Don't ask".

So, first take a quill of the thickness you need. Find the straight bit in the middle section of the quill, and cut off a piece of about 8" which is ideal for a straight waggler for dragging shots on the bottom. Often you can make two floats from the same quill if making insert wagglers. The amount of fine insert you cut from the thin end of the quill entirely depends on how long an insert you want. I like to use inserts of different lengths and try to carry a selection.

The base of the waggler is a bit fiddly to make but worth the effort. Take a piece of 1/8" diameter brass rod cut to 1" length. This should weigh at least 1.0 gram as a rough guide. Make a 1" hole in the bottom of the quill with a bodkin then carefully turn the brass rod into the hole, leaving about a ¼" sticking out. Remove the rod, smear it with Araldite or Superglue, then push it back in the hole. It will be secure.

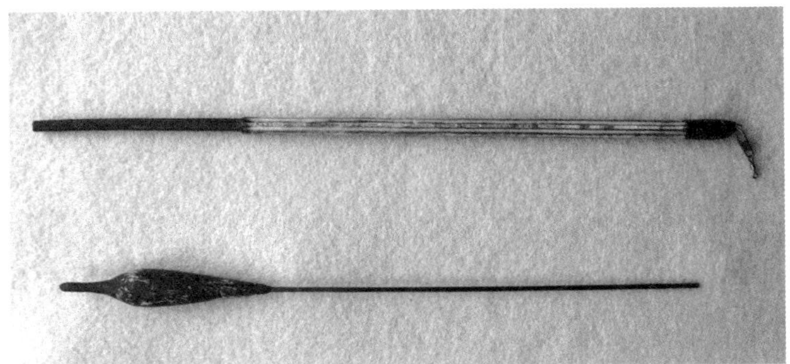

Roly's home-made floats – a waggler and a Bolognese. This waggler would be shotted with an AB shot either side of the float to lock it in place (made by Anchor these shots are green coated and slightly smaller than a AAA), and four no. 8s or four no. 10s evenly spaced out down the line.

Take some stainless wire, a fine pole float stem is suitable, and form a staple to fit closely around the end of the brass rod. Push this into the quill either side of the protruding section of brass rod, leaving enough 'bend' to first slide on a mini swivel. Glue in the wire (if using Araldite you can glue in the rod and wire together) and also smear and cover the exposed end of the peacock pith with glue.

Now mix a small amount of 'chemical metal' and, working quickly for it soon sets, mould around the base of the float and exposed brass, forming a teardrop shape which helps the float's aerodynamics. Use a little water on your fingers to make this shape as it stops the filler sticking to your skin. Allow the filler to set dry, then carefully sand into the required shape.

When you're happy with the float's base go to the tip or insert end. Carefully remove the pith from the quill with a drill bit held in the fingers, taking extreme care not to damage the quill walls. I find it safest to smear the top ½" with Superglue before doing this as this strengthens the quill. Go in about ¾" with the drill, far enough for the insert to hold firm in the body quill, and adjust until the insert is in a straight line, and finally glue the insert in place.

Take a plastic bag to protect your fingers, smear the whole quill with superglue and allow to dry. You may also wish to add a couple of coats of thin varnish, both coatings having the effect of sealing in all the fresh properties of the quill.

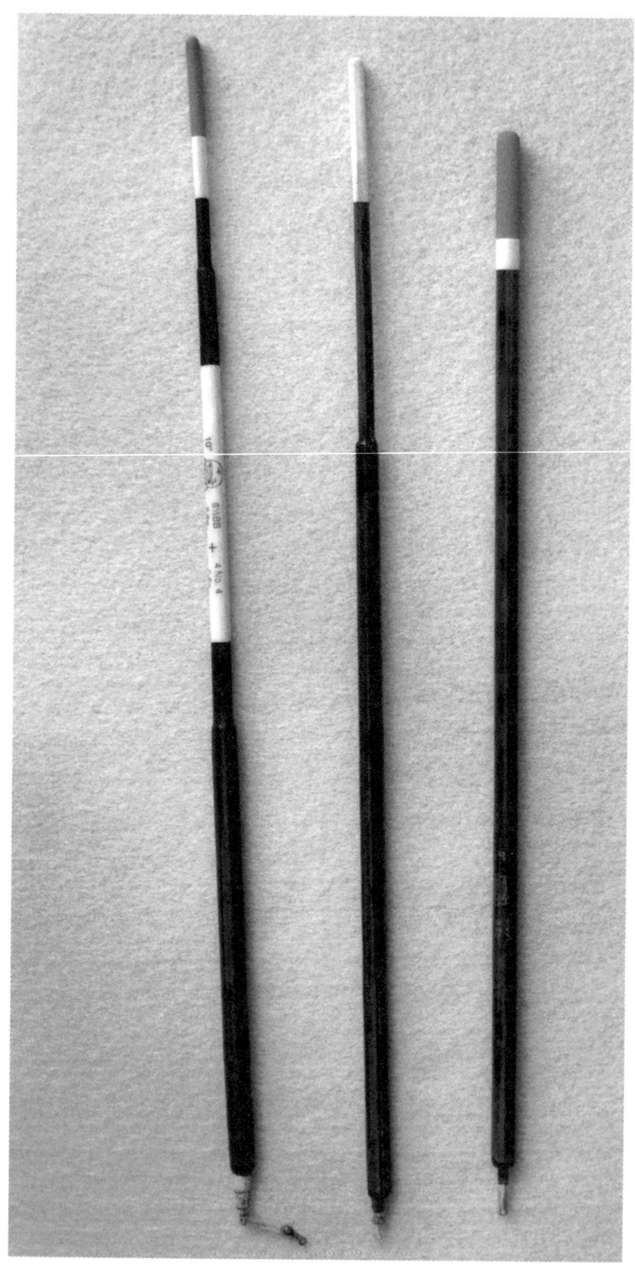

A selection of Drake wagglers.

Finally, take a permanent marker pen, mine are normally green, and colour the float, after checking to see if the float needs a little dusting with fine emery paper to smooth off any sharp edges left by the Superglue. Make a final check around the insert joint to see if it is sealed with glue or varnish, before painting the tip in base white and then the colour of your choice (mostly on the Trent it will be black) and VOILA, the float is done (see pic).

Yes, the job could be seen as a little time consuming, but well worth the effort surely. For when you take these floats to the river you can be confident that they will do the job. Straight wagglers, minus insert, are finished in the same way, white tips followed by the chosen colour.

I have sometimes spray painted then varnished the finished float, but could tell no difference in performance due to the weight of paint etc. And, if you do not fancy the task of making them at all, hunt down the float-maker Glen Bradley, of Drake Floats, who makes them commercially but only in small batches to order. I have used Glen's myself, especially the insert loaded ones, and they are good.

The float has to start fishing the moment it makes contact with the water, riding and ready to register bites. With the loaded float its sleek profile and build enters the water without splash or fuss when feathered in (that's checking the line at the reel just before the float hits the surface), and instantly the dropping shot are working on that insert.

Practice will tell you what to look for in a bite, and as often as not it is what the float does NOT do that gives the indication to strike. For you are not always waiting for a 'pull' to register, but more of a deviation from the float's normal behaviour. Sometimes as you get hold of the catapult to feed, having cast, the bite will come rapidly from a fish very close to the surface, and you must be ready to respond.

Beware, there is an imbalance with a lot of floats that just makes them unsuitable for the job. You possibly know what I mean, the splash factor, or the wobble as they set up. It is because of the loading that you can get rid of the bulky shot from around the base, and smaller locking shot mean a more aerodynamic flight – smoother and quicker through the air.

I like to think that when fishing the insert waggler I am at one with the river, and especially the swim I am on. I want to be quicker than other anglers, and smoother, and where possible swing in every fish. Some obviously you can't, but the catch rate can be hidden behind this action. If you have 'tamed' the hooked fish: got it moving towards you quickly and smoothly, fins by its side, align the rod in the down position and pull in sweeps, taking up line and bring it to a point in front of you then, without stopping, lift and swing.

You will have already have been able to assess its 'swingability', an art honed over many years of catching roach. But those splashy fish at your feet are a 'no-no' to lift, for valuable time is wasted if you lift and then the fish comes adrift and the rig tangles. The landing net is used on the latter, livelier and generally bigger fish.

There are days and times, of course, when, having hooked the fish down the peg, it is reluctant to move towards you due to its size, and just sits there 'nodding' until eventually you bring it upstream and net it. Dreams are made of this we might say, but all this evolves when fishing for roach. All the anglers I know who have fished for roach develop a similar style, but a very individual one. I suppose practice makes perfect but it's a mistake to copy others too slavishly.

Top Tip

When fishing the waggler for roach on the Trent, or anywhere else, now and again try slipping a grain of hemp on the hook. The best way still for me is to hook the hemp through the eye (that's the dot where the seed was attached to the plant), and sometimes several fish can be caught on one grain of hemp this way. Yes, the float is the boss, but feeding is also key, and maggots and hemp is a must for me. So give the 'hemp waggler' a try, you may like what you find.

Chapter 12

Dave Frost - Long Range Waggler

Pen Pic

David Frost is a retired police officer, age 58, from Treeton, Rotherham.

Most memorable matches: All at Willington, U.Trent, 1988 Derbyshire Police, 1st with 22lb from 200 anglers, 1989 Derby's Police, 3rd with 29lb, 1992 Derby's Police 1st 28lb, and 1992, South Yorks. Police 1st with 38lb both from 180+ anglers.
Favourite fish: chub, bream and roach.
All time angling heroes: Kevin Ashurst, John Dean, Alan Scotthorne and, one for the future, Matt Godfrey.
Favourite fishing team: Rotherham team of the early 1980s that won the Division 1 National.
Waggler choice: Rive carbon bodied and Cralusso.
Other Hobbies: Playing classical guitar.
Fishing ambitions: To reach the finals of either the Riverfest or Canal pairs competitions.

Dave Frost - Long Range Waggler

A catch of a lifetime put Dave Frost on the right track with the waggler float. Back in January 1984 he arrived at the River Trent at Farndon for a pleasure stint. It was a mild day but blowing a gale. He knew chub were in the area as three weeks before he'd taken a big weight on a stick float. But on this day he set up a peacock waggler, and caught fish almost from his first cast to his last. He totalled 45 chub for a tremendous 100lb 8oz and Dave never looked back from that day. Ten years later he enjoyed a purple patch on the upper Trent. Two great wins in particular came a month apart from entries of 180 anglers. Dave thought the first match had gone well with 27lb of fish on a stick float, but his second win was a bit special - a 38lb personal best match catch on the waggler and bronze maggot. Dave is a qualified NFA coach and has spent many hours putting something back into the sport by coaching youngsters...

There is one technique that has followed me through my angling life and that is waggler fishing. It is to me the essence of what angling is about. The cast is important and has to be mastered. The method of feeding is vital and has to be controlled and adjusted periodically. However, the sight of the float tip sliding under the water, or occasionally lifting when everything has been executed correctly, and the feel of a fish being contacted at distance, just provides that edge of excitement which to me no other form of angling does.

My love of waggler fishing grew as a result of frequenting places like Clumber Park in the 1980s, also the Rivers Welland and Witham, and especially the Trent. The advent of carbon rods played a major part, primarily because you could just stand with the rod in your hand all day, and the inspiration came from the books of Kevin Ashurst and Ivan Marks. Conversations with members of the great Rotherham team of the early 80s also helped. These anglers were masters of the method at a time when pole fishing was in its infancy, and the big lesson I learned from them was the way to catch at every depth by shotting fine coupled with light hooklengths.

Fast forward to the present day and my waggler rods are frequently in use at the delightfully picturesque Holmebrook Valley country park, near Chesterfield. Here I've applied my waggler style, which incorporates a blend of old technology with new innovative floats, modern lines and hooks, and is based entirely around the use of bronze maggots.

The target species are roach but I also look to catch perch, the odd bream and possibly an occasional tench. Although there are only

34 pegs on the lake, the closest angler on the opposite bank will be around 100 yards away. This gives the waggler angler a lot of water to cover and the option to fish one or more lines (ie. feed areas), wind permitting.

I disregard what could be a winning weight as this will more often than not be someone fishing the feeder, but as I have won matches from all areas of the lake and framed from almost any peg with the waggler approach, I look to just build a weight by taking fish at all depths and distances. Win or lose, the joy of seeing the distant tip of the waggler slipping under the surface becomes mesmeric even though these roach can be fickle.

During the 1990s I was fortunate to be able to afford Normark rods, and as the years have passed it has become more apparent to me that these weapons with their fine, forgiving 'roachy' tips are ideal for this lake. As many pegs are shrouded in trees I have supplemented the Normarks with a delightfully responsive and crisp 11ft Drennan Ultralight. But, not satisfied that the action was quite perfect for roach, I cut off the last 14 inches and replaced the tip with a solid carbon one and now have a perfect light action roach rod.

A good skimmer falls to the method.

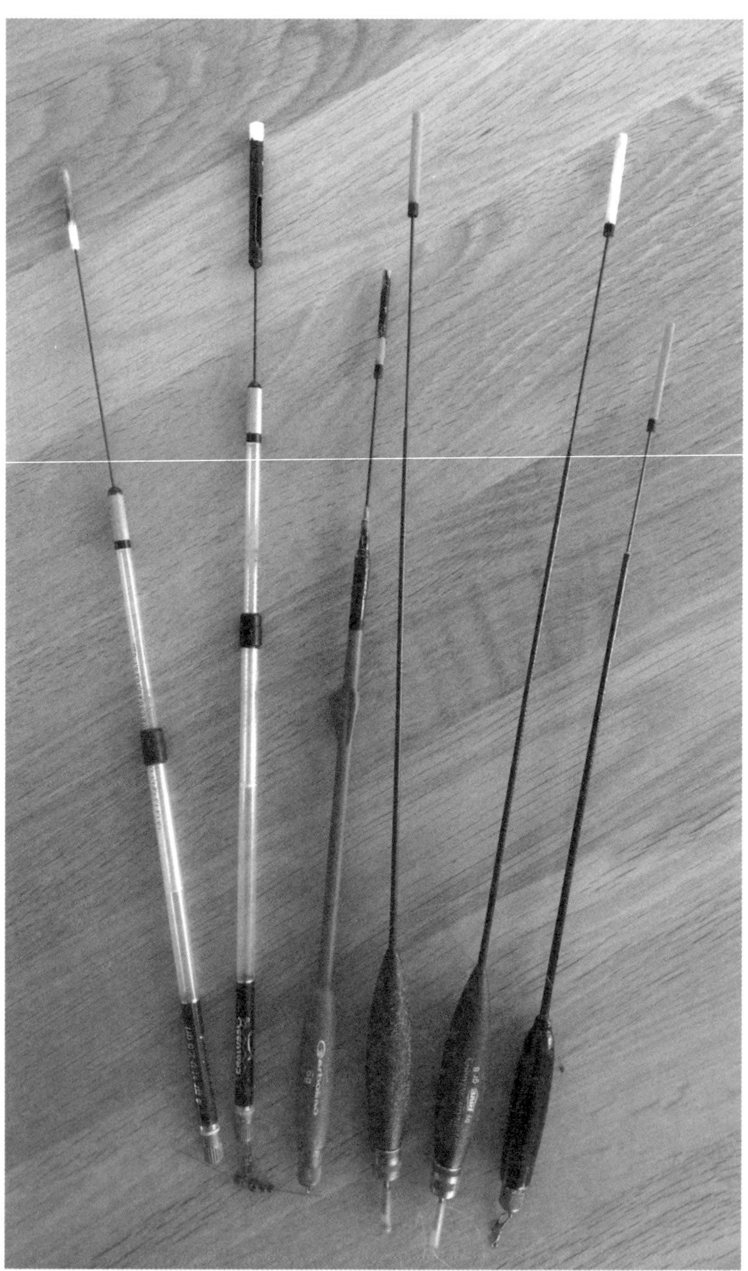

A selection of Dave's wagglers for fishing well out.

The majority of my wagglers have been home made over the years, but at this lake I have parted company with the past and use the more scientifically-designed modern floats. I have settled in the main for the large Garbolino multi-insert wagglers in 6g and 8g. I also use a Drennan Dart in 2.5 Swan (SSG) size. The Garbolino's are big floats, will easily cast 35 yards and, being loaded, they cut straight through the surface drift. They have sight tips built on the end of a slim 4-inch insert of carbon and are extremely sensitive. These floats are mostly set at depth which is around 8-9ft.

I prefer to lock the floats on the line with a small swivel and several no. 6 and 8 shot which allows me to slide some of this shot down the line should I think it necessary. To back up this float I use the Drennan Dart which still allows me to cast some distance, and this model also has a long thin insert which shows subtle bites up in the water. Just to give slightly more casting distance I have taken the odd antenna from a Drennan Dart and glued them into the end of some sarkandas reed wagglers, thus giving extreme sensitivity built into a float that cuts through the surface well and casts beyond the limit of the dart.

Main line is either Bayer 2.6lb or Maxima 2.5lb, both being robust and both tending not to sink too deep which counteracts the action of the shot. As for reels I use a Drennan 3000 reel with a smaller Daiwa 2508 on the shorter rod. On the large waggler I aim to place two no. 8 shot together at mid-depth with four no. 10 shot equally spaced out below it. The no. 8 shot are easily moved up and down or separated to either slow down or speed up the bait's descent. Some of the locking shot can also be separated and brought down to join these two shot should I want a faster drop.

I use a 0.09mm Shimano Aspire hook length which is the modern pre-stretched variety, but one I still think offers enough stretch and durability, tied to size 20 barbless Drennan Silverfish maggot hooks. With a size 18 there are too many false bites and a size 22 does not seem to improve the catch rate. The second waggler is normally set up with the same lines but only at half depth with just four no. 10 shot down.

The aim of this shallow rig is to take fish in the upper layers which the larger float/deeper rig might by-pass - predominantly a warmer weather rig. And this is generally the rig which catches the bream in the upper layers of water. Although bites on this are usually instant and positive, I maintain a four-foot minimum depth, as I just believe that the longer arc of fall through the water, presents the fish with a more natural-looking hook-bait.

Feeding is pure boy's stuff. Part of the satisfaction of this waggler method is the ability to feed accurately and consistently over the five hours. I can loose feed a fair distance with a soft blue elastic Drennan catapult, but these opportunities are rare. More often I have to struggle against tricky winds at any time of year, so this is when I turn to 'sticky mag' and Horlicks becomes the essential binder for the maggots.

Into a pint of maggots I add around an egg-cupful of Horlicks. I flick drops of water into this and 15 minutes later the maggots should be ready to be formed into sticky balls around 2/3 the size of a golf ball. If the bait sticks in the catapult just roll it in a little maize, or if you want it heavier add a little micro grit. I sometimes just give the ball a spray of water (from an atomiser) and roll in fresh maggots to allow maggots to break off on the drop.

I cast out using the line-clip on the reel to limit my cast, wind back two or three times to straighten the line, then catapult a ball of sticky mag directly at the float. If I believe that bream will feature, I feed groundbait that is mixed quite wet so that the balls just hold together. I add pinkies to this and roll the ball in dry groundbait before firing it. It lands with a slight 'puff' on the surface before filtering slowly through the upper layers of the swim.

Most of the feeding is done with the sticky mag, however, with small balls of maggot which are fired at the float. The normal routine is to cast the float out normally to 25 to 30 yards, wind back a couple of turns, dip my left hand into the maggots and grab a good pinch, roll them on the knee to form a small ball, then fire this at the waggler attempting a dart thrower's accuracy to try and hit the float. Practice is required. There is little chance of me achieving pinpoint accuracy for five hours; in fact I allow myself a rectangular target of three to four yards back to front and a couple of yards right to left.

There is just the odd time when I actually hit the float with the sticky mag ball and that gives me a little kick of pride, but usually there's never anyone looking on to share the moment! This feed area is big enough to allow me to drop short or overcast to pick up fish that have backed off or to just give them a pause to build up their feeding confidence. The spare waggler can be used to cast over this line but more often than not I feed a second, closer line to chase the roach along the near shelf. This is in the 17 to 20 yard range which is beyond the reach of poles and once again this offers a massive expanse of water to draw fish from.

The hookbait is 90 per cent bronze maggot, with a change to red or white occasionally to offer something different. The reason for this is a little scientific in case you are unaware of it. I learned from a fisheries management course a few years ago that the normal spectrum of light does not extend past six feet in depth and after that only colours in the red/yellow range are readily visible. Fish also see in the infra-red and ultra-violet spectrum which indicates to me that a bronze maggot should stand out above all other baits. True or not, I believe there is just a little something extra in a bronze maggot that white or red fails to match.

The roach vary in size from 2oz to 12oz. I gratefully take any size of fish knowing that over the course of the match I will get dozens of bites that are not hittable, so the float is being cast in and out repeatedly and allowed to settle for a short time. The roach will take the bait at any depth and the secret here is to try to work out where they are feeding and notice the subtle changes in feed pattern and adjust accordingly. Normally they will come up in the water, but the large waggler can be easily adjusted, and because they are remarkably fine in the tip there is no trouble hitting fast-biting roach at mid-water or less.

During the summer months bream play a major part in the results. Should I spot a bream topping or judge that it is warm enough, then I will add the 'puffs' of brown crumb and hope to catch a bream up in the water. This is quality sport when it happens. Instant bites are lovely but more often there is a wait for the roach. Yet once I have decided to fish the method my confidence is 100 per cent.

The Garbolino floats are provided with several interchangeable tips and I normally use the four-inch carbon insert to the float which cuts through the surface drift. I usually end up painting the tips with Sensas float paint, normally either yellow or black depending upon the light. Should I be faced with fishing into the sun these wagglers have a hollow, wide diameter tip. This reflects sunlight perfectly and glows away out on the lake with no lack of sensitivity.

Holmebrook Valley is a venue where catching the roach on waggler is a personal challenge. A good day's fishing is to have worked something out and made contact with the roach, always aiming to connect with that extra fish or two, trying to work out why the last bite was missed and to be constantly thinking through the processes: following the bait down through the water in the mind's eye and becoming one with the feeding fish.

From the start of the session I begin to count from the moment the waggler is in position. Although the visible float tip is important, the counting process allows you gauge when the bites are materialising. After a while actual counting stops and you just get a feel for the depth the bite will come at, having formed a mental picture of what is happening under the surface and at what depth the fish are feeding.

I have experienced days in the past, particularly on the Fenland rivers when a few meagre pounds of roach was enough to win money even in the largest matches. I look at this venue similarly and have to be content with what to many are very modest catches - anything from 8lb to 16lb. It's not the size of the catch that matters though, it's the construction of the plan and the execution that, win or lose gives me the thrill of waggler fishing. I can never be totally happy with a weight of roach as there are always missed bites, leaving questions in my head and small problems that have to be resolved. Strange how in over 40 years of match fishing it still feels like the roach have the upper hand.

To me waggler fishing has always been a joy. I tend not to fish the commercial matches, but there are great opportunities to fish waggler on these venues too, and in a manner that I have described. It can be challenging and at times frustrating, but equally rewarding when there are a few fish in the net. The best night's sleep of the week is still when I've had a busy day's fishing.

Top Tip

Always be prepared to adjust depths, shotting, and hook and line sizes. Presentation comes first, but all is lost without good feeding, and always try to feed instinctively.

Chapter 13
Terry Moroz - Reflections

Pen Pic

Born: 1956, Chesterfield.
Job: police officer.
Most memorable matches: Winning the National Champs team event with Notts Fed in 1987 and contributing 4lb of roach for 15th in the section from the Burton Joyce ferry field. Also, my first open win with 17lb of bream on the Witham caught on a swing-tip, circa 1976, Timberland Lane end.
Favourite venue: Derbys. Derwent at Borrowash – 'it used to be solid!'
Most enjoyable match: winning the 1995 Winter League Final with 35lb of chub and pommies, sadly tempered by the team finishing second.
Most respected angler: Wayne Swinscoe.
Influences: Wayne Swinscoe and Paul Goulding.
Waggler choice: depends on venue but generally a straight peacock.
Other hobbies: keeping fit and walking.

I consider myself fortunate to have been active on the match circuit during what must be considered the golden age of river match fishing: the 1980s. During this time attendances on the Trent exceeded 300 for the big summer matches and during the winter there would be two or three open matches every Saturday where attendances were 100-plus in each match. Winter leagues would have 200 anglers. Seems incredible now looking back as most of today's matches are tiny in comparison.

The big Fenland rivers, Nene, Welland and Witham also hosted huge matches, 400 or 500-peggers were not unusual, and the Thames Championship filled 1,100-plus pegs. There was also a thriving match circuit in the West Midlands on the Severn and Warwickshire Avon. Living in Chesterfield and later Nottingham, my main stamping ground was the Trent and Witham, with odd forays elsewhere. I did like the Warwickshire Avon in particular.

It was also around this time that the trend to fish further out took hold. I remember when first venturing onto the open match circuit that stick float and caster was the dominant method, often fished right under the rod end. Then gradually floats fixed bottom end only began to become dominant and maggot became top bait, and, of course, the feeder revolution also happened. The reasons for these trends have often been debated, but personally I think water clarity and fishing pressure were probably the main reasons why the fish started to shoal further out.

Luckily, I was fairly quick in joining the trend. I think the turning point was when I watched one of the winter opens at Burton Joyce, in the late 70s I believe, which at that time was quite literally a 'who's who' of running water match fishing talent. At this time all the talk in the angling press and on the bank was of stick float and caster, with such brilliant exponents of the art as Pete Warren. But that day the performance that struck me was Dave Thomas who was just starting a phenomenal run of results. He was fishing much further out than most with a waggler and, feeding heavily with maggots, dominated the area he was in and I think was third in the match with 15lb of roach.

The next day I won our club match on the tidal Trent with 13lb of roach on maggot fished well out. But that was on a stick float because the conditions were perfect for it with a slight back wind. This brings me nicely onto why the waggler float began to be the float of choice: weather conditions, namely the prevailing downstream wind on the usual venues, making distance fishing with anything other than a float attached at the bottom only well nigh impossible.

During my time in open match fishing, I have been lucky enough to compete against and rub shoulders with some of the great running water match anglers. In the early days I spent much time on the Witham and other Eastern rivers. In winter the main species to fish for was roach and because the rivers were controlled by sluices the flow would vary from quite strong to just creeping through, making both top and bottom float and wagglers necessary as the fish moved around the peg with the flow.

During this time Jim Baxter was one of the men to beat on the waggler. As I remember we used floats of around 3AAA size and fished a few number 8s down the line. I can remember seeing one of Jim's rigs and saw a mini bulk of 8s about a third of the way up from the hook. I adopted this style and found it very effective. The tactic at the time was to cast all around the area where the loose feed was landing, getting the bites instantly. The mini bulk seemed to get the bait down quickly to where the roach were hanging, particularly when you cast upstream of the baited area. Jim was also one of the men to beat on the Nene with roach and this tactic was most productive on there too.

I was chasing roach on these venues, of course, while anglers fishing the tip for bream would often win the match. However, after countless hours sitting watching a motionless tip, I realized that I was far more suited to a busy style of fishing, and the odds on putting a money-winning net of fish together were much better. This brings me on to a theme that has run through my match fishing, I have never been particularly flush with money and my fishing has at times had to at least pay for itself.

I've never turned my nose up at a section win or minor placing, I am always pleased with any brown envelope that comes my way. However, I do know I've probably chucked scores of winning opportunities away over the years by fishing a float and not the tip, yet I have enjoyed playing the percentages game. I know from talking to other match anglers, and from what I read it's not necessarily a common view, but I would sooner enjoy my five hours fishing with the chance of winning some money, than fish a method that is less active just for the kudos of winning the match. In one winter series for example, I came second four times with numerous other placings and section wins. Some might regard this as unlucky but my view was exactly the opposite, and I would have taken this over maybe two outright wins and numerous DNWs (did not weigh's).

Then came Deany (John Dean). He was a true legend. He took 'wag and mag' to new levels. He was also the master of every method he adopted. John was a quiet, unassuming bloke who just simply bagged up. I remember watching him on Welbeck Lakes winning with 20lb-odd of roach on waggler and caster in front of a large gallery who, like me, had packed up. The thought that struck me that day, and unfortunately I still cannot emulate it as much as I try, was his unhurried, calm approach.

He was catching quality roach and they were taking an age to take the bait properly and he waited several seconds, letting the bite develop before striking. I can remember him casting out, lighting a fag up, taking a drag or two as the float dipped and lifted, then making a nice smooth strike, steady wind, and 12-14oz of silver would hit the net. No rush, no hurried strike and bumped fish, truly the master. Even now when I'm having a bad day - iffy bites, cagey fish etc, when I mis-time my strike and miss or bump the fish, I have to give myself a talking to and think back to that day at Welbeck. With the number of roach in the Trent now it's a good job Deany is not entering the matches or I'm sure he would make me feel as though I don't really have a clue.

Wayne Swinscoe was another big influence on my fishing and outlook. I lived on the same street as Wayne in Nottingham, and we travelled to many matches together as well as socialising, talking fishing. The social circle also included other Trentmen greats such as Roy Toulson and Pete Palmer, I ought to be brilliant really didn't I?

Wayne could turn his hand to anything. As well as the Trent he had an amazing record of catching Fenland bream on waggler, feeding balls of groundbait.

Wayne moved on from Trentmen just as I joined them in the mid-1980s. What a mega gathering of river talent Trentmen were, even after Wayne, Frank Barlow and Don Slaymaker famously left to join the first ever 'super team', financed by Shakespeare. Ted Stokes was our captain, again a brilliant waggler angler and again someone who kept calm and kept it all in perspective. Long before I knew him I watched him catching roach on the waggler at Caythorpe. Fishing beyond those around him, his performance stood out immediately as I walked up the bank. I think it was the Trent Championship and we were on a recce trip for a second division National when I was with Chesterfield. I think he won the zone that day and I can remember his calm, effortless style - a class act.

Terry with a winning waggler catch from the upper Trent at Shardlow.

Ted had the ability to spot up-and-coming anglers and recruit them to replace those who were tempted away by lucrative sponsorship deals. I was lucky enough to be in two of the National winning teams on the Trent in 1987 and 1992. At the draw for the 1992 match I was stood with Pete Lee and some of the other Oundle lads, when our peg number came over the tannoy, and it sounded poor - peg 15, I believe, and I said we were going to struggle to win off it. Oundle had come second in the 1987 National off the end peg, and one of them said to me that they would have won that day if the Notts Fed team had been made up of the anglers about to fish the 1992 match. He clearly didn't know about Ted's skills as a team builder. We went on to win the 1992 National emphatically.

One of the anglers who fished that day in '92 was the enigmatic Jan Porter. Jan had left to join the great Essex County team who at that time were not in the Division 1 National, and I did oppose him fishing with us on the Trent National because of this. But Ted managed to smooth things over to pave the way for Jan to fish. Jan had actually been responsible for my joining Trentmen (I had been approached by several teams but was quite happy in my comfort zone, fishing with my mates in the Chesterfield team), persuading me to up the ante and for that I am eternally grateful.

As well as being the consummate showman, Jan was an immense angling talent. I got on really well with him and he's another one that I'm sure would put the waggler on flowing water right up there as a favourite method. I can remember Jan setting a bit of a trend christened the 'rod end waggler' when he had a string of good catches fishing small waggler floats close in on the Trent to beat the adverse wind conditions. At the time the rest of us were often struggling to make stick floats work. Another lesson learnt for yours truly.

On to the present day [2013] I can't believe how the Trent match fishing scene has revived recently. I now have the choice of fishing Wednesday Newark matches, on Newark Dyke or the main river, Thursday Scunthorpe matches on the tidal Trent at South Clifton, and frequent weekend matches on the tidal Trent, and Newark matches such as The Advertiser which regularly attracts over 100 anglers. On top of this there is a three-day tidal Trent festival, a three-day Trent festival at Burton-on-Trent, the River Fest matches, and every time I pick an angling paper up there is something about a river festival somewhere. Great times. There is also a thriving Yorkshire scene on the Rivers Calder and Ouse.

The Newark matches are run by the evergreen Colin Walton who still catches loads of fish. There are plenty of barbel and bream pegs on the Newark waters but there are also loads of roach to be caught and they love waggler and maggot. It is a very competitive circuit, the brilliant Tony Marshall can be unbeatable on a pole and hemp approach, or if there's extra water on it's got to be a feeder rig to win anything. But I have won matches and framed regularly over the last three years or so, with roach nets to 18lb on running line maggot methods, with the waggler seeming to outscore pole and hemp this season, largely, I think, due to a small roach explosion.

Roly Moses, another Trent legend, knows the tidal river like the back of his hand and can read the tide changes like a book. He is one of the most successful waggler anglers out there so, if you're thinking of going, be warned. So far this year I am lying in the frame places in the league and most of my results have been on the waggler. I have caught some perch nets including fish to 2lb on the waggler when these fish have shunned a pole and worm approach.

Still on the tidal there is a crop of younger anglers from the Lincoln area who are very talented, in particular Alan Henry, who is not only a brilliant angler he also has an equal talent for match organizing and has really got the match scene going down there. Alan pipped me by a point this year in the tidal Trent three-day festival. I did turn a few heads by fishing an 80 per cent float approach, taking advantage of the small fish explosion and the absence of the usual large numbers of feeder-caught skimmers. Again it's a waggler approach because of the depth close in on a lot of pegs, and the regular horrendous wind.

I have also discovered the Burton-on-Trent matches recently, an excellent circuit run by the amiable Tony Vandome and his Burton club colleagues. To me this is river roach fishing par excellence; there are few other species to target and the frame is tight. The clear water and shallow nature of much of this venue again leads to the success of the waggler method. The winner of the three-day festival each year will generally have caught a fair few fish on the waggler. I have framed in the festival several times and caught loads of fish on waggler. This year I qualified for the River Fest final at Burton with 21lb of mainly roach and dace, the bulk of which came to the waggler.

The versatile float – by Terry Moroz

I have been match fishing at various levels for at least 40 years and during that time I have seen a multitude of methods which have had periods of domination on a certain venue or species of fish. One method that I have found has stood the test of time is the waggler float, attached to the line at the bottom end only and fished primarily on a rod and reel set-up.

It used to be the case that to be a successful match angler, you had to master a number of disciplines on running line and pole, whip etc. But now on some of the circuits, dominated by commercial venues, there are some very successful anglers who put their faith in just one or two methods.

My match angling background was based mainly on natural venues, and where most people would be fishing a different venue every week, and even if it was a particular river series that they chose to fish, nature would often conspire to alter the conditions from one match to another. Versatility became doubly important if you were competing in a team, and some fish in your peg that you would ignore in individual events suddenly needed to be targeted. Individual leagues would also lead to this situation arising.

My own personal approach to match fishing often involves fishing more than one method during a match to take advantage of different areas of the peg and the different species present, to build a weight.

The reason I think the waggler method is such a great fish catcher is that it is extremely versatile. It is supreme in the way that it can be used to search a swim and overcome adverse wind conditions. Not only is it easily cast varying distances from the bank but it can be shotted, or adjusted to search the water column to find the depth the fish are feeding at. Finally, the boundaries of the peg can be explored by long trotting or distance casting.

Wagglers can be used in sizes carrying a shot capacity of just two or three BB shot, or 1.2 grammes right up to 10 or more grammes, and from three or four inches long to as long as you have a float tube to fit it in. I have won matches flicking the smallest size across canals in windy conditions that have defeated a pole, and casting 40 yards with the larger sizes to catch bream on lakes whose preference for midwater feeding has made feeder/ledger methods difficult. In fact I have won prizes with most species and on any type of venue that you could think of using waggler methods.

An observation I would also like to make is that I have found myself reaching for the waggler set-up more and more often during the last 10 years or so. This is because as a generalisation I have found that the fish I am after seem to shoal ever further from the bank, and also seem to move around the swim, refusing to feed confidently in the same spot for long periods of time. I have my own theories about this. Natural flowing venues have got clearer and even after floods the colour disappears quickly; arguably there are less fish to be caught in these venues as well. There is also an increase in predators, not only the dreaded cormorants, but also more grebes and herons than ever, and I'm lucky to get away without the attentions of pike during a match on any natural venue I fish. On commercial waters there is the factor of constant fishing pressure. All this affects the fishes' confidence leading to them backing away from bankside disturbance and reacting to their shoal mates being caught during a match by shying away from the commotion caused.

To summarise I would say: Gone are the days when a rigid feeding regime would eventually dictate to the fish where they'd shoal in the peg and all that was then required to make the most of the peg was a steady rhythm. Now the fish dictate far more how and where they can be caught.

So much has been written about shotting waggler-type floats that I do not propose to go into this, only to say that if you concentrate three quarters or more of the total shotting capacity of the float in the locking shot then the rig will be tangle free.

I currently fish five types of venue where I use a waggler. 1/ Medium pace flowing water with depths from 4 to 10 feet, typical of the middle or tidal Trent. 2/ Sluggish water with depths of 13 to 17 feet, such as is found on the navigable parts of the River Don. 3/ Pacey, running water of just 2 to 3 1/2 feet deep such as the upper Trent or River Calder. 4/ Commercial waters of 3 to 8 feet deep in autumn, winter and early spring where the target fish are predominantly silvers. 5/ Wide canals or drains of 15 to 18 metres across, eg. Stainforth and Keadby Canal.

The rod carrying cases available these days enable me to have ready-made-up rods and rigs for a particular venue. This really suits me as I am not one to spend hours in prep at home. What I aim to have set up for a particular venue is a float with enough shot carrying capacity to provide enough weight in the locking shot to easily reach the fish whatever the range.

I also aim to have plenty of extra dropper shots - 8s, 10s etc. - incorporated in the rig which gives me the versatility to tackle various depths and flows. The extra shot adjacent to the locking shot can then be spread down the line if the situation requires it.

Nearly all my rigs incorporate small swivels to prevent line spin on the hooklength; I don't tie this at the end of the main line I have found it works better if placed somewhere on the main line, and tend to put them about 18" above the hooklength.

All my wagglers are set up on quick-change adaptor, the type using silicone sleeving over a swivel or eyelet. I put a thin piece of silicone sleeving on the reel line before squeezing the heavy locking shot - SSGs, AAAs and BBs on. This prevents damage to the line and also allows the shot to be moved easily when making adjustments to depth whilst fishing.

All my wagglers are peacock quills, the only exception being those for canals/drains which are balsa, as the shot carrying capacity to length ratio is greater with this material making them ideal for the shallow water. Any bodies are balsa or polystyrene. One difference these days is that good quality floats can be bought over the shop counter whereas at one time I made all my own wagglers. All the float tips are matt orange in colour, if any other colour is required for visibility I put a piece of the appropriate colour silicone sleeving on the tip and just nip off one of the droppers to compensate for the little bit of extra weight if necessary.

As you can see from the above, my philosophy is to use rigs that are easily adjusted whilst fishing, to cope with changing situations, the thinking being to chase the shoals around, keeping fish dropping into the keepnet.

Rods and reels, lines and hooks are all personal choices really. My reels are any reliable fixed spool, and I use spliced tip rods of 13 to 15ft length as most of the fish I catch these days are less than 1lb except for still-water ide and skimmers which aren't hard fighters anyway. I'm happy to take my chances with the odd rogue chub or big perch that turn up.

I use 2lb Maxima main line and always carry cans of line floatant and sinker for varying conditions. I also carry a tub of Vaseline as I have found a heavily greased first yard or two of line behind the float aids presentation and positive striking, especially in heavier flowing water. I use Silstar Match Team line for hooklengths in 0.08mm or 0.10mm. Both Maxima and Silstar line are robust with good stretch qualities, and this I like because often when waggler fishing a hefty, sweeping strike is required due to fishing at distance, or line bow.

Often on flowing water in an adverse wind or heavy flow, the fish isn't felt on the strike and I only know there's one on after a couple of reel turns. Hooks tend to be Drennan Team England, Kamasan B511s or Preston PR333s in sizes 22, 20 and 18, depending on how well the fish are feeding.

I also always carry a non-spliced, beefier rod in the holdall and spare spools loaded with 3 and 4lb maxima, just in case I find myself on a peg where bigger fish need to be targeted.

Medium Pace Flowing Water

For the medium pace work I will have two rigs set up both with straight peacock wagglers. Rig 1 is a 6AAA straight peacock just shy of 12" long (28cm to be exact) with a 5mm thick tip. I have got one of the rigs out and checked the shotting as I'm writing this. It's set up with two Swan shot and a BB locking the float in place, plus 18 number 8 shot and three number 10 shot. Since I have used this rig over the last five years I have been surprised at how successful it has been. I call it 'Big Bertha' because at one time I wouldn't have dreamt of using so much lead.

I can even remember the day I first tried it during a match at East Stoke on the Trent. The river is wide here and, with a strong downstream wind blowing, I was struggling with the conditions. I had caught the odd small roach well out on a waggler probably two-thirds the size. I knew there were feeding fish out there so put the heavier rig on, cast down the peg and straightened everything up where the bites had been coming. A run of 4-6oz roach followed which was too late to do any damage in that particular match, but a lesson was learned.

Since that day I have been surprised how often the float has been effective. I use it in depths from 4 to 13ft and vary the number of droppers down the line accordingly. In the deeper situations the droppers tend to be concentrated in the bottom third, or they are evenly spread in twos until the last four or five which are singles. I rarely use a bulk shot, but I saw an experiment in a magazine article recently where strung out and bulked rigs were compared on the pole in flowing water and the bulk was far more effective. It's food for thought and I am going to do some experimenting with bulk shotting on the waggler.

Rig 2 is a 5AAA version of the same float, 23 cm long and 3mm thick at the tip. This takes 10 no. 8 shot and two no. 10s as droppers, plus an SSG, an AAA and a no. 4 locking shot around the float.

Often all that's required to get another burst of fish is to put the rig down that I'm using and chuck the other one to the same spot. I tend to set the lighter rig shallower and wouldn't hesitate to fish it at less than half depth. What I would say is that these days it seems to be much harder to keep catching up in the water and after a few fish I have to go deeper again. I sometimes use this rig with just three no. 8s and two no. 10s down the line in depths of up to 10ft. This can bring a run of fish on the drop. But I don't really like to spend too long fishing this light as it's not positive enough for me and I think a lot of bites go unseen.

Another thing that often happens when I swap rigs, is the stamp of fish or species that I'm catching changes with the different presentation, but it's hard to determine exactly why.

Deep Sluggish Water

Deep, sluggish water is often best tackled with a large 'topper' (named after the float's inventor: Mervyn 'Topper' Haskins), or Bolognese-type float, fished top and bottom with a long rod. However, when the fish are shoaling well out into the river or the wind is too strong to do this effectively, the waggler comes back into play.

For this style I modify my normal set-up by using a sliding float. One thing I learnt the hard way, was to use heavier main line than normal for this style and I now use 3lb Maxima. Lighter lines lead to far more tangles. I use two sliding stop knots and these would previously often kink the lighter main line when making depth adjustments.

The Rising Antenna

I usually use bodied wagglers as sliders to enable the shot-carrying capacity to cope with depths up to 18ft and to have some loading to be built into the base of the float. I have found that a loading of the equivalent of one quarter of the total shot carrying capacity of the float is about the right proportion. The loading helps the float to stay with the bulk shot on the cast; if the float slides up the line whilst flying through the air it will cause tangles.

Drop shots also need to be heavier than on my other rigs, and number 8 shot are the lightest I will use and often these are in pairs. The slider is a delight to use in deep water, coping with distance casts easily and offering little resistance to the strike, a massive bonus in water over 13ft deep.

Faster Flowing Water

The wagglers that I use for fast, shallow water need to be stumpy, that is, short but relatively thick to provide shot-carrying capacity and, more importantly, buoyancy. By their very nature the type of swim I am talking about will have weed patches and a gravelly bottom. There will be uneven pace in parts of the swim with the odd boil or swirl.

I did experiment at one time with hollow plastic floats for this style of fishing and although I liked their buoyancy, their durability wasn't good - they were brittle and would split easily. So I reverted to good old peacock. My favoured starting float would be a straight peacock of 7cm long and 8mm thick carrying a total of 2SSG. I would lock this with an SSG shot and two AAA shot. I would then use no. 8 shot to shot the float down with two no. 10s nearest the hooklength.

In this type of water I work on the formula of two no. 8s per 9 inches of water and I often have more of a concentration of shot in the top third of line immediately below the float, preferring to let the last 18 inches trail along the bottom of the river bed with minimum lead on it to catch obstacles. The perfect way to catch is to have evenly spread shot and just trip bottom but this does not always work or at least not for all the session.

Commercial Silvers

For this style of fishing I use wagglers with inserts. There is no flow to push the float under when a fish takes it, and species such as ide and skimmers, my main targets, can be extremely shy biters, so a sensitive tip becomes more important.

My typical rig is a peacock waggler 17cm long incorporating a 4cm long peacock insert 2mm thick. This is locked with an SSG, an AAA and a BB, and droppers are four no. 10 shot and four no. 11s. I often fish this with just two of the 11s down the line. Ide in particular will be fooled by this. But with the number of shot incorporated in the rig it is very versatile for chasing the fish, both around the peg and up and down in the water column. If the wind was in any way adverse I wouldn't hesitate to use a heavier version of the same float pattern, carrying up to two and a half SSG (or 4g).

The key is to have enough weight to cast accurately. Often on this type of water you need to cast to islands or far bank cover and get the line under control. Line sink spray is also vital for this style. Another reason for trying to keep as tight a line as possible, is because twitching and tweaking the rig to move the bait is a great bite inducer and I rarely sit there waiting for a bite to come along. I am constantly casting and twitching the float instead.

Wide Canals/Drains

Unlike most anglers these days I always take a waggler rod with me on canals and drains. On the wider waters in particular, if the wind is fierce, a waggler will give me access to parts of the swim that the normal pole approach won't allow.

I have used it to search far bank weed beds and the sides of far bank boats or tins. Some years back a popular method on the Grand Union canal was fishing squatts on a scaled-down waggler rig and I have done this occasionally on other squatt venues. Nowadays I use it on venues where there is a good head of stamp fish, with maggot, pinkie or caster hookbaits. Chub in particular are suckers for the method.

The method requires pin-point accurate casting to avoid getting caught up on far bank snags, and in order to get tight to these snags I tend to use a side cast to make the line below the float land parallel to the far bank. The same casting motion is used to cast top and bottom floats.

The float has to be compact with a good weight-carrying capacity to size. The pattern I use is based on the old squatt floats which

I bought in the early 90s. These were straight balsa wagglers which tapered sharply to a very fine tip. I have cut the tips off where the diameter of the balsa is only 2 to 3mm. This makes them more compact and buoyant. A typical rig incorporates a 13cm long balsa float locked with 2AAA shot with four no. 10 droppers built onto it.

As you can see, a range of waggler floats keep me catching fish through a multitude of situations, and the rigs discussed above are by no means the only ones that I use. I went into my tackle room and examined some of my set-ups to get the dimensions to write this chapter. Like many other anglers I'm sure, I have several float tubes full of wagglers not set up on rigs and no doubt some of these floats will never see the light of day.

What I would say to round off, is don't be a slave to the pole and feeder just because other anglers always catch well on these methods. The waggler float will put you in contact with fish that they won't. Don't just follow trends in other words. I have caught loads of fish by keeping the faith.

Top Tip

Don't struggle on regardless when bites are not coming in a particular swim and you have given it a fair chance. And if you can't put the bait where the fish are, try a different method. Less than perfect presentation in the right area of the swim is better than perfection where there are no feeding fish.

The author on Terry Moroz:

I first met Terry and his mate, John Haywood, on mid-70s Witham matches, two promising youngsters at the time from Chesterfield. We were all getting to grips with waggler fishing and trying to beat the more senior men, including good bream anglers who knew how to plunder a bream shoal on both swing-tip and float. Back then skimmers were often the target with groundbait and squatt feed and gozzers on the hook. Terry was as fiercely competitive as anyone but I think he disguised it with a smile and we managed to enjoy some good banter at the time. Terry then moved to Nottingham and switched more to Trent matches in the 80s. This paid off when the mighty Trentmen team signed him up. Terry once paid me a nice compliment when he walked over the floodbank one day at a Long Higgin match on route to his peg. I was the peg downstream of John Allerton and we were below the long bend towards the top end of Parkside – a good draw. Terry said 'a clash of the titans' and it made me smile. I probably tried harder than normal having been put on the spot, and I ended up winning the match with over 20lb, pushing John into second. The difference between us was that I found four chub to go with the roach but he didn't get one. A word of encouragement at the right time counts for a lot, so thanks mate. In later years we travelled to the River Don winter matches together. The river was often flooded or out of sorts, but win or lose we could raise a smile at the finish.

Chapter 14
Keith Hobson – The Attacker

When it comes to success and staying power, Keith Hobson and John Allerton – the latter a former member of Barnsley Blacks, the former who is still in the squad - have a touch of the 'Gary Player' longevity about them. They have both been winning matches for nigh on 50 years without any thought of slowing down or hanging up their rods for good; indeed the thought would horrify them. When the Trent declined before the turn of the century John chose to reinvent himself on commercial lakes and carp, while Keith has largely stayed faithful to flowing water and silver fish. Both anglers remain highly successful, but whatever the species or method, whether the water flows or not, they have each in their own way shown great versatility, able to switch from one method and species to another when it suits them.

One of Barnsley Blacks' longest-serving members and finest float anglers, Keith Hobson, 66, has always been a great fan of double maggot on the hook, and when the River Trent was at its peak he favoured dragging the bait along the Trent bed at all times. Although he had no exclusivity on fishing over-depth to slow the bait down (many other river anglers have won matches doing so) few I know have done it with such conviction and consistency.

Noted for being laid-back, Keith liked a pint or two in his younger days, and the joke within the Blacks team was he fished best when he'd had two paracetamol for breakfast to mend his headache.

He developed his rather individual style on the Trent where, in the chub explosion of the 1970s-80s, an attacking feeding regime with bronze maggot often paid off. The popular phrase at the time was: 'give 'em a gallon', which might have been an exaggeration, but certain anglers including Keith would blast it with anything from 4 to 6 pints or more of bronze maggots (plus a few reds as a change bait) over five hours and the fish usually obliged. It led Keith to multiple wins in the star-studded Burton Joyce winter matches and a host of other classy matches elsewhere.

His target species were the quality chub or roach that might want a good mouthful of bait presented slower than the speed of the current. Early in a match he would try double maggot on the hook and, if any bonus fish responded, he would always stick with it. It gave him an edge when others were fishing single maggot for smaller fish, but Keith could also adapt to harder days when a low winning weight was expected. He did not always fish maggot, however. On the tidal Trent at Dunham Bridge for example, he's preferred caster on the hook, and he has also fished caster on the Warwickshire Avon many times. But only very rarely has he ever bothered with hemp.

"I'd usually start on single maggot and then switch to double. Chub reckon to be greedy and prefer the double, but I once caught all roach on double and every chub on single in the same match which proves we know nothing about fish. This was a 16lb catch from what we call the coral at the bottom of the Burton Joyce road stretch," said Keith.

A long list of prestigious wins include the John Smiths and Wychavon Championships, both on the Warwickshire Avon at Evesham, the Avon Championship with 22lb of chub on waggler, two Soar Championship titles in consecutive years, and the Stratford Christmas match with 54lb of chub taken on both stick and waggler.

On route to his first Soar title in 1993 he caught 10 small chub in 10 casts and ended up feeding six pints of bronze maggot for a 16lb total. One spectator asked afterwards: *"Why did you feed six pints of maggots?"* (implying it was a lot) to which Keith retorted: *"Because that's all I had with me."* The following year he won the match with a net of bream.

Keith has also fished in four home international matches, including on Northern Ireland's River Bann, at Roath Park Lake, Cardiff, and Kilburnie Loch, Scotland, and been on the winning England side every time.

In a four-week purple patch at Burton Joyce he won a big open with 19lb, then followed up with another 19lb to win his section at Gunthorpe in the Trent National. Then he won both the Soar and Avon Championships over the next fortnight. That's as good as it gets.

It's fair to say that Keith for a long time was overshadowed by the achievements of his two Barnsley colleagues - England International Denis White and his pairs partner and one-time protégé, 1989 World Champion, Tom Pickering. Both were more versatile perhaps, but for his waggler and other float skills alone, Keith arguably had the beating of them both, and some might even say that as a river man his lasting success has no equal in Yorkshire.

It's curious how you draw next to some anglers on a regular basis but never draw anywhere near others. Certain paths never seem to cross even though the laws of chance say they should when the same group of people are fishing the same waters week after week.

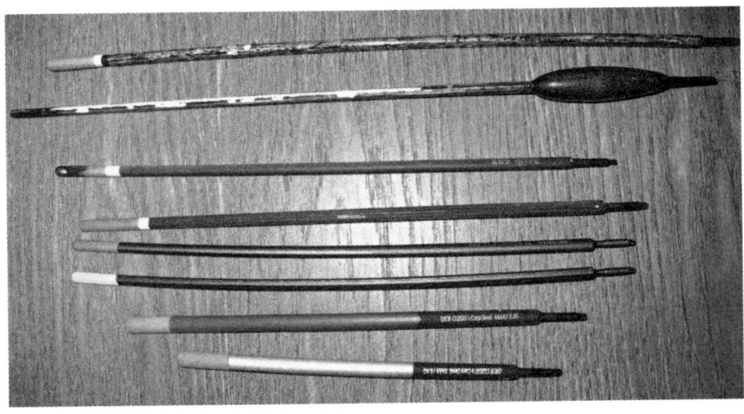

Keith's floats - short and stubby for R. Calder, longer for R. Ouse including a big slider.

I rarely drew next to Denis White or John Illingworth for example, yet Keith and I drew beside each other a good few times. I'm proud to say that we finished up with honours about even from those clashes on different waters because Keith at his best was, and by all accounts still is, a nightmare to beat.

I tried to learn more particulars about Keith's waggler method after meeting up at The Hind pub, Rotherham:

JB. Keith, tell me a bit about the waggler you used on the Trent at Burton Joyce when the Golden Mile lived up to its name and some great matches were staged?

KH. It was a straight peacock about 9" long, home-made and with a small balsa body at the base. The thinner end of the quill was at the tip and about 4mm diameter. It had a base peg of 3mm cane which inserted into a home-made float adaptor. This was simply a piece of electrical earth wire cover with a hole burnt through it with a hot needle. I also added a few turns of lead wire at the base and the float took 3AAA shot locking plus equivalent to four no. 6 shot down the line. The float was also slightly bent but this did not affect its performance.

JB. And the tip colour was usually black?

KH. Yes, but when fishing into shadows I'd add a short piece of red rubber to the tip, or later a hollowed out out piece of peacock quill, painted red which was better.

JB. How did you shot the float down the line?

KH. I placed a bulk of three no. 6 shot just below half-depth and two pairs of no. 10 shot below that as droppers. The bulk would always be clear of the bottom while the no. 10s dragged on the bottom. This always worked best for me. (see diagram on p342)

JB. I thought you said to me once that Nottingham's Roy Toulson, who also liked to fish over-depth, influenced your style, is that right?

KH. Not really, but I had a lot of respect for him. I drew next to Roy in the mid 70s in the Burton Joyce Ferry Field, and it was one of the first times I dragged on. I finished second or third in the match with 12lb-odd which was the first time I'd framed on the waggler. I'd be about 25 at the time so it was a milestone reached.

JB. Who became your main rivals at Burton Joyce?

KH. Dave Thomas, John Dean, John Allerton, Frank Barlow and Ted Stokes, to name a few. But many anglers could win from a good peg.

JB. How much float did you leave up top when you dragged on?

KH. About an inch usually seemed right, subject to the amount of line being dragged on.

JB. I know you were one of the first to scale down to a 24 hook on the Trent, what hook was it and what trace line did you use as a rule?

KH. I used a Mustad 90340 in a 24. I just changed down from a 22 one day and it made all the difference. I started getting lots more bites and won the match, and I never looked back from that day. Hooklength was 1.1lb Bayer in summer dropping down to 12oz in winter. As time went by I also started using the Kamasan B520 whisker barb. I liked Racine Tortue Nacrita line (the brown version) on the reel, 2lb for stick float, 2 1/2lb for waggler.

JB. Who taught you the ropes; did you get help from a mentor?

KH. Well not as such, I travelled with Keith Ashmore for a long time and we swapped ideas before and after every match. This helped us both I'm sure. Keith became a regular Barnsley Black of course, and he still fishes and still enjoys his sport.

JB. So how much line would you drag on the bottom in an average Trent swim?

KH. Well I'd start by plumbing the depth and then pull the float up at least a yard and set it there. I would never drag the bulk shot and this would usually be positioned around a foot off the bottom. Two no. 10s would be placed together around 18″-20″ from the hook then another pair of 10s around 18″ above that in an average 8′-9′ deep swim.

JB. What was your top weight on this deadly method?

Hobbo, all-out attack is his motto.

KH. It was 26lb of roach from the Mangold Field, Shelford.

JB. Moving up to present day, how has your waggler fishing changed on the Yorkshire rivers?

KH. I live about 15 miles from the Calder and so like to fish there, and on the Yorkshire Ouse. I use a straight fat peacock – 4AAA but little over 6″ long on the Calder which is mostly shallow water though can run fast in places. I find tripping the bottom works best or dragging no more than 12″ of line on the floor. What might surprise you is I now use a 0.16mm reel line Maver Genesis, with non-toxic shot locking the float. In most sections I fish three or four no. 8 shot down the line in the lower half of the rig.

JB. What would you say is your greatest asset?

KH. Confidence. I'd say it is 70% of the winning formula.
JB. Have you time for any other hobbies?

KH. I like to watch football and cricket of course, as a proud Yorkshireman. I won gold medals for football as a schoolboy, but that's when I was fit and could run!

JB. So as far as fishing goes then, we do live in God's own county?

KH. Absolutely. Yorkshire must have the best river scene in the country – both the Ouse and Calder produce fish consistently well and the match turn-outs are also above average.

Chapter 15
John Allerton - The All-rounder

For longevity at the top of angling few anglers anywhere can match John Allerton, of Selby. He has been winning matches for 50 years on all kinds of venues and, now 67, still has the drive and commitment to keep on doing so. It says much for his angling calibre that he has been sponsored by leading tackle company Tri-Cast for 20 years.

A true all-rounder, he established himself as a float wizard on running water with both stick and waggler, but was adaptable enough to win back-to-back Trent Championships on the feeder in 1993 and '94 – the only angler ever to achieve this feat. These days he's turned his hand to winning at commercials like Lindholme, where long pole is often his main weapon. And he's just put his name to a new range of pellet wagglers.

Arguably the best angler never to have fished for England, John progressed to become one of the UK's most consistent matchmen in the last quarter of the 20th century. He learnt his craft on the Yorkshire Ouse and Selby Canal, going on to discover the Trent, where he soon found the winning touch by topping a Castleford Open aged 19.

Travelling with Roy Duckett from Hull and Stan Brown from Goole (and learning a lot from Stan in particular), John's Trent apprenticeship was soon complete and he proceeded to win scores of matches on the river and conquered many other rivers and canals besides. BUT more recently, after crossing the river/commercials divide into the carp world of the new millennium, he is still winning with nets of carp topping 100lb. The venues where John has enjoyed his best success include: River Aire, the Trent – upper, middle and tidal reaches – R. Calder, R.Witham, Broomfleet Canal, Humberside Lakes, Selby Canal, Woodlands at Thirsk, Sessay Lakes, and Lindholme Fishery where he has won an incredible 175 times!

The many hundreds of rigs John has used over his career would fill a book on their own, but the one I'd like to concentrate on is from 1987 and a match on the Witham when I caught less than 2lb and he came second with 9lb of roach. This Eastern Region Winter League round at Kirkstead stands out for me because I had to report the result in my correspondence work for 'Angler's Mail' magazine. It left an entry in my diary of how John fished that was far more interesting than my own. From all my tackle changes on the day, it was obvious I'd not made the gap from the hook to the tell-tale shot anything like wide enough; not getting that natural-looking fall of the maggot that the fish demanded.

Interviewing John afterwards, all I knew in advance was that he had caught nearly double figures of roach on a waggler, while the majority of anglers had struggled for half that amount or less.

John began by explaining how he had tripped the bottom with his float set 9' deep, but the next snippet of information raised my eyebrows: how lightly he had shotted the bottom half of his rig. He had placed only two no. 12 shot in the bottom yard of line, then a no. 8, then a three no. 6 shot bulk two feet above that (ie. 5 feet total) just above mid-depth. (see diagram on p340). This was both surprising and revealing as I considered I usually fished my tell-tale shot a good distance from the hook, but a yard to an 8 with only two micro shot below, John's gap was 'miles' wider.

With the river pulling and a downstream wind not helping, he was casting downstream, then pulling the float back to keep as straight a line as possible, before trotting the bottom half of the swim only.

The Witham pegging was always fairly close compared to other major match rivers, which limited trotting distance. But despite this, John decided it was better to fish the last five yards of the peg in full float control than have a downstream bow develop in his line that would kill presentation.

John with a lovely net of big dace from Evesham on the Warwickshire Avon, gaining him second individual in a round of the McPherson's UK Championship.

Another interesting factor was his use of 1.7lb Bayer on his reel spool. This is a thinner reel line than most would use on a river, but was carefully considered as a way of minimizing the wind's impact in that downstream direction.

A summary of my Witham results for the season after it ended in March '88 briefly said: 'Thirteen times in the money but failed a few times – river very patchy all winter – too much rain'. But as far as this match went, the river improved as the day wore on which both ties in with John's feed adjustment in the second half, when he caught best, and suggests I put my shots too near the hook. The slow drop of John's hook-bait had seemed to make all the difference for, apart from those two micros in the first yard of line up from the hook, I'd not heard of such a light approach 'downstairs' other than the exceptional 5' of drop which helped Stockport's Dick Ward once win a Boston Open at Kirkstead (see Masterclass chapter 8). It left me with some soul-searching to do about whether I'd got complacent with my own shotting patterns.

In the feed department the match had been one of two halves for John. He went on to tell of how he'd fed only a pint of maggots, unlike many visiting Trentmen to the Witham who fed far heavier: *"I fed a quarter pint of maggots in the first half of the match for 3lb of small fish, at a rate of 4-5 maggots per cast, then more than doubled this in the second half with three-quarters of a pint of bait, feeding approximately 6-8 maggots twice per cast. And this brought me the better quality roach that made up two-thirds of my total."*

John says he can be both a light and heavy feeder with maggots or casters depending on the water and weather conditions. At the upper end of the scale he won one match with a good catch of roach from the tidal Trent at Girton. With the fish obviously hungry he fed three pints of maggots and two more of hemp that day. But on harder days he'll drop the hemp and cut right back on the maggot feed to only around a pint of bait total.

Regarding hemp feed, which some anglers like to pile in while others are reluctant to feed it at all, John will use it only when he thinks it necessary, at certain times in the season and depending on his estimated target weight. If he thought the river water was warm and a big catch was required to win he'd feed hemp, but rarely bothered with it in winter. "I have fed hemp many times on the Trent but for me it has been an attacking bait when looking for a big weight."

John was the first angler to describe to me the difference between fishing 'on the drop' and 'on the lift' and this is what he said:

"On the drop is what it suggests, casting to the target area – and for me that can be halfway down the peg on a river, dropping through the depth to where the fish are with as light a shotting as possible. I try never to use one more shot than necessary and the crucial bit is the bottom two feet of line. Catching on the lift is about holding back slightly to slow the float down, ideally when the bait has just touched the bottom, approximately five seconds after casting, but it varies depending on the amount of shot down, and this can lift the bait from 2"-3" which can be enough to prompt a bite."

The general message for anglers here is to consider every shot they put on the line and how it might make the bait react. But there is another shot option above the float that can improve presentation, and one that is perhaps neglected, namely the back-shot. In his river days John liked to place a no. 6 three-foot behind the waggler for straightening the line to the float when trotting. This magic shot makes sinking the line that bit easier with the rod tip underwater, and helps to minimize any bow in the line created by the wind.

"I have used this tactic many times, notably when I won the Calder Championship with a low double figure weight. It was a rock hard, hot summer's day with bright sunshine. I used a 24 hook (Kamasan B510), a small 3 1/2BB waggler and 1.7lb reel line, adding the back shot above the float to only four no. 8s below it. It helped me to 10-11lb of roach, and Dave Thomas above me came second with 8lb-odd. Never underestimate what this shot can do."

The Trent went through a bait transition in the 1970s when after over a decade of playing second fiddle the maggot started to regain the upper hand over casters. At this time it was not always clear to anglers which the best bait for the day would be. John would hedge his bets by alternating with caster and maggot on a 24 hook early in the match. Only after testing the fishes' response for an hour would he decide which bait to continue with.

John says his favourite rivers are the Trent, Witham and Calder, all of which have been happy hunting grounds for him on the waggler. Could he name a 'most memorable' match or day's fishing from any of them in what we call the golden era?

"For five hours of pure enjoyment I'd have to go for a Daiwa qualifier for a final in Denmark on the tidal Trent. I was drawn well upstream of North Clifton and fished the stick float for 30lb of roach. They were fish in the 8oz class and they kept coming all through on a six no. 6 stick."

How does John view the modern commercial fisheries compared to traditional river matches he loved for so long?

"I fish the commercial matches because of my competitive nature. I still enjoy it and Lindholme in particular has been good to me, but it's not the same, a far cry from the thrill of fishing the rivers at their peak. We only got better at it gradually, and it was more of a thinking man's game. In the heyday of the 300 peg matches around half the pegs had winning potential. One big difference to today was that if 10lb won the match there might be 50 anglers not far behind with 6-7lb. This gave them hope that they could win if they persevered and it kept them going back for more."

Chapter 16
Dave Ashmore - The Crafty Feeder

Feeding the swim is a subtle thing. It is about finding a balance between using enough bait to attract and hold the fish, but not too much to fill them up so they will leave the 'restaurant'. Some anglers are able to get this balance right more often than others. During my years fishing the River Witham, Grimsby's Dave Ashmore was down in my book as one such angler, with a kind of sixth sense for getting the feeding level right.

Dave had other skills to match. He was as good at catching roach on hemp in summer, he could also sit it out patiently with a feeder for bream when drawn on them. But I believe it was his feeding that made him such a consistent float angler, especially on the colder days of winter when the roach in a torpid state might not feed well for more than a couple of hours.

Born in Sheffield in 1951, Dave moved to the east coast aged 5, before spending his working life in the shipping industry based on the River Humber. In his words he "accrued enough money" five years ago to retire at 60, and now has the freedom to fish more often.

Of all the matchmen I came up against on the Witham, Dave was probably the hardest to beat on winter roach.* I am a little biased as he denied me a hat-trick of Witham Super League victories with a perfect section point score over the best six matches**, shading me by two points in year three! Those are times when we have to put our hands together and applaud the other guy.
(* Roger Wakenshaw took over as the main man later.)
(**60 anglers fished the league in the 1984/85 season comprising four sections of 15 pegs, and the best six results from 10 matches counted. Dave totalled 90 points to my 88.)

Former Oundle team angler and top Witham local, Edgar Purnell, agrees with me that Dave was underrated despite his exemplary match record, probably partly down to his modest and unassuming nature.

Dave pushed me down into second on another occasion back in late December, 1982. I thought I'd fished well for 16lb 11oz of roach, but Dave scaled 1oz short of the magical 20lb mark to beat me easily. Early that same year he topped 255 anglers to win the Lincoln Cathedral Open with 5lb 3oz when a facing gale seriously reduced the distance he could catapult feed. Yet he somehow found

All round skills: Dave with a bulging net of bream.

enough fish feeding from a swim beyond mid-river where few maggots ever reached.

Some anglers might remember Dave best though for one lucky incident, notably the time he won one of the Witham's grimmest ever matches. Pike are the scourge of match anglers, clever at thieving our best fish of the day with a surprise attack from the depths as we bring it to shore. But on this match Dave profited from a pike and at the same time we could say he cured its toothache.

It was the first round of the 1981 Eastern Region Winter League fished by over 300 anglers in early November. Chesterfield's Dave Nicholson, at upstream end peg 1, had a case for thinking he might win the match with 2lb 3oz, as he won the 50-peg Pound Length section (the first section of the match below Kirkstead bridge and a good one to draw, even though it was given its name years before when it fished so badly that a pound of fish was all one could expect from there!). The match grapevine was telling of failures everywhere, but Dave Ashmore put a spanner in the works.

At peg 103 on Timberland Lane end, he managed to hook and land a good pike but on close inspection he hadn't hooked the fish at all, but the eye of a swivel in a lure that had been lost in the pike's jaws by another angler - a million to one shot! As a bonus the 9lb 4oz pike had no chance of cutting his line with his teeth to escape. Dave could only add one tiny fish to it for a total weight of 9lb 6oz but won the match by a street and the £180 top prize. "Don't clap", he told the crowd as he walked up to collect his winnings later.

Here's how Dave recalled the capture:

"As I remember it was a nice day and the river was in good condition. The problem was it stood still all day [had no flow] and, as I am sure many river regulars will remember, that was often a recipe for disaster. After an hour I caught a 'tommy ruffe' and, as far as I was aware, this was the only fish that had been caught in my area around Timberland signpost. As the team event was decided on total weight in those days, and I figured I was winning my section, I decided to try for a bream. I put on the smallest feeder in my box, a 1.1lb hooklength and a size 20 hook with two red maggots, and cast to the bottom of the far shelf. After 20 or so minutes the tip went round and I was attached to something heavy. I can't be sure but I reckon it took about 20 minutes before I netted a pike.

*"Removing the pike from the landing net I noticed a wire trace hanging from its mouth and remember thinking that I had landed it on a 1.1 lb hooklength when a pike angler had lost it on far heavier tackle. To my amazement I then found that I had hooked the eye of the swivel on the end of the trace. Don't know what the odds are but reckon I'd have had a better chance of getting all the lottery numbers up any day! The pike also won us the team event on it's own."** (*Grimsby weighed 14lb 10oz to Rotherham's 8-12 for second).

But let's come back to reality now, and consider this business of feeding the swim. Dave obviously enjoyed many good results by feeding discreetly, just enough bait to keep the fish happy and no more. Others around him sometimes piled the bait in, but did this cost them fish? Some good Trent anglers in particular, used to feeding heavily on that bigger and faster river, possibly fell into the trap of overfeeding the fickle Witham roach.

Dave has a record three Witham Super League titles to his credit but has no idea of all the dates. He also finished in the frame a time or two and one of his biggest disappointments was finishing second one year after being miles in front with one match to go. It was when the river had started to decline and the further you were from Kirkstead Bridge the poorer your chances. Dave drew the penultimate peg downstream and didn't have a bite. As it turned out any kind of fish would have won him the league but Pete Bagshaw won the match and overtook him.

One career highlight for Dave was hauling in his biggest Witham bream weight of 47lb+ in a Grimsby open at Kirkstead, but his best roach weight from the river was an ever better achievement - 33lb 5oz no less, in a small match at Langrick, caught on the waggler with hemp and tares bait. The deep Langrick section of the Witham, near Boston, was a particularly good one when on form, but this was still a remarkable catch. Dave enjoyed many other wins on the waggler on the Witham during a long match career, both from the time when matches could boast 400 entrants pegged out all the way from Kirstead to Tattershall, through to the tiny matches in comparison in the new millennium.

Since the Witham's decline as a big match venue, Dave now spends most summers fishing the River Trent and 'Stainy' Canal, switching to the Fossdyke Canal in winter with an odd trip to the Rivers Steeping and Ancholme. Dave does a fair bit of cycling to keep fit.

He also plays lots of golf and snooker (the latter to a high standard - top break a 96 and ex-pro Mike Hallett is a regular opponent!). A long-time member of Grimsby Vikings, these days Dave has left team fishing behind to fish freelance...

In the following interview Dave explains more about his waggler approach...

Dave with a bunch of wagglers and two stick floats (left).

JB. Tell us how you started on the Witham Dave?

DA. I began fishing the river in the early Seventies when caster was 'the' bait but this soon changed largely through the success of Dave Thomas and his Leeds colleagues; the caster was superseded by bronze maggot. From that point my bait for an average open match would be two pints of bronze maggots with a few reds among them and, maybe, a pint of casters as back-up. By the mid-Seventies I started to catch better and get the hang of it.

Most of the fishing was on the waggler. I made all my own from peacock quills and most included an insert at the tip. I mainly fished from one third across to the middle of the river, and would kick off with the float set 3 or 4 inches over-depth, although I would change depth dozens of times in most matches and would catch a lot of fish off the bottom and on the drop. I also loved to throw a stick float onto the waggler line and found the different presentation would often bring bites if it had gone quiet.

I probably fed less bait than most and a pint of maggots would last most matches. My theory was the fewer maggots there were in my swim then the easier it was for a fish to find mine with the hook in it. That said, there were occasions that a few pouchfuls would revive a dying swim, or could also be used to feed off bits. I would always start (and usually finish) on a 22 hook to 12oz hooklength and, in the good old days, when they were allowed, would use six no. 6 lead shot down the line in a 3-2-1 pattern in normal conditions. This obviously had to change when the lead ban came in and no. 8 shot had to be used because I found the lead-free substitute shot too hard.

I eventually managed to win the Super League three times in all. The one that sticks in my memory however, was when I won it with a match to spare allowing me to enter another open, also on the Witham, on the day of the last Super League round. I was fortunate enough to win the open as well and went home with over a grand in my pocket - a lot of money in those days. I have no idea how many matches I won back then, nor since for that matter, but like to think I have had my share. One thing's for sure I have enjoyed myself and I think that's what it is all about.

JB. Would you say the Witham and waggler method were well suited?

DA. The waggler was my preferred method but I have also enjoyed a fair deal of success on the stick float and in later years a 6-8 metre whip. Before the pole arrived the only methods available, other than ledgering, were, I suppose, the stick or waggler. I had some success on the Trent using the waggler but probably more so on the fenland rivers and drains like the Welland, Sibsey Trader drain etc.

JB. Describe your Witham wagglers in a little more detail for me – the float's components, length and capacity etc?

DA. As mentioned I made my own wagglers, always from peacock quill in lengths varying from 8 inches to over 12 inches. I never used bodied wagglers, preferring to use longer ones in bad conditions. Obviously peacock quills have a thick and thin end so, by using different parts from the quill, many different permutations were possible. They could even be used, what you might call upside down, thin end at the bottom, thick end at the top, for holding up in a fast flow. That said, in normal conditions, I would always use an insert. These were usually made from thinner pieces of peacock quill, but I also used matchsticks which gave a thin and sensitive tip, sarkandas reed and plastic drinking straws - in fact anything that was light enough and of a suitable diameter.

I painted all the bodies black with mixtures of black, white, red, orange and yellow for the tips, depending on the background and position of the sun. All tips consisted of at least two colours to show lifts and other shy bites.

My Witham wagglers were between 3 and 5 AAA and not loaded. An average size would be around 10 inches long taking 3 ½ AAA. I preferred to use locking shot and used a small snap connector to attach them to the line. In the early days, when they were allowed I would start with 6 no. 6 shot down the line in a 3, 2, 1 pattern, obviously with the single 6 nearest the hook, probably 15 ins. away. The other two gaps up to the bulk shot would the same distance. When no. 6 shot and bigger was banned I started to use up to a dozen no. 8 shot down the line. The distribution was a bulk of four or five shot together and four droppers below that, with the rest placed just below the float.

By keeping three no. 8s directly under the float they could be dragged down if needed and, conversely, shot could be slid up to the float if I wanted to fish lighter down. I never used an olivette down the line but with these spare shot kept in reserve under the float a heavy bulk could be achieved if necessary. The pattern could change greatly during a match.

JB. Moving on to the hook, what pattern and size did you prefer, and do you think hook colour is important?

DA. In the early days I used a Mustad hook, the number escapes me but it was gold and quite a fine wire. Bear in mind we had nothing like the choice we have now back in those days. I don't think the colour matters much personally providing its the right hook. As time went on and more choice became available I tried a few different patterns and finally settled on a Tubertini series 2 for waggler. I never used barbless hooks but always flattened the barb. I would always start on a 22 but, depending what was happening, could go down to a 24 or up to an 18.

JB. What was your choice of reel line and hooklength?

DA. I had two lines for waggler fishing. One from Daiwa (I think it was called Harrier but not certain) in 2.4lb b.s., being a supple and fairly light line for use in 'normal' conditions, turning to good old Maxima in 2lb or 2.5lb if I wanted it to sink like a stone (very rare). I always carried a tube of vaseline to make the line float and some fullers earth and detergent to make it sink. Hooklengths were always Bayer Perlon, either in 12oz or 1.1lb (for bagging) strain, and I tied them 15 inches long.

JB. What would you say was your greatest asset as a Witham matchman?

DA. In a word, confidence.

JB. Who taught you the ropes; who did you study and learn from?

DA. No one in particular. My dad first took me when I was 5 or 6 but he was only a pleasure angler. I joined the Welholme AC when I was 16 and learnt from different anglers there, then after a year or two teamed up with a lad called Chris Brown. We travelled together and bounced loads of things off one another.

JB. As for the larger tools of the trade, what rods/reels/seat box do you favour? And was there anything unusual in your approach?

DA. Back in the day I always stood up to fish the float and a seat-box was only something to carry your gear in most of the time. I first had a Brennan and Hickman fibreglass 'coffin' then progressed to a Brilo (a bit more sophisticated). Rods were two 13' Shakespeare Presidents which I still use. No one has shown be anything better to this day. Reels were a bit more complicated. I started with the good old Mitchell match, like everyone, then moved onto the one with the automatic bale arm (was it a 410 or 440?). I also had a couple of Abu 507's closed face and finished up using the Daiwa Autocast. All excellent reels.

I don't think my method was much different to most others. The one thing I did, bearing in mind we were usually stood some distance from the bank, was to make sure everything I might need was to hand. On the soft Witham we'd stand on old wire bread trays for a time to stop sinking into it. When platforms came along they were a great help. I very rarely used one to sit on but it was great to have behind you with everything on it you might need. It used to annoy me watching guys pegged nearby paddling backwards and forwards to the bank during a match for bits of tackle.

JB. Bait requirements were simple 30 years ago compared to today's world, what was your average bait list for a Witham match?

DA. Casters were all the rage in winter matches in the early days, for hookbait and feed, with a handful of maggots for a change. Then came the bronze maggot revolution around 1974 and the roles were reversed. I reckon it was around 1980 before we started to see many bream caught in the winter and prior to that the bait list was quite simple to organise: three pints of bronze maggots with a handful of reds mixed in and maybe a pint of casters, and little else.

Starting bait was usually single bronze maggot on a 22 with double and red maggot being the obvious changes. I would often flick a few maggots or casters short of the main feed line. If I missed a bite I would leave the tackle over this closer area looking for a bonus fish.

As time went on and bream started to show in greater numbers I would also take some worms, a few more casters and a pint of squatts or if I couldn't get those, pinkies. Summer was different because to win a match you were usually looking for bream. Bait would have been: 2 pints casters, 2 pints squatts and some worms for the bream. Two pints of bronze maggots were also needed for the eels if you didn't draw on bream (not a particular strength of mine but it had to be done sometimes).

I much preferred to fish for roach and had a lot of success on hemp. I did win one or two large opens on hemp when the bream didn't feed but you were usually looking for a place or section win. The biggest winning weight I had in a big open on the roadside was (I think) 22lb 14oz, but 8-12lb was much more the norm; I'd frame or win sections with this sort of weight.

JB. Would you always start with maggot when targeting roach?

DA.--- Yes, a single bronze maggot to start, with red as a change colour, then would later try double maggot or caster. Most people had similar tackle and rigs etc. and I think one of the most important things that sorted the better anglers from the pack was feeding. I know I fed a lot less than most and would often use less than a pint during the course of a match, and never more than two pints. At the time we are talking about, the river was stuffed with roach, but the way I saw it was if six or eight maggots were falling through my peg a fish would find my hookbait quicker than if there were say fifty maggots going in.

If you were being plagued by small fish people used to talk about feeding them off to get the bigger ones. I personally found that if my swim was full of 'bits' that was what you were stuck with and the best solution was to find the best way of catching them quickest (this was where the whip often came to the fore). So I would usually feed very few maggots at a time but depending on the flow would feed two or three times a cast. This was, of course, not set in stone and if I felt more bait was required it went in. There were no rules and much of it was done on instinct.

JB. Did you feed hemp on the Witham?

DA. Only in summer, never in winter.

JB. Do you remember times when the anglers around you fed what you regarded as too much?

DA. Yes definitely. I drew next to Wayne Swinscoe in the Pound

Length 40s pegs once when it was a good area to draw. We both fished the 'wag and mag' and I felt it had gone well. We chatted after the match when Wayne asked me what I'd fed. *"A pint and a quarter,"* I said. *"I don't believe it!"* he said, *"I have fed six pints."* I had 18lb to Wayne's 11lb. The river had fished well and I think I was third or fourth with some bigger weights in the low numbers towards Kirkstead Bridge, but Wayne didn't make the money. Wayne's a marvellous angler but I thought he could not get away with ladling bait in in the manner they did on the Trent where there were more fish, or more willing fish.

JB. Did you plumb the depth, and whereabouts in the river did you usually target your feed?

DA. After selecting what I thought was the correct float for the conditions I would remove an AAA shot from under the float and nip a swan shot onto the hook to plumb up. I would have a little chuck around but, as I am sure you remember, the river didn't have many natural features and I would invariably start casting just short of the middle with the float set a couple inches over-depth. If the river was running I might start off feeding just a tad upstream but not too far as you didn't want the guy upstream pinching your fish. On a still river I would feed directly in front or just a little downstream.

If the river was still, or barely moving, I would be using an insert waggler with around 1/4 inch showing and this would increase depending on wind, flow or even bad light conditions. The other end of the scale would be a big 'upside down' waggler, one with the thicker end of the quill at the tip.

JB. How often would you slow the float's progress or wind back a turn/ twitch the bait to tempt fish?

DA. It is difficult to slow a waggler down effectively. Obviously, going over-depth works but I found the bottom was usually a bit too mucky to drag any shot, especially with an insert. The other way I found was to use the rod to ease the float down on a tight line but this was far more effective with a stick than a waggler, so if I thought the fish wanted the bait slowing down that's what I would use. I carried stick floats up to 10 no. 4 shot and loved using them. On either method anything that changed the bait's normal progression down the swim could bring a bite.

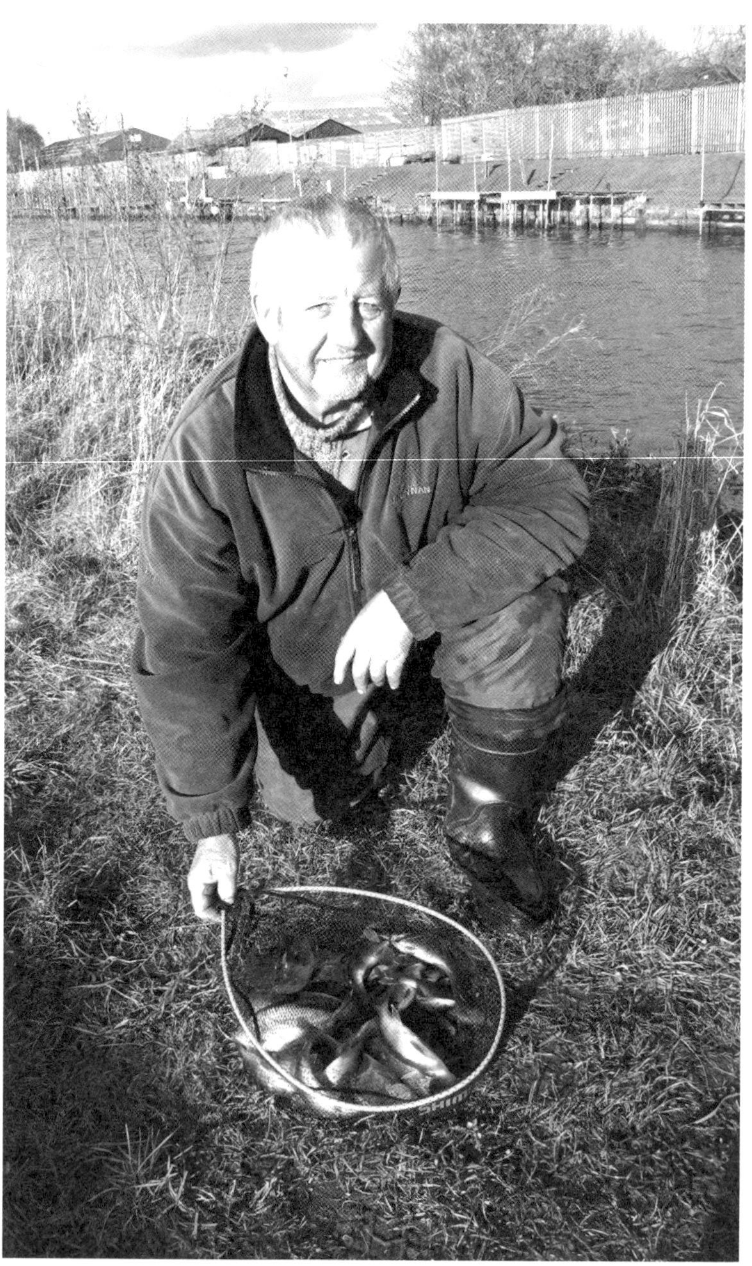

Dave with a hard-earnt perch catch from his local R. Ancholme.

JB. What subtleties of presentation would you say worked best for you and made you a regular winner?

DA. I don't know that I had any special wrinkles but I was constantly changing depth and it's amazing how many times a two-inch change of depth will bring bites when before none had been forthcoming. I also caught loads of fish off the bottom/on the drop and if this happened the shot would be moved around accordingly. This is where having around a dozen no. 8 shot on the line helped. If the fish started feeding off the bottom more shot could be slid under the float, or if nothing was happening on the drop more shot could be pulled down nearer the hook to get the bait down quicker.

Another thing was to watch the float like a hawk. Bites could be the tiniest lift or dip of the float or it could start to travel down the swim slightly faster or slower. I don't know how many times I have had someone stood behind me when I struck into a fish only for them to say they never saw the bite.

JB. Did you adapt your wag style at all when the long pole method grew more dangerous as a winning method?

DA. Well not that much. I would always make sure my waggler line was further than could be reached with a pole – say 18-20 metres, and, as mentioned earlier I would feed another line closer. This, hopefully, split up the pole anglers' fish and gave me a chance of nicking some of theirs; remember this was usually a second or throwaway line.

JB. How has your waggler approached changed in 2013 compared to the old Super League days?

DA. Not much at all really. I have been on the Witham today and the set-up was just the same as it would have been 30 years ago. The one major difference is, crazily, we (ie. six of us) fished in a line in what looked better than average conditions and NONE of us had a bite!"

JB. If you had just one fish to catch to save your life, and one bait to catch it, what would they be?

DA. Years ago it would have been a roach on a maggot, now I think it would be a perch on worm.

JB. What do you do when not fishing or thinking about it, other sports?

DA. I like a round of golf and a frame or two of snooker, and I try to keep fit by cycling a few miles every week. All these interests occupy my time when not fishing. I also love watching most sports on TV, particularly cricket and football, and enjoy a few pints (maybe a game of dominoes) down the local with my mates.

JB. What's your happiest memory?

DA/ None in particular but I've been lucky to have experienced over 40 great years of good fishing and made many friends along the way.

JB. Which angler do you most admire?

DA. Hmm, if pushed to name one I'd say Bob Nudd - a lovely guy who has been a great ambassador for our sport.

Top Tip

Always make sure your waggler is heavy enough to do the job you want it to.

Chapter 17
Roger Wakenshaw - The Witham Wizard

It takes something special to upset John Allerton's focus in a match to the point where he leaves his peg to watch another angler, but Roger Wakenshaw managed to do just this when winning a Witham Super League round on waggler back in the early 90s. Roger had that effect on others, they had to try to learn more about how he did it rather than struggle on regardless. He made a similar impact on the Trent, winning consecutive Kamasan British Open titles at Long Higgin in seasons 1992/3 and 1993/4. He caught 14lb of hybrids the first time and really made it count the second time with 53lb of bream.

As a mark of his consistency, Roger was also third overall in the prestigious Kamasan Matchman of the Year competition in 1993, which awarded points for all matches over 60-peg size in the UK. But barring a silly mistake he would have won it. A win in the Witham's 132-peg Grimsby Open didn't get reported and this proved costly. He realised too late when querying his points at the end of the season, only to learn points were also awarded for section placings in the National, where he'd scored a third for two more potential points. *"It was too late to complain and I ended up three points short of the title. Dave Vincent made it three titles on the spin to get a hat-trick, but I still enjoyed the year immensely,"* said Roger.

Roger, 58, was born and raised in Normanton, West Yorkshire. His formative years were spent on local rivers like the Wharfe, Swale and Ouse, along with lakes like the Half Moon at Kirkthorpe and Ryhill Reservoir. He left the county aged 20 to attend teacher training college in Lincoln where he met and married Karen, his wife of 33 years. Roger settled in Lincoln, and now has three sons all grown up - or he thinks they are! His match teams have included Kirkstead AC, Matchman Supplies and Lincoln Federation.

Roger, at times unbeatable on the Witham.

He has won two National Championship team medals, both on the River Witham – Division 4 in 1983 (which Kirkstead won with a record 978 points and their lowest score was a handy 55) and Division 2 in 1985. Roger led from the front with a section 3rd from Langrick in the first, and a section 2nd from the Timberland Lane section in the second. He won the Witham Super League title twice and enjoyed other placings in the top three, with most catches falling to waggler. He has also won big matches on the Trent and a string of events on his local Fossdyke Canal.

On the Fossdyke he'd fish a small waggler across the canal with caster for odd bream and big roach. The tidal reaches of the Trent have also been a happy hunting ground for him, including three successive Sunday open wins with weights from 14lb up to 26lb. His personal best weight came in an Embassy Pairs qualifier, on the non-tidal Trent at Holme Marsh peg 185 (the first below Winthorpe Lake) comprising 17 big bream on feeder for 93lb.

In his early years on the Witham Roger was taken under the wing of Witham ace Edgar Purnell, and was also helped by the late Eric Tattershall, a Lincoln team angler. By any measure they did a wonderful job. *"Eric was an ex-World War II fighter pilot and an angling perfectionist, who didn't even like catching fish in the lower lip and would change his rig to try and avoid it. We were teammates in the Nationals we won and I often travelled with him to the Witham,"* said Roger. *"As for maestro Edgar, I spent a lot of time sitting with him on the Witham learning about presenting the bait correctly, and getting the float to travel in a straight line – 'don't worry about a great bow,' he would say, 'the hook only has to move 2mm on the strike to get home.' "*

At his peak on the Witham Roger was nothing short of phenomenal, or *'at times unbeatable'* as Dave Ashmore put it. Roger now takes up the story...

Back in the early Nineties the River Witham from November through to March provided some of the best roach fishing in the country. As the summer level of the river was lowered, usually in early November, the Witham was transformed from a still drain to a flowing river. Providing it was not racing through, this flow was welcome as it made the fish feed.

The river was controlled by the lock gates which would open on the ebb tide. The flow depended on how much water was in the river, ie. flood conditions meant the gates would be fully opened, but on a low river with less force of water the gates might only be opened slightly. As the tide came the lock gates would close, presumably to prevent salt water getting into the river.

My favourite method by far during these winter months was the waggler, with the stick float and bomb the back-up methods. The obvious advantage of the waggler was its scope for covering a large area of river both across the river and downstream. The pole, though deadly on its day, was restricted by its length and could therefore not reach fish beyond the middle, nor further than halfway down the peg.

My rods were the original 13' Normark Microlites (which I still use) teamed up with a Daiwa 1600 XBM and later a Shimano when the Daiwa was no longer available. Reel lines included 2lb Maxima for waggler and 2.1lb or 1.7lb Bayer Perlon for stick float. My favourite hooks at the time were Drennan Fine Match – a light and sharp bronze pattern, later renamed the Polemaster. I'd also use the Drennan Carbon Canal Match, and these were tied to 12oz Bayer hooklengths for all float work, scaling up to 1.1lb or 1.7lb for bomb fishing.

The all-important float was a Drennan crystal insert waggler in 3.5AAA to 2SSG or 2-Swan size, with various interchangeable coloured tips. In a heavy flow or windy conditions I'd use the 2-Swan size, and being long and thin this gave stability and added casting weight. Confidence in your tackle is everything.

Shotting patterns would reflect the speed of flow. If the river was stood still, or flowing only gently, I'd hope to catch on the drop with the lighter float. For this I'd use a shirt button-style pattern with five no. 8s spaced out over the lower half of the rig – 6" to 10" apart depending on the depth, and three no. 10s spread out below that.

If the flow was stronger then the bigger float would be used with no. 6 shot instead of the 8s down the line, again shirt button-style. I never really bothered with bulking shots together.

I always began matches with the waggler set at dead depth. I expected to catch quicker this way, but my next move might be to drag up to 12" of line on the deck. I was less happy doing this as the bait could get masked by weed or debris, especially with fresh water in the river. As for positioning of the feed, depending on the river's flow, I'd generally feed at 1-o'clock or a yard downstream [note: anglers naturally face 12-o'clock when looking directly across the river on an imaginary clock-face, and the Witham at Kirstead flows left to right if fishing from the roadside bank]. The Kirkstead length often had a downgate wind too, so it would help bait presentation if the fish could be shoaled up a few yards downstream of the standing position.

Bait requirements included four pints of bronze maggots with a few reds mixed in them, plus a pint of casters, though I expected to use from two to three pints of maggots at most with any left over for the ducks. Only on the very odd occasion did I feed any groundbait, usually in small balls when the water was coloured and I was fishing stick float. I won a Lincoln Open one February on a coloured river with 24lb of hybrids fishing like this. Worms were saved for a rock hard day when I'd usually try a small bomb, twitching back a head of a redworm from mid-river. This would often attract a tommy ruffe or perch, though, of course, bloodworm was a better bait at such times.

My better results in this period gave me at least a double figure weight, and my best roach catch totalled 28lb. On this day I caught steadily for the first hour, a little better in the second, bagged up in the third and fourth hours, then back to a steady last hour. On less hectic days I often caught on straight lead [bomb] when the float swim was drying up, but these could be bigger roach from the tail end of the swim.

I never liked catching too well to start with as this usually meant the overall weight would be lower. On the good days I'd often fall behind the pole anglers after an hour, but as their swims slowed mine would get stronger and I was able to catch up and pass them.

I'd always feed nice and steady to start with, especially in the first hour, to see how the fish responded then take it from there. The better the fish fed then the more bait I fed. I didn't like to miss bites though, and found that when feeding too heavily the bites were less positive, and you could get line bite trouble [false bites]. We must always fine-tune the feed rate to give them the right amount for the occasion and quantity of fish in the swim.

Roger with a good tidal Trent barbel.

Feeding, I believe, is the big key to catching fish consistently. On some days just half a pint was more than enough. I remember winning a match by feeding this light between the old and new bridges at Tattershall with 22lb of roach on the waggler. There were so many fish in the peg that feeding more bait only produced loads of missed bites. Sometimes the fish do not need that much attracting and want to be where they are, and this was one such day. Very little was caught either upstream or downstream of the two bridges.

One exceptional season we caught lots of fish shallow and the river fished brilliantly all through the winter. These were 70-peg matches and I was able to feed heavily and catch at just three-foot deep. I would start my car on Saturday and Sunday and it was like it knew its own way to the Kings Arms pub match HQ. Happy days.

What a contrast it was then to how the river has declined now. I still often drive down the Kirkstead roadside in winter on route to work. If I see one angler over the four-mile stretch it is a rarity which is very sad. I have some great memories of great anglers and super matches, but can they ever return? I doubt it. The colour has dropped out of the river, excess weed makes fishing almost impossible during the summer months, and when the river drops to winter level the roach seem to disappear. The former regulars and younger anglers take refuge at the carp commercials, but at least us older generation have fantastic memories of the fishing and friends from this area.

Top Tip

Tackle preparation is the key to being organized on the day of the match, so get fully ready for business by doing your homework. Also, when the match starts ensure your float always goes through the swim in a straight line like the loose feed does

Further interview questions for Roger:

JB. Precise shotting positions - you do not consider this as vital?

RW. To be honest I'm not sure that shotting is as important to the fish as we humans like to believe. Lincoln's Les Smith, for example, caught loads of roach using a 1gm olivette down his line and nothing else. He was nicknamed 'Lead down Les' for his consistency with it. He won the Witham Super League doing it and his way could not have been simpler. I think, generally speaking, getting the float to go through the swim in a straight line is more important than shot placements. I did copy Les with the olivette for a short while when he was catching well. Maybe it slowed the bait a little better than an ordinary shotting pattern in cold water conditions but it didn't work for me on the Witham. I won a match on the Trent at Long Eaton with it however, with 35lb of chub and roach.

JB. But the tell-tale shot position matters surely?

RW. The tell-tale shot is the most critical one to get in the right place, of course. I'd use a hooklength of 18" on the Witham, ideally with a bit of stretch in it so not a pre-stretched brand, and would often put a no. 10 shot close to the hook in adverse/strong flow conditions. I always thought this added a bit of stability to the hookbait.

JB. How about dotting down the float?

RW. The amount of float showing once the shots had settled would vary between a mere pimple on calm days to an inch or more on rough days with 'rollers' on the surface. To give the line a twitch and thereby move the bait could tempt a bite on a still river, as could holding the float back a touch to lift the bait on a moving river.

JB. The pole is such an efficient method on hard matches. Did its advance in terms of length (to 16m) ever force you to re-think your approach?

RW. I don't think the pole influenced me that much, even a long time after other anglers were on it and scoring highly with it, except it possibly encouraged me to fish all-out waggler for longer. I just had so much confidence in the method that I never set the pole up. 'Why confuse a winning method?' was my reasoning.

JB. Roger, you were one Witham angler who broke the mould of the obsession with peacock wagglers by doing so well with the shop-bought Drennan crystals. I also think these are brilliant floats. But you still used peacock at times?

RW. That's right. For Trent matches I'd go for peacock - straight peacock quills, or with an insert included depending how much line I want to drag on the bottom. Obviously a thick tip holds up better and does not give false bites in faster swims.

JB. What do you regard as your best waggler match?

RW. It would have to be catching 28lb of roach [already mentioned] from peg 428 at Jimmy's Hill, Dogdyke, on the Witham, finishing second to a 30lb bream catch from the Bain mouth. Crazily, I actually gave away my two pints of casters to the guy who ended up beating me. After my first three casts I caught a small roach every cast for five hours. Les Smith, drawn next peg, said I had over 200 roach. He used to count the fish of the anglers either side of him, but don't ask me how or why.

JB. I thought I remembered you feeding casters at one time on the Witham, was this a plan B?

RW. No, not at all because I rarely carried them. I did have a bit of a run on a still, winter river feeding casters lightly and short (10m line), and trying the line after a few hours. It sometimes brought a few big roach but this was after the bagging days of the early 90s. I remember Edgar Purnell once telling me how he had often walked along with the scales-men after matches and could tell who had fished caster and who maggot by the size of the fish. But the bigger caster fish did not feed as reliably as the maggot fish in my time. I often used casters on the tidal Trent though, particularly after September when they definitely sorted out the better specimens.

JB. What was your greatest asset?

RW. Confidence I'm sure, and it has to be every angler's greatest asset. A confidence in everything you do is the secret, but your bait also has to be spot-on.

JB. Do you have an angling hero?

RW. My dad, George, and Denis White. Dad taught me how to fish in my early years (from age 5) on the Half Moon at Kirkthorpe. Denis because he is such a brilliant all- rounder. He once sat behind me upstream of Kirkstead Bridge when I won the Lincoln Hospital Cup with 15lb-odd of roach and hybrids. I felt really honoured, plus I love down to earth people like him.

JB. How has your match fishing changed in 2016?

RW. When I can catch on the float, which is less often now as I mostly fish the tidal Trent, my waggler set-up remains very similar. But the feeder and bream dominate the tidal river; only at odd times do the roach feed well enough to give the float a chance. My tackle has hardly changed for roach though, I'm still using the same rods, floats and rigs of 25 years ago – and size 22 hooks.

Chapter 18
Terry Payne & Jimmy Randell - The Innovators

In this joint chapter, two veteran matchmen have written short chapters describing the origins of the drinking straw float. It could hardly have been imagined that this idea for using lightweight plastic would eventually be refined into the transparent material of the popular Drennan Crystal waggler and others that we can buy over any tackle shop counter today.

First, Sheffield's Terry Payne. Terry is one of a select band of South Yorkshire anglers to win an England cap, in Poland back in 1975, the year Ian Heaps won his individual title. The team won the silver medal behind France but it was a personal disaster for Terry (see below). Here he describes some of his early wagglers made from a drinking straw.

Next up is Jimmy Randell, from North Walsham, Norfolk. Jimmy, is another former England International and writes about his own version of the straw which he used to good effect on the Grand Union Canal. He combined it with an attacking style to take on the canal's top man at the time: Billy Makin. Billy, for anyone too young to remember, was a Lancastrian by birth but moved to live in the Midlands where he dominated the Oxford canal and Grand Union matches. Together with his partner in crime, Ray Mills of Hinckley, they were deadly on small roach and gudgeon.

The Straw – by Terry Payne

In the early 60s the difficulty of finding good quality, straight peacock quills was a real problem for anglers. I think a certain chubby, left-handed angler from Coventry was to blame [aka the great Billy Lane, England's first World Champion in 1963]. Billy had just set up a float-making business [Ultra] apparently commandeering all the better quills being imported into this country.

Balsa wood could be made into a decent float, but unless a very dense balsa was used the resulting float was very fragile and could easily be cracked, allowing water to soak in when there was any slight chip on the paint seal.

A straight float is vital for accurate casting so, when seeking an alternative to peacock quills, most other bird feathers were a non-starter. We were looking for a float to be fished 'bottom only' or 'loose float'. After several attempts with plastic tubing the best solution I could find was the plastic drinking straw.

After many tries I managed to fashion a very crude but fishable float. Surprisingly, the float performed very well, much better than I expected. So maybe the bent peacock quills, which were all I seemed able to purchase, could be overcome?

Why is it so important to have this absolutely straight float you may ask? Well, consider an archer's perfectly straight arrows, similarly the darts player, and the answer is obvious, bent ones will not fly straight, and the same applies to a float. Not all plastic drinking straws are perfectly straight but they are so cheap that many can be discarded until some can be found for our purpose.

There are many different diameters of straws on sale today but in the Sixties and Seventies the only size available was about 3mm in diameter. But as more straws came onto the market we had a greater choice of diameter and length. But let's stay with one size for the sake of simplicity.

To make the float you first need to seal the top. To do this you need a candle and a wet finger and thumb. Hold the end of the straw near the lighted candle until it starts to melt, then with a twisting action (taking care not to burn your fingers) mould the softening plastic between finger and thumb until sealed. Suck on the open end to make sure it is airtight, then smooth away any sharp edges with glass paper.

Now for the bottom of the float which is going to be 'loaded' to take various weights. The best material for this job I found was brazing rod, on the basis that the more weight that is built into the float then the less shotting is needed on the line. Experience will tell you how much brass rod is needed for various float sizes, and I find it best to whip a float ring onto the brass rod before gluing it into the float with Araldite.

Now the float only needs painting. I use either black or green, with the tip always painted in the same colour. The tip colour is only the first stage because I use an ultra-sensitive interchangeable top, the colour of which can be changed at will to suit the light conditions/background colour.

Terry Payne and his first 2lb roach from Welbeck Lakes, Notts. He then added several more in a specimen boom at the water.

To make this top, or tip section, take a piece of straw the same diameter as the float stem about 1" or 25mm long. Then stretch one end of it for a length of approx. 6mm by forcing it onto a knitting needle which should be of a slightly larger diameter than the straw float. Now cut into the side of the tip about 7mm above the widened end a notch in the shape of a semi-circle [see hollow tip floats pic from Mark Wintle in chapter 6].

Do not make a seal on the top of this antenna, as it is obviously meant to accept water and this is important for sensitivity as only the plastic wall offers resistance to the taking fish. You can make several of these tips in various colours, all interchangeable, to suit different light conditions – red, yellow, black etc.

These straw floats can be made more robust by taking two different diameter straws and sliding one inside the other for strength, or you can even stack one on top of the other to double the length, which allows you to tuck the reel line deep under the surface to avoid wind drag. I also have in my kit some cork bodies for extra weight carrying. In fact the variations are almost limitless with this simple material.

The quality of shop-bought waggler floats nowadays is so good that it is hard to match them, but the personal satisfaction of using one's own creation to catch fish can't be overlooked. On one memorable occasion I used a straw waggler taking just four number 4 shots to catch 56lb of quality roach in an evening session at Damflask Reservoir. What could be more satisfying than that? [Fantastic. How did you do that? - Ed]

The Last Straw For Billy – by Jimmy Randell

My best period of fishing the Grand Union Canal was with a small form of waggler in the early 1970s. Fished around the Leighton Buzzard and Three Locks areas, the matches in those days were popular 100-peggers. I used to fish the canal, like everybody, for small fish in the edge with whips, and the squatt and pinkie method. This involved feeding with loose squatts with double squatt or a pinkie on the hook. The target fish were roach, skimmers and gudgeon. The best anglers on there at the time were Billy Makin and Ray Mills. You could win with about 6lb or 7lb. Sometimes bream would show but this was very rare. No-one ever caught a roach over 2oz.

One day at Three Locks I drew a peg with a bush on the other side. I had some casters with me from fishing the River Lea the previous day, and the bush looked just like one of the chub swims at Broxbourne [R.Lea]. I made up a small waggler because the canal was only about 16m wide. I started the usual way in close for the small fish. After about two hours I went across with a caster on the hook. I had been feeding with a catapult. The float went under first cast and I had a roach of about 12oz. I weighed in 14lb of big roach of the like nobody had ever seen before.

This was a 100-peg match and I won easily. Word got out after the match that I had caught bream. From then on I won virtually every match there for three years. Gradually other anglers found out what I was doing. Mark Pollard* used to come down with his dad and watch. With more and more anglers firing casters across, it became harder to win because they would stop the roach coming to me at some time during the day. I once waited three hours before I had a bite but still won with 7lb.
[* Mark Pollard was only a keen youngster then, but went on to become a top matchman himself and set up the Image tackle company in Luton.]

I used to fish with a homemade waggler which I made either from a plastic drinking straw or a biro inner tube. I made a small balsa body and glued it at the base of the straw, also filling the top with a small blob of araldite and gluing a swivel in the bottom. My floats had a hollow tip 30 years before this was thought of. [See rig on page 341].

The float took 3BB to lock to the line and three no. 8s down the line, two placed under the float and one halfway down. The hooklength was only 6" long, and kept short because when the canal ran I pushed all three 8s down to where the hooklength was joined to the main line. I used 1 1/2lb Maxima on the reel, 1lb Bayer hooklength and an 18 hook. The secret was to use dark casters that sank very slowly. I used no more than ½-pint in five hours. I would cast underarm to within a foot of the far bank. If there were brambles, or cover, and about 2' of water, that was ideal. Lock headings were also good.

Another thing I found out was that when the barges went through the locks the canal would pull quite fast and no-one caught at this time. This could happen five or six times a day. But by moving my three shots as near to the hook as possible as described, the caster would drag along the bottom and I'd expect to catch two roach every time the water moved. This trick usually gave me an extra ten roach at the end.

Things started to change when carp were stocked in several stretches by the River Board, much to Billy Makin's disgust. He said they would eat all his gudgeon. He was right. My run of success came to an end when poles got longer and could reach the far bank.

Spoilt for choice: Jimmy Randell with a boxful of wagglers.

More on Terry Payne, by Jim Baxter:

When first I nervously set foot into the world of open matches, the name of Sheffield and District AA's captain, Terry Payne constantly came up in discussions about the cream of the Fenland match circuit. On bream or roach he was known to be versatile. He surprised a few people, for example, by winning a big Damflask match with 6lb of roach taken on swing-tipped bloodworm, at a time when it was unheard of in Yorkshire to fish this bait with anything other than a pole.

Once described as an 'arch perfectionist', Terry was an innovator too, and found ways to improve equipment at a time when much of the good tackle we take for granted today was still in its infancy. His quick-change catapult elastic system where the elastic was threaded inside one hole in an aluminium frame and back out again through another hole then trapped with a small cane peg, was one typical brainwave.

As a young rookie Terry watched Coventry's Billy Lane finish third in the 1956 Witham National on the Witham at Kirkstead with 19lb of bream fishing a big ducker float. His teammate Norman Webb was second and they won the team title. Terry described the spectacle: *"Billy drew a peg opposite Horncastle Cut. As one of 200 spectators trying to get a good view behind him, I was impressed with how simple he made it look. From that day on if ever I drew badly on a match I'd try and find Billy and watch him. One day he said: 'You again? – come and sit down here.' I didn't need asking twice and it was always great to watch him."*

Never shying away from an attacking style in the manner of his early hero, Terry learnt how to plunder Trent chub with the deadly wasp grub and cake combination. Fishing a Mansfield Open at Besthorpe, he set up a 7-swan shot (SSG) waggler, equivalent to over 11g in metric. Five Swan went around the float as casting weight and two more down the line – *"The extra lead didn't bother them at all on this bait,"* he said. A mighty cast to within a rod-length of the far bank, some 60 yards out, got Terry to the chub shoal, and he won the match with 29lb. This was just one win of many in that period and, from a decent chub swim, Terry was always looking to 'frame'.

"The hardest part was reaching the far spot with the 'mulloch', our name for the groundbait mix," said Terry. *"This was a mix of caster,*

hemp and scalded, mashed up wasp cake. Fishing this method was great fun. We'd put six queen grubs on a size 10 or 12 size hook because with a big cast half of them might come off. We watched carefully as the float hit the spot and, being a white bait, you could see if too many grubs had come off on the way over and whether a re-cast was necessary."

Of all his victories, Terry regards his Tetley Gala win (800 entry) on the Welland in 1963 with 13lb 10oz as his finest victory. He caught bream on a ducker float, pushing Freddie Foster, known as the 'swing-tip king', into second by little over 1lb.

"It fished atrocious," recalls Terry, *'but I fished a big ducker which was not unlike a waggler but made from a cane stem and a balsa body. No shots were placed around the float, it all went down the line. The waggler was still a few years away. I fished 8' deep with a 3 SSG (swan shot) bulk at mid-depth and a BB tell-tale 15" from the hook. Billy had told me how to 'throw the shot and not the float'."*

In more recent years Terry has taken his share of specimen roach from Welbeck Lakes, Notts., with his two best each scaling 2lb 8oz. His first biggie weighed 2-1 and in one season he landed 15 over the magic 2lb barrier. *"They disappeared for a few years then, but I gather the big ones are making a comeback. Sadly, I have had to stop going there as I can no longer negotiate the banks."*

Perhaps the best illustration of Terry's analytical mind is his making of an eye for a sliding float, long before the host of clever accessories we now use were commercially manufactured. Using a French clip swivel, the silver type with a clip at one end and an eye at the other, he filled up this too-large eye with solder then drilled a 20 thou' [0.002"] hole in the solder. But it didn't end there. Terry countersunk the hole on either side, then took some cotton and Brasso [polish] and buffed up the new hole to make it smooth as silk. I call that smart thinking.

Terry's England experience:

To win an England cap and a silver medal has to be highlight of anyone's career but Terry finished the Poland match with just a small roach and a stickleback to show, and an empty feeling in his stomach at coming last in the section, knowing a few ounces more and the team's silver medal would have turned to gold. He drew the middle section of the five on what sounded like a peg from hell.

"My draw was in front of the access point where the teams and officials entered the match length and was therefore a bit noisy. But it got worse when I saw the activity on the lane meeting the canal bang opposite me on the far bank. Ice cream vans were in profusion and all sorts of other goods were being sold to the spectators there. Litter was strewn everywhere and an angler two pegs away pulled out a shopping trolley at one stage. This match was also the first time I'd seen bad gamesmanship at work. While I was trying to catch on my close line the Spaniard at the next peg dumped half a biscuit-tin's-worth of maggots as close as he could get to me and it killed the swim."

Terry proved he was fishing well by winning an open match back home only a week later, but his Polish match was not an easy one to forget, proving we can never take anything for granted in fishing.

More on Jimmy Randell, who sadly died in 2016 before the book was completed, by Jim Baxter:

Jimmy Randell, 74, a retired technical illustrator, considered himself an all-rounder, having won matches employing many different methods. He started fishing at the age of 5 on his local River Cam then, aged 14, he joined the Ilford and Wanstead AC, a club which took its members every weekend by coach to fish matches on the River Thames. By the age of 17 he was the club champion. But the Ilford club was affiliated to the London Angling Association whose strict match rules only allowed fish over a certain size to be weighed in. Jimmy saw no sense in this and rebelled.

"A few young blokes in the area were getting fed up with the LAA's dictatorial attitude and they decided to form Roding Valley AC. We started going to the Ouse and Cam where every fish we caught could be weighed in. My next step was to join Essex County with Dennis Salmon in 1964. [Dennis Salmon worked as a London stockbroker and was to go on to become team coach of the talented Essex County side.] My greatest rival in London at the time was Ray Mumford," said Jimmy.

"I was now fishing Winter Leagues and Nationals and gaining more experience. I went to the River Severn at Stourport for the first time on a 95-peg midweek match and won with 20lb-odd of dace. I had two other wins that year on the same venue which got me noticed by Stan Smith, the England manager, and in 1972 I was picked for the England team to fish in Czechoslovakia in the World Championships. The team came 2nd. I was 7th in my section. This was my only call up for England."

Jimmy's impressive record includes: regular wins on the Rivers Lea, Medway and Thames; winning The People (newspaper) Angling Championships on the River Avon at Pershore in 1964; won R. Lea Championship (when 200 bleak an hour was possible), several wins at Coombe Abbey Lake, Coventry; individual winner in North v South Easter Festival on N. Ireland's River Bann two years running; numerous wins on Grand Union Canal; 2nd individual on Division 2 National on the Cam and Ouse [*see endnote]; Many match wins on the R. Wensum – on his debut in 1970 he won with 38lb of roach; won Broads Open Champs on R, Bure with 20lb of roach - 450 pegs; and made 3rd on the first 1971 Woodbine Challenge final (80 fished) on Denmark's River Guden with 66lb of roach.

Jimmy had adapted to commercial fisheries and was a consistent winner on carp venues. He had also landed some impressive big fish, targeting them at the end of each season. Personal bests: Four chub in one hour on the River Wensum in 2012 – from 6lb 12oz up to 7lb 2oz; also: Dace 1lb 2oz, Wensum 2010; Roach 2lb 14oz, Bure Valley 2010; Bream 9lb 15oz, Wensum 2010; Tench 8lb, Rackerhayes 1980; Perch 3lb 6oz, Barford; Carp 19lb 12oz, Hockwold; and Barbel 11lb, River Trent 2010.

Endnote: The longest walk to fish a match...

I'd never met Jimmy until 2013, but had heard plenty about the former Essex County team man who was in their victorious Ancholme National Champs winning squad in the 1980s. One remarkable story was how he missed his section bus on the 1974 Welland National and was forced to walk over five miles to his peg, pulling a trolley and all his tackle behind him, not arriving until midday, long after the match had started. He had no option but to make the long trek as he was obviously late for the section coach and, because 'rules are rules', it had set off without him. The incident spoke volumes to me that here was a man prepared to go to any length not to let his team down, even though at the finish Jim weighed in only ounces for his trouble. As for his talent, I'd read about his winning performances with big roach on the famous Riverside road stretch of the Wensum in Norwich years before. Right up to his death Jimmy was still beating anglers half his age, and doing particularly well at Cobble Acre, a commercial carp water, near Norwich.

Endnote:

Surprisingly, Jimmy did not class this as his worst fishing experience: *"The day I came 2nd in the 1997 Division 2 National was the worst of my fishing life. I caught 45lb of bream and rudd on the waggler on the Cam and beat 400 other anglers, only to find that my teammate, Rodney Finch had 50lb on the Ouse. He won £10,000, I won £2,000. He reminds me of this when I see him every week as he sponsors my bait... the wind-up is always painful!"*

Chapter 19

Brian Halliwell interview – The sliding waggler - by Jim Baxter

Brian Halliwell made his name as a float angler in the Sheffield area back in the 60s, the decade most associated with the swing-tip method for bream. Most of the big Fenland matches of the time were won with bream because in any contest of at least 400 anglers someone would draw on a shoal and make a winning catch. To win on the float was hard in summer but at the back end of the season the bream would take a backseat. This is when anglers like Brian could make it pay.

But he was no slouch on swing-tip either. In the 1966 National Championship, Brian, aged 27, enjoyed his finest hour on the then match mecca the River Witham, with 20lb 9 1/2oz for third individual. He represented Sheffield Amalgamated, while his 'steel city' colleague Bill Bartles came a few ounces behind in fourth with 20lb 4oz fishing for local rivals Sheffield and District. Boston's Roy Jarvis won the National title convincingly, while Brian was shaded by a mere 1/2oz for the silver medal by Leicester's Roy Marlow. It earnt Brian and the other three top scorers a bonus of an England cap in the 1967 World Championships in Dunajvaros, Hungary.

Despite the team going on to win a bronze medal which equalled England's best ever performance, having been in the medals only twice before since the inaugural competition in 1957, Brian recalls how it was a hard match personally and that England got their tactics wrong:

"The team plan was to fish the first hour for big fish, then go for bleak as 'plan B'. But this meant giving the continentals an hour's start on small fish and to catch up would have been nigh-on impossible. Without any bream showing I was left scratching to do just that and finished 11th in my section. Bill Bartles, however, had other ideas and took the rings off his rod on the eve of the match and fished it like a pole for small fish, ending up a respectable 4th in his section. We were placed thanks to Roy Marlow and Roy Jarvis who both caught bream, with Roy Marlow (with 100 fish) just missing out on a bronze medal as 4th individual."

Brian was happy to return to normality in the big Witham matches, and enjoyed a good run of results on punched bread flake for bream. But his float skills often brought equal success especially in deep swims with his own version of a sliding waggler which has no loading at all at the base of the float. What makes all Brian's sliders unique is the special angled float adaptor he pushes them into. I interviewed Brian, a keen tackle maker and innovator, about his approach...

Question: For river or lake swims as deep as a rod length - 12′ or 13′, especially where casting is tricky due to overhead trees, bankside bushes etc., fishing a slider is surely the answer? This gives a practical and comfortable casting length from float to hook of less than 8′. Shouldn't more anglers turn to the slider instead of struggling to cast a longer line in deep swims?

Answer: Yes, of course. I'm surprised more anglers don't make life easier by using one.

Q. What depth of swim would make you fish the slider method?
A. 10′ or even shallower.

Q. You slide the float up to a nylon stop knot and down to a bulk of shot - what's your optimum casting depth, the bulk to hook distance?
A. Just 4′ 6″ to start with then work from there. Occasionally if the wind is opposite to the flow or undertow and is putting rollers on the water, I will adjust the bulk position to make sure the float is moving with the flow against the wind, the way it should travel.

Q. How do you tie the stop knot?
A. It's really quite simple. First, thread the reel line through the rod rings then cut off about a ten-inch piece. Lay this piece alongside the reel line a foot or so from its end, though the exact position is immaterial as the knot will slide once tied. Taking the right-hand end of the line piece (if you are right-handed), form a full loop, laying the tag end back against the main line pointing right. Trap this loop in position on the reel line between left-hand finger and thumb. Ensuring this tag end is long enough to do so, make five turns around both the main line and loop line, in and out of the loop formed. Now pull on both tag ends, closing the loop into a knot, and tighten so it will not slide easily. What you have is a half-blood knot, but it's the angle between the knot's lower tag end and the reel line that traps the float in place when it slides up to the knot. Cut off the excess line either side of the knot.

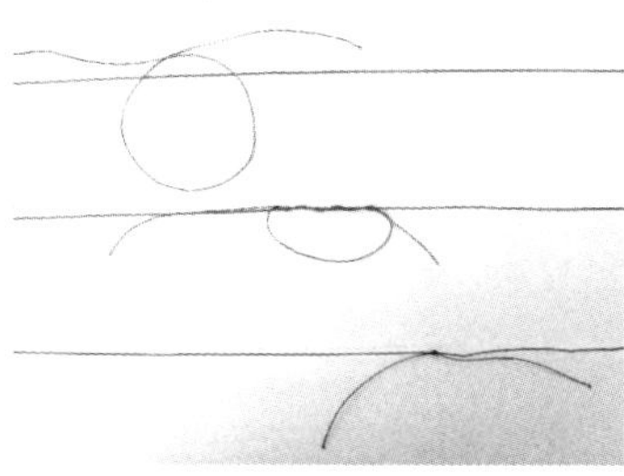

Q. How long do you leave the tag ends of the knot, so they don't catch in the rod rings when casting?
A. About 1 ½ inches is right.

Q. What shotting capacity of slider would you regard as minimum?
A. 2 Swan (or SSG), or 4AAA is about standard, but for very close in work 3AAA is enough.

Q. What's the heaviest you'd consider?
A. About 5 Swan for fishing most waters in the UK.

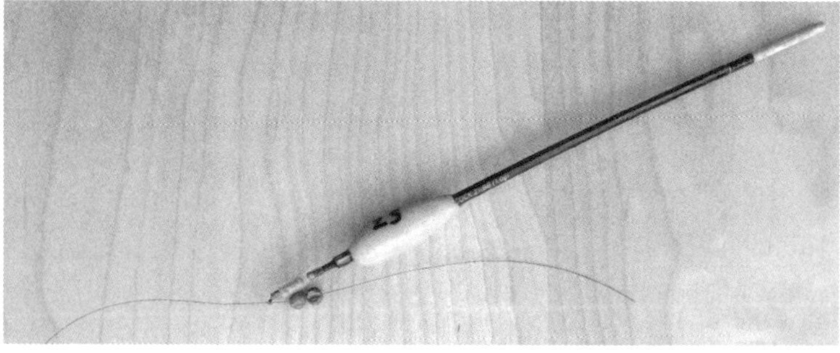

The angled eye helps the float fold round the bulk shot for a neat cast.

Q. Now let's discuss the special angled eye in the float adaptor you have developed, please describe it and why it works so well? (Including eye diameter.)
A. It is an extended three-turn eye in 15 thou' fuse wire, whipped onto a piece of 3mm cane, and angled to 45 degrees. It only works right when slid onto the line one way so that the float angles downwards and folds around the bulk shot in the casting position. The effect helped by the eye's width helps the float stick to the bulk when casting, so tangles are rare, and the line also slides through the eye smoothly up to the stop knot. A four-turn eye might work even better but it's good with three.

Q. Billy Lane pioneered the sliding antenna and it was a breakthrough for which all anglers must be grateful. But, talking to slider float fans, his float's base ring of 0.015 of an inch (15 thou') has always seemed tight for the line to pass through smoothly. It has led to many modern anglers using heavier sliders possibly heavier than necessary to ensure the weight pulls the line through to the stop knot. What's your view?
A. Well my eye is 27 thou' and it has served me well. With the greatest respect to Billy, and he was the original, along with the Webb brothers who I believe had a hand in its development, their eye diameter was too small. I've tried such an eye and the float quivers as the line is sliding through it. Even if the float reaches the set depth it can take a while to get there, and that is wasted fishing time. I think some anglers have gone to extremes as a result, using floats that are too big for a given depth or distance with unnecessary weight built into them as partial loading.

Q. So you don't see the need for a loaded float, Brian?
A. No, with the angled eye the dreaded bird's nest tangles are avoided.

Q. Wouldn't a loaded float help the float stay in contact with the bulk when casting?
A. In my opinion it's unnecessary and casting can be just as accurate with the angled eye of the right diameter.

Q. Moving on to the so-called 'rest shot' - what was its real purpose as I still don't know why Billy did not rest the float on the bulk for casting. Ian Heaps fishes similarly though, to be fair, he tells me he never gets tangles with his method. Most Yorkshire slider fans I know slide down to the bulk which looks to me like all the casting weight is in an aerodynamic single unit, so which way is right?

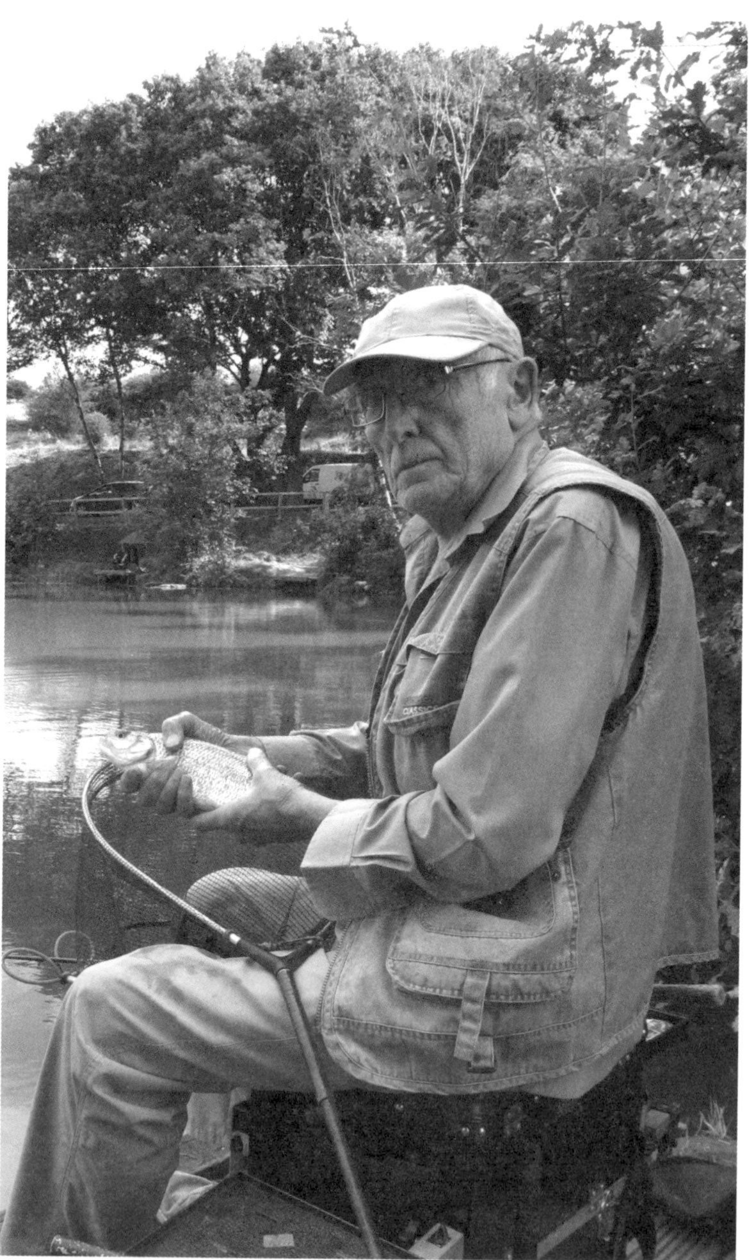

Brian with an ide from Aston Park, Sheffield.

A. There's no logical reason I can think of for a rest shot either; sliding down to the bulk is the best way.

Q. Billy Lane recommended an underhand cast to avoid tangles and I personally like to cast this way. What's your preferred cast?
A. I cast overhead unless under trees.

Q. What's the deepest water you have fished the slider in?
A. I've rarely fished very deep waters and more fish can be expected to live in 15′ of water or less than any deeper. The Middle Level drain and Relief Channel [in Cambridgeshire] were as suited to the method as anywhere, and they both produced well for me in depths of 12′ to 14′.

Q. I know you shot up simply, what's an average pattern?
A. 2 Swan as bulk and 3 no. 8 bunched as a single dropper, or sometimes using four no. 8's as a long dropper spaced up to an inch apart. The fish decide how they want it on the day, but the basic idea is that a medium sized dropper will show bites better than a small one. It's a case of simple shotting works best, but I do also add a small size 18 swivel below the bulk to prevent line twist.

Q. Do you mostly fish a little over-depth with it, just tripping the bottom?
A. Again the fish decide, but ideally just over-depth.

Q. Some say slider fishing demands a more durable reel line than standard waggler fishing which makes sense - what diameter line do you favour?
A. An 8 thou′ line, eg. 4lb Maxima, or 0.16mm/0.18mm approx.

Q. Presumably you add wash-up detergent to sink the line easily?
A. Yes, always.

Q. Do you usually groundbait with solid balls when fishing a slider say 12′ deep, or loose feed like with a normal waggler and simply shallow up if the fish come up in water?
A. The former, to try and keep the fish down.

Q. Where's your favourite slider venue?
A. Locally its KJS Aston's no. 2 lake or 'big pond' which has always been a good venue and has a suitable depth for the method.

Q. What's your best win on the method?
A. My most enjoyable I'd say was a catch of 30 fish, mainly small bream, for 30lb from the River Delph at Welney, all coming to gozzer hookbait in the last 90 minutes, feeding groundbait and squatts.
Author's Footnote: I have used Brian's special slider float eye and not once suffered a tangle. If you have any reluctance to trying the sliding float you should pick a suitably deep venue and try this method at once, for two reasons. First, plumbing the depth in a near or far swim is easy, and you can either add a plummet or use just the bulk shot and the sliding stop knot. Second, when striking at a bite the line pulls through the float smoothly instead of feeling the bump when the line connects with a fixed waggler and the shots around it. This can reduce the dreaded knock-off on lightly-hooked fish.

Top Tip

Always clip-up the reel line when fishing the slider. When the float hits the surface plunge the rod tip underwater and turn the reel four times to straighten and sink the line. By casting to the line clip it propels the bulk and droppers in a straight line beyond the float, and by giving the reel four turns every cast it means you are fishing as accurately as possible. As the shots descend, with the rod pointed straight out, the float will creep back up the line towards the stop knot, and be on your guard as a bite can occur before it gets there.

Chapter 20
Light Slider, River Weaver Style - by Jim Baxter

When I first set eyes on Cheshire's River Weaver at Hartford Bridge, Northwich in 1985 I felt immediately at home. A mid-match shotting change (referred to elsewhere) paid dividends with a 1lb 6oz roach putting me on course for second place. Fishing my Witham style, the Weaver, with its abundance of green chickweed, was a hard but fair test and not unlike the Witham. The locals were always friendly and helpful too, from Tony Waterman, Mal Scott and the Northwich gang, to the pie munchers on the midweek Winsford contests, where the tradition was to enjoy a hot meat pie before the afternoon contest. A waggler locked in place roughly a foot deeper than most Witham swims and light shotting down the line was my approach, and for three or more seasons life was good. Then came a day of reckoning when I drew next to one of the better locals, John Shellam, and got thrashed. He used a short, waggler slider and, despite it being a low weight match, he won the section and doubled me – 4lb to 2lb. He also struck at and missed many more bites. I was left scratching my head. 'There has to be something in this?' I thought, and so from then on I started trying a slider myself. A Drennan Crystal with one AAA shot as bulk worked to some extent, but I never quite got the old confidence back from that point on as the roach were suddenly taking fewer prizes and the float men losing out to the ledger and bream. The Weaver matches always kicked off at a civilised 1pm, but the journey over the Pennines was hard; there was simply no easy route to and from Northwich. I decided to move on, but this chapter looks at reasons why a sliding waggler can out-perform the standard version with shots either side...

The River Weaver is ideally suited to a small to medium weight slider thanks to its slow-moving nature and good average depth of 9' -11'. The late Brian Lees made the method his own, and river

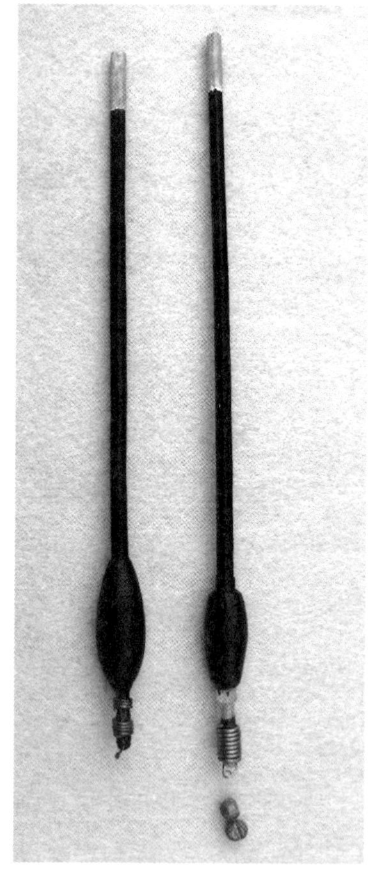

Halliwell-style (unloaded) sliders (left), and dumpy (part-loaded) Weaver-style (right).

regulars like Pete Clements, a Barlow's Tackle-sponsored angler from Macclesfield, and Chris Simmons of Northwich, have kindly given me details of his approach and their own versions of it.

Brian Lees was arguably the master of the slider on the river for years, enjoying many match successes with a small waggler which he rarely found necessary to slide much more than a yard. This was far enough to get the bulk shot below any wind action on the water and, if the wind was upstream, ensured the float travelled in the right direction with the river's flow. Both Pete and Chris learnt the method from Brian then became winners in their own right.

Brian, from Swinton, Manchester, had for a time mixed in the best of company as a travelling partner of the Ashursts, Benny and Kevin. His preferred peacock slider was just 7" long with a small 1" long cork body at the base, and only a light float at a shade over 3BB capacity. One BB approx. equated to lead wire loading at the float's base, leaving two BB (0.8g) together as bulk shot down the line and three no. 10 droppers below that. He'd generally cast this rig out to mid-river which is about 16m range.

Chris Simmons observed how Brian was a *"brilliant bloke and helpful"*, and he also had a knack of including a 1lb roach in his catch that would often give him the edge when the leading weights in a match were bunched tightly together.

With a waggler locked in place with shots either side, there is a noticeable 'bump' on the strike when the float is hit either a fraction of a second before the fish is felt or simultaneously. With a sliding waggler this bump is overcome as the line pulls through the float instead, giving a smoother contact with the fish. This can keep a fish on the hook with a fragile hold that might otherwise be knocked off.

I got to know Pete Clements as a winner both on the float and the tip, and he was good enough to give me up to date information on pegs wherever I drew. He also helped renew my interest in the spring-tip method for ledgering, a popular technique on the Weaver where double hooking is allowed, with a top hook set 18" or more away from a bottom hook, offering two chances of a bite every cast. Using springs from ring binders, Pete made tips that were more sensitive on the bite than any quivertip I knew, and combined them with a home-made rod from the top two sections of a soft-action float rod. He and other Weaver tippers were good at waiting for two indications on the tip before striking and winding two roach back. But back to the slider.

Pete lists four advantages the slider offered on the river:

"1. The slider seems well suited to presenting a bait at any depth in the water column. If sliding from a bulk shotting at 4' deep and fishing on the bottom in 10' of water, the bait gets down to the fish quicker than from a float set 10' deep. This is more the case in the colder months.

"2. In summer when looking to catch fish on the drop the float can easily be converted to a fixed waggler by adding a small back shot just above the float to fish it 4' deep, or the stop knot can be slid down to the bulk, though I would advise the first option.

"3. With four no. 10 shot droppers spread out over the end four feet of line, one or two of them can be slid up to the bulk to give an even slower fall to the bait. Brian Lees used to say 'you want 'em (ie. the roach) chasing the bait and then a good catch is likely'. It's regular feed that makes the roach chase or compete, of course, and if the fish are ever swirling as the feed goes in that's the time to consider shallowing up.

"4. You hit bites better as the strike is more direct to the fish, through the float not into it. In matches at Rudyard Lake, Staffs., for example, I have used the slider in 8' of water, sliding from a bulk set at half-depth and found it successful."

Pete warns that not all bites take the float under, he also gets some lifts from good fish, but he always dots his float down to 1/8" of show on the surface. The peacock is approximately 1/8" diameter at the tip. As for the all-important wire eye, he whips this onto a short cane peg at the bottom of the float having filed down the cane first to flatten it slightly. As for the eye's diameter, without checking he believes it is just over 1mm. To complete the rig Pete's hook is mostly a size 20 - a B510 barbless – to which he impales a single bronze maggot.

"It is important to keep the feed going in as a swim can come alive at any time. I usually get through 1 ½ to 2 pints of bronze maggots in a five-hour match," adds Pete.

Chris Simmons fishes the float only slightly different to Pete: *"I liked to fish a bit heavier than Brian [Lees] did and slide 3BB, the float being a 3BB Drennan straight peacock (grey-painted type) for fishing on the bottom, and an inserted version for off the bottom. I liked these floats as the paint stopped on them, unlike today where the paint comes off many shop-bought wagglers too easily.*

"Below the bulk I had 2 no. 8s and three no. 10 droppers. The bulk would be set around 6' from the hook, or 5' minimum, and we'd slide from there to full depth. We would always slide at the start of the match but if the fish came up in the water we had the option of locking the stop knot against the bulk shot to fish 6' deep.

"The float and method is versatile. In the deeper part of the river at Northwich we might sometimes fish 15' deep and slide the float 5' to the stop knot, while at shallower Winsford Marina we'll slide from 8'-10' deep only, or even lock the float on the bulk at 6'.

"The key to a frame catch is finding the quality roach of 6oz-8oz size, and it means shopping around the feeding zone. Sometimes the best fish are found on the edge of the feed, and they might be at a level below the bits or feeding above them. You have to search and find out where they are on the day."

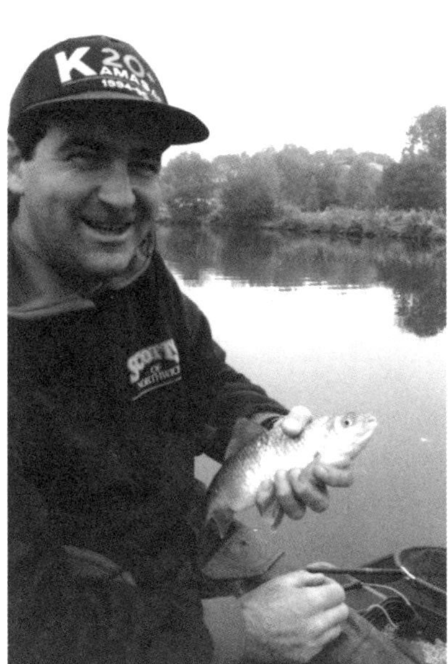

Pete Clements with a 1lb Weaver roach.

Chris is not exactly sure what size eye he uses in the float base. For a long time he used an adaptor he found which had a small, stainless wire eye attached, later changing to a small swivel bound to the float. Rod choice was a Shakespeare President 12' combined with a Mitchell 'Match' or a '300'. *"Mitchell should have made the 'Match' so the bale arm could be closed manually, my one criticism of an otherwise lovely reel,"* said Chris.

His preferred reel line is 2.6lb Bayer and hooklength Shakespeare Omni 1/2lb which is more like 1lb breaking strain but may be off the market and hard to find these days. Chris makes a habit of tying two stop-knots together above the float as a single one has a tendency to slip with the friction of winding it through the rod rings.

Chris always prefers to loosefeed maggots, at times attacking with 'double feed' or two pouchfuls when they are really hungry, with a single bronze or white maggot on a size 20 Colmic B957 hook. He also likes to add turmeric to his maggots which gives a fresh white maggot a yellow tint. When the roach are slow at coming to the float like when the river is out of sorts or pulling hard, Chris turns to Plan 'B', which is a light ledger rod and bomb with a long 6' tail. He'll cast this down the swim and will pick up roach or sometimes bonus skimmers and eels.

Top Tip

Cast the slider out slightly beyond the target zone and wind back into it with a couple of reel turns to straighten everything out. Quickly dropping the rod in the rod-rest ready to feed with the catapult, the float will slowly slide back up the line towards you and the stop-knot. Watch the float closely when firing the bait out, as just before the bulk settles a bite is likely. Whenever the fish climb up the column of feed towards the maggots' point of entry, these bites can result in the bigger roach, the sort Brian was so good at conjuring up. - **Chris Simmons**

Top Tip

Add curry powder and turmeric to your maggots, roach love it! They degrease the maggots but they also wriggle more which must be a good thing. The smell must also appeal. I wouldn't say the same additives work for bream, but roach and spice go together for me. – **Pete Clements**

Chapter 21
Simplicity is the Key to Successful Slider Fishing – by Matt Godfrey

Matt Godfrey, 25, from Sheffield, has achieved more in his young life to date than most anglers do in a lifetime, with a meteoric rise to fame over the last 11 years. Fishing for England at Youth and Intermediate level since the age of 14, he has won three individual gold medals and a silver to sit in his cabinet alongside seven team medals! Now as a senior angler he has just been rewarded for his progress by selection for the 2016 European Championships squad. He has also been proud to represent England in the World Club Championships for his Barnsley Blacks team in 2014 and 2015, which brought another team medal. While Matt is as capable on running line as well as pole, the sliding waggler was curiously once a method he dreaded using. Now it has become his favourite style of fishing. In this chapter he explains why…

What could be worse than slider fishing, I once thought? A complicated, tangle-prone rig, a float that is difficult to shot-up, and the need to accurately feed groundbait with a catapult - quite frankly an out of date technique that was far too difficult to master. If you had asked me about slider fishing some 10 years ago, that was my view and I'd have told you that feeder fishing was far easier. Now, however, I fish the slider at every opportunity I possibly can. In my opinion, it is the most enjoyable method of fishing. Interestingly however, it took me a while to realise just how simple slider fishing is. The simpler you make it, the more enjoyable it is, and the more fish you'll catch on it.

I was thrown in at the deep end when it came to the slider, when I travelled abroad to fish the Junior World Championship at the age of 14. In international rules, you must fish with a float, and anything that slightly resembles ledgering or feeder fishing is strictly prohibited. This means that the slider is the only way of tackling deep water on these matches. If you want to fish in a lake that is 20 feet deep without using a feeder, you would need a rod at least 20 feet in length. Casting out with a float set at that depth is the kind of challenge you'd be presented with in a gladiator game show.

The slider involves having a float that slides on the line. The weight of the rig is towards the terminal end of the rig, and sinks down taking the hookbait with it. Meanwhile, the float slides up the line, only stopping when it reaches a stop knot set at the required depth. This may be 9 or 10 feet, but at the same time could be 40 feet. You can simply wind your stop knot through the rod rings and onto your reel.

You will hear all kinds of theories about slider set-ups - rigs, casting techniques, floats and more, but I'd like to promote a very simple, well-considered and what I believe is the most effective way to fish a slider. A conversation with Alan Scotthorne (five-times World Champion) totally changed my thinking about slider fishing, and much of what I'm about to explain was inspired by him. I'm sure you'll agree he's one man who has authority on this method.

The Rod

First, let's start with the rod. I use a 14-foot Drennan Acolyte Plus. This little bit of extra length and power in the rod enables you to punch a weight out smoothly and effortlessly, and helps you pick up line when you strike.

Main line

The main line is the next vital part of my rig. I always use a very thick reel line. My choice is 8lb Daiwa Hyper Sensor – 0.23mm in diameter. The main reason for this is because it eliminates tangles. Try and use anything much less than this in diameter, and I can

Boss floats that give presentation options.

Main line of choice.

assure you that you'll suffer tangles. I can honestly say I can count on one hand the number of tangles I've had in the last 18 months with this method. This main line is stiff, and prevents any kind of wrap-over around the bulk and float. It's also very durable to withstand casting a heavy weight constantly. It also comes on a bulk 3,000m spool, so for a Yorkshire lad like me it's cost effective too.

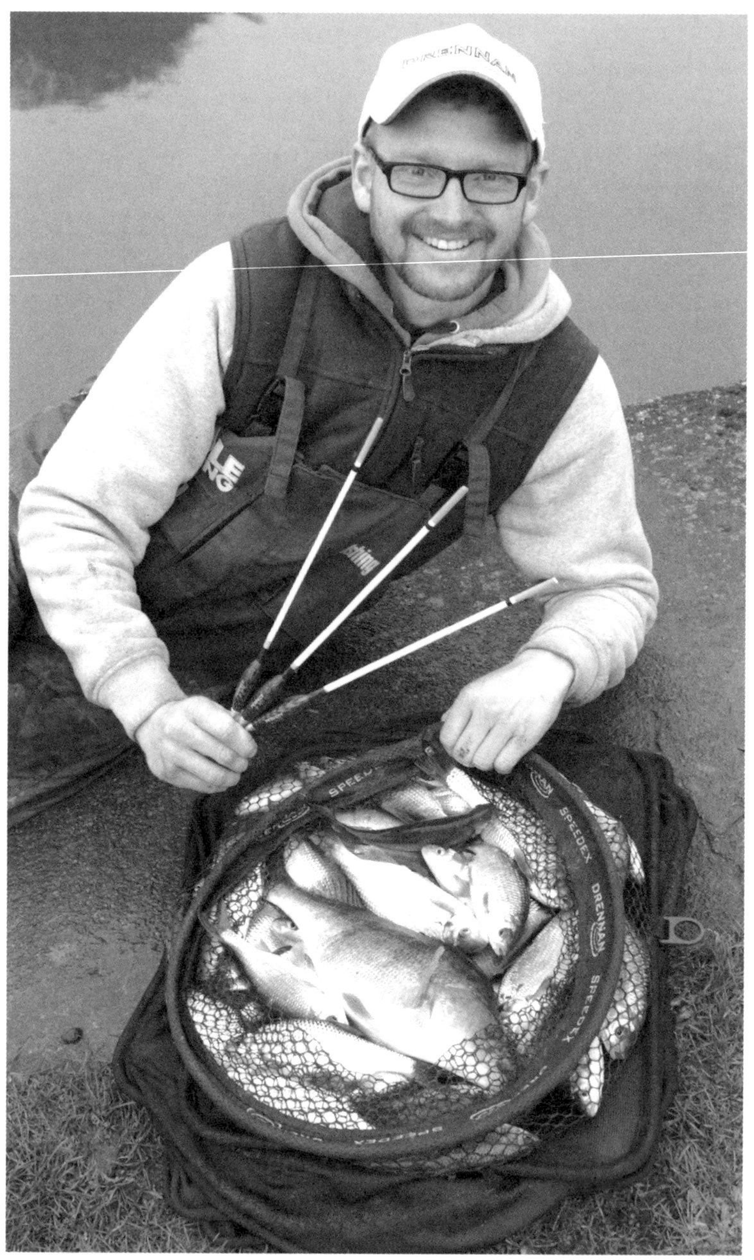

A slider catch to be proud of.

Floats

I only use one kind of slider float, and they are the Hungarian-made 'Perfect Sliders'. A good friend of mine, Szilard Magyar, makes these semi-loaded floats, which are quite literally 'perfect'. The semi-loading is important, as a small amount of loading helps the float sit tight to your bulk when you cast. You can also alter the loading of these floats by adding or taking away little brass disks that slip in place. This is important for my set-up, as it allows me to shot the float very precisely, as you'll see later.

The floats also come with interchangeable tips. The first is a thin, hollow plastic insert, while the second is a thick, hollow plastic bristle. The thin one is ideal on calm days when you want just a small amount of line on the deck, while the thicker one is perfect in rough weather, when dragging lots of line for big fish. I simply attach the float using the eye provided on its base, and prevent it running over the stop knot with a tiny plastic bead (the bead's internal hole is approx. 1mm diameter). The stop knot is tied in 0.15mm or 0.17mm Reflo Power line, not too thick so it will slide easily through the rod rings on the cast.

Beads.

The bulk, leader and droppers

Rather than using shot for my bulk, I use an in-line Drennan olivette. It's simply a case of finding a size that is ideal for the float you are using. I find that 8g, 10g and 12g olivettes cover all my slider work.

Olivettes are much neater and far less tangle prone than big bulk shot. I actually place mine upside down on the rig, so the float kicks out from the top of the olivette to further eliminate tangles. This is locked in place by a loop. At the base of the rig I have a one-metre length of 0.22mm fluorocarbon as a mini leader. This is loop-to-looped onto the main line, and the olivette wedges onto this.

Below the olivette I place four No. 8 shot to play with (can slide them down to add extra weight near the hook if necessary) and these add further security to the olivette to stop any chance of it sliding out of position. At the bottom of the leader I place a swivel with three No. 8 shot bulked next to it. This makes a super stiff and inconspicuous leader thanks to the fluorocarbon. There's no scope for strung-out shot or lots of droppers to my mind. You're asking for tangles, and it's too negative to register lift bites. When a fish moves the three No. 8s and swivel, the float either lifts right up or sails away. I have some spare leaders tied up on a foam spool with the swivel and shot in place should anything go wrong. To this, I attach a 30cm hooklength to complete the rig.

The 8g olivette with six brass disks screwed under the float and the shotting I've described is perfect for the 3+10g float size. A 10g olivette with five brass disks under the float is perfect for the 3+12g float. Then a 12g olivette with four brass disks screwed under the float is ideal for the 3+15g float. Now you can see where the disks come into play.

The 'Perfect' floats.

Olivettes.

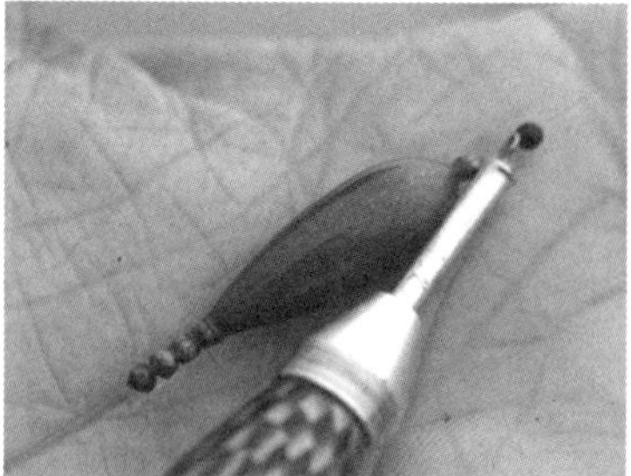

This is how the float sits on the olivette ready for casting.

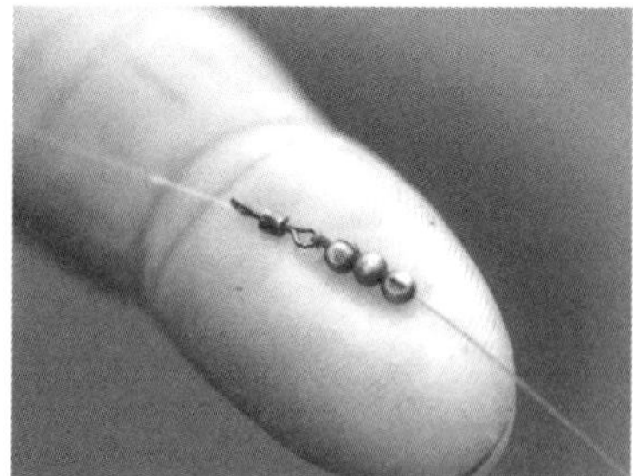

The end of the leader where the 3 no. 8s and swivel form the tell-tale shot.

Feeding techniques

I am terrible at feeding groundbait with a catapult. I can feed it all down the same hole, but often that is not around my float, sadly. However, once again I was given words of wisdom from Alan Scotthorne about feeding accuracy. He actually fires in his groundbait first, and then fishes on top of it.

I have several catapults set up that will fire groundbait to different (approximate) distances. Some have green Drennan elastic for 25m, others orange for 35m, and the big boys come with black elastic for 45m-plus. When stretched to full extent, equal-sized balls of groundbait will go near enough to the same place every time. I gauge roughly where I want to fish, and proceed to feed my bait. If the first three balls I feed land a metre and a half short for example, I'll reel back to that spot, place a mark on my line at the reel in that spot using a Sensas Line Marker Pen, and proceed to feed the rest right there.

The most important thing is that you know where your bait has gone, and that you fish on top of it. With the three catapult set-ups I've described, I can normally get within a couple of metres every time.

The flexible system of adding weight to the float base.

Plumbing up

I have a foolproof method for plumbing up when slider fishing. The key to finding the true depth of the swim is to use a very heavy 30g plummet (just over 1oz), and a very buoyant 20g float. That way the plummet sinks and the float pops up very positively. Whatever size waggler I might have attached beforehand, I can simply unscrew it (another benefit of Szilard's Perfect floats) and replace it with a great big 20g version. By putting the plummet on the hook, I can cast out and find the depth, altering the stop knot position until the float shows the depth inch-perfect.

Once the depth is found I will then move the stop knot a few inches up the line to fish over-depth. Then I simply screw the original float back in place together with the right number of brass disks so the float is shotted perfectly. But why not start by fishing the bait just touching the bottom, you may ask? Well, I prefer to err on the side of having more line on the deck than less with this method. It is positive, and often you are fishing for quality fish, so a static bottom bait is normally a good form of presentation.

A handful of slider-caught roach.

A quality roach.

Memorable Slider experiences

I've been lucky enough to fish the slider in some stunning venues all over the world. I also love fishing it in the UK too, of course. There's something so lovely about casting out the float, letting your line peel off the reel spool as the weight falls, before seeing the float cock and droppers set. When it bobs, and then slowly dips under, you get an indescribable adrenalin rush, before leaning back into a firm strike and feeling that solid, nodding resistance of a fish. It's making me want to go and have a fish with the slider just writing about it.

One venue that sticks in my mind is the River Vilaine in Rieux, France, where I fished an intermediate World Championship. The river was around 60 metres wide and had a huge drop-off around 20 metres out, below which the river's stocks of bream and skimmers were living. It was around 20 feet deep there and, with the river only gently pulling, the slider was a key method. In fact, come the weekend of the World Championship, our team each set up just four slider rods and that was it.

We were in contention after the first day, but halfway through the second day, there was a huge thunderstorm and the match was stopped for over an hour. When it was re-started, the river suddenly picked up pace and we were virtually running our sliders through like stick floats. It seemed all wrong, but by attacking the swims by feeding a heavy ball of soil and groundbait every cast, each of us began to catch mullet on the slider. Yes, you heard...mullet! I managed six, which fought amazingly in the flow, and in such hard conditions we managed to win a silver team medal. It was a one of the craziest matches I've ever fished, but I'll always remember it.

More recently, I was lucky enough to fish the Daiwa Silverfest festival on Loch Ken, Scotland. This was float only, and after having a practice session up there the day before the event began, teammate Lee Kerry and I twigged that the slider was a great way to catch roach early in the match before they moved in on the pole swim.

Unlike normal slider fishing, however, this venue required a little more finesse; we missed many bites if we had too much, or too little line, on the bottom. Three inches of line on the bottom was ideal. It may sound picky, but that's how particular I'd be on the pole for roach, so why should it be any different on the slider?

The trip taught me the importance of plumbing-up accurately, which is where the big plummet and big float came into play. I went on to have two of the best day's fishing I've ever had. The first day I tipped 25lb of roach onto the scales to win the match, and on the second day a lower 20lb confirmed another win and overall festival win. Of course, I drew some very good pegs too. Fishing the slider for the first two hours out in the deeper water put me well ahead of the anglers around me, and the enjoyment factor of fishing such a beautiful method in stunning surroundings was sublime. If you've yet to explore the slider, please don't leave it too long. Keep things simple and positive, and it could become your favourite method too.

Chapter 22
Big Catches on the Waggler Today - by Warren Martin

Modern wagglers have tended to get shorter and fatter to suit the growth and popularity of shallow commercial fisheries, and fishing for carp with hair-rigged, banded pellets on the hook is now a common sight. Norfolk's Warren Martin, aged 36, from Dereham, has made the method his own and taken some huge catches on commercial waters. His big match breakthrough came in 2012 when he claimed the £25,000 cheque for winning the prestigious Fish'o'Mania title. Sponsored by Matrix/Barford Tackle, he's a quantity surveyor who seems gifted at putting large quantities in his keepnets. Warren now describes his pellet waggler approach...

The term 'pellet waggler' is used to describe both a float and a method of fishing, and has developed into a proven match winner since its inception around the start of the new millennium. Prior to that anglers around the UK had for many years caught carp on peacock wagglers and similar, going right back to the original days of match carping at places like Layer Pits, near Colchester, but this was traditional type waggler fishing with natural baits.

Big Catches on the Waggler Today - by Warren Martin

Being an angler whose early days were spent on natural waters in and around the Broads and Fens, I have always enjoyed running line fishing, and when the change to fishing predominantly commercial waters largely with pole came along, I always tried to integrate it into my fishing. In the early days this was still using basic traditional wagglers. Those days spent pleasure fishing in my teens and my early years match fishing are, I believe, what have stood me in good stead for pellet waggler fishing. I'm sure it's because all the principles of efficiency, smoothness and presentation are the same.

The introduction of specialist wagglers for fishing shallow, and the use of hair rigs by match anglers, opened up endless new variations of waggler fishing not previously known about and, with thought, huge catches can be taken. Personally I've had catches of big carp on it up to 363lb with countless weights over 200lb, but my most pleasing catch was 175lb of small carp on it to qualify for the 2012 Fish'O'Mania final. This was at Messingham Sands in North Lincolnshire, a catch which felt like a reward for the hard work I'd put in mastering the method.

It's a method that is still evolving and in just a few years we have gone from heavy obtrusive floats that unwary carp would hook themselves against, to more refined, delicate floats to outwit the fish, while always searching for better and better presentation.

When we talk about pellet waggler fishing, we are predominantly talking about catching carp up in the water on pellets and this is what we will talk about here. These wagglers do have other uses such as fishing on the deck up to islands out of pole range, and there are days when a waggler-fished pellet over loose feed on the deck will out-fish the feeder, but these are secondary to the main tactic.

The basic principle is regular feeding, and by that I mean almost non-stop of a very small amount of pellets to bring the fish up in the water and competing for the feed. A usual starting point would be three or four 8mm pellets, with a hair-rigged 8mm on the hook. If fishing for F1s rather than proper carp then 6mms come into play, and on large waters where the carp are at range then heavier 11mm pellets are used.

To start a match I would generally set the float at around half depth, feeding 8mm pellets, three at a time every 20 seconds, and then read the swim from there. By that I mean if there are swirls as the bait falls or I'm getting line bites, then I would shallow up. Conversely, if there were no signs then I would go deeper 6" at a time until I found the fish. There are of course days, like with all methods, when it simply won't work.

As with all methods the fish soon wise up to it, and whereas in the beginning it was just a case of chucking a big waggler out, feeding, then seeing the rod go round with a fish on, it's now a much more skilful, refined method that carp have become wary of, so tackle and tactics have to be thought about far more.

The anglers who do well on the method are those who are prepared to work, and those with a background on traditional venues, running wagglers or stick floats down rivers, seem to understand the necessity for good presentation on all types of float fishing. These anglers also seem to have the necessary coordination, and be able to handle their gear in the correct way to be efficient.

As mentioned, in the early days you could have your rod on a rest and the fish would hook themselves against the heavy float; now however, the single most important factor, which is of the utmost importance, is that you must hold your rod at all times, and in a manner that means you are able to strike at every indication or dip even whilst feeding. Anglers who cast, rest their rod down to feed, then pick it up again, miss countless indications that could have been hit had they been holding their rod. Some of the tiniest, sharpest dips are proper bites and the only way to hit these is by striking the very second they occur.

If you think about what's happening underwater, the fish are sitting in a tight area where the feed is landing, and usually stationed at a set depth where they feel comfortable. They are not therefore going to pick up your bait and charge off giving a good bite, as they will just be waiting for the next pellets to fall, and the second one takes your pellet it might feel something wrong and reject it. That split second beforehand, where you may only see a tiny dip on the float, may be all you will get from that fish.

There are still the red letter days when the fish are very shallow, and snatching at the bait the second it hits the surface where they will bolt and hook themselves, and on these days the striking element isn't as important. But the holding of the rod is still important, as you will be looking to feed then cast, feed then twitch the float back, reel in and repeat, all within 30 seconds. It is just not possible to put the rod down between each step as there is no time. Other than practice, the best tip for being able to hold the rod at all times is to have your knees slightly higher than you normally would as this gives extra support and balance.

The biggest issue once the actual physical difficulties are overcome is float choice. There are now hundreds of different designs and materials on the market and are all aimed at doing different things.

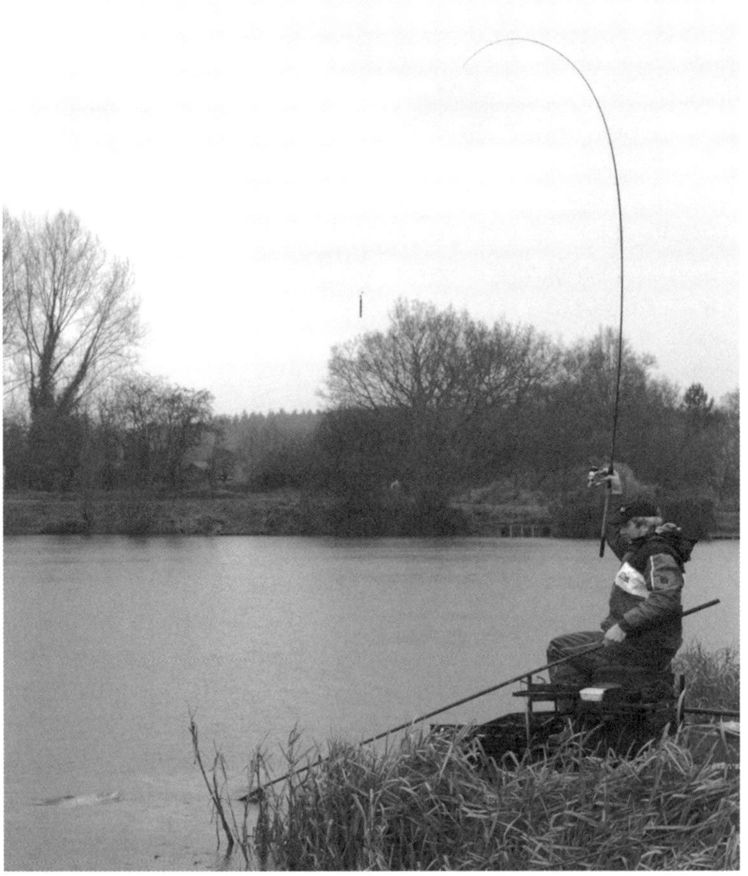

The moment of truth. Warren is in perfect position to net the carp.

Poly Wags (made with a polystyrene body) are probably the most widely used and can be loaded or unloaded. These floats usually take between 2 and 6 grammes and are used for fishing very shallow at close to medium range. These are my personal preference for fishing very shallow, but being made from such a lightweight material they are only of use in good conditions when the wind is kind, as any tow will cause them to drag instantly.

I use unloaded floats, with the shot around the float placed on fine silicone to protect the line. My theory for using unloaded floats goes along with my theory for pellet waggler fishing in general which is that simplicity is the key. Loaded floats can have issues with the loading moving or breaking, as can the stops (ie. rubber stops holding the float in place) that are used with them. Any break in the feeding routine can cause the carp to drift off so time spent re-tackling is costly. The worst that can happen with an unloaded float is a shot falling off which takes seconds to replace. The pale blue coloured wagglers from J-Range, or the black models from Preston Innovations, are both excellent. Unlike some other models, the width/length/weight ratio seems right, giving them a nice balance and helping them cast and land straight.

Longer balsa-type wagglers come into their own for fishing slightly deeper or for fishing shallow when there is tow. These are almost a cross between traditional wagglers and the poly wags mentioned above and commonly models taking 6 to 10g would be used. My personal choice are the silver Garbolino models. Although a shallow water method, there are days when the fish will sit at half depth or even lower, and a longer, more stable waggler offers better presentation for longer periods than a shorter, lighter waggler would.

Some of my best weights have come in winter, when I've found the fish sitting at a certain depth, for example at 7′ in 10′ of water. In cooler water, the fish will find levels they are happy to sit at. These are called thermoclines, and may just be a layer of water a fraction of a degree warmer than the rest of the water column. When the fish are shoaled tightly it is possible to fish 6″ shallower or deeper and not even know any fish are there. But find this layer in winter and a bumper day can be had as the fish will be tightly shoaled and won't move. A longer waggler like those described, fished at this depth, will produce bites providing it is not pulling off line.

When fishing like this it is more akin to traditional waggler fishing as the bites won't be on the drop, but will come after the rig has settled. When fishing this way, or for that matter anything over 4 feet, I like to incorporate shot down the line. This may go against everything that's been written about the method, but I believe it's vitally important. Some days I will have been getting a bite every cast then they suddenly stop. When I've checked, a shot has come off; I put one back on and bites restart, and this has happened too often to be coincidence. I believe this works as the loose feed sinks uniformly, at a rate which may differ slightly between the pellets if sizes are not the same, but each pellet will fall unhindered at its own constant speed. But with anything over 4' of line between float and hook unshotted, that line will hang in the surface tension for periods before sinking, then another bit may hang and so on, meaning the hookbait isn't falling evenly and will look unnatural amongst the loose offerings. Three or four no. 9 or 10 shot are all that's needed to sink the line and counteract this.

On larger venues bigger floats are required. These come in many shapes and sizes and, due to the amount of shot that's required, this is when we need to use loaded floats. British Waterways venues like Boddingtons, Earlswood or Clattercote have become specialist venues as the fish live at huge distances from the bank. Big loaded wagglers up to 15g are needed with 11mm pellets. Commercially made models are available but the cult pattern to use are the hand-made versions from John Bonney. They look slightly rough around the edges but, I repeat, there is a perfect length/weight/diameter ratio for every waggler to work properly and these achieve that.

Other variations have sprung off from pellet waggler fishing. In hot, still weather mugging (or dobbing) has long been carried out on the pole. This is fishing a long line and simply flicking the rig at cruising fish with no feed. As with all methods on heavily fished commercials, the carp are wising up to this now, but by accurately casting a waggler at them, landing the float short and feathering it so the pellet flips over into the path of the fish, it can be devastating as there is no pole to spook them. For this as small a float as possible is needed as the splash can spook them. A traditional waggler that wouldn't make a big splash is no good though, as with thick reel line - and my main line for pellet waggler work is 6lb Maxima - they will not cast well.

The answer is to cut down a 4g J-Range Poly wag to a third of its length. This will now take around 2AAA but it somehow defies the laws of physics by still casting straight and up to 30m distance even with 6lb line, and it makes little disturbance on landing; again the correct weight/length/diameter ratio. A week before writing this I won a match at Barford Lakes with 240lb, all casting at fish I could see with this float and I never fed anything all day.

There are days, especially in spring and autumn, when the fish will be shallow, but with the water clear they will be spooked by the pole. At these times of year big pellets and big weights might not be possible, but by fishing a traditional insert waggler, but with 4 or 6mm pellets and light line, casting 13m or 14m and feeding small pellets, fish that may not be catchable on the pole are possible on the waggler.

As with all styles of float fishing, presentation along with feeding are the keys. Whatever style of pellet waggler fishing I'm doing, I will always dot my float down as much as I can while still being able to see it. I will strike at any indications and by dotting it down these are seen easier. Also, and this is something many people don't think about, when you are fishing off bottom, many bites will be hold ups - carp which intercept the bait but do not move off with it. This will usually happen when fishing deeper, and by using the shot down the line as mentioned earlier, and having the float properly dotted down, these bites can be seen, bites that many anglers do not see. To further show these on floats that don't come with them, I draw on a black line in marker pen under the coloured tip so I can spot when it's held up.

Along with the floats, good hooks and line are needed to aid presentation. As mentioned, 6lb Maxima is always my choice for carp, with 4lb Maxima for F1s. Maxima is ever-reliable and very strong, the other bonus is untreated it will float, perfect for calm days, but on windier days it can easily be sunk. Hooklengths need to be the lightest the day allows to get more bites, but strong enough to cope. Typically these will range from 0.11mm for F1s on the traditional waggler mentioned, through to 0.18mm for big carp. I have never needed to fish heavier than this and in fact the 363lb weight I had was on 0.15mm line.

Reels need to be smooth with a wide spool to aid casting and I use the Matrix Ultrons in a 3000 size for short casts and 4000 for longer distances. These are paired with Matrix Carpmaster rods, an 11-footer for the 3000 reel and a 12-foot for the 4000 reel. These are both very balanced set-ups. Hooks are always Matrix Riggers, tied with a knotless knot and a hair-rigged band - a size 16 for 8mm pellets, and an 18 for 6mms.

Top Tip

One of the main considerations with pellet waggler fishing is feeding ACCURACY. A good catapult is therefore vital for a pellet waggler session. The tighter and more accurately you can group and land the pellets each cast the more bites you will get. For this an old-style catapult with a mesh pouch seems to work best for me, I use the Middy 321 which is very strong and one can last a whole match which is something most catapults struggle with after non-stop use for five hours. And don't forget, keep hold of that rod at all times. Practice firing the catapult while holding the rod with the two smallest fingers and the cattie pouch between forefinger and thumb.

Chapter 23
Darren Moyle – The Carp Bagger – by Matt Godfrey

Darren Moyle, 48, from Eckington, Sheffield, is a self-employed landscape gardener formerly in the military with the Royal Engineers. Originally specialising in barbel on rivers, he decided to try his hand at match fishing and soon found the winning touch. Darren believes that fishing is a science and he certainly puts lots of thought into his methods. He broke the 150lb match record at Aston Springs No. 2 lake with 164lb in 2010, then broke his own record in 2012 with 171lb which stands as his best win to date. Favourite venue: Trent at Newark. Most memorable fishing session: nine barbel including seven double figure fish up to a personal best 12lb 9oz in a five-hour Trent night stint.

The pellet waggler is a method in the armoury of many commercial anglers throughout the warmer months. However, many anglers I know use the pellet wag to quickly mug a few fish at the start of a match, or reach for their rod as a last gasp bid to catch when their pole and method feeder lines don't throw up the goods.

It became apparent that one local angler, Darren (or 'Daz') Moyle, had become rather feared on the pellet waggler method. People in tackle shops around Sheffield were trying to find out what he'd been doing differently to other anglers. Many of them were astonished to discover that he had made the decision to sell all his pole fishing gear, and become a rod and line specialist.

This turned out to be a smart move. His successes at KJS Aston No. 2 Fishery suddenly escalated, and in one year he framed in every single match he attended between April and August, and many of these results saw him take first place. In eight consecutive matches, Darren caught over 1,000lb of fish, broke the match record with 164lb 2oz, and recorded wins from every bank of the lake. I caught up with him on a short session to get a little insight into what he was doing...

The set-up

On arriving at the lake, Darren was set up and ready to go. It was immediately obvious why he has an advantage over other anglers. He was prepared with two identical waggler rods – Preston Carbonactive 11' pellet waggler models, together with a bomb (ledger) set-up, and a slow-sinking 'bubble' (see panel below for details), both attached to Carbonactive 10' mini rods. All four reels were Daiwa TDR's and his waggler rigs were very interesting and simply arranged.

His waggler choice is either a 6g, 8g or 10-gram Middy Popper, which is painted in a grey colour to blend in with the sky when wary carp are looking up. At Aston, the water is particularly clear and, as will become clear, Darren's big weight tactics revolve around tricking the wiser fish. As a reserve float he also uses a Drennan crystal pellet waggler.

The float is attached with a metal Maver waggler adapter, and is locked in place with a Drennan grip-stop above the float, and three more below. These stops are to prevent any slippage of the float on casting, but it also allows quick and easy depth changes without damaging the line. There are no shots on the rig at all, and the only weight down the line is a tiny size 24 swivel to prevent line twist during the intense casting sessions that take place.

The bomb rig is a little bit special, and doesn't actually involve what most anglers regard as a bomb – the Arlesey version. Darren's river specimen background has led him to develop a rig incorporating a drilled bullet, with a very short hooklink from 6

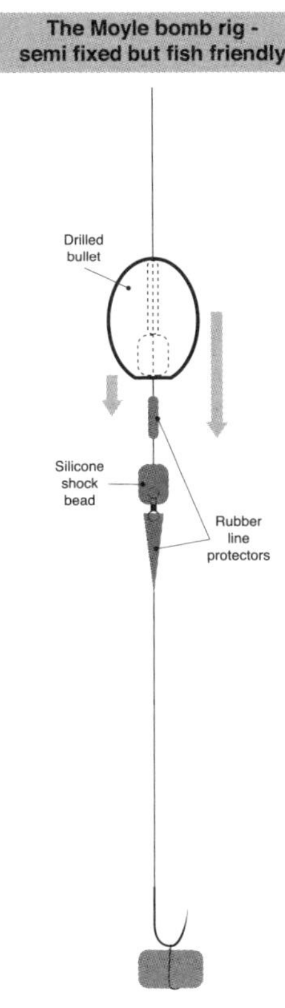

to 8 inches long. This is a semi-fixed lead with a Drennan Grip-stop built inside the bullet, which covers the rule of most commercial fisheries that requires a lead or feeder to be fished in-line or sliding, but because it slides under tension it is still in effect a bolt rig whereby all taking fish are likely to get hooked. With a conventional bomb, there is lots of movement around the swivel and bomb link. Darren believes the bigger, wiser carp use this to their advantage and can eject a hookbait without a bite being seen (see diagram, left).

The third rig is the slow-sinking bubble – the Fox bolt bubble version – which is used to search the depth layers during quiet spells. The bubble is semi-fixed in the same way as the drilled bullet. However, the big difference is in the bubble's slow-sinking capacity. Darren can also make minor adjustments to the sinking speed which can make all the difference to bites. This is done by simply dripping a few drops of water in or out of the bubble until the right speed of fall to suit the fish is found. Note that on some days this has to be done several times to keep the fish coming.

Finesse

Despite catching huge weights, Darren's tackle is remarkably light, and is another key aspect of his approach. He feels that by fishing light, he gets a lot more bites, which enable him to read his peg and work out what is going on much better than if he was getting very few bites. His hooklengths are in 0.11mm, 0.13mm and 0.15mm Powerline, and he uses either an 18 or 20 Guru MWG or Pellet Waggler hook. To this he attaches a hard pellet in two different ways: 1/ pushed inside a pellet band tied on hair rig and the no-knot knot if fishing the waggler or bubble; and 2/ by a noose (or slip knot) on the hair when fishing the bomb.

The most common hook-link is the 0.13mm, which is strong enough to pull most of the carp in easily, but light enough to get more bites than others. Setting the clutch correctly enables Darren to strike and play fish without worry, and on striking you can actually hear his clutch ticking. This works on a similar principle to using elastic in a pole, and means that nearly all fish hooked end up in the net.

Machine-like Feeding

Feeding is by far the most important part of Darren's approach. Two sizes of pellets – 6mm and 8mm - are all that is present on his side tray, but he has developed a further edge with these on closer inspection. In his tubs of pellets, there is a wide variety of shades and colours - from deep red, to light brown and even dark green. These have different oil contents, and therefore different sinking speeds, which hold fish at different layers in the water.

"Changing the colour of the pellet on the hook is I believe another important part of catching extra fish," says Darren. *"A change of hookbait often results in short bursts of fish, and I have found that certain colours work better at certain depths."*

Grey-painted Middy poppers, 8mm and 6mm pellets, and enough catapults to survive a busy session.

Darren keeps the rod low while pumping the fish in to shore.

There is no scope for negativity in Darren's feeding, and he opts to make more noise, feed more often and feed larger quantities than everyone else on the lake. Aston is a big expanse of water, and it can sometimes take two hours before the fish are in the peg. A defensive approach gives very little chance of drawing in fish, so Darren does everything in his power to pull fish into his peg. It won't be unusual for him to get through six pints of pellets in a match, and sometimes even more.

His routine is machine-like, and he'll feed before casting, after casting, then, after winding his float into the feed, he'll feed again on top of the float while twitching his rig, and finally, will feed again before reeling it in. He always tries to feed an area about the size of a small saloon car like a Mini. There he'll create a constant column of bait in the peg, and it will get fish feeding at all depths.

Sometimes it is not obvious where the fish are in the swim and how many pellets they're willing to accept. Instead of feeding cautiously like some would advise, Darren will often bravely step up the feed to a heavy rate. This has the effect of sending the smaller stockie carp to the bottom and any bigger fish to the far edge of casting range. He then feeds pellets in ones and twos to try to bring the fish back up into midwater. If he gets bites at 4' deep or less he'll immediately grab the float rod, but any deeper he'll opt for the bubble. All the time he is exploring the edges of his feed area as this is where the bigger fish tend to patrol.

He does point out that his whole approach is for catching fish that are willing to feed and looking for bait. Realistically, these are the only ones you are going to catch anyway, and with this approach on an open water venue, a two hour 'window' of feeding fish is often enough to win the match.

The Session

Today's session at Aston could not have been a better example of Darren's winning approach. His first fish came within minutes of starting - a small F1 of around 2lb. As the session developed, short bursts of bites resulted in runs of three or four fish. After two hours, Darren was able to step up a gear and underline why he has been so successful. He looked completely at one with the peg, and would pick up the bomb rod whenever he felt the fish were shy or backing off. He'd nick a few fish on this before returning to the waggler.

He changed his depth over 20 times during the four-hour session, where most people will fish just one depth all day. Out of the blue, he'd have a chuck with the bubble, and several times, this resulted in bigger fish to the 6lb mark.

"The bubble is a good tactic whenever I'm not sure what depth the fish are at, as the extra slow fall of the hook-bait compared to the feed seems to trick the bigger ones into having a go. It's also the method that set the lake's weight record some time back," added Darren.

After planning on fishing five hours, he decided to cut the session short, as he had only brought along two keepnets. He finished the day with over 130lb of carp to 6lb, as well as some smaller stockies, F1s, and even a few big skimmers. By employing a positive feeding approach, with finesse rigs, and an active mind to work at the peg, Darren showed just why he has gained himself his unbeatable reputation at Aston.

Result: another 100lb-plus catch for Daz.

What is a bubble?

The bubble deserves further explanation as one third of Darren's three-pronged attack, as the waggler alone would not have caught so many fish. In short, the bubble is a slow-sinking ledger weight. Many versions of this handy device have been tried over the years and Captain Leonard Parker even wrote about one in his book 'Roach - How to catch them' of 1954.

In the Sheffield area two anglers in particular pioneered what became known as the bubble feeder. Eddie Outram in the 1960s began using an oval plastic capsule (the type containing novelties sold from dispensers outside newsagents) to fish Damflask Reservoir. He'd put three or four holes in each half of the capsule, attach it to a short boom of line with a swivel and run this on the line, only shotting it enough to sink very slowly (see pic in colour section).

Eddie put squatts in the feeder to fish all depths of this deep water and won two Damflask Championships doing so. Tony Wills, who learnt the basic principle from Eddie when they were work-mates, developed it further and he in turn won many matches at the difficult, gin clear reservoir, also setting the three-hour and five-hour weight records with catches of big roach and perch up to 24lb, with many fish taken on the drop. Tony used a Shakespeare Sigma Wand rod to fish the method but any light feeder rod will suffice. Their bubbles would be half-filled with maggots which gave the casting weight, though a bubble does not have to contain bait for it to be effective.

The modern bubble is made from various raw materials but all work on the same principle. Plastic grapes sold for decoration in garden centres, balls of hard wood like beech, or a commercially made bubble float, can all be weighted to sink at the right slow speed, and they will catch both carp and silver fish at every depth level. The pellets or other baits are fired to the target zone by catapult. Another bubble similar to Darren's is built from a plastic widget from an empty beer can. Water is added until the bubble sinks but the level is adjustable via a tiny plug. This type is sold in some local tackle shops.

Ten Top Tips For Successful Pellet Waggler Fishing – by Andy Sellars

Andy Sellars, 58, is a prison officer, formerly of Sheffield now living in Doncaster. An ex-Barnsley Black and Sheffield National Championship angler, he has many good match wins on silver fish under his belt, but now fishes freelance on local waters Hallcroft and Hayfield. His personal best Hallcroft catch is 244lb 14oz consisting of 24 carp to 14lb on waggler and bomb and an 8mm pellet bait. At the same venue he recently broke the weight record for the Leegem league, run by a Chesterfield tackle shop of the same name, with 183lb of carp, and he is acknowledged as being very tough to beat on the pellet waggler...

1. Use a pellet waggler that will cast accurately. Some floats are sadly lacking in this department, not enough attention paid to the aero-dynamics in my opinion! I mostly use a loaded Garbolino float of 4g-8g depending on the distance required. It has a peacock quill stem and a small body and measures anything from 6″ to 10″ long depending on the cast I need to make. They cast beautifully. Most of the quill is left as its natural white colour by the manufacturer and I like to blacken it with a permanent marker pen.

Andy's crystal waggler set just 12″ deep.

Andy with a quality carp from Hallcroft, Retford.

2. Use some FINESSE as this method is not always as easy as some people claim. A good fish will not always give a bold bite and a slight dink of the float can mean a 12-15lb fish has got the bait. My float is fully loaded and, light and wind permitting, I'll dot it down to ¼" of show. I only place shots around the float, none down the line for a nice slow and natural fall of the hook-bait.

3. Use the sharpest hook you can find. I like the Guru Pellet Waggler hooks in size 16 or 18. They are quite simply the best hook there is for the job. I fish a hard 6mm or 8mm pellet in a band on a hair rig tied to the hook with the no-knot knot.

4. I use 6mm or 8mm hard pellets. There are many good brands on the market but I don't like the rule that states: 'must use fishery's own pellets'. This is simply a con, one of the worst in match fishing, as it has nothing to do with fish welfare.

5. Feed little and often with two or three pellets only, but occasionally vary the sequence. A few minutes lay off, or even up to a 10-minute one, can sometimes induce a fish to take the hook-bait. In the meantime try a slight turn of the reel handle to twitch the bait back as this can also do the trick.

6. Make sure your reel line sinks because any drag that pulls the float off line unnaturally can be detected by those bigger and wiser fish that have been caught before. I use 6lb Maxima on the reel and a 0.16mm hooklength in summer, dropping to a 0.14mm when the water turns cold. But even in winter a 0.14 line can be risky anywhere there are double figure fish living near a potential snag, eg. an island or spinner/aerator. Always be wary when near this type or other feature as the smarter carp will head for them, and beef up your tackle if necessary.

7. Make up your end rigs to suit the depth of the water you fish, but also let your experience guide you to the best taking depth. My local Hallcroft is an average 6.5' deep and I might set the float at 3.5' - 4' to start then work from there. Sometimes I have to fish near the deck at 6' deep but in summer I'd expect to shallow up. I put my rigs, all different lengths, on winders and attach them to a clip swivel tied on the end of the reel line. This allows me to change depth quickly.

8. I advise the use of silicone float stops to hold the float in place as these are kinder on the line than shot. And watch for signs of big fish chafing and weakening the last few yards of reel line, and replace a short section if and when necessary.

9. Use a rod and reel that will handle good fish if there are double figure size and upwards expected. My rods include a 14′ and a 13′ Daiwa Matchwinner, and I combine them with Daiwa TDI reels, and the blue version of this reel is the one I prefer as it's the most robust.

10. Always have a back-up plan. I usually set up a bomb rod as a standby. In a recent league match I caught three good carp on bomb in the last 20 minutes and it put me third with 28lb.

Chapter 24
Float Diagrams

The following shotting diagrams show some tried and tested patterns for river or lake from several contributors. Depending where you fish and for what species, you may find one of them suits your style.

The first group (next page) offers four river rigs, each showing a good gap between the hook and tell-tale shot. The second set (p.341) includes a light canal rig and three examples of light shotting for river or lake. The third group (p.342) includes a medium weight Trent rig set overdepth, a heavier Witham rig and a heavy slider rig for very deep water.

Float Diagrams

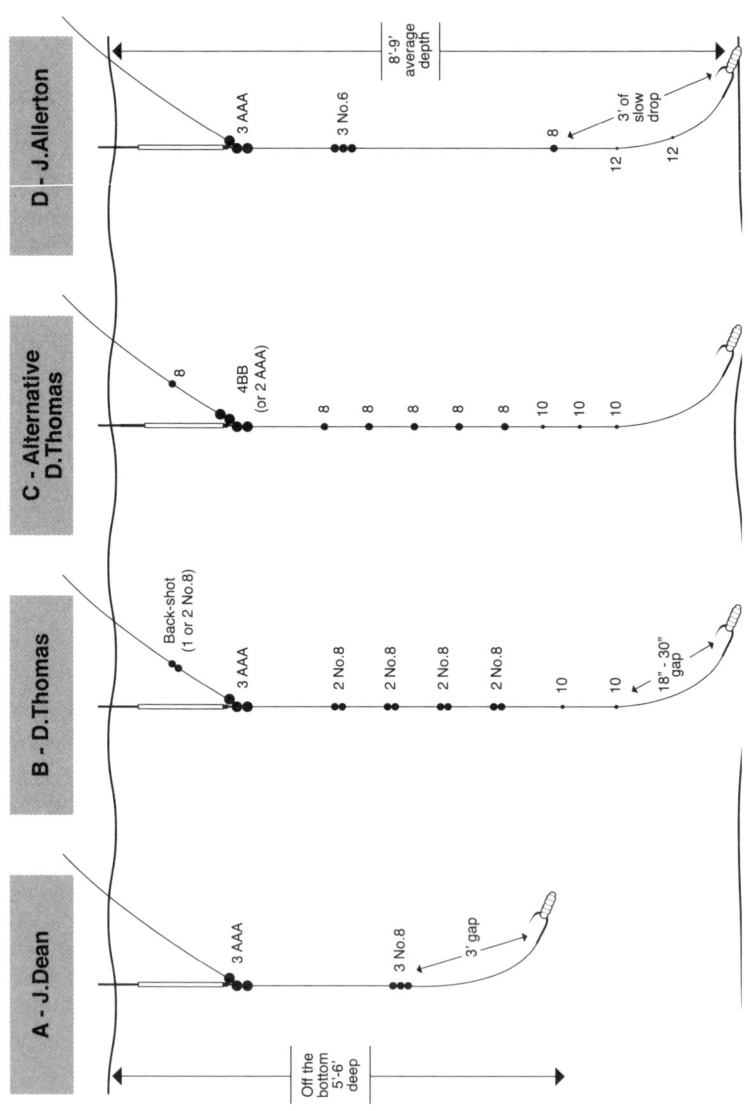

A - J.Dean
3 AAA
3 No.8
3' gap
Off the bottom 5'-6' deep
B - D.Thomas
Back-shot (1 or 2 No.8)
3 AAA
2 No.8
2 No.8
2 No.8
2 No.8
10
10
18" - 30" gap
C - Alternative D.Thomas
8
4BB (or 2 AAA)
8
8
8
8
8
10
10
10
D - J.Allerton
3 AAA
3 No.6
8
12
12
3' of slow drop
8'-9' average depth

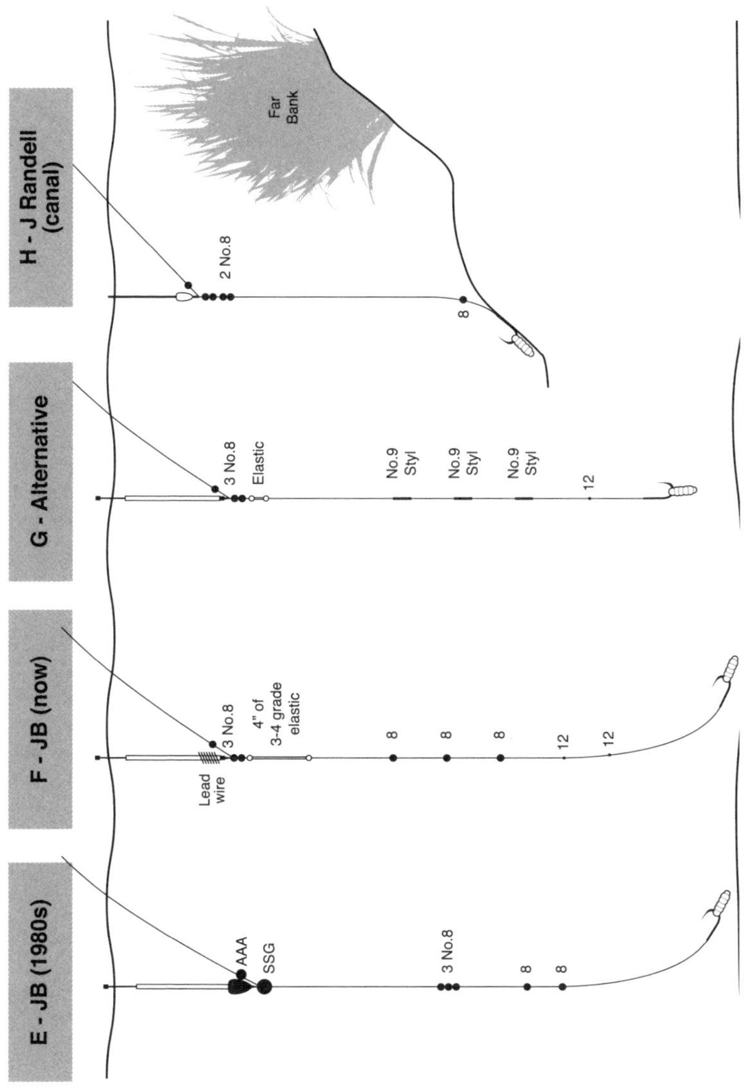
E - JB (1980s)
AAA
SSG
3 No.8
8
8
F - JB (now)
Lead wire
3 No.8
4" of 3-4 grade elastic
8
8
8
12
12
G - Alternative
3 No.8
Elastic
No.9 Styl
No.9 Styl
No.9 Styl
12
H - J Randell (canal)
2 No.8
8
Far Bank

Float Diagrams

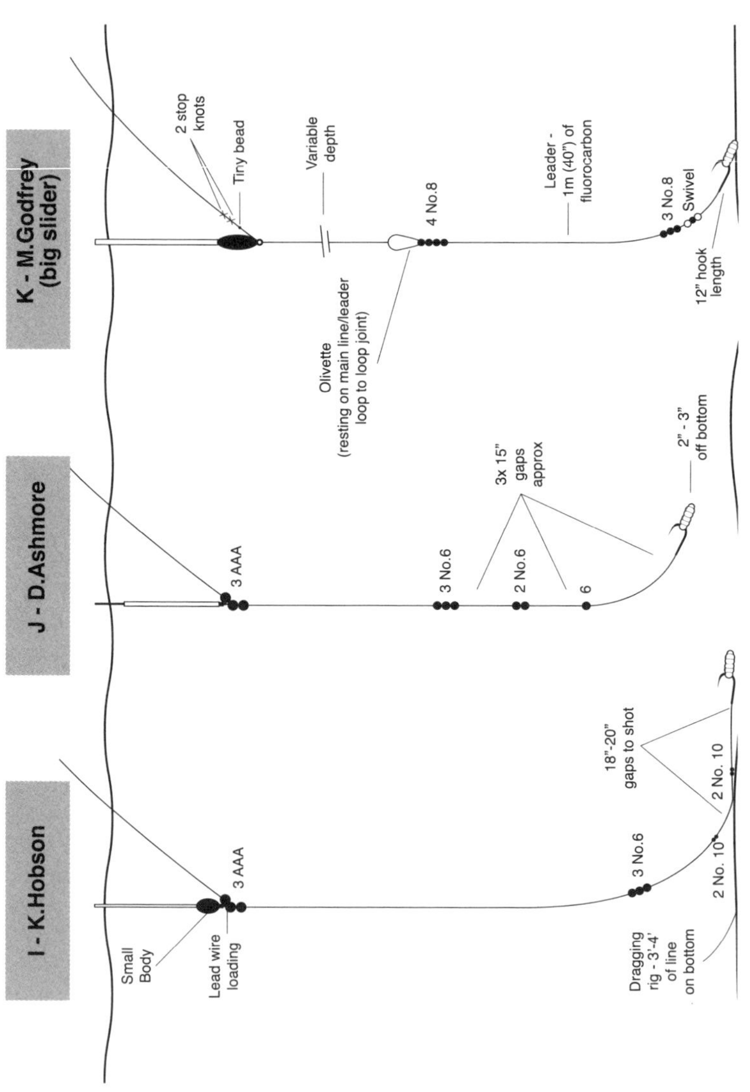

I - K.Hobson
Small Body
Lead wire loading
3 AAA
3 No.6
2 No. 10
2 No. 10
18"-20" gaps to shot
Dragging rig - 3'-4' of line on bottom
J - D.Ashmore
3 AAA
3 No.6
2 No.6
6
3x 15" gaps approx
2" - 3" off bottom
K - M.Godfrey (big slider)
2 stop knots
Tiny bead
Variable depth
4 No.8
Olivette (resting on main line/leader loop to loop joint)
Leader - 1m (40") of fluorocarbon
3 No.8
Swivel
12" hook length

Chapter 25
The Author - A Look to the Future

What does the future hold for my type of waggler with its slim antenna - can it continue to rise in that slow, deliberate way on a good roach bite like it has so often? Well I believe yes, absolutely, as long as there are redfin lovers and waters where they abound. But the waggler experience is not restricted to roach of course, not that it really ever was.

Carp are the fish with a cult following amongst younger anglers, and while some of its fans might only ever reach for the pole or feeder rod, there are others who still fish my way. Having read the latest 'Middy' tackle catalogue I was nicely surprised to find it crammed with 50 varieties of waggler for today's market. Pellet wagglers, bagging wagglers and large feeder floats have each emerged to meet the demands of catching carp on a float.

The ingenuity of anglers never fails to amaze me. Thanks to Glen Bradley at Drake Floats, I was introduced to Ian Heaps' compact version of a pellet waggler. In appearance it's hardly like any roach waggler I have always used but, resembling a 3" bullet made from balsa, it also zips through the air but lands flat and ever so quietly on the water. Ian got the idea from an old canal float on which he placed some lead wire loading halfway up the float so it wouldn't dive deep in his local, shallow Peak Forest Canal. The casting power of his pellet waggler comes from a lead ball inside the float which runs along a channel to sit in the tip of the float when cast, but it momentarily hits the water flat before it cocks - a useful feature on a float made to catch fish very shallow.

Similarly, John Allerton has come up with his own original thinking to break all float-making rules only recently. His new 'crystal' pellet waggler is unique in that it has a tiny hole in it. This float is also designed to land quietly on the surface before water enters the hole and the float cocks. Brilliant.

A third subtle but clever idea for a float tip is an inch-long 'pin' of lead inserted and glued into the tip of a peacock waggler. This reduces the buoyancy of the peacock antenna, but allows a relatively fat tip to be seen by the older angler with failing eyesight. These examples are from only three anglers I know, but there are thousands of other innovators out there pushing back the boundaries every hour of every day. It continues to give us new tackle inventions, including modern wagglers that are looking more versatile than ever.

Of the latest slim wagglers I've seen, the Hungarian Cralusso models are excellent and must rank with the best around. All of them carry highly visible plastic tip (or sight bob) on top of a slim insert of solid carbon fibre. A choice of tips is offered, in different diameters and colours, and all are inter-changeable. The floats are also telescopic so the length can be adjusted by several inches (see p. 166). One Cralusso is called the 'Rocket' and it is a fitting label as so many wagglers from mainland Europe are built for distance casting.

In the UK we have the Drennan brand which continues to change and adapt to today's market; many of their famous crystals have now been shortened to suit shallower swims for example. Drake Floats, based in the North West, is a smaller company but, as the pictures in our colour section reveal, their floats are top drawer and 'bespoke'.

From the many different float tips now available, the fluted plastic type takes some beating. This offers a good width for the eye to see out on the water, but in any diameter the overall tip volume is reduced by at least a third, hence more sensitivity (see colour section).

Having been re-acquainted with the feeder float in the book research, I can imagine an improved version of this float being introduced sooner or later. If 'sticky mag' is a fine way of catching fish at a distance beyond a catapult's range, then an improved feeder float must surely do the same but more accurately. A streamlined version of the original float would prove a winner, I feel.

Danny Shaw and his winning bag in the 2012 Lord Mayor's Cup junior match - making it a hat-trick of titles.

The waggler may never regain its old popularity over the modern long and lightweight carbon pole, but diversity should be angling's strength as no single method can do everything. Coarse angling is big enough for all methods to work in harmony depending on the water type and species within.

In finding the right balance of methods for different waters/species, we must constantly be looking for new tricks. What starts out as an experimental way of catching fish can soon become standard practice, and tackle keeps on improving to suit. Plastic baits is one area where great advances have been made in recent times, and the big fish anglers have led the way with artificials like 'zig rigs'. On a recent trip to Holland I used a version of artificial corn, combining one of the small kernels with three maggots or a worm. It seemed to catch me more bream than without it, probably because it neutralised the weight of the natural bait and the fish could suck it in easier. And the vivid yellow, pink or red colour of the corn possibly attracted them too.

Better still is the 'banded caster'. I have only known about this clever dodge for less than two seasons but it is a great time saver for matchmen. Instead of using a hard pellet inside the standard mini pellet band (hair-rigged to hook as usual), a caster is carefully slid inside the band. Providing the bait does not reach the fish's throat teeth before it's hooked, the caster will come back intact meaning re-baiting is unnecessary and many fish can be caught on the same bait. The oval caster shell has some strength to it but it's said this reduces considerably once a hook pierces it, which gives credence to this new hooking method.

Regarding the trolling method (or puller) described earlier in the book, I never had a clue about this until my late 40s after I'd been fishing for over 30 years. A sliding stick float for catching roach on the drop on lakes did sound bizarre, but it worked. Sheffield's Bernard Bryan pioneered this technique at small waters like Howbrook Dam and Ecclesfield Dam. He experimented endlessly and reached his goal by purposeful practice. I now think I have developed the method to a decent standard – stick and waggler versions - and it has won me many prizes. But harking back to some of the easier venues I fished, like Holme Pierrepont when it was good in the 80s, and Roundhay Park, Leeds at times, I now know that trolled baits would have worked. What big catches did we miss out on back then - potential record breakers even – if we had only known about trolled baits at the time?

To accept that angling can never be fully learnt and we can never totally master it is a wonderful thing, because the challenge never diminishes - or it shouldn't as long as we avoid waters that are too easy. I've taken the waggler as far as I'm able to in this book, but no doubt some whizz kid out there is already working on improved designs that we cannot yet contemplate.

As for the general spread of methods, we learnt the long pole from our continental friends at the same time as they took to our rod and reel methods like ducks to water, after importing wagglers from the UK. The long carbon pole revolutionised our sport, but the waggler has still played a big part in our World Championship record which is now second to none (since manager Dick Clegg's first win in 1985 in Italy). Some of the French and Italian stars, inspired by what they saw at those same championships and in friendly events, have become champions in their own right at waggler fishing. But there is always scope for improvement and new techniques at every level, and they must naturally evolve further.

Former Sheffield Lord Mayor, Coun. John Campbell, and the Mayor's Cup winning team, 2012.

The Author - A Look to the Future

When French teams were winning nearly all the World Championships in the 60s and 70s, Guy Hebert, the leading French international, said that the best anglers in future would be those who combined the UK's running line methods and the pole skills of the continentals. They could then claim to be true all-rounders: "able to cope with any fishing eventuality". I think those wise words are worth keeping in mind by any aspiring match angler. Angling continues to develop with the objective of catching more fish and doing so more easily, but where does it leave the variety of methods and species? I'm not sure we are always fully conscious of where new trends are taking us and if they are a good or bad thing. I am the last person to ever want fishing to be too difficult - having always been impatient for a bite, but must question where the regular filling of four keepnets with 200lb or more of carp for example, is taking us. I'm far more comfy with the other end of the scale and a big fish angler sitting for a fortnight for the chance at one good specimen, if that's his passion.

In these times of hundredweight catches to win an average commercial match, and often from a swim only a yard from the bank, I must question how hard the challenge is? If all our improved equipment and techniques tip the balance so far that there's no challenge left to catching fish, what then? We surely owe it to future generations to keep the sport fresh, looking for variety and using our craft to build up a net of fish without having it all our own way. It would be nice to see a promoter bring in a match where five methods would be compulsory to put a winning catch together. That would get the juices flowing, or maybe I am getting sentimental. But angling's greatest strength to me is its variety and unpredictability, and I'll drink to that as a final thought.

Appendix i
Hooks and Knots

The point of the matter – barbless hooks

When analyzing tackle presentation it makes sense to me to study the angler-fish 'chain' backwards from the hook (commonly described as the 'business end') up to the rod, which Benny Ashurst called the least important piece of equipment.

The baited hook and line are the links of the chain we cannot afford to break. If we get these just about right for a given situation, and assuming we have located some fish, catching them should become easier. Add the right float, suitably shotted, and we move another step in the right direction, and much of the rest revolves around correct feeding. There are many other elements to efficient angling of course, but the best-laid plans will quickly unravel if the hook and line are not right for the job.

I recently fished a local pond with an old pole and light elastic and an even older Mustad 5713 fine wire hook size 20. This hook is generally too feeble for any fish over 2lb (in truth it is a good gudgeon or bleak hook) yet it held onto a lovely 5lb common carp in mint condition. The battle tested the fine elastic and hook to the limit but the hook held, despite some scary moments when the fish charged around the fringes of two lily beds. Would I have hooked the fish with a bigger or stronger hook? Well possibly, but I would not have bet on it. Though fishing too light for strong fish that may smash up tackle can never be recommended (my target fish on that session were roach), we learn more by hooking a fish and losing it than we would by not hooking one at all.

I sometimes grieve for anglers I see struggling to catch anything on my easiest local water. I am sure it is down to two basic mistakes: a/ they do not feed bait regularly enough to attract the fish, and b/ they probably use too big a hook. I believe that if a magic wand could be waved to change every hook that every angler used to a size smaller at least, the total number of fish caught would double.

Hooks have improved greatly since they were first given a chemical sharpening treatment, and the choice of quality hooks is now also vast. But an old hook pattern is not necessarily an obsolete one. The Mustad hook referred to (including barb which I flattened) is a close cousin of the barbless 5715 which has caught me stacks of fish over the years.

So what makes a good hook? From all the patterns I've tested, I've narrowed it down to four criteria that tell me on whether a hook is good, bad, or a maybe. I am ever willing to try new and unusual patterns, but the main features considered are: size, sharpness, weight/wire thickness and shape.

1. The size of the hook ideally matches the size of the bait. A big maggot or caster fits neatly on a 20, where a pinkie matches a 22 or 24, and bigger baits like sweetcorn or a dendra' worm suit a size 16 or 14. This can be our starting point when entering a shop with a view to buy, but we should trust our eyes more than the number on the packet. Hook sizes printed on some packets are not always accurate, and it can be hard to determine the true size from the information given. Fox hooks for example, have not always been known for being accurately sized. I have some claimed to be size 21 that are more like an 18. Even the odd-numbered sizes can cause mild confusion, so the answer could be to visualize the hook you need before entering the shop.

2. Sharpness of the hook point is essential in any pattern, and the hook should not get blunted by catching a hard object like a stone

A selection of hooks, old and new.

or even a bony-mouthed perch. Hooks with the correct temper should be tough enough to stay sharp throughout many days of catching. But accidents will happen. In bigger sizes it pays to use a carborundum sharpening stone to quickly replenish a blunted point, while in smaller sizes it's easier to replace the hook. Always replace a hook with a damaged point immediately.

3. A hook's exact weight is not easy to determine unless you own or can access some very fine laboratory scales, and the weight is rarely found printed on a hook packet. I have only known it given once, on a Mustad hook range, but if you drop two similar hook patterns onto a hard surface from a couple of inches height it is sometimes easy to tell which one is the heavier. Experience can also tell us that certain hook wires are neither the right temper, or too brittle or springy for the job in hand. In the finer wires I like to (carefully) check a hook's strength against the thumbnail, to see if it keeps its shape under pressure.

Wire thickness is obviously linked to the hook's weight but never take it for granted that the finer of any two wires is the weaker hook. The modern Gamakatsu black hook for example, is a fine grade wire but also extremely strong. Nine times out of ten I'd opt for the finest wire possible for the majority of fish I'm likely to catch on a given water, but the exception is what I call heavy water - deep and/or strong flowing where the pressure on the hook increases. This requires a thicker wire than normal.

4. Regarding a hook's shape, there's a multitude of choices available which can seem confusing to the untrained eye – long shank v short shank, round bend v crystal bend, or narrow gape v wide gape. For my regular maggot fishing a crystal bend is the standard where the bait hangs at the bottom of the point. A round bend shape is less powerful for an equivalent wire grade but I still use them occasionally. The Sensas 3405 is one such hook, a very sharp black nickel pattern. In terms of shank length I prefer a medium. A long shank is said to penetrate better than a short one but the downside is that the extra wire length can make the fish turn away. A short shank on the other hand is not as easily seen by the fish but the science says the angle of penetration is less efficient. This does not stop me using a short shank in some patterns however, as some good maggot hooks have short shanks (see favourite patterns).

Moving onto the question of barbs: most of my hooks are barbless patterns like almost all modern fisheries insist on, as they do no harm to the fish. We have come a long way since the days of the hooks with crude, big barbs that were both inefficient and did damage fish. Any that are still around should be thrown in the nearest dustbin. If I ever use a barbed hook it is always a micro-barb (aka whisker barb), but I will flatten the barb first with fine-nosed pliers.

Some big fish anglers still prefer barbed hooks as it gives them more confidence that a hooked fish will not come adrift, and some of the latest barbs are tiny, but a barb is still more of a hindrance than a help for my styles of fishing. I have total faith in a barbless penetrating better, and the hole it makes in the fish is smaller than that made by any hook with even a tiny barb on it.

Barbed hook fans do say that if a hook penetrates so easily it will come out just as easily, so more fish will be lost? It can happen but I don't buy the argument. Providing you keep your line taut during the fight I'm certain that the barbless advantages outweigh the barb's claimed holding power. I have a friend who does well with a micro-barb and disputes my strong belief, but in all my years of catching roach, providing there was good elasticity in my rod and line set-up, I say fewer fish have come astray my way.

Fashions do come and go with hook design. Carp anglers long ago introduced the 'bent' hook that was given an inward bend in the shank to make the point line up with the eye. They resembled a question mark shape upside-down and this curving of the shank helps a barbless hook stick when it goes in. The shape is now also used for match carp and some anglers report that fish cannot shed the hook once it is embedded in the flesh. When it comes to specimen fish, a strong and thick-wired hook is required. This will need more power to strike home than a small, fine wire one, and powerful rods and sturdy line fit the bill, though with a bolt-rig a big fish will usually hook itself anyway.

Some anglers like to take the risk of opening up a hook slightly to make it catch the fish's flesh easier. I am not keen on this idea as it takes the shape closer to a v-shape and this has cost me fish in the past. Wider gaped hooks are being used more than ever on modern fisheries, but care must be taken not to use one with a shank that's too short or they get out of balance. Another interesting idea is the off-set point. This is where the hook point is not perpendicular with the shank but set at a slight angle for increased hooking power. If you test this with the hook tied to nylon by gently pulling it between finger and thumb the off-set hook does tend to catch skin easier than a straight one. This makes a lot of sense for a bolt-rig but I do not use them myself.

Another useful feature on some hooks is the 'beak', or curved point. My original Mustad 5715 barbless hook had a slight beak on the point - like an avocet's beak in miniature – and I think it helped it to stay secure in the fish. For some reason the beak disappeared from later hooks in the same model at the same time as the point got a fraction shorter. Good hooks can change from one year to the next, or suddenly they become obsolete for no apparent reason, so it might pay to stock up well if you have a favourite hook that never lets you down.

Finally, a good hook for 'silvers' for my kind of fishing – for roach and bream mainly, sometimes perch, chub, crucians, rudd or ide - must be of a fine enough wire so the fish will not detect the weight like they would a heavier wire when they suck in the bait. If we study fish in an aquarium we soon observe how rapidly they can blow out an unwanted food item, and it's no different with fish in the wild. For this reason I have always tried to use the lightest weight hook I can get away with.

A few years ago while working on the Sheffield 'Angling Star' magazine I was sent some French VMC Vanadium 9035 size 30s. They were the smallest hooks imaginable: about 5mm total wire length from spade to point, and the point length was only 1mm.

It took me five minutes to tie one on to .05mm line under my lamp. Armed with five hooks tied up at a local pond, and fishing with a tiny float and single joker in a winter setting, I expected bites BUT was less than confident I would land many fish. I anticipated the minute gape – ie. The space between point and shank – was a test for my good eye and would not hold the fish. In short the 'hooking power' looked powerless.

But remarkably, from 20 bites struck I brought 19 fish back to the waiting landing net. This high average was because every fish had the hook at least 1" down its throat and more, and needed the disgorger to remove. My response time on the strike was no different to any other day. The same strike with a larger hook, say a 22, would have seen me lip-hook fish I was certain. Conclusion: the roach had not felt the weight of the hook.

Top Tip

Never be afraid to try hooks of different colours. I would only use bronze hooks at one time as they gave me confidence. I had no faith in silver hooks until one evening at an angling roadshow when I heard French international, Jean Desque give a talk. He claimed that silver hooks 'attracted' fish. This was new and different. From that moment on I tried the Drennan B511 pattern and caught fish and my attitude to silver changed totally. John Dean used a standby gilt hook (yellow finish) to win Trent matches. I have also caught on green, red and black hooks, and hemp anglers have been known to paint a hook white. So most hook colours catch fish at times.

A selection of favourite hooks:

The following hook makes/patterns have all worked well for me in different situations:

AU LION D'OR 1217B blue – in sizes 24 and 22 this was my standard Witham stick float pattern and occasional waggler hook, sporting a long spear point. The 24 was reserved for fishing a bomb for a handful of fish on the worst days of winter.

MUSTAD 5715 – my Witham waggler hook for difficult days, in ex-fine wire and with a long beak point, a 22 was the one size that fitted all fish I was ever likely to encounter on low weight matches.

DAIWA MLB size 20 only – a super Trent roach hook, the best I could find at one time (an Ivan Marks design). These have long since gone off the market. Jan Porter once joked the points were longer than he was and he was at least 6′ tall!

MUSTAD 314 or 313 – a blue round bend, with a rather narrow gape and long shank, it was like a scaled up 5715 in strength but still fine enough. At some point in time the model number was changed. I used it when produced in odd sizes and the smallish 21 was an ideal size for roach.

KAMASAN B511 – this was the first silver coloured (nickel) hook I used with confidence in a size 24 from about 1990. It could be the lightest 24 I have ever tied on. It is a shade springy but good for shy roach. When this hook became popular I think any edge I might have had with the old 5715 pattern was lost.

KAMASAN B510 – this hook was probably introduced as a rival to the famous Mustad 90340. A well-proportioned barbless with a crystal bend, my mate, Steve Koc, won the Welland Championship on one in size 22 soon after the hooks came out in the mid-1980s, and he hardly lost a fish, on the way to 11lb 0 1/2oz of roach.

More recent additions:
MIDDY 6313 teflon barbless – a consistently mega-sharp roach hook with a slippy Teflon coating, the way that this hook goes in the fish and doesn't come out confirms once again that barbless is best. All the smaller sizes have performed well for me.

GAMAKATSU 1510 green – a modern hook which has replaced the finer hooks like the 5715 and B511 in recent years for roach. Extra fine wire with a wide gape but still offering a fair strength, it is perfect for small fish in sizes 20/22/24. Size 18 is a slightly thicker wire and stronger and a good caster hook for easy fish.

GAMAKATSU black nickel – This pattern is a fraction short in the point, but remarkably strong for the wire grade and I don't lose many fish with it. It caught me a 7lb 10oz carp on a size 20 to 0.10mm line that won me the big fish prize in a match where many carp were lost on bigger hooks/stronger gear.

MUSTAD 90343 – an old hook and a good all-rounder for easy fish in size 19 (a 20 in reality).

MUSTAD 90340 – the cult Trent hook when the river produced stacks of chub back in the 80s in sizes 20/22/24, often with double maggot. It has a long spear point that usually stays put in the fish.

COLMIC NUCLEAR 957B – a reasonably fine wire but still a strong hook for a round bend, this hook is well-proportioned.

SENSAS 3405 (black nickel) – an extremely sharp hook, surprisingly strong for a round bend, and a bit longer point that the Gama black. The 20 is a good size for roach, a shade small, more like a 21.

TUBERTINI 808 – a gilt/gold tint to this pattern and a recently tried hook, strong with a good beak point which is slightly off-set.

PRESTON PR30 – at first sight of this pattern it was like a remake of the old MLB, an excellent hook, fine but strong in sizes 20/22 and accurately marked up for size on the packet.

PRESTON 311 – formerly the PR26, this is a lightweight maggot hook (sports a barb which I flatten), a similar shape to the PR30 above but a finer wire.

GURU MWG – For carp and other big fish, this hook brand is the tops with a lot of thought gone into its design. Considering the full Guru range is about strength, and these are as strong as I personally ever need, they seem sharper than any other forged hooks I've used. Where once for barbel the old Super Spade was my choice, now I'd say check out these in the orange and black packet and you won't be disappointed.

APACHE SF1 and SF2 hooks are sharp and strong and another black nickel made in the right proportions.

TRIANA TAKARA include several silver nickel patterns, all made in Japan and marketed in Italy. The 711 and 540 are particularly good models.

Knots – that crucial link

For as long as man has worked with rope or string, many clever minds have invented some wonderful knots. From the Polynesians with their braided flax fibres, to other shore dwellers who must catch fish to survive, on to mariners and mountaineers, some of these ingenious knots can give 100% strength, a seamless link.

While big game anglers should be more than grateful for the more complex knots – the Bimini twist for example, they can be tricky to tie. The average freshwater angler on the other hand can get away with simpler knots that are still secure. It is essential to be able to tie a good knot and know it will not let us down at the critical moment when landing the fish of a lifetime, so we must tie them properly.

For readers with a little dexterity in the fingers, tying knots for fishing is easy, and below are a few good ones. I've narrowed them down to reliable knots that are straightforward to tie. All will give secure connections without any awkward, multi-stepped tying methods.

For anglers with less than nimble fingers, or who suffer from poor eyesight (and I have known some very good anglers who could not tie a spade end by hand if someone offered them a fortune to do it), I can only suggest using a hook-tyer. There is always a way. The diagrams show three knots starting with the double loop knot which is very easy to tie for attaching the reel line to trace 'loop to loop'. The spade end hook knot might need more patience to learn, but a little practice with big hooks and thick line and you should get the hang of it.

1. Single or double overhand loop knot – It is elementary to tie a loop in the end of any line, and this gives us the popular loop-to-loop connection that joins the main line to trace (or hooklength). Take the tag end of the line and double it back on itself. Form a circle with the doubled up section. Insert this doubled tag end once or twice through the circle formed and tighten and there you have it. The doubled version of the knot sits straighter than a single one (see pics p.359). I placed my faith in single overhand loops for years with no trouble, but now use the double overhand loop as it is stronger and neater. Keep your loops small – 1cm long max. – which is easy to do with practice. A cocktail stick point can be used for pulling finer lines through the circle to make the knot.

2. The spade end knot or 'snell' – for tying spade end hooks by hand this is the only knot that is really worth knowing about. A good spade end knot when complete should not have any line running down the outside edge, and this one mimics a neat whipping on a rod ring. If you prefer using a hook-tyer and find it easier that is your choice, but the hand-tying method is given below.

Always start with a big enough loop to get half your finger and thumb tip inside comfortably, and place the hook point upwards and the line next to the shank, but with wire on the outside, line inside, so each turn of line will touch the metal first (or the line can slip). Then it's a matter of working from the spade end down the shank in touching turns, guiding the line over the hook with the thumb to make each turn.

Method: 1. Trap the line loop against the spade and half the shank with left-hand forefinger and thumb tips.

2. Place half the right forefinger and thumb tip inside the loop pointing downwards and pull to the right edge of the loop to catch hold of the line and tighten it slightly.

3. Turn the wrist clockwise 90 degrees to bring the finger and thumb tip upwards and put a half-turn in the loop. Your thumbnail now faces you with the line hanging over it.

4. Rotate the hand to guide the line over the hook with the thumb and make one line turn over the shank. The thumb is now below the hook holding the line down, and both thumb and fingertip stay inside the loop.

5. Rotate the wrist again to bring your finger/thumb pointing up again and the line back in the starting position.

6. Repeat until you have made sufficient turns – seven on average.

7. Holding what is left of the loop tight to the hook with the forefinger, transfer it to the middle finger to free up the forefinger and thumb to trap the knot.

8. Pull any loose line back through the knot both ways - standing part and tag end - while still pinching the knot firmly, and it's done! Finally, slide the knot up to the spade carefully with fingernails checking that the line leaves the knot on the inside of the spade, and if not, lever it around the wire so it does, and tighten fully (see pics p.360).

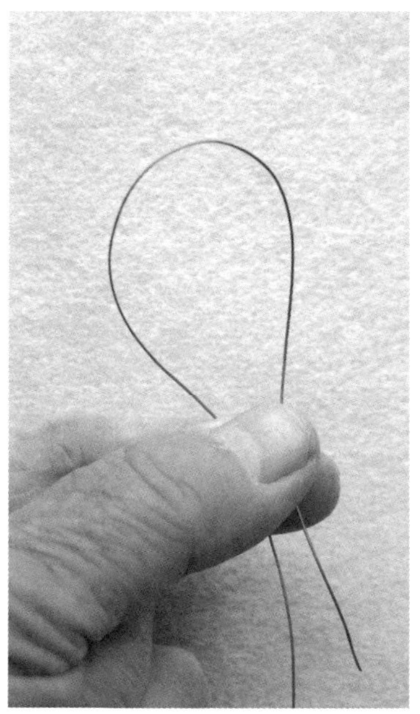

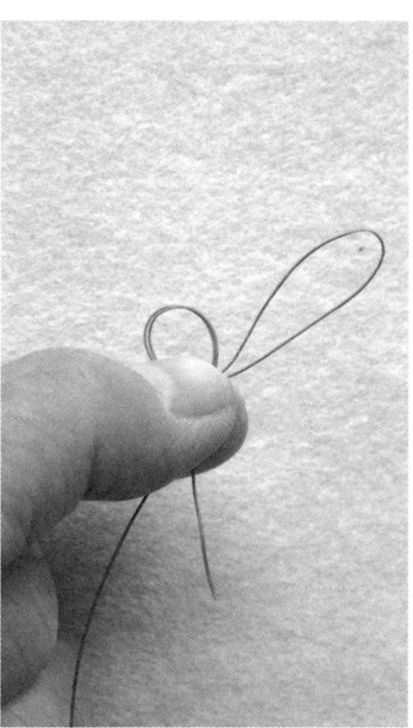

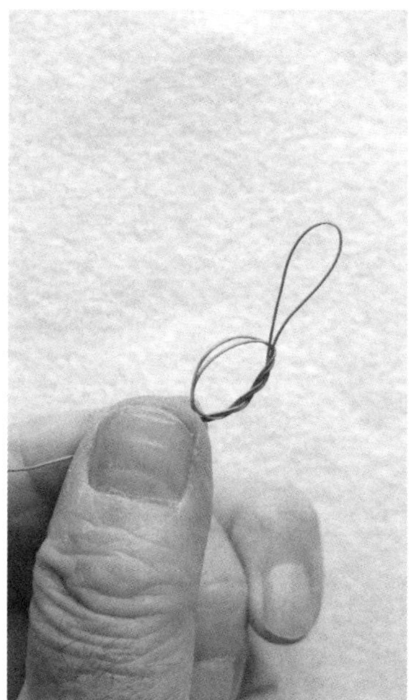

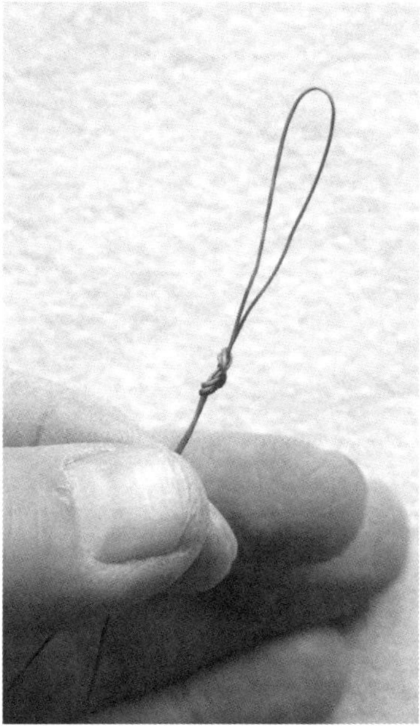

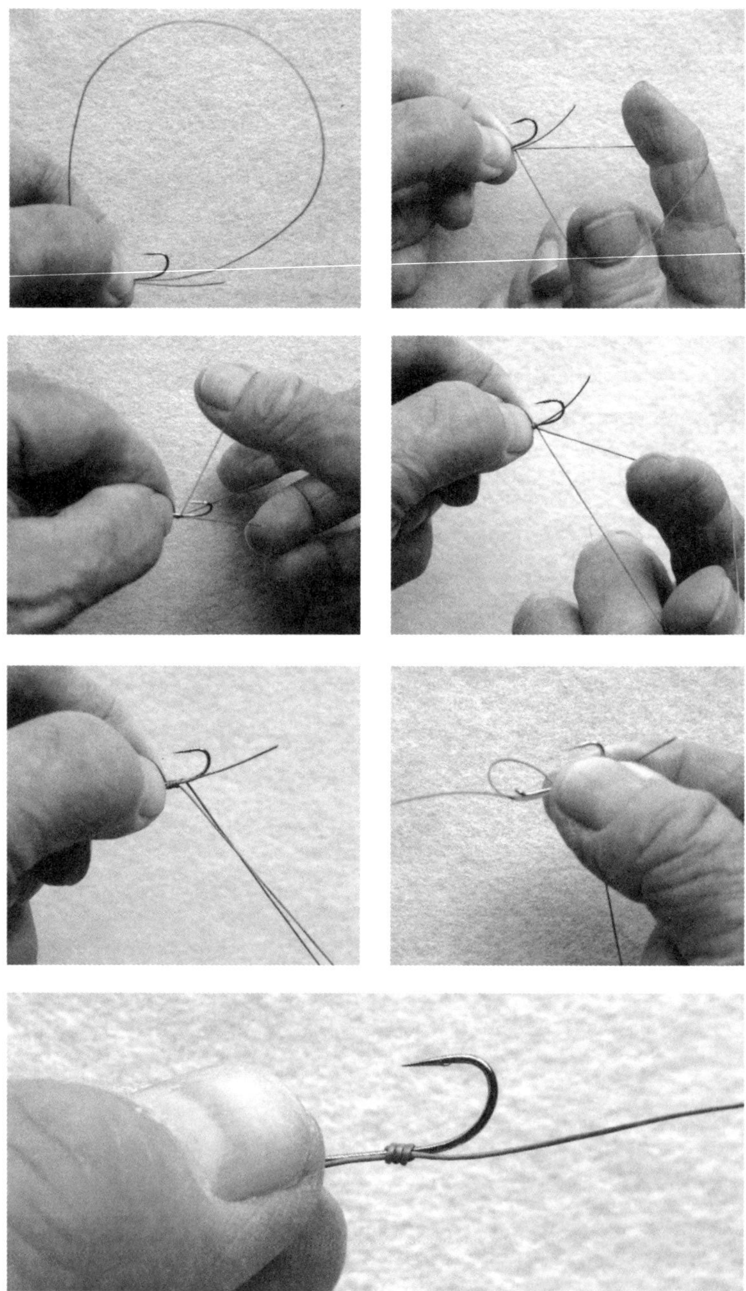

3. Knotless knot – no, this is not a confusion in terms, but an excellent hook to line connection. It is now the common knot for carp fishing with an eyed hook, or any situation where an eyed hook is tied in a kind of back to front manner to enable a pellet band (tiny elastic band) to be mounted on a hair rig. The trick with this knot is to insert the line through the back of the eye, whipping the knot with seven or more turns down and back up the shank, then pushing the tag end through the back of the eye once again (see pics).

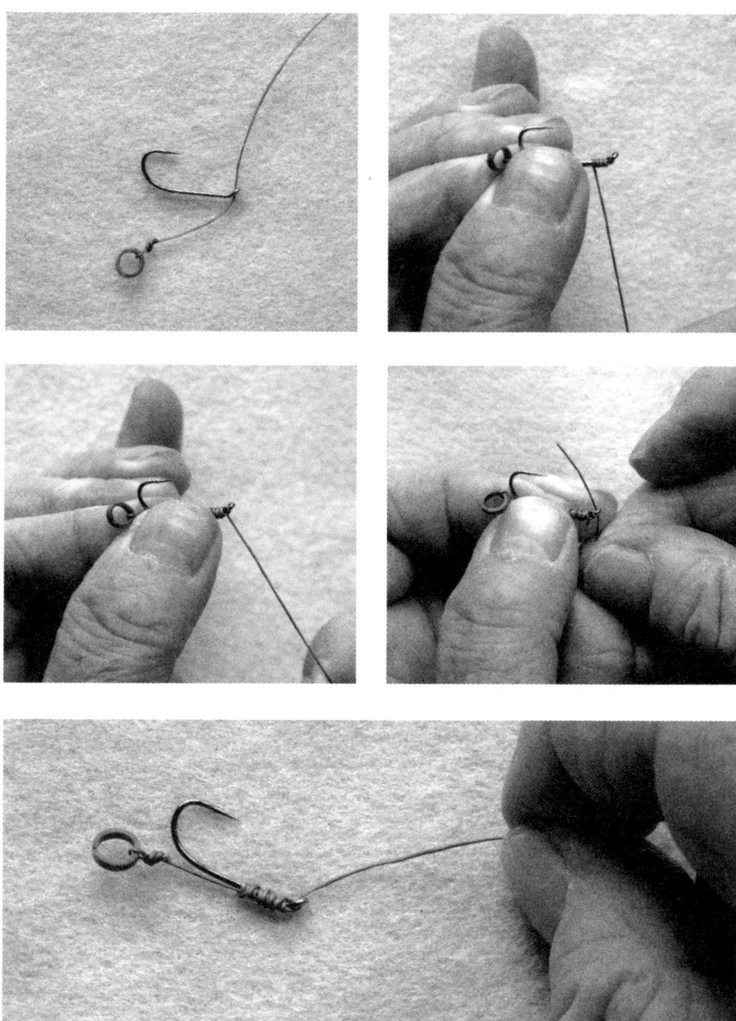

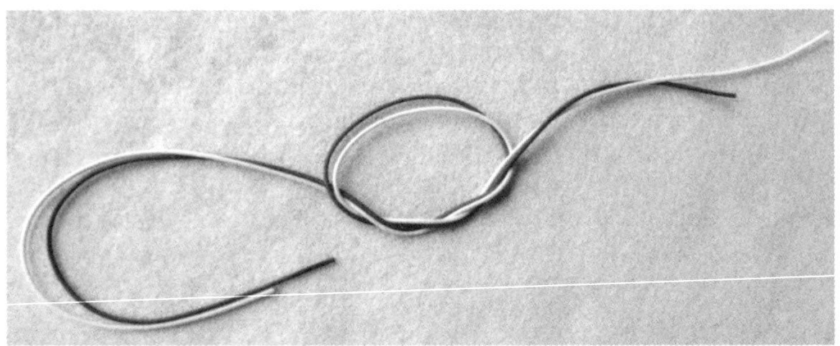

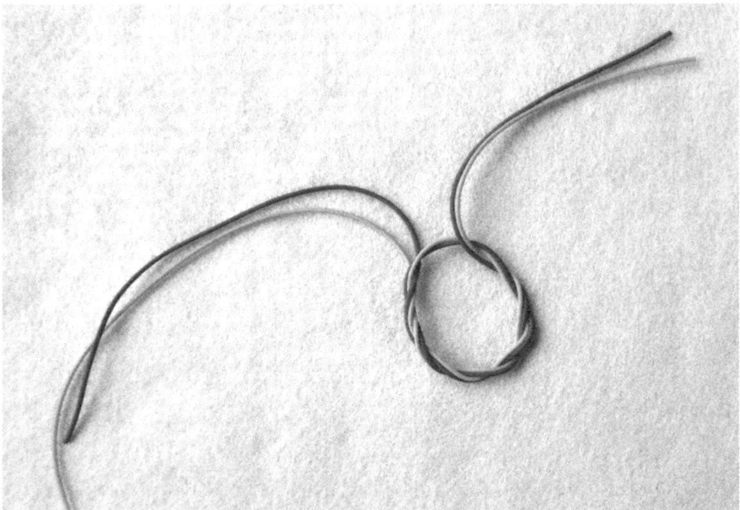

4. Four-turn water knot – an alternative to the loop-to-loop connection for joining reel line to the finer hooklength is a single knot. This one gives a neater finish than loop-to-loop, and is easier to tie than a blood knot (or 'fisherman's knot') for example. The one drawback is if you break on a good fish at the knot then your depth setting changes with the re-tying. To tie the knot simply place the two pieces of line side by side. Form a loop, pinch both lines together with finger and thumb, then insert both lines through the loop four times. If both ends are the same length you can take them through the loop simultaneously; if one line is longer than the other pass them through individually with care not to miss a turn. A quicker tied two-turn or three-turn water knot will still stand up to considerable pressure without slipping (pics of 2-turn and 4-turn shown in elastic for easy guide)

5. Trilene knot – the best knot I know for tying an eyed hook when a hair-rig is not required. I also use for attaching flies to a leader when fly fishing. It puts two turns of line through the eye which makes for a strong connection, and serves for floater fishing for carp etc. The grinner is a very similar knot but I use the Trilene, a safer knot than the 'tucked half blood' knot in my experience. For small fish however, the half-blood knot when tied to a loop of line is not one to feel nervous about as long as it's pulled tight, and I sometimes use one at the end of the reel line (basis of knot shown in elastic. The tag end feeds through the double loop before moistening and pulling tight).

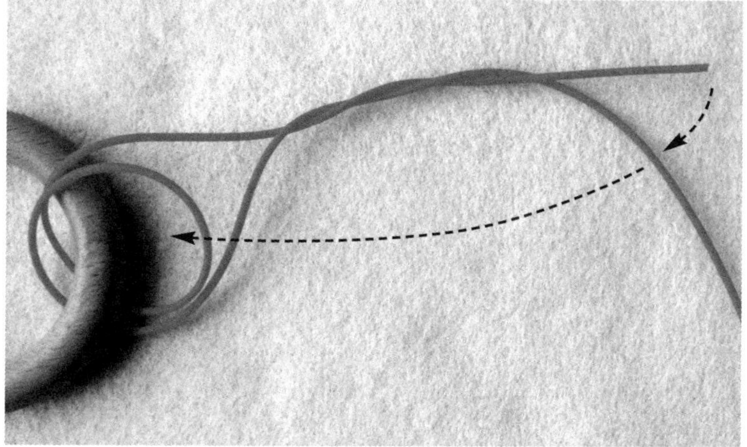

6. Crow's foot knot – simply a double overhand loop with the loop cut away to leave a knot with three tag ends, hence the name. Used to form the leading end of internal elastics for pole fishing.

7. Arbor knot – a slip-knot used for securing a line to the reel spool (or arbor of same).

8. Noose slip knot – Simply a bite of line pulled through an overhand loop to form a secondary loop which can then be slipped over and drawn tight over a knot.

As good as I think my spade end knots are, there have still been times when I've lost a fish through a hook slip. With eyed hooks I switched from the tucked half-blood knot to the more reliable Trilene knot some time ago, but we are always learning. Five or more winters back, thanks to a tip from John Moroz, I started applying a light brush of Super glue to all spade end knots. It offers a 'belt and braces' safety system, and with no more slips it has been worth the little extra trouble.

Footnote:
An alternative to the double loop knot is the figure of eight loop knot where a twist is put in the line before pushing the loop through to finish. This is rated as a more reliable knot. But for most of the fish I target the difference seems negligible.

Top Tip

Check out the book 'Practical Fishing Knots' by Mark Sosin and Lefty Kreh, published by Batsford.

Appendix ii
Author's Match Record

River Witham (at Kirkstead unless stated)

1975 Tom Sails Memorial, Kirkstead 6-15 4th and section win - 275 fished*

(* mentioned only because the result demonstrated real progress on the waggler 12 months after a beating from John Dean)

		lb-oz-dms	Pos
1977	Tom Sails Memorial, Southery	1-10-8	1st - 100 fished
1978	Boston Clayton Pearson Mem.	13-4-0	1st - 300 fished
1980	(No matches, spent the year in West Germany)		
1981	Newark Federation	7-11-8	1st - 200 fished
	Boston Clayton Pearson Mem.	4-1-8	1st - 150 fished
1982	Witham Championship	12-4-8	1st - 100 fished
	Lincs. Fed Championship	9-7-8	1st - 200 fished
1983	Witham Super League Rd.6	11-9-8	1st - 75 fished
	(Won Super League 160 points / 168 max)		
	Doncaster AA	6-10-0	1st - 50 fished
	JB Open	7-2-0	1st - 44 fished
1984	Witham Super League Rd. 8	15-2-0	1st - 50 fished
	(Defended Super League title (145 points /150 max)		
	Scunthorpe AA	9-15-8	1st 150 fished

1984	Sheffield AAS Pairs	8-14-8	1st pair with G. Newby - 200 fished
1985	AT Eastern.Region Winter Lge	14-2-0	1st - 240 fished
	(2nd in Super League 88 points from 90 - 15-peg sections – a perfect score by Dave Ashmore denied me hat-trick!)		
	Witham Super League Rd.2	6-7-8	1st - 75 fished
1986	Grimsby ASA	14-6-0	1st - (entry unrecorded)
	Sheffield AAS	15-0-0	1st - 150 fished
1987	Witham Super League Rd.4 (including a 2-1-8 roach!)	5-7-0	1st - 60 fished
1989	Batemans	6-1-0	1st - 132 fished **
	(** tied with Pete Bagshaw – see below)		
	Witham Super League Rd. 3	10-8-0	1st - 44 fished
	(2nd overall in League, lost by 1 point to Tony Woods)		

Notes:

The Witham winning weights (including the 1984 Sheffield pairs) totalled 183lb 7oz for an almost 10lb per match average, more than I recalled catching but they were the best of the good days. Other days on the Witham could indeed be tough. An Easterly wind could be the kiss of death and the Kirkstead pegging was closer than other rivers, cramped when the river was flowing hard on an outgoing tide at Boston.

Eels figured in some summer catches though I never managed to win with eels alone. I'd include them in a catch when they invaded the swim after an hour of roach sport. Approximately three-quarters of all fish caught were roach.

I considered myself a 5lb to 10lb specialist and that worked well in the 80s. By the turn of the 1990s though, Rog Wakenshaw emerged as the Witham no. 1 and my defensive style was less effective; heavier feed was required as the winning weights improved for a time. Also, other methods like long pole and whip were now producing more fish than ever in the right hands and both these factors affected my consistency.

The Clayton Pearson was obviously lucky for me, winning my first with bream on swing-tip (my one bream win in the list) then with roach in '81 on a tough October day.

After a disastrous Tom Sails Memorial in 1974, drawn next to the emerging force that was John Dean, this event, named after the famous Lincoln skipper turned out lucky after all. When it was switched from Kirkstead to upstream Southery it gave me my first Witham win with my lowest ever winning Witham weight and I made the top 10 in this event three times.

In 1977/78 season my methods were starting to work well and from 64 matches I made the prize list in half of them - averaging 1+ Witham wins per year in the 14 years 1977 to 1991, then stopped fishing the river.

When the Witham Super League entry dwindled to less than 50 it was because: a/ the river was patchier than ever, and b/ the roach had seemed to become more migratory. Parts of the popular 'Pound length' section returned to fishing as hard as when it was originally named for being worth only a pound of fish. Pegs adjacent to bridges became the only reliable ones for bites in winter, while the high numbers downstream in the Pound (towards peg 50) did not guarantee a bite when things got rough. More cormorant predation was also reported at this time.

After my first two Witham wins – 1/ small roach on short pole and squatt; and 2/ bream on ledgered worm - the winning methods were waggler, stick float and bomb in that order, with long pole only figuring seriously from around 1987 onwards. But I did catch a 2-1-8 specimen roach on pole on a flooded river to help win one Super League round. A rare creature.

Throughout the second half of the 80s the big Witham associations were dwindling in size and the days of the 'big' Witham matches would soon disappear as falling match entries confirmed. The old sections of 50 anglers had reduced to 25, and soon this would be an average match size. As the new millennium dawned, with so many venues/matches available, the 'cake' was cut so small that if 20 anglers turned up to fish it was seen as a fair number.

** The tie with Chesterfield's Pete Bagshaw in the Bateman's meant we shared a winner-take-all pool. One fish either way would have left one of us with regrets, so it has to be better to tie than lose by 1/2oz. I also won a Half Moon Trent Open when Leicester man, Ivor Bilson forced a tie, but the payout was good. And I have twice tied and shared winnings with Dennis Pinkos, on the River Don and the Derbyshire Derwent at Matlock.

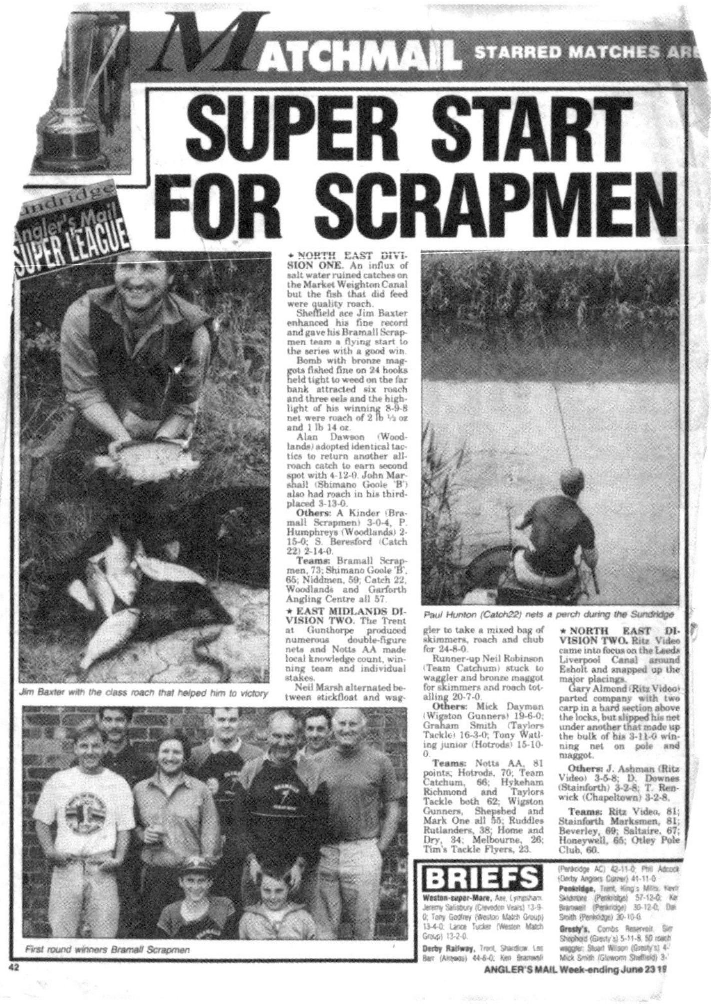

MATCHMAIL STARRED MATCHES AR

SUPER START FOR SCRAPMEN

★ **NORTH EAST DIVISION ONE.** An influx of salt water ruined catches on the Market Weighton Canal but the fish that did feed were quality roach.

Sheffield ace Jim Baxter enhanced his fine record and gave his Bramall Scrapmen team a flying start to the series with a good win.

Bomb with bronze maggots fished fine on 24 hooks held tight to weed on the far bank attracted six roach and three eels and the highlight of his winning 8-9-8 net were roach of 2 lb ½ oz and 1 lb 14 oz.

Alan Dawson (Woodlands) adopted identical tactics to return another all-roach catch to earn second spot with 4-12-0. John Marshall (Shimano Goole 'B') also had roach in his third-placed 3-13-0.

Others: A Kinder (Bramall Scrapmen) 3-0-4, P. Humphreys (Woodlands) 2-15-0; S. Beresford (Catch 22) 2-14-0.

Teams: Bramall Scrapmen, 73; Shimano Goole 'B', 65; Niddmen, 59; Catch 22, Woodlands and Garforth Angling Centre all 57.

★ **EAST MIDLANDS DIVISION TWO.** The Trent at Gunthorpe produced numerous double-figure nets and Notts AA made local knowledge count, winning team and individual stakes.

Neil Marsh alternated between stickfloat and waggler to take a mixed bag of skimmers, roach and chub for 24-8-0.

Runner-up Neil Robinson (Team Catchum) stuck to waggler and bronze maggot for skimmers and roach totalling 20-7-0.

Others: Mick Dayman (Wigston Gunners) 19-6-0; Graham Smith (Taylors Tackle) 16-3-0; Tony Watling junior (Hotrods) 15-10-0.

Teams: Notts AA, 81 points; Hotrods, 70; Team Catchum, 66; Hykeham Richmond and Taylors Tackle both 62; Wigston Gunners, Shepshed and Mark One all 55; Ruddles Rutlanders, 38; Home and Dry, 34; Melbourne, 26; Tim's Tackle Flyers, 23.

★ **NORTH EAST DIVISION TWO.** Ritz Video came into focus on the Leeds Liverpool Canal around Esholt and snapped up the major placings.

Gary Almond (Ritz Video) parted company with two carp in a hard section above the locks, but slipped his net under another that made up the bulk of his 3-11-0 winning net on pole and maggot.

Others: J. Ashman (Ritz Video) 3-5-8; D. Downes (Stainforth) 3-2-8; T. Renwick (Chapeltown) 3-2-8.

Teams: Ritz Video, 81; Stainforth Marksmen, 81; Beverley, 69; Saltaire, 67; Honeywell, 65; Otley Pole Club, 60.

Jim Baxter with the class roach that helped him to victory

Paul Hunton (Catch22) nets a perch during the Sundridge

First round winners Bramall Scrapmen

BRIEFS

Weston-super-Mare, Axe, Lympsham. Jeremy Salisbury (Clevedon Vets) 13-9-0; Tony Godfrey (Weston Match Group) 13-4-0; Lance Tucker (Weston Match Group) 13-2-0.

Derby Railway, Trent, Shardlow. Les Barr (Airways) 44-6-0; Ken Bramwell (Penkridge AC) 42-11-0; Phil Adcock (Derby Anglers Corner) 41-11-0.

Penkridge, Trent, King's Mills. Kevi Skidmore (Penkridge) 57-12-0; Ke Bramwell (Penkridge) 30-12-0; Dai Smith (Penkridge) 30-10-0.

Gresty's, Combs Reservoir. Sir Shepherd (Gresty's) 5-11-8, 50 roach waggler; Stuart Wilson (Gresty's) 4- Mick Smith (Glowworm Sheffield) 3-

42 ANGLER'S MAIL Week-ending June 23 19

Setbacks on Witham...

The late Howard Robson, Leeds National Championship skipper at his peak, inflicted my worst ever defeat from the next peg, circa 1970 at Kirkstead. I was still a raw Witham rookie, fishing an inferior quality stick float with caster bait, while he fished centre-pin and a light porcupine quill, with caster presented well over-depth, inching his float through on a cold October river. I caught one roach, he'd 6lb+ for fourth overall. Lessons: never underestimate a shabby-looking set of tackle (Howard's black wooden seat box looked a relic), and practice the stick float more on flowing water. I was well impressed with what my experienced adversary did but must say he was less than sociable afterwards. The late Alan Mayer, of Stockport, also put me in my place in one early Pound length, Witham encounter. Alan caught roach steadily to win the section but I could not get them going at all from two pegs away.

My all-time nightmare match was when drawn beside the stranger that turned out to be John Dean in the Tom Sails Memorial, 1974. The thrashing he gave me was a shock, but had I known anything about his silky skills it wouldn't have been. Probably the only time I felt as demoralised after a match was when the bank collapsed under me at Swarkestone on the upper Trent an hour after the start. That left me and all my tackle in an 8′ deep, swirling eddy and, saturated and mud-encrusted from crawling out, I spent the rest of the day drying off. The only consolation was the sun beamed down.

Jinx matches? Living on the Sheffield/Chesterfield border, just four miles from the crooked spire, I fish more against North Derbyshire anglers than Yorkshiremen. Chesterfield boasts some fine angling talent, but Opens run by their former Association (long defunct) were never that lucky for me. I could frame but never managed to get over the line first.

1979	Chesterfield Open (Witham)	7-13	3rd from 200
1981	Chesterfield Open (Witham)	11-14	2nd from 70
	Chesterfield Open (Witham)	8-9	3rd from 100
	Chesterfield Fur & Feather (Trent)	3-4	2nd from 30
1984	Chesterfield (Holme Pierrepont)	13-6	3rd from 100
1985	Chesterfield Bob Fuller Memorial (Welland)	7-2-8	6th from 150

Results on other waters:

1973	Newark Fed, Trent at Winthorpe and Holme Marsh	8-10	1st
1981	British Sugar Open, R.Nene's North Bank	14-6-0	2nd - (350 pegs)
1981	Woodhouse Syndicate, Nene's North Bank	7-10-8	1st - (200 pegs)
1982	Leeds-Liverpool Canal Champs, Bingley	7-3-6	1st
1982	Green Un Top 200 – Trent, Burton Joyce	15-10	2nd
1982	England Trial 1, Newry Canal – 4th in leg 1 (and 7th overall)		

Appendix ii - Author's Match Record

1983	England v Select, Long Higgin	14-9	3rd
1983	Sheffield & Dist.AA Joe Emmens Memorial, Coronation Channel	8-8-8	1st
1983	Parkgate AC Champs, R.Welland	9-10	1st
1983	Angling Times England v Select, Rod v pole invttn, Mallory Park	27-11-8	1st
1983	Toone Open, R. Trent at Long Higgin	21-8	1st
1984	RAF A and B v Press v Trade (10-a-side), Nene's North Bank	6-5	2nd & team win
1984	Toone Open, Long Higgin	21-2-8	1st
1985	Toone Open, Long Higgin	6-9	1st
1985	Toone Open, Long Higgin	15-5-8	1st
1985	Rolfe Open, Long Higgin	13-6	1st
1985	Shardlow Marina Open	10-12	1st
1985	Regal Home Care Invitation, River Weaver	8-9	2nd
1985	Greenall Whitley Big 'un, R. Weaver	14-3	3rd (792 entry)
1985	Whitbread UK Theale Lagoon, Reading	17-11	1st
1985	Stainforth Open, S/K Canal	1.750kg	1st
1985	Rudyard Lake Open	12-6-8	1st
1985	Rudyard Open	14-12-8	1st
1986	Rudyard Open	6-9-4	2nd
1986	Rudyard Open	5-4	1st
1987	Rudyard Open	12-8	3rd
1987	Rudyard Open	9-7-12	2nd
1987	Rudyard Open	13-10-8	1st
1987	Rudyard Open	9-12	2nd
1987	Rudyard Open	9-6-12	1st
1986	Eastern Region Winter League, Trent, Winthorpe	6-3	2nd
1986	Damflask Res. evening series – 1st overall		
1986	onwards Damflask Opens – several 1sts		
1986	Spalding FC, Coronation Channel	2.700kg	1st
1986	Normark League, Evesham, Warks Avon	14-0	1st (league 2nd over 6 rounds)
1987	Courage Championship qualifier, Evesham	9-8-8	1st
1987	Rotherham Open, Trent, Dunham	17-12	1st
1987	Half Moon Syndicate, Barton in Fabis	17-6	Jt 1st
1988	Hampton Ferry Pole Champs	11-5-12	1st
1988	Courage Championship qualifier, Evesham	8-7	1st
1989	Winsford Open, Weaver	14-1	3rd (200 entry)
1989	Northwich Open, Weaver	7-15	1st
1989	Courage Championship qualifier, Evesham	7-6-8	3rd
1989	Sundridge Super League – Trent at Dunham	22-12	1st
1980s	Holme Pierrepont Opens - several 1sts		
1989	onwards, Combs Reservoir Opens - several 1sts		
1990	Northwich Open, R. Weaver	8-3-8	1st
1990	Fossdyke Canal Open (and 3rd overall in series)	10-5	1st

1990	Damflask Championship - 5-9 - 1st		
1990	Sundridge Super League – Market Weighton Canal – 8-9-8 - 1st		
1990	Northern Bait Farm invitation, Queen Elizabeth Lake, Ashington	4-4-4	2nd
1991	Ron Russell Memorial, Belper, Derbys Derwent	28-12	1st
1992	Drennan League – Trent at Dunham	14-10	1st
1992	Winsford Winter League – R.Weaver	6-9-8	1st

(One summer in new millennium?) Whizzo Open weekend, R.Spui, Holland - 1st in match 1, and 1st overall

2008	KJS Aston Ponds Spring Lge, Aston – 1st in round 1 and 1st overall
2009	KJS Aston Ponds Spring Lge, Aston – 2nd Aston Park Opens, several 1sts
2014	Holme Brook Valley Park – John Shillito Shield – 1st pair with Dave Frost
2014	HBVP teams of 3 – 1st team with Dave Frost and Kev Hodkinson
2000s	Fusion Ponds Winter Leagues: 3 league wins Poolsbrook Country Park (40-pegger) – 1st and 2nd

Chances missed?

The River Don at Sprotborough is a good float venue but a very deep section of the river that I never really conquered in my time spent there. The waggler rarely worked well and I should have fished the stick float or pole more often.

Recent results:

2012/2013 Barlow Farm evening matches, 10 wins from 12 matches, best weights 51lb and 56lb* – bream/roach/perch and odd crucian carp. Excellent sport, mostly enjoyed with one pint of casters. (*three-hour match record)

2014 - 24 open matches fished, 21 times in money* (see footnote)

Fusion Ponds Lge 5lb+ - 3rd

Fusion Ponds Lge 5lb+ - 1st and 2nd overall

Barlow select v Mosborough 6-a-side challenge	22-8 - 2nd and team win	
Barlow select v Holme Brook Valley 6-a-side	40-8 - 2nd and team win	
Barlow evening match 1	12-15	4th
Barlow " " 2	20-0	2nd
Barlow " " 3	49-15-8	1st
J. Moroz Charity Open, Holme Brook Valley Pk team win (no thanks to my performance!)	2-8	and 5-man
Fusion Ponds Open	10-0	5th
Holme Brook Valley Open	6-5	4th
Poolsbrook Evening Open	15-15	2nd

Alan Dawson's match, Horseshoe Lk	39-15	2nd
John Shillito Mem'l Pairs match at H.Brook Valley	10-6	2nd and team win
Poolsbrook Evening Open	14-4	3rd
Poolsbrook Evening Open	15-3	4th
Poolsbrook Evening Open	19-8	2nd
Gary Skelley Mem., Fleets Dam	15-8	2nd
Bernard Bryan Mem., Howbrook Dam	16-4	4th
Poolsbrook Open	13-13	1st
Holmebrook Teams of 3	7-9-8	jt.3rd and team win
Poolsbrook Autumn Lge	15-10	section win
Poolsbrook Autumn Lge	10-0	section 3rd
Poolsbrook Autumn Lge	17-0	section win

(*A most enjoyable season and a consistent one, after discovering a brilliant local venue – Markham Lake at Poolsbrook, Staveley – 10 minutes from home and prolific for bream, roach and perch. This is a water that suits the waggler style but have also used puller float, long pole and whip here).

Appendix iii

An Inspiring Poem

Thinking –by Walter Wintle, first published 1905

If you think you are beaten, you are
If you think you dare not, you don't,
If you like to win, but think you can't
It is almost certain you won't.

If you think you'll lose you're lost
For out of the world we find,
Success begins with a fellow's will
It's all in the state of mind.

If you think you are outclassed you are
You've got to think high to rise,
You've got to be sure of yourself before
You can ever win a prize.

Life's battles don't always go
To the stronger or faster man,
But sooner or later the man who wins
Is the man who thinks he can.

Appendix iii - An Inspiring Poem

Credit for this poem goes to an old snooker pal, Pete Holbert. He was a good player, but whenever he lost a match he'd say how he needed to re-read 'the poem', and this was the one he used to psyche himself back up. It is all about self-confidence, and perfect for anyone looking for the belief that what he/she has done before they should be able to do again. Anglers spend a lot of their time thinking and it is important that we have positive thoughts – thinking 'high to rise'.

Apologies to female readers. Written in the Victorian age, the poem does have a male-only tone even though our sport is male-dominated, but as a motivational piece of writing, brilliant.

Appendix iv

Bibliography

Roach – How to Catch Them, Capt. L. A. Parker (Herbert Jenkins, 1954)

Match Fishing, How to join the ranks of the experts, Frank Oates (Herbert Jenkins Ltd., 1957)

Coarse Fishing Baits, Their Preparation and Use, Frank Oates (Herbert Jenkins Ltd., 1958)

Rod and Line, Arthur Ransome (Sphere Books, 1967)

Match Fishing with Benny Ashurst, Peter Collins (Ernest Benn Ltd., 1968)

Freshwater Fishing, Bernard Venables (Panther Books, 1969)

Freshwater Fishing – The Trent & the Witham, Clive Brett and Albert Garfoot (Ernest Benn, 1969)

Woodbine Angling Yearbook 1972, edited by Colin Graham (Queen Anne Press, 1972)

Appendix iv - Bibliography

Billy Lane's Encyclopaedia of Float Fishing, Billy Lane and Colin Graham (Pelham Books, 1972)

World Class Match Fishing, Kevin Ashurst and Colin Dyson (Cassell, 1977)

The Witham Story 1946-1980 (a text never published), Alan Baynes

There's More to Fishing, Martin Read (Shadowline Publishing Ltd., 2008)

Ivan Marks - The People's Champion, Ivan's stories compiled by Bauer Media (m press Ltd., 2011)

Ivan Marks and the Likely Lads, Mark Wintle (m press (Media) Ltd., 2015)

And various magazine articles selected from: the original Midland Angler, Coarse Angler, Coarse Fisherman and Angling Star.